Diasporas and Exiles

The publisher gratefully acknowledges the generous contribution to this book provided by the David and Susan Wirshup Endowment in Jewish Studies of the University of California Press Associates.

Diasporas and Exiles

Varieties of Jewish Identity

EDITED BY

Howard Wettstein

UNIVERSITY OF CALIFORNIA PRESS

Berkeley   Los Angeles   London

University of California Press
Berkeley and Los Angeles, California

University of California Press, Ltd.
London, England

Library of Congress Cataloging-in-Publication Data

Diasporas and exiles : varieties of Jewish identity / edited by
Howard Wettstein.
    p.   cm.
    Includes bibliographical references and index.
    ISBN 0-520-22864-2 (cloth : alk. paper)
    1. Jewish diaspora—History. 2. Jews—Identity. 3. Jews—
Civilization. I. Wettstein, Howard.

DS134.D52245   2002
909'.04924—dc21   2002002826

Manufactured in the United States of America

10 09 08 07 06 05 04 03 02

10 9 8 7 6 5 4 3 2 1

The paper used in this publication meets the minimum
requirements of ANSI/NISO Z39.48−1992 (R 1997) (*Permanence
of Paper*).♾

CONTENTS

ILLUSTRATIONS

Introduction

This volume represents and extends the work of a fall 1997 University of California Humanities Research Institute (UCHRI) residential research group on Jewish identity in the diaspora. The group was multidisciplinary; members represented anthropology, art history, comparative literature, cultural studies, German, history, philosophy, political theory, and sociology. General agreement within the group was rare, even on the nature of our topic. The disagreements, however, proved to be a source of great stimulation. This introduction will be something of a roadmap of the terrain covered by our papers.

Our topic was Jewish identity, which one can hardly mention without reference to *diaspora*. Jews, whatever else they have been, have been wandering. Early in our discussions, however, it emerged that the term *exile* rather than the more modern *diaspora* better translates *galut,* the traditional Hebrew expression for the Jews' perennial condition. The distinction between *diaspora* and *exile* proved controversial, difficult to analyze, but focal to our discussions.[1]

The original *galut,* as Arnold Eisen points out in his seminal work, *Galut: Modern Jewish Reflection on Homelessness and Homecoming,* was the expulsion of Adam and Eve from the Garden of Eden.[2] Turning from mythology to history, the paradigmatic *galut* is the dispersion of Israel after the destruction of the second Temple in 70 C.E. The destruction of the first Temple—in 587 B.C.E.—and the subsequent Babylonian exile was calamitous, of course, but that exile lasted only half a century. As Eisen notes, at that time exile could still seem unusual, an exception to the order of things. With the events of 70 C.E. and the subsequent defeat of Bar Kochba in 135, *galut* became not an exception, but the rule for Jewish life.

To be in *galut* is to be in the wrong place; it is to be dislocated, like a limb out of socket. Indeed, it is tempting to suppose that *exile* suggests, in Erich Gruen's words, "a bitter and doleful image, offering a bleak vision that issues either in despair or in a remote reverie of restoration."[3] Or, as Bluma Goldstein puts it, it is "a condition of forced homelessness and an anguished longing to return to the homeland."[4] However, whether a view of Jewish identity that emphasizes exile, *galut,* is necessarily so negative is controversial.[5] What is not controversial is that the term *exile,* as opposed to *diaspora,* suggests anguish, forced homelessness, and the sense of things being not as they should be.

Diaspora, on the other hand, although it suggests absence from some center—political or religious or cultural—does not connote anything so hauntingly negative. Indeed, it is possible to view diaspora in a positive light. Gruen discusses the view that Jews and Judaism requires no "territorial sanctuary or legitimation"; as "the people of the Book, their homeland resides in the text." Diaspora would then impose no special burden. It might even facilitate the spread of the word.

Let us turn from the diaspora/exile distinction to the concept of identity proper. If the former is controversial and resistant to analysis, the latter is even more so. As for the controversy, this volume presents the reader with a wide variety of perspectives on Jewish identity. This raises a general question about this controversy, about the multiplicity of views. Are these genuinely competing answers to a single question, about the nature of Jewish identity? Is there such a phenomenon, Jewish identity, about which different theorists proffer competing accounts?

Another possibility exists. We might see the "competing accounts" to be expressions of alternative Jewish identities. Such a possibility is suggested by the fact that questions about Jewish identity—like questions about other ethnic, religious, or cultural identities—seem to be largely concerned with the meaning or significance of one's Jewishness. Seen this way, it no longer is tempting to suppose that there is a right answer to the question of Jewish identity, that something or other actually constitutes *Jewish identity.* Who is to say, after all, that there is only one way in which Jewishness can matter, or legitimately matter? Who wants to get into the business of limiting the ways in which Jewishness might matter?

In philosophical language, questions about Jewish identity are not questions of metaphysics—of the constitution of Jewishness. Instead, they are in the domain of the theory of human values. This contrasts with classical philosophical questions about "personal identity," which are easy to confuse with our concern. Those classical questions are not about significance but about constitution, for example, John Locke's time-honored view that a person is constituted by temporal stages—time-slices, as it were—linked by memory. Even if Locke is on the right track, we would still have no help with the questions of significance that are our concern. We would not be a lick closer to understanding the character of Jewish identity. Questions of religious/cultural/ethnic identity, as Cora Diamond writes, are "hardly visible to the philosophical tradition."[6]

Our roadmap begins with the historian Erich Gruen. It may be tempting to suppose that a positive conception of diaspora comes into its own with modernity and Jewish Emancipation, that until modern times, Jews lived under the cloud of *galut*. Gruen, in "Diaspora and Homeland," challenges this presumption.[7]

Gruen distinguishes what he calls the gloomy approach to Jewish dispersion, which is more common, from a positive approach. The former resolves diaspora into *galut* and sees salvation exclusively in terms of homecoming, the reacquisition of a homeland. The latter sees Jews as "the people of the Book," the text as a "portable temple," and restoration to a homeland as superfluous. In the end Gruen suggests that both approaches are too simple, too stark. "The whole idea of privileging homeland over diaspora, or diaspora over homeland, derives from a modern, rather than an ancient, obsession." If we attend closely to the ancient world, another conception emerges.

Jewish dispersion, Gruen emphasizes, did not begin with the destruction of the Temple in 70 C.E. What Gruen has in mind is not only the destruction of the First Temple and its attendant diaspora. Rather he means to stress that for a host of reasons, largely including voluntary migration, Jews lived outside the Center. Indeed, there was a vibrant diaspora of some three to five million Jews in the roughly four centuries from Alexander the Great to Titus. Jerusalem was no more a home for them than it is for many diaspora Jews today. Diaspora communities were stable and had opportunities for residents to take part in the social, economic, and political life of their adopted lands, and often even to gain citizenship.

Few of these Jews ever saw Jerusalem, yet it was still their spiritual Center. Never was the sanctity of Jerusalem in question. Indeed, Jerusalem was, in Gruen's words, "the principal emblem of their faith," and "a critical piece of their identity." The tithe to Jerusalem was a ritual that bonded the far-flung diaspora. And they felt great solidarity with fellow Jews, both in the homeland and abroad.

If Jerusalem was critical to the Hellenistic diaspora Jews' sense of themselves, what becomes of Jewish identity when Jerusalem is no more? Here *galut* arguably comes into its own as a touchstone, at least until modern times. In "Coming to Terms with Exile," my own paper in this volume, I explore a Jewish identity for which *galut* is one central pillar. My contention is that even in modern times, *galut* cannot and should not be avoided. Rather than steering clear of the almost inbred Jewish sense of dislocation—one that we cannot quite lose even in our own Western diasporic setting—*galut* must be reckoned with. But such a reckoning does not necessarily issue in a bleak outlook. An ultimately positive take on the human and Jewish conditions requires that we give substantial weight to unpleasant, stubborn facts about human and Jewish dislocation.

I distinguish two *galut* phenomena. First there is in the human condition that which I call "normal dislocation." Being the sorts of all-too-human creatures that we are, living in the sort of world we find ourselves in, has always meant big trouble. The second and specifically Jewish *galut* phenomenon is not normal; it is extraordinary. I have in mind the cataclysmic sequence of events mentioned above: the *churban,* the destruction of the Second Temple in 70 C.E., the defeat of Bar Kochba in 135, and the attendant dispersion. The prospect of living without the foci of national and religious life must have been experienced as threatening, if not destroying, the very conception of a partnership between God and Israel. The *churban,* by contrast with normal dislocation, constituted a cosmic jolt.

My paper sketches aspects of the Rabbinic response to the cosmic jolt and explores how a tradition smitten by and obsessed with *galut* develops practices and an outlook to cope. My focus is on a crucial theological aspect of the rabbinic response, specifically the super-anthropomorphizing tendency one sees so clearly in the commentary, *Midrash Rabbah,* on the Book of Lamentations. This tendency culminates in an anthropomorphic quantum leap, the idea that after the *churban,* God Himself is in exile; dislocation is cosmic. The outcome is a religious sensibility better equipped not only for history's great catastrophes, but also for the normal travails of the human condition.

We turn now to Bluma Goldstein's "A Politics and Poetics of Diaspora: Heine's 'Hebräische Melodien.'"[8] During the first half of the nineteenth century, Central European Jews struggled both to free themselves from the constrictions of the *halakha* and to become fully integrated citizens. The golden age of Spain—perhaps somewhat idealized in the nineteenth century—served Jewish critics of the oppressive exilic life as the basis of a much more palatable model of Jewish identity. In this context, Goldstein sees in Heine's work an inviting positive conception of diaspora as well as a critique of "the devastating consequences of an oppressive exilic life."

Negative images of *galut,* of exilic life, inhabit the three poems that constitute "Hebräische Melodien." In the first poem, "Prinzessin Sabbat," Heine portrays the miserable situation of the "weekday Jew" imprisoned by traditional ritual. In the second, "Jehuda ben Halevy," the narrator-poet feels the stirrings of the ancient Babylonian exile. The final poem, "Disputation," dramatizes, as Goldstein writes, a kind of exilic "intellectual and cultural immobility." The rabbi and Jews are forced, on pain of death, to defend sterile traditional dogma, though they knew that successful defense of Jewish doctrine may also issue in death.

Goldstein's view, however, is that the specter of *galut* in these poems serves to highlight Heine's suggestion—most fully developed in the middle poem, "Jehuda ben Halevy"—of a different model, that of "an integrative diaspora that promotes interactive dialogue across borders." Heine thus makes available to us the prospect of "integrating substantive aspects of Jewish tradition and secular culture." The result is a picture of diasporic life in which the modern Jew might thrive as a Jew and as a European.

One who emphasizes a positive conception of diaspora, as does Goldstein, can readily agree that throughout Jewish history there has been exile, dislocation, and homelessness. But how central to contemporary Jewish self-perception is the sense of ourselves as in exile? By contrast with, for example, my own emphasis on *galut*, Goldstein directs our attention to an attractive and very different way of construing Jewish identity.

In "Dancing at Two Weddings: *Mazel* between Exile and Diaspora," Murray Baumgarten comes at our subject as does Bluma Goldstein, from a literary direction. His focus is Rebecca Goldstein's 1995 novel, *Mazel*.[9] To a certain point, Baumgarten's treatment of *galut* and diaspora parallels that of Bluma Goldstein and to some extent Erich Gruen. *Galut* is characterized by powerlessness, *halachic* constriction, dislocation, and anguish, in contrast with the diaspora's possibility of empowerment and integration. Baumgarten reads *Mazel* as identifying the movement from *galut* to diaspora with the Emancipation movement from the *shtetl* to the city.

But here is the twist: *Mazel* goes farther than the movement from *shtetl* to city. It is the story of four generations of Jewish women, beginning in the *shtetl* (Shluftchev), proceeding to the city (Warsaw), winding its way through Israel to New York, and ending in the suburbs (Lipton, New Jersey). This suburb, largely populated by the traditionally religious, is no more than "Shluftchev with a designer label," as Sasha, the central character, puts it.

Baumgarten sees this movement to the suburbs—it involves both Jews and, if Baumgarten is correct, a new direction in Jewish writing—as subtle and complicated. The city promises a newfound and heady freedom, spontaneity, and meaning born of enjoying the prizes of modernity—in Warsaw "there were so many ideas in the air you could get an education simply by breathing deeply"—but it is incapable of providing salvation.[10] So Baumgarten reads *Mazel*. Warsaw is, as Baumgarten says, "but another stop in the long Jewish journey of homelessness."

This is, of course, not to say that the life of the *shtetl* provided salvation. As noted above, its shortcomings are legend. But Baumgarten emphasizes the complexity of the *shtetl*: It was a bounded and constricting world, but at the same time dream-like (as suggested by the name Shluftchev, which roughly means "Sleepy Hollow"), possessing the "completeness of meaning of a classical work of art." Think here of a Mozart symphony as opposed to a twentieth-century atonal work of striking spontaneity. The world of Warsaw was more open and as Baumgarten says, "clangorous," with subtle but blaring meanings. Another aspect of the *shtetl* was that it was "a world desperately trying to articulate and safeguard, in a polluted, corrupt environment, a space of sacredness even at the cost of obsessive behavior." Thus Baumgarten locates the power of the *shtetl,* deadening as it may be.

The ultimate destination—ultimate for now—is the suburb, a context that appropriates values of both *shtetl* and city. Not that the suburb represents a smooth assimilation of those values and virtues; there is no Hegelian synthesis, as it were. Indeed, Baumgarten notes that his title, "Dancing at Two Weddings," intimates both the impossibility of a synthesis and the power of the pursuit. Many of *Mazel*'s central characters are unable to abandon either world. They are caught between exile and diaspora.

This leads to something to which most, perhaps all, members of our research group could agree: Jewish Emancipation allowed and even encouraged the transformation of the constricting *shtetl* version of exile into something more creative, open, and cosmopolitan. That much seems relatively uncontroversial. But, while agreeing with this, some would argue—there are suggestions of this in Baumgarten's paper as there are in mine—that there is in the newfound worldliness something of a new form of homelessness, of rootlessness, one that has been widely shared since the advent of modernity. As we will see below when we discuss Louise Tallen's essay on *baalot teshuvah,* this homelessness has taken its toll and sometimes leads to a desire to reengage with at least some of the values of the *shtetl.*

The costs of Emancipation are illuminated from another direction by art historian Catherine M. Soussloff in "Portraiture and Assimilation in Vienna." Soussloff sketches the history of Jewish portraiture and points out that assimilation, one of the effects of Emancipation, issued in portraits of Jews in which there are no overt signs of their Jewishness. This was so in colonial and federal America as well as in central Europe in the eighteenth and nineteenth centuries. But to deny Jewish content to such portraits—and Soussloff's work is pioneering here in its identification of Jewish content—is to abstract these portraits from their historical and social contexts. It is also, argues Soussloff, to fly in the face of both recent work in museum studies and a historical interpretation of art.

Soussloff's contextualism views portraiture as a transaction between the artist, those who sit for the portrait, and the audience. A crucial component, stressed by Soussloff, is the placement of the work of art. The portraits in question, free as they are of overt Jewish content, were viewed in the parlors and living rooms of emancipated American and European Jews. The portraits thus represent an ideal of assimilation, "unmarked," as Soussloff says, "by dress, no longer residents of the ghetto." But viewed in context—including both their social history and their placement—these portraits signify both the desire not to signify their subjects' Jewishness, and at the same time (and for this very reason) their subjects' Jewish identity.

That Emancipation engendered assimilation is, of course, a commonplace. And that portraits of assimilated Jews abstract from the ethnic and religious dimensions is no surprise. Soussloff's provocative point is that the same assimilationist tendency is at work in the interpretation of the art. Writers about portraiture have participated in what Soussloff calls the ethics of assimilation. They view the portrait as if it were simply an image, something contained in the picture frame. Soussloff's emphasis is not simply the visual product, but on portraiture itself, and she sees this as occurring "along an axis perpendicular to the image's frame." Emancipation not only leads to assimilation, but it also contributes to the adoption of a universalistic—context-insensitive—view of art.

The papers thus far have explored Jewish identity in ancient or modern Western diasporas. As noted, one important agreement between the essays is that there is no single account of Jewish identity, no uniquely privileged Jewish identity. The lesson is brought home with force by Daniel J. Schroeter in his study of a non-Western diaspora, "A Different Road to Modernity: Jewish Identity in the Arab World." Indeed, as Schroeter explains, there is no single story even for the Arab world, though the multiple Asian/North African Jewish identities are unified by shared contrasts with Western Jewish identities.

Schroeter explores the meanings and effects of modernity for the Arab world generally—not only with respect to Jews. For example, the development of the modern nation-state in the Arab world was quite a different affair than that in Europe. In the former, the nation-state is somewhat artificial. The earlier rise of Islam as both a political and religious entity meant that, by contrast with the Catholic Church in Europe, "the Muslim community, the *umma*, never had to define itself in relation to the state." This changes with the Ottoman Empire in the nineteenth century and even more so in the later Colonial period. These political movements attempted to establish a civil society, but the enormous influence of the Muslim past meant that secularism never took hold as it did in Europe. Accordingly, even with the rise of the Arab nation-state, the hold of religion and the cohesiveness of religious minorities remained strong. Unlike Europe, Arab lands never developed a secular common ground. Jewish assimilation thus was not a major threat to Jewish identity and survival.

The lack of a secular common ground is also related to the lack of a pressing need felt for religious reform. Thus one does not find any analogue to Reform Judaism in the East. But where there is no Reform, there is also no Orthodoxy. (*Orthodoxy* here does not refer to a rigorous commitment to traditional religious practice, but rather to the movement that arose in Europe to counter Reform.) In the East one does not find the tension that existed in Europe between the demands of traditional Jewish religious practice and technological innovation and secular education. The rabbis could be more relaxed about modernity; it was considerably less threatening.

Similarly, Zionism was not needed to fill the gap left by the move from *shtetl* to city, the meaning-gap left by the rejection of the old ways. Zionism thus arose not as an all-embracing new modern Jewish identity but as one thread, sometimes an important one, among many; a new aspect of a more smoothly and slowly evolving Jewish identity.

In Europe, modernization dismantled the virtually self-governing Jewish *kehillah* [community], and granted citizenship to Jews. This in turn had a dramatic impact on Jewish identity. A Jew became, Schroeter writes, "a German or a Frenchman of the Hebrew or Israelite persuasion or faith." The rise of colonialism and its attendant weakening of Jewish self-government in the East often had a dramatically different outcome, in part due to the factors mentioned above, such as the lack of secular common ground. Jews largely continued to maintain strong attachments to local community and local religious practices.

Schroeter's essay raises important implications for the concept of diaspora. Consider Moroccan Jews living in Israel. The category "Moroccan Jew" is not one that Jews applied to themselves in Morocco. Given the linking of the modern Arab nation with Islam, it was implausible for Jews living in Morocco to identify themselves as Moroccan. They were Jews whose home was Morocco; Home was another matter. Indeed, their situation is in some ways similar to that of the more comfortably assimilated Hellenistic Jews described by Erich Gruen.

Jews living in Morocco were certainly members of a Jewish diaspora, but unlike the Hellenistic Jews, they emigrated to Israel in significant numbers. Such people saw Israel as their new home, but Morocco—especially their local community, with its distinctive modes of Jewish practice—was also their home. Israel, partly because of its powerful Ashkenazi roots, was still another diaspora for its Moroccan Jews. Like Jake in Diane Wolf's narrative, discussed below, they live in multiple diasporas.

Let's turn to the effects of recent history on Jewish identity. To what extent has the experience of the Shoah been formative?[11] This is a question both for those people who have been directly affected by it and for those most removed from the horror. Can the identity of a late-twentieth-century Jew *not* be affected by the Shoah?

Similarly, can a contemporary Jew's sense of himself or herself be unaffected by the existence of the State of Israel, the first politically autonomous Jewish entity in millennia? No doubt for many Jews, the State of Israel constitutes a factor in self-perception. But how important a factor is it, and what precise role does it play?

The historian Irwin Wall addresses these questions in "Remaking Jewish Identity in France." One thing that is striking in Wall's paper is the central place he gives to another thesis upon which there was universal agreement within the research group. Any attempt to locate anything like *the* correct account of Jewish identity, or *the* correct Jewish identity, is doomed to failure. There is no—and from the ancient world there never has been—single or uniquely correct Jewish identity. One is reminded of the old joke concerning *n* Jews and *n*+1 synagogues.

Wall gives primacy of place to this insight. Both in postwar France—Wall's main focus—and elsewhere, one can find many pegs on which to hang one's Jewish identity: the consciousness of a shared history; a sense of Jewish community as having survived all manner of disasters, most notably the Shoah; a sense of solidarity with the State of Israel; minority status vis-à-vis Christianity; the political and cultural prophetic tradition of social justice; solidarity based upon shared language (Hebrew, Yiddish, Ladino); finally and quite prominently for some, traditional Jewish religious identity.

Wall strongly criticizes views of identity that fail to observe this multi-identity stricture, for example, the "essentialist" characterizations of non-Jewish thinkers like Sartre and Lyotard who attempt to fashion an identity for Jews from the outside. As Wall explains, Lyotard "characterizes the Jews as the quintessential other. . . . [they] have the role of remaining in exile and spreading the word of Kant to the world." The Jews of France, Wall insists, fit no such neat picture.

Wall's project, particularized to France, is that of finding significance in one's Jewishness. How is this to be done? How or where is one to find the elements to remake a contemporary Jewish identity in the diaspora? There is a sense in which this question is already answered once one notes the multiplicity of contemporary Jewish identities in France. If there is such a multiplicity then somehow French Jews have found a way to construct such identities.

But Wall's question goes deeper. He is worried about the plight of those largely secular Jews for whom Jewish identity is problematic. At the heart of his worry is the sense he shares with Alain Finkielkraut that the two most prominent candidates for pillars of Jewish identity, the Shoah and the State of Israel, are in the end unsatisfying. To make the Shoah a pillar is unsatisfactory since this would, in effect, make Jewish victimization focal. This, as Wall notes, would be a poor substitute for a rich identity. Solidarity with Israel is unsatisfying to the contemporary French Jew since it depends on a perception of the justice of Israeli policy, risky in a country whose foreign policy is so often pro-Arab. What makes Israel an even shakier pillar is the increasing polarization in Israel of the religious—read "Orthodox"—and secular.

Where then is the secular French Jew to turn for a rich Jewish identity? Wall discusses a number of modern French thinkers who have addressed the issue. Two of the most prominent, and the two in whom Wall is particularly interested, are Finkielkraut and especially Finkielkraut's teacher, Emmanuel Levinas.

Finkielkraut's own ambivalent position is quite telling. On one hand, he feels a powerful sense of being a Jew. His Jewishness, Wall says, is "proclaimed from the rooftops with pride." But Finkielkraut himself cannot discern any real content to this sense of identity. It is an identity without substance. Finkielkraut's somewhat quixotic idea that the revival of secular Yiddish culture might constitute a real basis for a diaspora Jewish identity. The only remaining native speakers of Yiddish, however, are the Hasidim, hardly advocates of secular Yiddish culture.

For Wall and the French thinkers he explores, the project is to unearth something from the history of Jewish culture that might engender Jewish renewal. This is significant—and highlights something controversial among our contributors—since it suggests that what is in hand at the moment in the Jewish cultural or religious repertoire will not suffice. The most powerful voice in favor of such an approach—his voice extends considerably beyond France—is Levinas, a prominent French philosopher and critic of Husserl and Heidegger.

Levinas reaches out to the Talmud, specifically to talmudic ethics, recast through his "Greek," that is, Western, lens. His interest is not in full-blown Jewish religiosity, but in abstracting and to some extent reconstruing the ethical insights of rabbinic Judaism. The problem with talmudic ethics as a pillar of Jewish identity for the diaspora is the inaccessibility of Talmud to all but its Orthodox students, who approach it in quite a different way than does Levinas. The situation is parallel to that of Finkielkraut's dilemma with Yiddish—the language is owned, as it were, by Hasidim who are not interested in Finkielkraut's secular agenda.

Where Wall contends that the Shoah cannot underpin a rich, contemporary identity for most Jews, Diane Wolf, in "'This Is Not What I Want': Holocaust Testimony, Postmemory, and Jewish Identity," presents a case study of a survivor for whom the Shoah is indeed central. Wolf's subject is Jake, a Polish Hasid, for whom a bitter taste of *galut*, rather than an empowering diaspora, is pivotal to his sense of himself as a Jew.

Wolf speaks of "collective memory," the product of the transmission of a group's history and culture from one generation to the next. Collective memory, she argues, is crucial to individuals' identities as members of the group and products of its culture and history. Since the Shoah figures centrally in recent Jewish history, it has become a crucial component in the transmitted collective memory.

Wolf draws on Jake's postwar life to accomplish two goals. She illustrates the difficulties that characterize the lives of many survivors. For Jake the end of the war marked the beginning of injustices created by family members.

Wolf's other goal is to demonstrate that the methods used in Spielberg's Shoah Visual History Foundation can undermine the richness of survivors' stories, while perhaps encouraging a Jewish identify based on victimization. A more nuanced oral history, one that examines the reactions of Jewish kin and the Jewish community, might yield a richer set of images.

Jake's testimony is powerful, moving, painful. The story begins with Jake as a young Hasidic boy in Poland, a classic *galut*. It moves through the Shoah with the horrors of concentration camps and a death march, to still another *galut* in upstate New York. It is difficult to consider oneself in exile if one lives the privileged lives that most of us lead. For Jake, however, it was as if the universe was constantly reminding him that he was in the wrong place. He and his wife—survivors who met and married right after the war—relocated to New York State to be near his wife's few living relatives, only to find that these relatives exploited them economically and in many respects treated them worse than strangers. A devout Jew, Jake was unable to practice his religion as he wished, as his relatives/employers required him to work on Shabbat and on holidays. The long hours he worked left him little time for his family, which was especially painful for him, having grown up in a world where family was of primary importance. Only once did his (almost sweatshop) work hours permit attending his son's baseball game; he arrived as the game ended.

Jake's life in America, writes Wolf, was thus multidiasporic. In prewar Poland, Jake was like Gruen's Hellenistic Jews in diaspora: Jake's home was Poland even if his Home was Jerusalem. His later life in America—hardly experienced as the "goldenah medinah"—was one of dislocation, not because of a religious yearning for messianic times or places, but rather simply because America did not work for him. This is not to say that it was a vale of tears, that he lived a miserable existence. Wolf is careful to present a balanced picture. His was in many ways a success story. He is warm, lively, optimistic, and humorous. He eventually owned a successful business, raised two children who became professionals, and is an active member of the Jewish community. At the same time, Jake has lived his life in a palpable *galut;* indeed, sometimes in several at once. Wolf's discussion, like Daniel Schroeter's, thus directs attention to the phenomenon of multiple diaspora, but in a very different context.

In "The Ideology of Affliction: Reconsidering the Adversity Thesis," Bernard Susser is concerned with victimhood. The "adversity thesis" maintains that anti-Jewish prejudice and oppression have been the key to Jewish identity and survival over the last millennium, at least in the Ashkenazi world.

Susser is happy to advocate the adversity thesis when it is restricted to the pre-Enlightenment period. Indeed, for much of Jewish history there has been a kind of marriage between adversity and theological ideas, specifically the dominant theodicy that sees suffering as punishment for waywardness from God. Jewish religious thinking has thus made sense of and given meaning to Jewish suffering. In return, oppression has given power to, even confirmed, as it were, the theological ideas. This worked well for a time—a long time. Indeed, oppression, given its theological interpretation, served to foster solidarity and survival.

But the Enlightenment, with its support for religious skepticism, and post-Shoah developments—specifically the character of Western, democratic, pluralist societies—have caused trouble for the adversity thesis and the marriage of theology and Jewish oppression. To begin with, once the theodicy loses its grip, oppression no longer has any clear or specific significance. Once we stop thinking of oppression as punishment for our waywardness from God or as purification on the way to messianic liberation, it can come to mean many different things. Perhaps it has no special significance at all. In any case, adversity no longer automatically yields group solidarity. Indeed, oppression may encourage assimilation, a "massive silent exit."

The problem posed by post-Shoah political developments is that the historic reality of Jewish adversity is, in Susser's view, dramatically diminished. Many Jewish communities in North America, Europe, and Israel are flourishing, and Gentile oppression seems a remote possibility. If adversity was a central element of Jewish identity, then once the reality of political tolerance and pluralism rises to consciousness, the "Jewish ethno-religious civilization would need to undergo fundamental reformulations." Nevertheless, Jews still very much have a sense of themselves as embattled. Susser writes, "Embattledness as an instinct has outlived embattledness as a reality." Adversity has been *"reified* {. . .} transformed into a static mental picture that is independent of its empirical referent."

Susser makes Jewish victimhood central in historical and contemporary Jewish identity. This might appear to be at odds with, say, Finkielkraut and Wall, but there is a deeper level of agreement. Susser thinks that there is not much more to Jewish identity—at least for the nonreligious American Jew, his main focus—than the sense of himself or herself as part of an embattled minority. But this is to describe the current state, not to advocate an ideal. The deeper level of agreement is that Susser, no less than Finkielkraut and Wall, maintains that adversity will not support a rich, contemporary identity. Adversity, no longer theologically significant for many and increasingly incongruous with Western realities, will surely not support long-term Jewish survival. Survival is clearly a more central focus for Susser than for many of the others represented here.

Jewish identity is, thus, doubly problematic for Susser. First, because it has not liberated itself from its traditional association with adversity. This outdated picture stands in the way of the development of a positive one that can give significance to Jewishness. But second, even if we could throw off the burden of adversity, how might we construct a significant Jewish identity? What might replace the enormous role of adversity?

Susser ends his paper with what one might think of as Finkielkraut's problem: If one isn't a religious Jew or an Israeli, what rich content can there be to one's Jewish identity? One has the sense that Susser is not optimistic about Jewish survival outside the ambit of Orthodoxy and the borders of the State of Israel.

Along the way, however, Susser raises important questions about the positions he defends, questions that the reader may want to ponder. First, is it so clear that historically the adversity thesis has played such an enormous role? Susser alerts us to the dangers of reducing a major cultural tradition to a mere defense mechanism or social reflex. One might suppose that there is more to Jewish identity—pre- or post-Enlightenment—than the instinct to circle the wagons. Second, Susser feels that Western civilization has turned a corner in regard to Jewish oppression. Nevertheless, he wonders: Given the facts of the Shoah and its cultured German perpetrators, indeed, given the events of the last decade with harrowing images of ethnic cleansing, dare we suppose that humanity has come of age?

The anthropologist Louise Tallen, in "Jewish Identity Writ Small: The Everyday Experience of *Baalot Teshuvah*," emphasizes, as does Susser, that for many American Jews, Judaism is hardly at the core of their identity. It is one facet—often a rarely surfacing one—of who they are. But there is a countervailing tendency that is the subject of Tallen's paper.

Tallen's study concerns formerly secular Jewish women who have become Orthodox Jews, *baalot teshuvah*, through the outreach efforts of Chabad Lubavitch Hasidism. Despite the emphasis in our culture on self-actualization and freedom of choice, Orthodoxy—even Chabad-style Orthodoxy, which involves great sacrifices in personal autonomy—is staging something of a return. For increasing numbers of Jews, Jewishness has become a focal element of their identity.

Tallen is interested in identity formation, a process that she sees as usually taking place below the level of consciousness. Her focus here is in people who undergo radical life changes, since in such cases the process of identity formation and negotiation becomes conscious, as it also does, says Tallen, for those living in cultural margins. Here we can perhaps obtain a glimpse, even a model, of what we all do unconsciously.

The *baalot teshuvah* in Tallen's study typically experienced a sense of "not fitting in" in their earlier lives. Some were troubled by experiences with organized Judaism or with a Christian-dominated society. Some were seeking meaning after growing up in families troubled by divorce, traumatic deaths, or mental illness. They report a sense of betrayal and/or disillusionment before their finding their new Orthodox lifestyle. For these people, embracing

Chabad-style Orthodoxy made the difference; they found a home and the beginnings of a meaningful identity.

Leaving the old ways of being in the world, however, and embracing and maintaining the new is almost always painful and difficult. Specifically, it is difficult to unlearn the old ways and values, to shed, as Tallen says, "an ill-fitting but sticky identity." And then there are inevitable conflicts between one's personal desires and the communal ideals. Many of these conflicts, Tallen suggests, are of the kind every individual faces—the need to mediate a compromise between self and community. This is at the heart of identity construction and reconstruction.

Other difficulties arise from the Chabad community itself. Tallen explains several respects in which *baalei teshuvah*, both men and women, are not quite accepted as full-fledged members of the community; they bear a stigma. They thus occupy a "borderland, caught between secular and religious worlds, unable to fully enter the religious world and still feeling the pull of the secular world." The reader will want to ponder the obvious connection with Murray Baumgarten's discussion of the modern Jewish plight, the need to dance at two weddings at once, the inability to abandon either of two incompatible worlds. Ironically, Tallen's *baalot teshuvah* stand modernity on its head; it is the modern and postmodern world from which they are running. And it is a world of considerable constriction they enter.

The papers in this volume range over a variety of views of Jewish identity and, indeed, a variety of identities, as well as a variety of diasporas. But the myth of an essential Jewishness—and the related idea of an essentially unified Jewish people—dies hard. Our volume concludes with the art historian Kerri P. Steinberg's contribution, "Contesting Identities in Jewish Philanthropy."

Steinberg directs our attention to the reluctance of mainstream Jewish philanthropies to allow for the reality of Jewish diversity. Steinberg contrasts the univocal conception of Jewish identity that informs the work of the Joint Distribution Committee (JDC), the overseas arm of the United Jewish Appeal (UJA), with the emphasis on diversity of the New Israel Fund (NIF). Her project is to scrutinize the photographs that appear in the 1995 annual reports of these funds. These photos, reproduced in this volume, with their different portrayals of donors, philanthropic officers, and recipients, present the contrasting conceptions of identity.

The UJA sprang into existence in January 1939, the offspring of the merger of the JDC and United Palestine Committee as a response to *Kristallnacht*. The UJA thus represented the unification of competing American philanthropic interests. Accordingly, built into the fabric of the UJA is an impulse towards unification as a way to resolve crises, an impulse that in the past has been highly effective.

By contrast, the NIF began in the late 1970s, a response to the social, cultural, and intellectual upheavals of the 1960s and 1970s in Europe and America. A central concern was the desire for social justice in Israel and peace in the Middle East. From its inception, it has been a joint effort of Americans, Europeans, and Israelis, and tends to attract more progressive donors.

Steinberg analyzes the visual culture of each organization as revealed in their annual reports. The JDC photos prominently portray donors and officers—the latter sometimes in formal portraits. The report thus pays tribute to the American donors, but it often leaves the beneficiaries anonymous. The JDC photos also correspond to mainstream American Jewish notions of social progress. The underprivileged are often shown as being Westernized and modernized. The NIF photographs, by contrast, emphasize cultural differences and the subjects' autonomy. Donors do not appear. Instead we find profiles of casually attired activists involved in a variety of causes supported by NIF funds. Tribute is paid to those fostering social justice in Israel. Further, compared to the JDC's more journalistic style, the NIF's photos are artistic and compelling. There is thus the implication that donors have something of an artistic sensibility and that issues of race, gender, and class matter to them.

Again and again, the JDC photos return us to the influence of American Jews and to its conception of progress. Clearly, argues Steinberg, there is an agenda here to propagate the myth of Jewish unity. Although in the past such a myth has functioned for the organization, perhaps the myth has outlived its utility. Indeed, Steinberg associates the insistence on a univocal portrayal of Jewishness with a yearning for an essence that unites Jews. The NIF is, of course, not without its own agenda. This is revealed by an emphasis on diversity, on the marginalized, and by the polemical character of some of the NIF photographs, such as one of women studying traditional religious texts. Steinberg concludes that where the photographs of the JDC portray difference as opposed to sameness, for the NIF "difference is recast into a softened motif of diversity."

We conclude with remarks on an arresting but so far unremarked feature of Jewish identity phenomena, the powerful irony they exhibit. A glance at Jewish history provides a study in irony, and so does even the first glance taken in this introduction at the perplexities of Jewish identity. For a taste of the irony of Jewish history, consider novelist Walker Percy's remarks,[12]

Where are the Hittites?

Why does no one find it remarkable that in most world cities today there are Jews but not one single Hittite, even though the Hittites had a great flourishing civilization while the Jews nearby were a weak and obscure people?

When one meets a Jew in New York or New Orleans or Paris or Melbourne, it is remarkable that no one considers the event remarkable? What are they doing here? But it is even more remarkable to wonder, if there are Jews here, why are there not Hittites here?

Where are the Hittites? Show me one Hittite living in New York City.

Such ironies are easily multiplied. Woody Allen suggests that there ought to be still another Jewish holiday, this to commemorate all the promises that God broke to the Jews. More seriously, there is the specter of a people of whom many considered themselves chosen by God, subjected to millennia of horrors. Perhaps the ultimate and most painful irony is that of the Shoah, perhaps the greatest of those horrors, inflicted by a modern nation of otherwise truly high culture.

But the ironies of post-Enlightenment Jewish identity are as notable. We might begin with an example of a Jew who sees no point in his Jewishness and wants out. Indeed, cultural/religious/ethnic identity can be constricting. But often at least, getting out is no trivial matter. One has limited control over how others think of one, and many such people cannot escape thinking of themselves as Jews who want out. Next—a kind or ironic variation—there is Finkielkraut (and he is not alone in this) who in a way also sees no point in his Jewishness, but declares his Jewish identity from the rooftops. Then there is the case of the Israeli Moroccan Jews, who never thought of themselves as Moroccan. There is Heine, who converts to Christianity only to later write with great passion and warmth about the Jewish experience. There is the irony of those steeped in post-Enlightenment culture returning to traditional religious practice, Louise Tallen's *baalot teshuvah* being a striking case. My argument in my paper, that *galut* be seen as a pillar of a contemporary religious Jewish identity, furnishes another example, emerging as it does from a post-Enlightenment outlook for which supernaturalism is problematic. And irony is underscored by Murray Baumgarten's image of the postmodern Jew as attempting the proverbially impossible: dancing at two weddings. As with the ironies of Jewish history, these ironies may be easily multiplied. For the ironically inclined, Jewish identity, as Jewish history, provides a gold mine.

The members of the fall 1997 research group at the University of California Humanities Research Institute wish to extend special thanks to the institute's then director, Dr. Patricia O'Brien, and to her wonderful staff for their especially generous hospitality and for providing the sort of context in which our research was able to flourish. We are also grateful to the Lucius N. Littauer Foundation for making it possible for Israeli scholars Asa Kasher and Bernard Susser to participate with us.

NOTES

1. Murray Baumgarten introduced the distinction into our discussions. Baumgarten attributed it to Cynthia Ozick.

2. Arnold Eisen, *Galut: Modern Jewish Reflection on Homelessness and Homecoming* (Bloomington: Indiana University Press, 1986).

3. See his essay below. Gruen does not endorse such a view of exile.

4. See her essay below.

5. See my own paper, "Coming to Terms With Exile," for another view.

6. "Sahibs and Jews," in *Jewish Identity,* ed. David Theo Goldberg and Michael Krause (Philadelphia: Temple University Press, 1993).

7. See his essay.

8. See her essay.

9. He also discusses her 1983 novel, *The Mind-Body Problem,* and her 1993 collection of short stories, *Strange Attractors.* Here we attend to his discussion of *Mazel.*

10. *Mazel,* 206.

11. A number of contributors point out the problematic character of the terms *Holocaust* and *Shoah.* For purposes of this introduction, *Shoah* has been chosen, since it at least does not suggest sacrificial offering.

12. See "The Delta Factor," in *The Message in the Bottle* (New York: Farrar, Straus and Giroux, 1954), 6.

1

Diaspora and Homeland

Erich S. Gruen

Diaspora lies deeply rooted in Jewish consciousness. It existed in one form or another almost from the start, and it persists as an integral part of the Jews' experience of history. The status of absence from the center has demanded time and again that Jews confront and, in some fashion, come to terms with a seemingly inescapable concomitant of their being.[1] The images of uprootedness, dispersal, and wandering haunt Jewish identity throughout. Jews have written about it incessantly, lamented it or justified it, dismissed it or grappled with it, embraced it or deplored it.

At a theoretical level, that experience has been deconstructed from two quite divergent angles. The gloomy approach holds primacy. On this view, diaspora dissolves into *galut,* exile, a bitter and doleful image, offering a bleak vision that issues either in despair or in a remote reverie of restoration. The negative image dominates modern interpretations of the Jewish psyche. Realization of the people's destiny rests in achieving the "return," the acquisition of a real or mythical homeland.[2] The alternative approach takes a very different route. It seeks refuge in a comforting concept: that Jews require no territorial sanctuary or legitimation. They are "the people of the Book." Their homeland resides in the text—not just the canonical Scriptures but an array of Jewish writings that help to define the nation and give voice to its sense of identity. Their "portable Temple" serves the purpose. A geographical restoration is therefore superfluous, even subversive. To aspire to it deflects focus from what really counts, the embrace of the text, its ongoing commentary, and its continuous reinterpretation.[3] Diaspora, in short, is no burden; indeed, it is a virtue in the spread of the word. This justifies a primary attachment to the land of one's residence, rather than the home of the fathers.

The destruction of the Temple in 70 C.E., of course, constitutes a principal watershed for the Jews of antiquity. Both of the above analyses apply primarily as constructs to comprehend Jewish mentality in the generations, even centuries, after that cataclysmic event. The elimination of the center, source of spiritual nourishment and preeminent symbol of the nation's identity, compelled Jews to reinvent themselves, to find other means of religious sustenance, and to adjust their lives to an indefinite period of displacement. That story has been told many times and in many ways.[4]

But another story demands closer attention. Jews faced a more puzzling and problematic situation prior to the loss of the Temple. Diaspora did not await the fall of Jerusalem to Roman power and destructiveness. The scattering of Jews had begun long before—occasionally through forced expulsion, much more frequently through voluntary migration. The major push came with the arrival of the Greeks, the Hellenistic period. Alexander the Great's conquests stimulated wholesale settlements of Greek veterans, merchants, travelers, and adventurers in the lands of the eastern Mediterranean and the former subject areas of the Persian empire. That development proved to be an irresistible magnet. Jews migrated to the new settlements and expanded communities in substantial numbers. A Greek diaspora, in short, brought the Jewish one in its wake. Perhaps three to five million Jews dwelled outside Palestine in the roughly four centuries that stretched from Alexander to Titus.[5] The era of the Second Temple brought the issue into sharp focus, inescapably so. The Temple still stood, a reminder of the hallowed past, and, through most of the era, a Jewish regime existed in Palestine. Yet the Jews of the diaspora, from Italy to Iran, far outnumbered those in the homeland. Although Jerusalem loomed large in their self-perception as a nation, few of them had seen it, and few were likely to. How then did diaspora Jews of the Second Temple conceive their association with Jerusalem, the emblem of ancient tradition?

In modern interpretations a dark picture prevails. Diaspora is something to be *overcome*.[6] Thunderous biblical pronouncements had presented it as the terrible penalty exacted by God for the sins of the Israelites. They will be scattered among the nations and pursued by divine wrath.[7] Spread among the lands, they will worship false gods and idols and enjoy no repose from the anger of the Lord.[8] Abandonment of ancestral precepts means that the children of Israel will have to enter the servitude of foreign lords in foreign parts.[9] They will be dispersed among peoples unknown to them or to their fathers and will suffer God's vengeance until their destruction.[10] Failure to heed the divine commandments or the warnings of prophets produces the scattering of Israel at the hands of the Lord.[11] The dismal character of exile seems reinforced by the words of the learned Hellenistic Jew Philo in the first century C.E. For him, banishment far exceeds death as the most feared penalty. Death at least puts an end to one's misery; exile perpetuates it, the equivalent of a thousand deaths.[12] No solace lies in adjustment. There seems nothing worth adjusting to. Only a single goal can keep flickering hopes alive: the expectation, however distant, of returning from exile and regaining a place in the Promised Land. The Bible offers that possibility. Obedience to the Lord and eradication of past errors will induce him to re-gather the lost souls spread across the world and restore them to the land of their fathers.[13] He will raise a banner among the nations and assemble the people of Judah from the four corners of the Earth.[14] Given such a tradition, it causes no surprise that the grim sense of diaspora and a correspondingly gloomy attitude are conventionally ascribed to Jews of the Second Temple.[15]

Yet that convention ignores a grave implausibility. It is not easy to imagine that millions of ancient Jews dwelled in foreign parts for generations mired in misery and obsessed with a longing for Jerusalem that had little chance of fulfillment. Many of them lived hundreds, even thousands, of miles away from Jerusalem, in Memphis, or Babylon, or Susa, or Athens, or Rome. To imagine that they repeatedly lamented their fate and pinned their hopes on recovery of the homeland is quite preposterous. Signs of a shift in scholarly attitudes are now discernible. Some recent works tip the balance away from the center to the periphery. It seems only logical that Jews sought out means whereby to legitimize a diaspora existence that most of them had inherited from their parents and would bequeath to their descendants.[16] As is well known, large and thriving Jewish communities existed in numerous areas of the Mediterranean with opportunities for economic advancement, social status, and even political responsibilities.[17] The essential facts are not in dis-pute.[18] Does it follow then that the displaced and dispersed had recourse to the thesis that mobility takes preference over territoriality, that the nation is defined by its texts rather than its location?

The dichotomy is deceptive. Hellenistic Jews did not have to face the erad-ication of the Temple. It was there—but they were not. Yet they nowhere developed a theory or philosophy of diaspora. The whole idea of privileging homeland over diaspora, or diaspora over homeland, derives from a mod-ern, rather than an ancient, obsession. The issue is too readily conceived in terms of mutually exclusive alternatives: either the Jews reckoned their identity as unrealizable in exile, and the achievement of their destiny as de-pendent upon reentry into Judaea; or they clung to their heritage abroad, shifting attention to local and regional loyalties and cultivating a permanent attachment to the diaspora. Those alternatives, of course, have continuing contemporary resonance.[19] But Second Temple Jews did not confront so stark a choice.

Hellenistic texts, upon initial examination, would appear to support a sol-emn conclusion: life in foreign parts came as consequence of divine disfavor, a banishment from the homeland. The characterization of diaspora as exile occurs with some frequency in the works of Hellenistic Jewish writers.[20] And this has prompted what seems to be a natural assumption: that the gloom represents Jewish attitudes in the contemplation of their current fate. But that assumption is shaky and vulnerable. A caveat has to be issued from the start. The majority of these grim pronouncements refer to the biblical misfortunes of the Israelites, expulsion by Assyrians, the destruction of the Temple, and the Babylonian Captivity. Were they all metaphors for the Hellenistic diaspora? The inference would be hasty, and it begs the question.[21]

Ben Sira laments the sins of his forefathers and records the fierce retaliation of the Lord that brought uprooting from their land and dispersal into every other land.[22] The reference, however, is to the era of Elijah and Elisha, to the ills of the Northern Kingdom, and to the Assyrian conquest that scattered the Israelites. It may, indeed, have contained a warning to Ben Sira's contemporaries, whose shortcomings paralleled those of his ancestors—but it did not condemn the current diaspora. The Book of Tobit tells a tale that ostensibly takes place in the Assyrian Captivity as well. Tobit bewails his own fate, prompted by the sins of his forefathers, and the fate of his countrymen, now an object of scorn and a vulnerable prey to those in the nations whither they have been dispersed.[23] A later prayer by Tobit once again labels the diaspora as a penalty for Israel's abandonment of tradition, but looks ahead to divine mercy and redemption.[24] And a final prediction anticipates another calamity, the loss of the Temple, the desolation of the land, and yet another dispersal abroad.[25] To suppose that the author of Tobit sees in all this a reflection of his present circumstances is a simplistic leap. Tobit also forecasts the recovery of the Temple and portrays the outcome as the culmination of Israelite dreams, a happy ending to endure indefinitely.[26] That hardly suggests that the Hellenistic diaspora is a vale of tears.

The same can be found in the Book of Judith. Achior, the Ammonite leader, briefly sketches the highlights of Israelite history to Holofernes and includes the deportation to Babylon and the scattering of Jews as a devastating penalty for waywardness. But the penalty was canceled with the return from exile and the rebuilding of the Temple.[27] Nothing in Judith suggests that subsequent dispersion, when the Temple remained intact, derived from sin and punishment.

The dire predictions that occur in the Testaments of the Twelve Patriarchs include the calamity of dispersal to the four corners of the Earth, wrought by the wrath of God, the equivalent of captivity among the nations. Here too the sons of Jacob foresaw the capture of the Temple and the grief of their people in Babylon—but also the renewal of divine compassion and eventual restoration.[28] This makes no direct, and probably no indirect, allusion to diaspora Jews of the Greco-Roman era.[29] Similar conclusions apply to various other statements in Second Temple texts. Jubilees reports the afflictions suffered by Israelites who succumbed to idolatry and were scattered by

God into captivity amidst the nations.[30] The Psalms of Solomon include a hymn praising the righteousness of the Lord in expelling Israel's neglectful inhabitants from their land and sending them into exile around the world.[31] The Greek additions to Jeremiah, incorporated as I Baruch in the Septuagint, echo the self-reproach for misdeeds that produced the Lord's dispersal of the Israelites and landed them in an accursed exile.[32] And the thunderous forecasts of the Third Sibylline Oracle contain a segment on abandonment of the Temple, enslavement by Assyrians, desolation of the land, and distribution of the despised throughout Earth and sea.[33] This repeated theme runs through the texts, extending over a lengthy stretch of time. The biblical allusions are stern and severe, reminders of past punishments and warnings against future apostasy.[34] Diaspora dwellers in the Greco-Roman world are put on notice, lest they lapse again. But a notable fact needs emphasis. The texts do not make the current scattering itself a target of reproach or a source of discontent.[35]

Our sources do, it can be conceded, make reference to Jews in Ptolemaic Egypt who did not arrive there of their own free will. Convoluted and controversial evidence applies to the transfer of Jews to Egypt in the wake of Ptolemy I's campaigns in Palestine. The *Letter of Aristeas* reports that some Jews migrated south after being removed from Jerusalem by the Persians and a far greater number, more than one hundred thousand, came as prisoners of war after Ptolemy I's invasion.[36] Josephus, however, preserves a different version, ostensibly drawn from Hecataeus of Abdera, but almost certainly composed by a Jewish writer cloaking himself in the persona of Hecataeus. In this happy account, the Jews accompanied Ptolemy voluntarily and enthusiastically, impressed by his gentleness and magnanimity, making a contented home for themselves in his country.[37] The truth of the matter may be indeterminable. It is, in any case, irrelevant for our purposes. Even the harsh version in the *Letter of Aristeas* is immediately softened. Ptolemy I employed the newly arrived Jews in his army, paid them handsomely, and set them up in garrisons.[38] His son went much further. Ptolemy II excused his father's severe actions as necessary to appease his troops and then proceeded not only to liberate all Jewish captives in Egypt, but to enroll many in the forces and even to promote the more trustworthy leaders to official positions in the realm.[39] The reality or unreality of this rosy picture makes no difference. This was the image conveyed by Egyptian Jews. They did not portray themselves as laboring under the yoke. Josephus, extrapolating from the narrative of "Pseudo-Hecataeus," pointedly contrasts the forcible expulsion of the Jews to Babylon by the "Persians" with their migration to Egypt and Phoenicia after the death of Alexander the Great.[40]

The inventive tale of III Maccabees places the Jews of Egypt in the gravest peril. Thrice they were almost annihilated by the wicked schemes of the mad monarch Ptolemy IV. The text alludes to a precarious existence at the mercy of their enemies. They were to perish unjustly, a foreign people in a foreign land.[41] But the dire forecast did not come to pass. The Jews triumphed in the tale, their enemies thwarted and their apostates punished. More significantly, their vindication would be celebrated by an annual festival—in Egypt.[42] The diaspora existence, in III Maccabees as in the *Letter of Aristeas*, could go on indefinitely and contentedly.

What of restoration to the homeland, the presumed sole remedy for the anguish of exiles? Such a promise derives from the Pentateuch: the Lord who issued the banishment will eventually return the children of Israel from the most remote regions to the land of their fathers.[43] That happy ending recurs in the same Hellenistic writers who bemoan the transgressions that brought about dispersal in the first place. Tobit affirms that God's fury will be followed by his mercy, thus to produce an ingathering of the exiles and even conversion of the Gentiles.[44] Achior, in the Book of Judith, informs the Assyrian general that the Israelites have regained their city and their temple. To be sure, they might lose them again if they go astray—but that anticipates perilous times in Palestine, not the drawbacks of diaspora existence.[45] The prophecy in Asher's testament foresees the same reinstatement of the scattered faithful through the benevolence of God.[46] Similar sentiments are expressed in the Psalms of Solomon.[47] And God himself makes the identical promise to Moses in the text of Jubilees: after consigning his people to captivity among their foreign enemies, he will reassemble them once more in the place of their origins to revere their newly rebuilt sanctuary.[48] But in each instance the termination of exile and return to the homeland is connected to the reconstruction of the Temple. Its demolition as symbol of the faith had rendered foreign enslavement—or its representation—especially wrenching. A comparable condition, however, did not hold in the Hellenistic diaspora.[49] The Temple stood again in Jerusalem, and few Jews abroad were held there by constraint.[50]

Just one text takes up this theme and applies it to the ingathering of exiles in the Hellenistic age. The preamble of II Maccabees contains a letter purportedly sent by Judah Maccabee, the council of elders, and the people of Jerusalem and Judaea to the Jews of Egypt. The vexed questions of whether or not the letter is authentic, whether Judah ever sent it, whether it was composed by the author of II Maccabees or attached later, and what parts are original and what parts interpolated can all here be set aside.[51] It is, on any reckoning, a Hellenistic composition. The missive concludes with the hope that God, who has now delivered Jews from great evils (the persecutions by Antiochus IV) and has purified the sanctuary, will show compassion and reassemble Jews from all regions of the world to the holy place.[52] Do we have here then a reflection of a continued wish for dissolving the diaspora and repopulating Judaea with those languishing abroad?

The inference is far from inevitable. This concocted letter, whatever its genuineness, represents a Maccabaean line. Judah deliberately and point-edly echoes the biblical theme.[53] The final lines of the epistle follow closely the wording in Deuteronomy 30.3–5. And they are not the only allusion to this motif of regathering the dispersed. Earlier in the letter Judah cites Nehe-miah, recently returned to Jerusalem, issuing a prayer after the erection of the Second Temple that God liberate the enslaved among the nations and reassemble those in the diaspora.[54] Later he adverts to Jeremiah at the time of the exile and the prophet's promise that God will show pity and bring his people together again.[55] The latter two passages are inventions by the com-poser, without authority in the Scriptures. The purpose plainly is to link Ju-dah's achievement in the purification of the Temple to grand moments of the Israelite past. The letter alludes not only to the rebuilding of the Temple in the time of Nehemiah but to its initial construction by King Solomon himself and even to divine signs vouchsafed to Moses.[56] Judah is set in the line of the grand figures of biblical antiquity. That context accounts for the phraseology of regathering the exiles, a dramatic plea with scriptural reso-nance, not a mirror of contemporary longings by diaspora Jews.

The point can be strengthened. Judah's epistle directed itself to the Jews of Egypt. Its principal objective was to declare the celebration of Hanukkah (or its original version as a Feast of Tabernacles) and to encourage the Ju-daeans' Egyptian compatriots to celebrate it as well.[57] The message con-templates no dissolution of that diaspora community, but rather presup-poses its continued existence.

A consistency holds amidst these texts. Dismal memories of misery and exile recall the biblical era, sufferings under Assyrians and Babylonians. But redemption came, the promise of a new Temple was kept. The lamentations do not apply to current conditions. Hellenistic constructs have Jews thrive in Egypt, overcome their enemies, and enjoy festivities that celebrate tri-umphs won in Palestine and the diaspora alike.

How compelling was the notion of a "homeland" to Jews dwelling in distant and dispersed communities of the Mediterranean?[58] In principle, the con-cept held firm. The sanctity of Jerusalem retained a central place in the con-sciousness of Hellenistic Jews, wherever they happened to reside. They had not wrapped themselves in the text as the real meaning of their identity, em-bracing their location in the diaspora and indifferent to their territorial roots. Judah Maccabee labels Jerusalem as the "Holy City" in his epistle to the Egyptian Jews, as one might expect.[59] The phrase also appears several times in the work of the Alexandrian Jew Philo, who never doubts the pri-macy of Jerusalem.[60] And the Jewish devotion to their sacred "acropolis" is observed even by the pagan geographer Strabo.[61] Numerous other texts characterize Palestine as the "holy land." That designation occurs in II Maccabees, the Wisdom of Solomon, the Testament of Job, the Sibylline Oracles, and Philo.[62] Most, if not all, of these works stem from the diaspora. They underscore the reverence with which Jews around the Mediterranean continued to regard Jerusalem and the land of their fathers.[63]

Loyalty to one's native land was a deep commitment in the rhetoric of the Hellenistic world.[64] A striking passage in the *Letter of Aristeas* pronounces that precept in unequivocal fashion. Amidst the myriad questions put to his Jewish guests by Ptolemy II at his week-long symposium was one that asked "how to be a lover of one's country." The respondent made as strong a contrast as can be imagined between a native land and residence abroad, between *patris* and *xenia*. It is a noble thing, he said, to live and die in one's own country; by contrast, *xenia* brings contempt to the poor and shame to the rich—as if they had been expelled for criminal behavior.[65] The statement, surprisingly enough, has received almost no comment from commentators.[66] Prima facie, it looks like a *locus classicus* for Jewish belief that life in Palestine alone is worth living and that diaspora existence is mere despair and disgrace.

Philo more than once endorses the idea that adherence to one's *patris* has compelling power. He speaks of the charms of kinsmen and homeland; trips abroad are good for widening one's horizons, but nothing better than coming home.[67] Failure to worship God is put on a level with neglecting to honor parents, benefactors, and *patris*.[68] Defending one's country is a prime virtue.[69] And, as Philo has Agrippa say to Caligula, love of one's native land and compliance with its precepts is deeply ingrained in all men.[70]

Palestine as the *patris* appears as a recurrent theme. The diaspora author of II Maccabees brands the Jewish villains of his piece, Simon, Jason, and Menelaus, as betrayers of their homeland.[71] Judah Maccabee, on the other hand, is a preeminent champion of his *patris* and its laws.[72] The Hebrews, according to Philo, had migrated to Egypt as if it were a second fatherland, but eventually they conceived a longing for the real thing, their ancient and native land.[73] A comparable formulation can be found in Artapanus' recreation of the Exodus,[74] and in the Greek drama on that theme composed by Ezekiel.[75] That the term *patris* is no mere shorthand expression for traditions, practices, the site of their faith, or even Jerusalem is clear from an unambiguous assertion in II Maccabees. Judah Maccabee called upon his troops to fight nobly and to the death for their laws, their temple, their city, their *patris,* and their way of life.[76] *Patris* is not synonymous with any of the rest. The native land is Palestine.

So, Jerusalem as concept and reality remained a powerful emblem of Jewish identity—not supplanted by the Book or disavowed by those who dwelled afar. How then to interpret this tenacious devotion? Do these pronouncements entail a widespread desire to pull up stakes and return to the fatherland? It might seem logical, even inevitable, to conclude that diaspora Jews set their hearts upon such a return. Fulfillment could come only with a re-connection to the *patris*.[77]

Logical perhaps, but not inevitable. Broad pronouncements about love of one's country accord with general Hellenistic attitudes and expressions.[78] They do not require that residence abroad be abandoned and native envi-rons reinhabited lest life remain incomplete. References to the Hebrews' migration to Egypt from the fatherland and subsequent recovery of that fa-therland are perfectly reasonable and acceptable—without imposing upon them the burden of masquerading for aspirations by Hellenistic Jews. It is noteworthy that the texts that speak of reverence for the *patris* do not speak of the "return."

The bald and forceful statement in the *Letter of Aristeas,* noted above, of-fers an ostensibly formidable obstacle. The Jewish spokesman, in a Hel-lenistic composition and a Hellenistic setting, draws a stark contrast between the nobility of living and dying in one's *patris* and the ignominy of dwelling abroad.[79] Is the reference here to Palestine? Not an obvious conclusion. In the context of the whole work, a disparagement of Egypt as residence for Jews would be absurd. The main message of the *Letter* directs itself to Egyp-tian Jews for whom the Hebrew Scriptures are rendered into Greek, an ac-complishment they greet with fervid gratitude. Indeed, they insist that not a word be changed in the translation, so that it remain forever inviolable.[80] The entire tale rests on the premise that diaspora Jews will now have direct access to the tenets of their faith and a solid foundation for enduring com-munities abroad. Why then this statement in the symposium? It is well to re-member that each question posed by Ptolemy II seeks advice from a Jewish sage on some aspect of how to govern his kingdom or how to lead a good life. In this instance, the king asks how he might be a genuine lover of his coun-try.[81] The first part of the answer, that which contrasts native land and for-eign residence, seems curiously irrelevant. And the last part, which advises Ptolemy to bestow benefits on all, just as he regularly does, and thus to be reckoned a real patriot, presupposes (if it carries any substantive meaning) the continued and contented community of resident aliens. Like so many of the swift and brief retorts by Jewish sages at the banquet, this one is bland and unsatisfying, containing statements that barely pertain to the king's query. The passage, whatever its significance, can hardly serve as a touch-stone for the thesis that diaspora Jews were consumed with a desire to for-sake their surroundings.

Did Jewish settlements abroad carry a stigma? A term sometimes em-ployed to characterize them might, at first sight, seem to suggest it. They were reckoned as *apoikiai* [colonies]. That designation presented them as offshoots from the metropolis, secondary to the original. But the term in customary Greek usage lacked pejorative overtones and, as employed by Jewish writers, its implications were, in fact, decidedly positive.

The Jews hounded and herded in Alexandria faced nearly certain death in the fantasy depicted in III Maccabees. A final prayer reached God from the elderly and respected priest Eleazer. Among his pleas Eleazer included a reference to possible impieties committed by Jews in their *apoikia*.[82] But the sins, not the location, provide the grounds for potential destruction. And the happy ending vindicates and perpetuates the colony. The new festival instituted by the Egyptian Jews to celebrate their rescue and triumph would hold for generations to come and throughout the time of their settlement abroad—here designated as *paroikia*.[83]

Philo uses the word *apoikia* with reference to Moses leading the Hebrews out of their abode in Egypt. No negative overtones characterize that statement. The same phraseology in the same context was employed three and a half centuries earlier by the Greek writer Hecataeus of Abdera.[84] Indeed, Philo elsewhere makes clear his very positive assessment of Jewish "colonies" abroad. God reassured Moses that Jews dwelling abroad in future generations would be on the same footing as Jews in Palestine with regard to fulfilling sacred rites. The diaspora Jews, he affirms explicitly, live at a distance through no transgression, but through the need of an overpopulated nation to send out *apoikiai*.[85] The philosopher reiterates that statement in fuller form in Agrippa's letter to Caligula, proudly detailing the colonies that had been sent out from Judaea over the years to places all over the Mediterranean and the Near East.[86] Josephus echoes Philo in asserting that Jewish participation in colonies sent abroad by other nations gave them an honored presence in those settlements from the start.[87] In a most revealing passage, Philo, in fact, asserts that in the case of those sent to a colony, by contrast to those simply away from home, the *apoikia*, rather than the *metropolis*, becomes the *patris*.[88] Jerusalem was indeed the mother city.[89] But, as is clear, the expression "colony" had a ring of pride and accomplishment, signaling the spread of the faith and its adherents, not a fall from grace.[90]

Jews formed stable communities in the diaspora, entered into the social, economic, and political life of the nations they joined, aspired to and often obtained citizen privileges in the cities of the Hellenistic world. Adequate evidence attests a Jewish striving for full and acknowledged membership and a genuine sense of belonging. Philo expresses the principle of the matter clearly enough. He declares that *xenoi* should be reckoned as residents and friends eager to enjoy privileges equal to those of citizens and, indeed, as being hardly any different from the indigenous people themselves.[91] Josephus maintains that Jews have every right to designate themselves as Alexandrians, Antiochenes, Ephesians, or whatever name belongs to the city in which they have settled.[92] Further, in discussing elsewhere the Jews of Ionia who sought redress from Rome against their opponents in the time of Augustus, he claims that they established their status as "natives."[93] Philo, indeed, referred to his city as "our Alexandria."[94] That form of identification emerges more poignantly in the petition of an Alexandrian Jew threatened with loss of his privileges. He labels himself an "Alexandrian" at the head of the document, alluding to his father, also an Alexandrian, and the proper education he had received, and expresses his fear of being deprived of his *patris*. The petitioner or the scribe who composed the letter in its final form then altered the term "Alexandrian" to "a Jew from Alexandria."[95] Whatever legal meaning this terminology might have carried, it signals the petitioner's clear affirmation of his roots in the community.[96] A comparable sentiment might be inferred from an inscription of the Phrygian city Acmonia, alluding to fulfillment of a vow made to the "whole *patris*." A Jew or a group of Jews must have commissioned it, for a menorah appears beneath the text. Here again the "native city" is honored, presumably through a gift for civic purposes. The donor pronounces his local loyalty in a conspicuous public manner.[97]

The most telling statement comes in Philo's *In Flaccum*. The passage is often cited for its reference to the impressive span of the Jewish diaspora, the spread of Jews to many places in Europe and Asia, including the most prosperous, whether on islands or on the mainland. But Philo proceeds to offer a striking depiction of Jewish attitudes both toward Jerusalem and toward the lands where they (and previous generations) had made their home. As Philo puts it, they considered the Holy City as their "metropolis," but the states in which they were born and raised and which they acquired from their fathers, grandfathers, and distant forefathers they adjudged their *patrides*.[98] That fervent expression eradicates any idea of the "doctrine of return." Diaspora Jews, in Philo's formulation at least, held a fierce attachment to the adopted lands of their ancestors.

Jews around the Mediterranean appear unapologetic and unembarrassed by their situation. They did not describe themselves as part of a diaspora. They did not suggest that they were cut off from the center, leading a separate, fragmented, and unfulfilled existence. They could eschew justification, rationalization, or tortured explanation for their choice of residence. They felt no need to construct a theory of diaspora.

Commitment to the community and devotion to Jerusalem were entirely compatible. That devotion had a public and conspicuous demonstration every year: the payment of a tithe to the Temple from Jews all over the Mediterranean.[99] The ritualistic offering carried deep significance as a bonding device. Its origins are obscure and require no investigation here. That it rests on a biblical prescription, the half-shekel imposed by the Lord upon Israelites counted in a census in the wilderness, may be questioned.[100] A more direct link perhaps comes with Nehemiah's establishment of a one-third shekel tax to help finance maintenance of the new Temple's operations.[101]

When such a contribution was first expected of Jews in the diaspora can only be guessed at. The Seleucid overlords of Palestine had subsidized the financial needs of the Temple in the early second century B.C.E., as the Ptolemies may have done before them, and the Persian kings before them.[102] At some time after installation of Hasmonaean rule, support for the Temple came in from abroad, soon a matter of established practice and an accepted obligation of the faithful.[103]

The fact impressed itself notably among the Romans. Events of the mid 60s B.C.E. brought it to their attention in a forceful fashion. Economic circumstances in Rome and abroad had prompted a series of decrees forbidding the export of gold. The Roman governor of Asia, L. Valerius Flaccus, enforced the policy in various ways, including a ban on the sending of gold by the Jews of Asia Minor to Jerusalem.[104] The action not only prompted resentment among the Jews in Flaccus' province but stirred a hornet's nest of opposition among the Jews in Rome itself. Cicero, who conducted Flaccus' defense at his trial for extortion in 59, comments bitterly about the horde of Jews crowding around the tribunal, exercising undue pressure upon the proceedings and passionately exhibiting their "barbaric superstition."[105] The account, of course, is partisan, rhetorical, and exaggerated, but it also conveys some precious information. First, Cicero indicates the earnest commitment of Jews to provide funds annually to the Temple from Italy and from all the provinces of the Roman empire.[106] Next, his record of Flaccus' activities indicates that tribute for the Temple was collected by Jewish communities, city by city, wherever they possessed sufficient numbers in Asia Minor.[107] And, most revealingly, Cicero's speech, however embellished and overblown, shows that the plight of Asian Jews who were prevented from making their wonted contributions to the Temple stirred the passions of their compatriots far off in Rome and provoked impressively noisy demonstrations on their behalf. Cicero remarks both on the pressure and size of the Jewish assemblage and on its community of interests—features, he claims, well known in Rome.[108] The whole episode exhibits the solidarity of sentiments among diaspora Jews from Italy to the Near East in the matter of expressing their allegiance to Jerusalem.[109]

The centrality of Jewish commitment to the tithe is demonstrated again and again. Philo reinforces the testimony of Cicero. His comment on the large Jewish community in Rome at the time of Augustus once again associates it with zeal for gathering the sacred tithes for Jerusalem—a fact with which the *princeps* was well acquainted.[110] The size of contributions over the years had brought substantial wealth to the Temple. Josephus proudly observes that the donations had come from Jews all over Asia and Europe, indeed from everywhere in the world, for a huge number of years.[111] When that activity was interfered with by local authorities, Jews would send up a howl to Rome. So, for instance, when M. Agrippa, overseeing the eastern provinces for Augustus, appeared in Ionia, Jews from various Ionian communities complained loudly of Greek interference with their prerogatives, naming first and foremost the seizure of cash destined as contributions to Jerusalem.[112] If Josephus' collection of Roman decrees be trusted, the emperor Augustus himself intervened to assure the untroubled exercise of Jewish practices in the province of Asia. In promulgating an edict to put Roman muscle behind the protection of Jewish privileges, Augustus placed at the head of the list the inviolability of sacred monies sent to Jerusalem and designated for the treasury officials of the Temple.[113] That prerogative and that alone is noted in the emperor's letter to the proconsul of Asia.[114] Agrippa followed it up with directives to officials in Ephesus and Cyrene, as did the Roman governor in a message to Sardis.[115] The active support by Augustus and Agrippa for Jewish interests on this matter is attested also by Philo, a close contemporary.[116] Monies collected for Jerusalem form the centerpiece in each of the Roman pronouncements. That emphasis must come from Jews pressing their claims upon the imperial government. Indeed, areas beyond the reach of Roman power also contained Jews who pursued the same practice with rigor and consistency. Communities in Babylon and other satrapies under Parthian dominion sent representatives every year over difficult terrain and dangerous highways to deposit their contributions in the Temple.[117] Even if the documents are not genuine, they reflect the order of priorities expressed by the Jewish sources of Philo and Josephus. The issue of paying homage to Jerusalem was paramount.[118]

Proof, if proof be needed, is provided by a hostile witness with no axe to grind on this score. Tacitus, in a list of depraved and deplorable Jewish habits, sets in first place the institution of collecting tribute and donations to increase the resources of the Jews.[119] And there is ironic significance in the fact that when the Romans destroyed the Temple they refrained from destroying this institution; rather, they altered its recipient. The annual tithe would no longer go to the nonexistent sacred shrine; it would metamorphose into a Roman tax. The cash would now serve to subsidize the cult of Jupiter Capitolinus.[120]

The stark symbolism of the tithe had a potent hold upon Jewish sentiment. That annual act of obeisance was a repeated reminder, or rather display, of affection and allegiance. Jerusalem cast the most compelling image and gripped the imaginations of Jews everywhere in the Mediterranean and the Near East. The repeated, ritualistic contributions emblematized the unbroken attachment of the diaspora to the center. Even the Romans recognized the symbolic power of the payment. Its transformation into a subsidy for the preeminent deity of the empire would serve as dramatic signifier of a new loyalty.

What implications does the tithe possess for our question? Did the outpouring of cash for the Temple by Jews from Italy to Iran imply that the diaspora was reckoned as fleeting and temporary, an interim exile or refuge, an affliction to be endured until restoration to the Holy City? In fact, the reverse conclusion holds. The continuing pledge of allegiance proclaimed that the diaspora could endure indefinitely and quite satisfactorily. The communities abroad were entrenched and successful, even mainstays of the center. Diaspora Jews did not and would not turn their backs on Jerusalem, the principal emblem of their faith. Their fierce commitment to the tithe delivered that message unequivocally. But the gesture did not signify a desire for the return. On the contrary, it signaled that the return was unnecessary.

A comparable phenomenon demands attention: the pilgrimage of diaspora Jews to Jerusalem. How often and in what numbers is unclear.[121] Major festivals could attract them with some frequency and in quantity. If Philo be believed, myriads came from countless cities for every feast, over land and sea, from all points of the compass, to enjoy the Temple as a serene refuge from the hurly-burly of everyday life abroad.[122] The most celebrated occasion occurred after the death of Jesus. The feast of Pentecost had brought numerous persons into the city from far-flung and diverse locations: peoples from Parthia, Media, and Elam, from Mesopotamia and Cappadocia, from Pontus and Asia, from Phrygia and Pamphylia, from Egypt and Cyrene, from Crete and Arabia, and, indeed, even from Rome, all witness to the miracle of the disciples speaking in the whole array of diverse tongues.[123] When the Roman governor of Syria visited Jerusalem at the time of Passover in the mid 60s C.E. he encountered crowds of incalculable numbers.[124] Even the Great Revolt did not discourage pilgrims from coming at Passover. A large number found themselves trapped in the city and perished in the Roman siege.[125] Huge crowds from abroad, including Gentiles, at Passover were evidently common.[126] The women's court at the Temple was large enough to accommodate those who resided in the land and those who came from abroad— a clear sign that female pilgrims in some numbers were expected.[127]

The delivery of the annual tithe itself brought diaspora Jews to Jerusalem on a regular basis, a ritual performance analogous to, even identical with, a pilgrimage. Philo attests to the sacred messengers who not only deposit the monies but perform the sacrifices.[128] And they might be accompanied by many others, especially when arduous and perilous journeys required numbers for protection.[129] The adherents of Paul who went with him to Jerusalem from Greece, Macedon, and Asia may also have been performing a pilgrimage.[130] The Holy City exercised tremendous force as a magnet. Josephus' romantic tale about the conversion to Judaism by the royal family in far-off Adiabene, whatever its authenticity, illustrates the point nicely. The queen mother, Helena, an ardent proselyte, felt that confirmation of her new status required a visit to the sacred site and worship in the Temple. Helena proceeded to shower Jerusalem with gifts, a gesture duplicated by her son Izates, the king of Adiabene. Izates sent his five young sons to Palestine to receive training in Hebrew language and culture. And both mother and son were buried not in Adiabene but outside Jerusalem in monuments whose construction Helena herself had directed.[131] The experience of the royal house, at least as represented in the tale, recapitulates the behavior of diaspora Jews, which they had, in effect, become.[132] The visits to Jerusalem and gifts to the Temple followed the appropriate mode of expressing homage, but that demonstration of devotion did not entail a desire for migration. Pilgrimage, in fact, by its very nature, signified a temporary payment of respect. The Holy City had an irresistible and undiminished claim on the emotions of diaspora Jews. It was indeed a critical piece of their identity. But home was elsewhere.

The self-perception of Second Temple Jews projected a tight solidarity between center and diaspora. The images of exile and separation did not haunt them. They were not compelled to choose between restoration to Eretz Israel and recourse to the Word as their "portable homeland." What affected the dwellers in Jerusalem affected Jews everywhere. The theme of intertwined experience and interdependent identity is reiterated with impressive frequency and variety.

Many of the texts already noticed, and a good number of others besides, fortify this conclusion. The author of II Maccabees—or at least of the letters attached to the beginning of that work—gives pointed expression to the idea. The Jews of Jerusalem take for granted the intimate relationship that exists with their brethren in Egypt. The preamble of the first letter greets them as "brothers" to "brothers" and alludes to their common heritage, God's covenant with Abraham, Isaac, and Jacob.[133] The central message of both missives is that the Egyptian Jews should celebrate the new festival honoring the recovery and purification of the Temple after the desecration by Antiochus IV.[134] The concluding lines of the second letter make reference to the desired reunion of all Jews in the holy site. As argued above, that is not a call for an end to the diaspora. It represents the party line of the Maccabaeans.[135] But even if pressed, it signifies no more than a summons to a festival—and thus a reaffirmation of solidarity among Jews everywhere. It reflects the practice of pilgrimage rather than a program to dissolve the dispersal.

The *Letter of Aristeas* makes the connection between Jerusalemites and other Jews still more forcefully and unequivocally. King Ptolemy's letter to the High Priest in Judaea asserts that his motive in having the Hebrew Bible rendered into Greek was to benefit not only the Jews of Egypt but all Jews throughout the world—even those not yet born.[136] And it is fitting that, when the scholars from Jerusalem completed their translation and it was read out to the Jews of Egypt, the large assemblage burst into applause, a dramatic expression of the unity of purpose.[137]

The narrative of III Maccabees depends on that same unity of purpose. It presupposes and never questions the proposition that the actions of Jerusalemites represent the sentiments of Jews anywhere in the diaspora. After Ptolemy IV was thwarted in his design to enter the Holy of Holies in Jerusalem, his immediate reaction upon his return to Egypt was to inflict punishment upon the Jews in Egypt. The king had determined to bring public shame upon the *ethnos* of the Jews generally.[138] A few were prepared to yield to his offer of civic privileges in Alexandria in return for apostasy. But most of them held firm, reckoning the apostates as enemies of the nation and refusing them any part in communal life and mutual services.[139] Whatever Ptolemy IV may in fact have thought, the author of III Maccabees certainly presumed a commonality of interests within the Jewish *ethnos* as a whole. Egyptian Jews were "fellow-tribesmen" of those who dwelled in Judaea.[140]

The Book of Tobit offers a parallel episode. A principal theme of that work concerns proper burial rites. Tobit, dwelling in exile at Nineveh, felt it incumbent upon himself, despite the dangers and difficulties involved, to bury the bodies of all Jews executed on the orders of the Assyrian king Sennacherib. Like the wicked Ptolemy of III Maccabees, Sennacherib wreaked vengeance upon Israelites in Assyria because of a rout he had suffered at the hands of their compatriots in Israel.[141] Once again, the assumption of solidarity among Jews in the center and those abroad underpins the narrative.

Apart from the pagans of fiction, real ones found Jewish solidarity as well. The notorious passage of Cicero, treated earlier, offers a vivid example. When a Roman governor sought to prevent export of gold from Asia for the Temple in Jerusalem, a large crowd of Jews in Rome protested vociferously and exerted heavy pressure on the public proceedings.[142]

In the perception of Philo and Josephus, no breach existed, no discernible difference even, between the practices of Palestinian Jews and of those abroad. The priestly classes in the diaspora maintain the same rigid adherence to genealogical purity as do those in the homeland. Moreover, the scrupulous records of the family lines are regularly sent to Jerusalem as a token of esteem and a sign of solidarity. Josephus here employs the term διεσπαρμένοι [scattered]—and plainly without any derogatory undertone.[143] Philo asserts the equivalence of diaspora Jews, with regard to the ritual of honoring the dead, in still more forceful terms: those who settle abroad have committed no wrongs and cannot be denied equal privileges. The nation has simply spilled over its borders and can no longer be confined to a single land.[144]

The community of interests could have direct effect on the events of Jewish history. In the late second century B.C.E., Cleopatra III, the queen of Egypt, gained the upper hand in a war against her son Ptolemy Lathyrus and was urged by some of her advisers to seize the opportunity for an invasion of Judaea. The plan never materialized because better advice came from another quarter. The Jewish military man Ananias, a loyal and effective general in Cleopatra's army, dissuaded her with a compelling argument. He counted the High Priest in Judaea, Alexander Jannaeus, as his own kinsman. And any attack on the High Priest, so he claimed, would make enemies of all the Jews in Egypt. Cleopatra reconsidered the matter, dropped plans for an invasion, and instead concluded an alliance with Jannaeus.[145]

A half century later, the close ties of Judaean and Egyptian Jews and the prestige of the High Priest once more had a telling effect on the course of historical events. At the height of the Roman civil war, Julius Caesar found himself besieged in Alexandria in 48/7 B.C.E. A troop of three thousand Jewish soldiers marched to his rescue under their general, Antipater, who had rounded up additional support from Arabia, Syria, and Lebanon. But their path was blocked by Egyptian Jews who dwelled in the Oniad district, that is, in the enclave of Leontopolis, the site of a long-standing Jewish community. Antipater, however, overcame any resistance by appealing to their common nationality and, indeed, their loyalty to the High Priest Hyrcanus. Antipater wielded a letter from Hyrcanus requesting that Egyptian Jews support the cause of Caesar. No further persuasion was necessary. The Jews both of Leontopolis and of Memphis declared themselves for Caesar and helped to turn the tide of the war.[146] The sense of Jewish solidarity and the respect for the High Priest's authority in Jerusalem had an impressive impact. No sign of an "exilic" mentality here. Leontopolis itself endured as an autonomous center of Judaism with its own temple for well over two hundred years, until its destruction by the Romans in the wake of the Great Revolt. But, as this episode indicates, there was no schismatic separatism here. The Jews of Leontopolis continued to acknowledge the ascendancy of Jerusalem.[147]

One might note also the active involvement of Roman Jews in pressing Augustus to put an end to Herodian rule in Judaea after the death of Herod the Great. Fifty envoys came from Judaea for this purpose and eight thousand Jews resident in Rome joined in their lobbying efforts.[148] When a pretender to the throne emerged, claiming to be a reincarnation of one of Herod's sons, he found widespread support from Jews in Crete, in Melos, and in Rome itself.[149] These events provide a revealing window upon the lively interest and occasionally energetic engagement of diaspora Jews in the affairs of Palestine.

The affiliations and interconnections emerge perhaps most dramatically in the grave crises that marked the reign of the emperor Caligula. Harsh conflict erupted in Alexandria, bringing dislocation, persecution, and death upon large numbers in the Jewish community of that city. Philo's accounts of these events contain their own bias and agenda, but they do convey the reflections of an eyewitness and participant and they afford an insight into the attitudes of articulate Jews in the diaspora. The attacks upon the Alexandrian Jewish community came under the authority of the Roman prefect of Egypt, A. Flaccus. And when they came, so Philo maintains, the word spread like wildfire. Once synagogues were destroyed in Alexandria, reports would swiftly sweep not only through all the districts of Egypt but from there to the nations of the East and from the borders of Libya to the lands of the West. Jews had settled all over Europe and Asia, and the news of a pogrom anywhere would race through the entire network.[150] So Philo says. And, although his claim of such speedy communications might stretch a point, the concept of tight interrelationships among Jews of the diaspora can hardly be gainsaid. Flaccus, of course, eventually perished for his misdeeds, an appropriate ending to the morality tale. And Philo makes sure to emphasize that this was no peculiar Alexandrian affair: Flaccus is described as the "common enemy of the Jewish nation."[151]

Philo himself headed the delegation to the emperor that would plead the cause of the Jewish community in Alexandria. The timing of their arrival in Rome only heightened the drama. Word soon arrived of the larger crisis: Caligula's decision to install his statue in the Temple at Jerusalem. The initial motive for the embassy now seemed paltry by comparison. Philo's words are arresting: this most grievous calamity fell unexpectedly and brought peril not to one part of the Jewish people but to the entire nation at once.[152] Indeed, Philo berates himself for even thinking about parochial Alexandrian matters when a much greater catastrophe threatened the very existence of the Jewish polity and the name common to the nation as a whole.[153] The magnitude of Caligula's decision had already occurred to P. Petronius, the legate of Syria, whose task it was to oversee the erection of the statue. Petronius dragged his feet and reached for excuses to postpone the job. For he knew (or so Philo reconstructs his thoughts) that such an act would outrage Jews everywhere and provoke resistance not only in Judaea, where their ranks were especially strong, but from the large number of Jews dwelling across the Euphrates in Babylon and all the provinces of the Parthian empire, indeed almost throughout the world.[154] The letter of Agrippa I, a friend of the emperor who had recently been accorded a kingdom among the Jews, urgently alerted Caligula to the severe gravity of the situation. Agrippa's plea to the Roman ruler maintained, among other things, that an affront to Jerusalem would have vast repercussions: the Holy City was the metropolis not only of Judaea but of most nations in the world, since Jewish colonies thrived all over the Near East, Asia Minor, Greece, Macedon, Africa, and the lands beyond the Euphrates.[155] No matter how self-serving Agrippa's statement—or indeed the account of Philo in which it is embedded—the image of Jerusalem as binding together Jews everywhere in the *oikoumene* surely held a prominent place in the self-perception of the diaspora. And, in Philo's account at least, that perception is not confined to Jews. If Gentiles in any city received authorization to attack Jews, their counterparts in all cities would take it as a green light to conduct their own terrorist activities.[156]

The consistency of this portrait leaves a potent impression. Philo articulated an unbroken bond among diaspora Jews and between them and Jerusalem. No trauma in one community would go unfelt in the rest. And the ripples from any threat to Jerusalem would quickly extend throughout the Jewish world.

A moving passage elsewhere in Philo's corpus neatly encapsulates the theme of this essay. It stands outside the context of crisis and turmoil, outside the fears of pogrom in Alexandria or the megalomania of a Roman monarch. Philo, who thrived in the diaspora, enjoyed its advantages and broadcast its virtues, nevertheless found even deeper meaning in the land of Israel. In his discussion of Jewish festivals, he interprets the Shavuot Festival as a celebration of the Jews' possession of their own land, a heritage of long standing and a means whereby they could cease their wandering over continents and islands and their existence as foreigners and vagabonds dwelling in the countries of others.[157] Philo saw no inconsistency or contradiction. Diaspora Jews might find fulfillment and reward in their communities abroad, but they honored Judaea as refuge for the formerly displaced and unsettled, and the prime legacy of all.

Josephus makes the point in a quite different context but with equal force. In his rewriting of Numbers, he places a sweeping prognostication in the mouth of the Midianite priest Balaam. To the consternation of the king of Moab, who had expected a dark oracle for the Israelites, Balaam projected a glorious future. They will not only occupy and hold forever the land of Canaan, a chief signal of God's favor, but their multitudes will fill all the world, islands and continents, outnumbering even the stars in the heavens.[158] That is a notable declaration. Palestine, as ever, merits a special place. But the diaspora, far from being a source of shame to be overcome, represents a resplendent achievement.

The respect and awe paid to the Holy Land stood in full harmony with commitment to local community and allegiance to Gentile governance. Diaspora Jews did not bewail their fate and pine away for the homeland. Nor, by contrast, did they ignore the homeland and reckon the Book as surrogate for the Temple. The postulated alternatives are severe and simplistic. Palestine mattered, and it mattered in a territorial sense, but not as a required residence. Gifts to the Temple and pilgrimages to Jerusalem announced simultaneously a devotion to the symbolic heart of Judaism and a singular pride in the accomplishments of the diaspora. Jewish Hellenistic writers took the concurrence for granted. They were not driven to apologia. Nor did they feel obliged to reconcile the contradiction. There was none.

NOTES

1. See the stimulating discussion by A. Eisen, *Galut* (Bloomington, 1986). Eisen recapitulates his thesis in A. A. Cohen and P. Mendes-Flohr, eds., *Contemporary Jewish Religious Thought* (New York, 1987), 219–25.

2. See, in general, the important works of Y. F. Baer, *Galut* (New York, 1947); Y. Kaufmann, *Exile and Estrangement* (in Hebrew), 2 vols. (Tel Aviv, 1962); Eisen, *Galut*. See also D. Vital, *The Origins of Zionism* (Oxford, 1975), 1–10; E. Levine, "The Jews in Time and Space," in E. Levine, ed., *Diaspora: Exile and the Jewish Condition* (New York, 1983), 1–11. For the notion of exile and return as a construct invented by the composers of the Pentateuch, dominating Jewish self-definition ever thereafter, see J. Neusner, "Exile and Return as the History of Judaism," in J. M. Scott, ed., *Exile: Old Testament, Jewish, and Christian Conceptions* (Leiden, 1997), 221–37, summarizing his lengthier presentation in *Self-Fulfilling Prophecy: Exile and Return in the History of Judaism* (Boston, 1987). In a similar vein, with specific reference to the Assyrian and Babylonian "exiles," see R. P. Carroll, "Exile! What Exile? Deportation and the Discourses of Diaspora," in L. Grabbe, ed., *Leading Captivity Captive: "The Exile" as History and Ideology* (Sheffield, 1998), 62–79; T. L. Thompson, "The Exile in History and Myth: A Response to Hans Barstad," in Grabbe, ed., *Leading Captivity Captive*, 101–18; P. R. Davies, "Exile? What Exile? Whose Exile?" in Grabbe, ed., *Leading Captivity Captive*, 128–38. This concept of the Jewish experience has become a paradigm for the diaspora mentality everywhere. Cf. W. Safran, "Diasporas in Modern Societies," *Diaspora* 1 (1991): 83–99. The use of such an ideal type is rightly criticized in the acute discussion of J. Clifford, *Routes: Travel and Translation in the Late Twentieth Century* (Cambridge, Mass., 1997), 244–77.

3. See especially G. Steiner, "Our Homeland, the Text," *Salmagundi* 66 (1985): 4–25. On the ambivalence of exile and homecoming in recent Jewish conceptions, see the comments of S. D. Ezrahi, "Our Homeland, the Text . . . Our Text, the Homeland," *Michigan Quarterly Review* 31 (1992): 463–97.

4. The recent article by C. Milikowsky, "Notions of Exile, Subjugation, and Return in Rabbinic Literature," in Scott, ed., *Exile*, 265–81, argues, most interestingly, that early midrashic texts do not single out the Roman conquest as a pivotal turning point, but conceive a more continuous period of exile and subjugation, stretching through the Second Temple era and beyond. The notion of the Temple's fall as a caesura emerges only in later rabbinic writings.

5. Cf. Strabo, *apud* Jos. *Ant.* 14.115. For population estimates, see S. Baron, *Encyclopedia Judaica*, 13 (Jerusalem, 1971), 866–903; L. H. Feldman, *Jew and Gentile in the Ancient World* (Princeton, 1993), 23, 468–69, 555–56. Much uncertainty remains.

6. A doleful portrait of diaspora for Hellenistic Jews is drawn most forcefully by W. C. van Unnik, *Das Selbstverständnis der jüdischen Diaspora in der hellenistisch-römischen Zeit* (Leiden, 1993), a posthumous publication of papers actually delivered in 1967. Van Unnik shows that the term "diaspora"—or more usually its verbal form—is

almost always employed with a negative connotation in the Septuagint (which uses it to render various Hebrew words); *op. cit.*, 89–107. It has a negative meaning also in the large majority of its appearances in Hellenistic Jewish writers; *op. cit.*, 108–47.

7. Lev. 26.33.

8. Deut. 4.26–28, 28.63–65.

9. Jeremiah, 5.19.

10. Jeremiah, 9.15.

11. Daniel, 9.4–7.

12. Philo, *Abr.* 64.; cf. *Conf. Ling.* 120–21, 196.

13. Deut. 30.2–5; cf. I Kings, 8.33–34, 8.46–51; II Chron. 6.24–25, 6.36–39; Jeremiah, 29.10–14.

14. Isaiah, 11.12.

15. Baer, *Galut,* 9–13; Eisen, *Galut,* 3–34. As noted above, the most sweeping argument on melancholy Jewish attitudes toward the diaspora in the Second Temple era is made by van Unnik, *Das Selbstverständnis.* See also the useful survey by W. D. Davies, *The Territorial Dimension of Judaism* (Berkeley, 1982), 28–34, 61–100.

16. Davies, *Territorial Dimension,* 116–26, endeavors to resolve the "contradiction" between commitment to the Land at the center and the realities of life on the periphery, concluding that, although the pull of the Land is personal and powerful, it is not territorial. In the view of A. T. Kraabel, "Unity and Diversity among Diaspora Synagogues," in L. Levine, ed., *The Synagogue in Late Antiquity* (Philadelphia, 1987), 56–58, Jews shifted from an "Exile theology" to a "Diaspora theology," although he appears to believe that this really took hold only after the destruction of the Temple. The trenchant review article of J. Price rightly stresses the diversity of diaspora communities and the successes enjoyed by Jews therein; "The Jewish Diaspora of the Graeco-Roman Period," *SCI* 13 (1994): 170–79. But he plays down too much the power still wielded by the concept of the Holy Land. J. M. G. Barclay, *Jews in the Mediterranean Diaspora* (Edinburgh, 1996), 418–24, offers a sensible and balanced statement, arguing that attachment to the "motherland" could coexist with rootedness in regions abroad, although he regards the degree of attachment as dependent on circumstances. The fine study of I. M. Gafni, *Land, Center, and Diaspora* (Sheffield, 1997), 19–40, explores various strategies whereby diaspora Jews sought to account for or legitimize their situation. He places perhaps too much emphasis, however, upon the apologetic character in Hellenistic Jewish representations of local patriotism; *op. cit.*, 42–52.

17. The classic study is J. Juster, *Les Juifs dans l'empire romain,* 2 vols. (Paris, 1914). Among recent treatments, see M. Stern, "The Jewish Diaspora," in S. Safrai and M. Stern, eds., *The Jewish People in the First Century* (Philadelphia, 1974), vol. 1, 117–83; E. Schürer, *The History of the Jewish People in the Age of Jesus Christ (175 B.C.–A.D. 135),* rev. ed. by G. Vermes, F. Millar, and M. Goodman (Edinburgh, 1986), vol. 3, part 1, 1–176; Barclay, *Jews in the Mediterranean Diaspora,* 19–81, 231–319; I. Levinskaya, *The Book of Acts in its Diaspora Setting* (Grand Rapids, 1996), 127–93.

18. On the variety of motives and circumstances that induced Jews to settle in various parts of the Mediterranean, see the evidence assembled and the discussion by A. Kasher, "Jewish Emigration and Settlement in Diaspora in the Hellenistic-Roman Period" (in Hebrew), in A. Shinan, ed., *Emigration and Settlement in Jewish and General History* (Jerusalem, 1982), 65–91.

19. See the contrasting views expressed by E. E. Urbach, "Center and Periphery in Jewish Historical Consciousness: Contemporary Implications," in M. Davis, ed., *World Jewry and the State of Israel* (New York, 1977), 217–35, and J. J. Petuchowski, "Diaspora Judaism—An Abnormality," *Judaism* 9 (1960): 17–28. Davies, *Territorial Dimension,* 91–100, usefully summarizes the positions.

20. Not that the two terms were reckoned as equivalent in antiquity. Indeed *galut* or *golah* is never translated as *diaspora* in Greek. The Septuagint employs a variety of Greek words, including ἀποικία [colony], μετοικεσία [change of abode], παροικία [residence abroad], and αἰχμαλοσία [captivity]. See van Unnik, *Das Selbstverständnis,* 80–85. Van Unnik, *op.cit.,* 150–52, even argues, paradoxically and implausibly, that diaspora was a grimmer concept for Jews than exile. See the just criticisms by J. M. Scott, "Exile and the Self-Understanding of Diaspora Jews," in Scott, ed., *Exile,* 180–84.

21. Scott, in Scott, ed., *Exile,* 185–87, notes certain passages in the Septuagint on the expulsion of the Jews to which the translators added phrases such as "until this day"; Deut. 29.28; II Kings, 17.23; II Chron. 29.9. It hardly follows that these were intended to apply to the Hellenistic era.

22. Ben Sira, 48.15: ἕως ἐπρονομεύθησαν ἀπὸ γῆς αὐτῶν / καὶ διεσκορπίσθησαν ἐν πάσῃ τῇ γῇ. Elsewhere he offers up a prayer for divine deliverance in an ostensibly contemporary context, including a plea for gathering all the tribes of Jacob and restoring their inheritance as from the beginning; 36.10. But Ben Sira here echoes biblical language and by no means implies a longing for return felt in the diaspora.

23. Tobit, 3.3–4.

24. Tobit, 13.3–6, 13.10–11.

25. Tobit, 14.4.

26. Tobit, 13.10–11, 14.5–7.

27. Judith, 5.18–19.

28. Test. Levi, 10.3–4, 15.1–2, 16.5; Test. Judah, 23.3–5; Test. Iss. 6.1–4; Test. Zeb. 9.6–8; Test. Dan, 5.8–13; Test. Asher, 7.2–6.

29. The Testament of Naphtali, 4.1–5, speaks of two separate calamities inflicted by God, an exile and a scattering, after each of which he restores his favor to the children of Israel. For van Unnik, *Das Selbstverständnis,* 119–20, the second actually refers to the Hellenistic diaspora. But it may well allude to the aftermath of the destruction in 70 C.E.; so M. de Jonge, *The Testaments of the Twelve Patriarchs* (Leiden, 1978), 85.

30. Jubilees, 1.9–13.

31. Ps. Solomon, 9.1–2.

32. I Baruch, 3.8.

33. III Sibyl, 266–79.

34. Even Josephus, who rarely indulges in this form of outburst, expands on Deuteronomy and has Moses warn his people of dispersal and servitude everywhere in the inhabited world as consequence of their rebellion; *Ant.* 4.189–91. In the view of B. Halpern-Amaru, "Land Theology in Josephus' *Jewish Antiquities,*" *JQR* 71 (1980/81): 219–21, Josephus here obliquely alludes to the Jewish revolt of 66–70 C.E. So also van Unnik, *Das Selbstverständnis,* 141–42.

35. As is assumed, e.g., by Price, *SCI* 13 (1994): 172.

36. *Let. Arist.* 12: τοὺς μὲν μετῴκιζεν, οὓς δὲ ἠχμαλώτιζε; 35: ἀνασπάστους . . . ὑπὸ Περσῶν . . . αἰχμαλώτους. Similarly, Jos. *Ant.* 12.7.

37. Jos. *CAp.* 1.186; cf. *Ant.* 12.9. That this is the work of a Jewish "Pseudo-Hecataeus" is cogently argued by B. Bar-Kochva, *Pseudo-Hecataeus "On the Jews": Legitimizing the Jewish Diaspora* (Berkeley, 1996), 71–82.

38. *Let. Arist.* 13–14, 36. Josephus even adds that he bestowed citizen privileges equivalent to those of the Macedonians; *Ant.* 12.8.

39. *Let. Arist.* 19–27, 36–37.

40. Jos. *CAp.* 1. 194: ἀνασπάστους εἰς Βαβυλῶνα Πέρσαι πρότερον ἐποίησαν μυριάδας, οὐκ ὀλίγαι δὲ καὶ μετὰ τὸν Ἀλεξάνδρου θάνατον εἰς Αἴγυπτον καὶ Φοινίκην μετέστησαν. On the truth of these matters, see the discussion by Bar-Kochva, *Pseudo-Hecataeus*, 101–5, 143–44.

41. III Macc. 6.3: λαὸν ἐν ξένῃ γῇ ξένον ἀδίκως ἀπολλύμενον. Cf. 6.10: κατὰ τὴν ἀποικίαν; 6.15: ἐν τῇ γῇ τῶν ἐχθρῶν αὐτῶν.

42. III Macc. 6.36, 7.15, 7.19.

43. Deut. 30.1–5; cf. Jeremiah, 23.8; Ezek. 11.16–17. Philo's reference, *Praem. et Poen.* 115, to the change from a "spiritual diaspora" to wisdom and virtue, allegorizes the prophecy in Deuteronomy but does not refer to Hellenistic expectations or desire for return to Judaea. Nor does his gloss on Deut. 30.4 at *Conf. Ling.* 197.

44. Tobit, 13.5, 13.10–11, 13.13, 14.5–7.

45. Judith, 5.19.

46. Test. Asher, 7.7.

47. Ps. Solomon, 8.28.

48. Jubilees, 1.15–17. Cf. the analysis of B. Halpern-Amaru, "Exile and Return in Jubilees," in Scott, ed., *Exile*, 139–41. See also I Baruch, 2.29–35.

49. The arguments of Scott, in Scott, ed., *Exile*, 209–13, for a continuing hope of return through the Greco-Roman period lack foundation in the evidence. The texts cited do not derive from the diaspora.

50. Philo, in a puzzling passage, does make reference to Jews in Greek and barbarian islands and continents, enslaved to those who had taken them captive, and ultimately to strive for the one appointed land; *Praem. et Poen.* 164–65. He draws here on the texts of Lev. 26.40–45 and Deut. 30.1–10. But the language must be metaphorical and the sense is allegorical, with messianic overtones, as the Jews will be conducted by a divine and superhuman vision; 165: ξεναγούμενοι πρός τινος θειοτέρας ἢ κατὰ φύσιν ἀνθρωπίνην ὄψεως. Cf. van Unnik, *Das Selbstverständis*, 132–36. It is unjustified to see here a concrete concept of the return, as does J. M. Scott, "Philo and the Restoration of Israel," *SBL Seminar Papers* (1995), 567, or a belief in the eventual disappearance of the diaspora, as proposed by J. J. Collins, *Between Athens and Jerusalem*, 2d ed. (Grand Rapids, 2000), 134–35. The passage is best understood as a symbolic voyage to God or true wisdom. Philo expresses a closely comparable idea in *Conf. Ling.* 81. In any case, Philo's references to the ingathering of the exiles, even in an obscure fashion, occur almost exclusively in the *De Praemiis et Poenis*. Cf. the treatment by B. Halpern-Amaru, "Land Theology in Philo and Josephus," in L. A. Hoffmann, ed., *The Land of Israel: Jewish Perspectives* (Notre Dame, 1986), 83–85. On Philo's messianic ideas, see the valuable discussions with surveys of earlier opinions by R. D. Hecht, "Philo and Messiah," in J. Neusner, W. S. Green, and E. Frerichs, eds., *Judaisms and their Messiahs at the Time of the Christian Era* (Cambridge, Eng., 1987), 139–68, and P. Borgen, "'There Shall Come Forth a Man': Reflections on Messianic Ideas in Philo," in J. H. Charlesworth, ed., *The Messiah* (Minneapolis, 1992), 341–61.

51. II Macc. 1.10–2.18. See, e.g., E. Bickermann, "Ein jüdischer Festbrief vom Jahre 124 v. Chr.," *ZNW* 32 (1933): 234–35; J. Bunge, *Untersuchungen zum zweiten Makkabäerbuch* (Bonn, 1971), 32–94; C. Habicht, *2 Makkabäerbuch*, Jüdische Schriften aus hellenistisch-römischer Zeit, vol. 1, part 3 (Gütersloh, 1976), 201–2; B. Z. Wacholder, "The Letter from Judah Maccabee to Aristobulus," *HUCA* 49 (1978): 89–133; J. A. Goldstein, *II Maccabees* (Garden City, 1983), 154–88.

52. II Macc. 2.18: ἐλπίζομεν γὰρ ἐπὶ τῷ θεῷ ὅτι ταχέως ἡμᾶς ἐλεήσει καὶ ἐπισυνάξει ἐκ τῆς ὑπὸ τὸν οὐρανὸν εἰς τὸν ἅγιον τόπον. ἐξείλετο γὰρ ἡμᾶς ἐκ μεγάλων κακῶν καὶ τὸν τόπον ἐκαθάρισεν.

53. See, most recently, T. A. Bergren, "Nehemiah in 2 Maccabees, 1:10–2:18," *JSJ* 28 (1997): 249–70.

54. II Macc. 1.27: ἐπισυνάγαγε τὴν διασπορὰν ἡμῶν, ἐλευθέρωσον τοὺς δουλεύοντας ἐν τοῖς ἔθνεσιν.

55. II Macc. 2.7: ἕως ἂν συναγάγῃ ὁ θεὸς ἐπισυναγωγὴν τοῦ λαοῦ καὶ ἵλεως γένηται.

56. II Macc. 8–12.

57. II Macc. 1.9, 1.18, 2.16.

58. This, of course, is not the place to examine the concept of the "Land of Israel" in Jewish thought generally, a vast topic. See the succinct and valuable study by Davies, *Territorial Dimension.*

59. II Macc. 1.12: ἐν τῇ ἁγίᾳ πόλει.

60. Philo, *Leg.* 225: κατὰ τὴν ἱερόπολιν; 281, 288, 299, 346; *Somn.* 2.246. See also his emphasis upon the centrality of the Temple in Jewish practice and allegiance; *Spec. Leg.* 1.66–68. Cf. A. Kasher, "Jerusalem as 'Metropolis' in Philo's National Consciousness" (in Hebrew), *Cathedra* 11 (1979): 48–49.

61. Strabo, 16.2.37.

62. II Macc. 1.7; Wisdom, 12.3; Test. Job, 33.5: ἐν τῇ ἁγίᾳ γῇ; III Sib. 267: πέδον ἁγνὸν; 732–35; V Sib. 281; Philo, *Heres,* 293; *Somn.* 2.75; *Spec. Leg.* 4.215; *Flacc.* 46; *Leg.* 202: τῆς ἱερᾶς χώρας; 205, 330. Cf. Zech. 2.16. On Philo and the "Holy Land," see B. Schaller, "Philon von Alexandreia und das 'Heilige Land,'" in G. Strecker, ed., *Das Land Israel in biblischer Zeit* (Göttingen, 1983), 175–82, who finds the philosopher's appeal to this concept largely determined by the particular circumstances in which he was writing—most of the references coming when Judaea was under threat. Cf. R. L. Wilken, *The Land Called Holy* (New Haven, 1992), 34–37; G. Delling, *Die Bewältigung der Diasporasituation durch das hellenistische Judentum* (Göttingen, 1987), 37–39.

63. Philo, in fact, indicates that even the migration of Abraham to Canaan was more like a return to his native land than a movement to foreign parts, thus associating the Jews with Palestine from the dawn of history; *Abr.* 62: καθάπερ ἀπὸ τῆς ξένης εἰς τὴν οἰκείαν ἐπανιὼν ἀλλ᾽ οὐκ ἀπὸ τῆς οἰκείας εἰς τὴν ξένην. Cf. Artapanus, *apud* Euseb. *PE,* 9.18.1; Wisdom, 12.2–7; Jos. *Ant.* 1.159–60.

64. Cf. Polybius, 1.14.4: καὶ γὰρ φιλόπλιον εἶναι δεῖ τὸν ἀγαθὸν ἄνδρα καὶ φιλόπατριν.

65. *Let. Arist.* 249: ὅτι καλὸν ἐν ἰδίᾳ καὶ ζῆν καὶ τελευτᾶν. ἡ δὲ χενία τοῖς μὲν πένησι καταφρόνησιν ἐργάζεται, τοῖς δὲ πλουσίοις ὄνειδος, ὡς διὰ κακίαν ἐκπεπτωκόσιν.

66. Cf., e.g., the standard commentaries, R. Tramontano, *La lettera di Aristea a Filocrate* (Naples, 1931), 211–12; H. G. Meecham, *The Letter of Aristeas* (Manchester, 1935), 290–91; M. Hadas, *Aristeas to Philocrates* (New York, 1951), 197; A. Pelletier, *Lettre d'Aristée à Philocrate* (Paris, 1962), 212, 250.

67. Philo, *Abr.* 63, 65.

68. Philo, *Mos.* 2.198; *Mut.* 40; cf. *Spec. Leg.* 1.68; *Plant.* 146; *Ebr.* 17; *Fug.* 29; *Deus Imm.* 17.

69. Philo, *Cher.* 15; *Abr.* 197; *Leg.* 328.

70. Philo, *Leg.* 277: πᾶσιν ἀνθρώποις, αὐτοκράτορ, ἐμπέφυκεν ἔρως μὲν τῆς πατρίδος, τῶν δὲ οἰκείων νόμων ἀποδοχή. Cf. *Migr. Abr.* 217; *Spec. Leg.* 1.68, 4.16–17. Philo's references to πάτρις in the metaphorical sense, as abandonment of the territorial homeland for the true πάτρις, are not, of course, relevant to this point. See, e.g., *Spec. Leg.* 1.51–53; *Conf. Ling.* 78, 81. Other references in S. Pearce, "Belonging and Not Belonging: Local Perspectives in Philo of Alexandria," in S. Jones and S. Pearce, eds., *Jewish Local Patriotism and Self Identification in the Graeco-Roman Period* (Sheffield, 1998), 100.

71. II Macc. 4.1, 5.8–9, 5.15, 13.3.

72. II Macc. 8.21, 13.10.

73. Philo, *Mos.* 1.36; *Hyp.* 6.1.

74. Artapanus, *apud* Euseb. *PE*, 9.27.21.

75. Ezekiel, *Exagoge, apud* Euseb. *PE*, 9.28.12.

76. II Macc. 13.14: παρακαλέσας τοὺς σὺν αὐτῷ γενναίως ἀγωνίσασθαι μέχρι θανάτου περὶ νόμων, ἱεροῦ, πόλεως, πατρίδος, πολιτείας.

77. So, e.g., Kasher, *Cathedra* 11 (1979): 52–56.

78. Cf. I. Heinemann, "The Relationships between the Jewish People and Its Land in Jewish-Hellenistic Literature" (in Hebrew), *Zion* 13–14 (1948): 3–6; Kasher, *Cathedra* 11 (1979): 45–50.

79. *Let. Arist.* 249. See above, n. 65.

80. *Let. Arist.* 308–11.

81. *Let. Arist.* 249: πῶς ἂν φιλόπατρις εἴη.

82. III Macc. 6.10: εἰ δὲ ἀσεβείαις κατὰ τὴν ἀποικίαν ὁ βίος ἡμῶν ἐνέσχηται.

83. III Macc. 6.36: ἐπὶ πᾶσαν τὴν παροικίαν αὐτῶν εἰς γενεάς; 7.19: ταύτας ἄγειν τὰς ἡμέρας ἐπὶ τὸν τῆς παροικίας αὐτῶν χρόνον εὐφροσύνους. The latter may be a doublet of the former. These passages do not imply that the author emphasized the temporary character of the sojourn in Egypt and looked ahead with enthusiasm to the "ingathering of the exiles," *pace* Heinemann, *Zion* 13–14 (1948): 7; Scott, in Scott, ed., *Exile*, 192.

84. Philo, *Mos.* 1.71: ἡγεμόνα τῆς ἐνθένδε ἀποικίας; Hecataeus, *apud* Diod. 40.3.3: ἡγεῖτο δὲ τῆς ἀποικίας.

85. Philo, *Mos.* 2.232. On this passage, see Gafni, *Land*, 58–59. Cf. Josephus' reference to the same principles that apply to priestly practices both in Judaea and wherever there is a community of Jews; *CAp.* 1.32, employing the term σύστημα.

86. Philo, *Leg.* 281–82. Y. Amir, "Philo's Version of the Pilgrimage to Jerusalem" (in Hebrew), in A. Oppenheimer, U. Rappaport, and M. Stern, eds., *Jerusalem in the Second Temple Period* (Jerusalem, 1980), 154–57, presses the analogy with Greek colonization a little too far.

87. Philo, *Flacc.* 46; Jos. *CAp.* 2.38. The view of Kasher, *Cathedra*, 11 (1979), 49–53, that this sets "colonies" in a lower or dependent status with regard to the metropolis, misplaces the emphasis.

88. Philo, *Conf. Ling.* 78: τοῖς μὲν γὰρ ἀποικίαν στειλαμένοις ἀντὶ τῆς μητροπόλεως ἡ ὑποδεξαμένη δήπου πατρίς, ἡ δ' ἐκπέμψασα μένει τοῖς ἀποδεδημηκόσιν, εἰς ἣν καὶ ποθοῦσιν ἐπανέρχεσθαι. Scott, *SBL Seminar Papers* (1995), 562–63, misses the contrast between

the μὲν and the δὲ clauses and wrongly sees the passage as a negative comment on the contemporary diaspora.

89. Cf. Jos. *BJ*, 7.375; *Ant.* 3.245.

90. Cf. Philo's use of the term in a very different context; *Spec. Leg.* 4.178. J. Mélèze-Modrzejewski, "How to Be a Greek and Yet a Jew in Hellenistic Alexandria," in S. J. D. Cohen and E. Frerichs, eds., *Diasporas in Antiquity* (Atlanta, 1993), 66–70, rightly points out that the Septuagint often translates *galut* [exile] or *golah* [the collective exiled] with *apoikia*, thus, in effect, offering an *interpretatio Graeca*. His further assertion, however, that Jews, unlike Greeks, invariably expected a return to the land of their fathers, is questionable. Scott, in Scott, ed., *Exile*, 189–93, unconvincingly takes the connotation of ἀποικία in a negative sense.

91. Philo, *Mos.* 1.35.

92. Jos. *CAp.* 2. 38–39.

93. Jos. *Ant.* 16.59: οἱ δὲ ἐγγενεῖς τε αὑτοὺς ἐδείκνυσαν.

94. Philo, *Leg.* 150: τὴν ἡμετέραν Ἀλεχάνδρειαν. Cf. *Leg. All.* 2.85. On Philo's attitude toward Alexandria, see, most recently, Pearce, in Jones and Pearce, eds., *Jewish Local Patriotism*, 97–104. He was, of course, fiercely hostile to Egyptians, their practices, institutions, and beliefs. This served him well in distinguishing the superior qualities of the Jews and their association with Greco-Roman culture. Cf. K. Goudriaan, "Ethnical Strategies in Graeco-Roman Egypt," in P. Bilde, ed., *Ethnicity in Hellenistic Egypt* (Aarhus, 1992), 81–85; Pearce, *op. cit.* , 83–97. But that would not compromise his affection for Alexandria; it might indeed reinforce it.

95. *Corpus Papyrorum Iudaicarum (CPJ)*, II, #151. Just what this change signified has been much debated and need not be explored here. See, e.g., V. A. Tcherikover, *CPJ, ad loc*. The discussion of Kasher, *Cathedra* 11 (1979): 53, concentrates only on the political aspect.

96. Cf. also the epitaph of a young woman from Leontopolis, so evidently a Jewess, which refers to her "homeland and father"; *CPJ*, III, #1530 = W. Horbury and D. Noy, *Jewish Inscriptions of Graeco-Roman Egypt* (Cambridge, Eng., 1992), #38, line 2: πάτραν καὶ γενέτην. To be sure, the *patris* here is the land of Onias, a Jewish enclave in Egypt, but the inscription discloses an unequivocal local allegiance. Cf. Gafni, *Land*, 48.

97. *Corpus Inscriptionum Iudaicarum (CIJ)*, #771: ὑπὲρ εὐχῆ[s] πάσῃ τῇ πατρίδι. The *patris* here almost certainly refers to the city of Acmonia, not to the Jewish community; see P. Trebilco, *Jewish Communities in Asia Minor* (Cambridge, Eng., 1991), 81–82. Gafni, *Land*, 49–50, questions the degree to which conventional formulations of this sort disclose any genuine feelings of local patriotism.

98. Philo, *Flacc.* 46: μητρόπολιν μὲν τὴν ἱερόπολιν ἡγούμενοι ... ἃς δ᾽ ἔλαχον ἐκ πατέρων καὶ πάππων καὶ προπάππων καὶ τῶν ἔτι ἄνω προγόνων οἰκεῖν ἕκαστοι πατρίδας νομίζοντες, ἐν αἷς ἐγεννήθησαν καὶ ἐτράφησαν. Cf. Schaller, in Strecker, ed., *Das Land Israel*, 174–75.

99. See the useful summary of testimony and the discussion by S. Safrai, "Relations between the Diaspora and the Land of Israel," in Safrai and Stern, eds., *The Jewish People*, vol. 1, 186–91.

100. Exodus, 30.11–16; cf. Philo, *Heres*, 186; *Spec. Leg.* 1.77–78.

101. Nehemiah, 10.32–34.

102. For the Seleucids, see II Macc. 3.3; Jos. *Ant.* 12.138–44; cf. II Macc. 9.16;

Jos. *Ant.* 11.16. For the Ptolemies, see Jos. *Ant.* 12.40–41. For the Persian kings, see Ezra, 6.8–10, 7.18–21.

103. It was certainly well entrenched by the early first century B.C.E.; Jos. *Ant.* 14.110–13; Cic. *Pro Flacco,* 67.

104. On possible reasons for Roman policy here, see A. J. Marshall, "Flaccus and the Jews of Asia (Cicero, *Pro Flacco* 28.67–69)," *Phoenix* 29 (1975): 139–54.

105. Cic. *Pro Flacco,* 66–68.

106. Cic. *Pro Flacco,* 67: cum aurum Iudaeorum nomine quotannis ex Italia et ex omnibus nostris provinciis Hierosolymam exportari soleret.

107. The Ciceronian speech singles out Apamea, Laodicea, Adramyttium, and Pergamum; *Pro Flacco,* 68. Cf. Philo, *Spec. Leg.* 1.78.

108. Cic. *Pro Flacco,* 66: scis quanta sit manus, quanta concordia, quantum valeat in contionibus.

109. Modern discussions of Cicero's attitude toward the Jews pay little attention to the implications of his statements on this score. So, e.g., Y. Levi, "Cicero on the Jews," *Zion* 7 (1942): 109–34; B. Wardy, "Jewish Religion in Pagan Literature during the Late Republic and Early Empire," *ANRW* 2.19.1 (1979): 596–613.

110. Philo, *Leg.* 155–56.

111. Jos. *Ant.* 14.110; cf. 18.312–13; *BJ,* 7.45.

112. Jos. *Ant.* 16.28, 16.45.

113. Jos. *Ant.* 16.163: τά τε ἱερὰ εἶναι ἐν ἀσυλίᾳ καὶ ἀναπέμπεσθαι εἰς Ἱεροσόλυμα καὶ ἀποδίδοσθαι τοῖς ἀποδοχεῦσιν Ἱεροσολύμων. Cf. further a ruling by Julius Caesar that also appears to guarantee the Temple tithe; Jos. *Ant.* 14.202: ἔστησε κατ᾽ ἐνιαυτὸν ὅπως τελῶσιν ὑπὲρ τῆς Ἱεροσολυμιτῶν πόλεως.

114. Jos. *Ant.* 16.166.

115. Jos. *Ant.* 16.167–71. Another similar letter by the governor of Asia to Ephesus is preserved by Philo, *Leg.* 315.

116. Philo, *Leg.* 291, 312.

117. Philo, *Leg.* 216.

118. Cf. Philo, *Spec. Leg.* 1.76–77. In addition to the annual contributions felt as an obligation by all Jews, there were more substantial gifts by wealthy diaspora donors to express their reverence; Jos. *BJ,* 4.567, 5.5, 5.201–5; *Ant.* 18.82, 20.51–53.

119. Tacitus, *Hist.* 5.5.1: cetera instituta, sinistra foeda, pravitate valuere; nam pessimus quisque spretis religionibus patriis tributa et stipes illuc congerebant, unde auctae Iudaeorum res.

120. Jos. *BJ,* 7.218; Dio Cassius, 66.7.2.

121. The biblical prescription indicates three times a year; Exodus, 23.17; cf. Jos. *Ant.* 4.203. But actual practice varied widely; cf. Safrai, in Safrai and Stern, eds., *Jewish People,* vol. 1, 191–94; A. Kerkeslager, "Jewish Pilgrimage and Jewish Identity in Hellenistic and Early Roman Egypt," in D. Frankfurter, ed., *Pilgrimage and Holy Space in Late Antique Egypt* (Leiden, 1998), 106–7.

122. Philo, *Spec. Leg.* 1.69: μυρίοι γὰρ ἀπὸ μυρίων ὅσων πόλεων . . . καθ᾽ ἑκάστην ἑορτὴν εἰς τὸ ἱερόν.

123. Acts, 2.1–11; cf. 6.9.

124. Jos. *BJ,* 2.280. Josephus' figure of "no less than three million" is, of course, preposterous. Cf. also Jos. *BJ,* 6.422–25.

125. Jos. *BJ,* 6.420–21.

126. Jos. *BJ*, 6.426–27. Cf. *Ant.* 17.214. On the numbers, see J. Jeremias, *Jerusalem in the Time of Jesus* (Phildelphia, 1969), 77–84.

127. Jos. *BJ*, 5.199.

128. Philo, *Leg.* 156: χρήματα συνάγοντας ἀπὸ τῶν ἀπαρχῶν ἱερὰ καὶ πέμποντας εἰς Ἱεροσόλυμα διὰ τῶν τὰς θυσίας ἀναξόντων. So also 216, 312; *Spec. Leg.* 1.78. Philo could also, of course, employ the concept of pilgrimage in an allegorical sense; cf. Amir, in Oppenheimer et al., eds., *Jerusalem in the Second Temple Period*, 158–65.

129. See Jos. *Ant.* 18.312–13; cf. 17.26.

130. Acts, 20.4, 21.29.

131. The tale of the royal house of Adiabene and its conversion is told in a long excursus by Josephus, *Ant.* 20.17–96. For the attachment to Jerusalem, see 20.49–53, 20.71, 20.95; cf. *BJ*, 5.55, 5.119, 5.147. The desire to be buried in Jerusalem is attested also by epitaphs recording the transferral of bones to the Holy City. See, e.g., J. A. Fitzmyer and D. Harrington, *A Manual of Palestinian Aramaic Texts* (Rome, 1978), #68 (first century B.C.E. or first century C.E.). Cf. I. M. Gafni, "Reinternment in the Land of Israel," *The Jerusalem Cathedra*, 1 (1981): 96–104.

132. For additional evidence, including rabbinic texts, and discussion of diaspora pilgrimages to Jerusalem, see S. Safrai, *Die Wallfahrt im Zeitalter des Zweiten Tempels* (Neukirchen, 1981), 65–97. A condensed version is in Safrai and Stern, eds., *The Jewish People*, vol. 1, 191–204. Cf. Delling, *Die Bewältigung*, 36–37. On visitors to Jerusalem generally, see the testimony and discussion by Jeremias, *Jerusalem*, 58–77. The speculation of M. Goodman, "The Pilgrimage Economy of Jerusalem in the Second Temple Period," in L. I. Levine, ed., *Jerusalem: Its Sanctity and Centrality to Judaism, Christianity, and Islam* (New York, 1999), 69–76, that large-scale pilgrimage began only in the reign of Herod, encouraged by the king for economic reasons, rests on little more than an argument from silence.

133. II Macc. 1.1–2: τοῖς ἀδελφοῖς τοῖς κατ᾽ Αἴγυπτον Ἰουδαίοις χαίρειν οἱ ἀδελφοὶ οἱ ἐν Ἱεροσολύμοις Ἰουδαῖοι . . . εἰρήνην ἀγαθήν.

134. II Macc. 1.9, 1.18, 2.16–17. A similar promotion of a festival advocated by Jerusalemites for diaspora Jews occurs with regard to Purim. See the Greek supplements to Esther, Addition, F, 11.

135. II Macc. 2.18. See above. It does not follow that the letter represents Hasmonaean policy to claim ascendancy over diaspora Jews, as is argued by U. Rappaport, "Relations between the Jews of Eretz-Yisrael and the Jewish Diaspora in the Hellenistic and Hasmonaean Period" (in Hebrew), in B. Isaac and A. Oppenheimer, eds., *Te'uda* 12 (Tel Aviv, 1996–97), 3–4.

136. *Let. Arist.* 38: βουλομένων δ᾽ ἡμῶν καὶ τούτοις χαρίζεσθαι καὶ πᾶσι τοῖς κατὰ τὴν οἰκουμένην Ἰουδαίοις καὶ τοῖς μετέπειτα.

137. *Let. Arist.* 307–11.

138. III Macc. 2.21–27: προέθετο δημοσίᾳ κατὰ τοῦ ἔθνους διαδοῦναι ψόγον.

139. III Macc. 2.28–33: . . . ὡς πολεμίους τοῦ ἔθνους ἔκρινον καὶ τῆς κοινῆς συναναστροφῆς καὶ εὐχρηστίας ἐστέρουν.

140. III Macc. 3.21: τοὺς ὁμοφύλους.

141. Tobit, 1.18: καὶ εἴ τινα ἀπέκτεινεν Σενναχηριμ, ὅτε ἀπῆλθεν φεύγων ἐκ τῆς Ἰουδαίας, . . . ἔθαψα. The subject of ἀπῆλθεν is certainly Sennacherib, as observed by C. A. Moore, *Tobit* (New York, 1996), 120. Cf. II Kings, 19.35.

142. Cic. *Pro Flacco*, 66–67, 69.

143. Jos. *CAp.* 1.32–33.

144. Philo, *Mos.* 2.232: μὴ χωρούσης διὰ πολυανθρωπίαν τὸ ἔθνος μιᾶς χώρας.

145. Jos. *Ant.* 13.352–55: ὅτι τὸ πρὸς τοῦτον ἄδικον ἐχθροὺς ἅπαντας ἡμᾶς σοι τοὺς Ἰουδαίους καταστήσει. Cf. M. Stern, "Relations between the Hasmoneans and Ptolemaic Egypt in Light of the International Relations of the Second and First Centuries" (in Hebrew), *Zion* 50 (1985): 101–2.

146. Jos. *Ant.* 14.127–37. See, especially, 14.131: πείθει δὲ καὶ τούτους τὰ αὐτῶν φρονῆσαι κατὰ τὸ ὁμόφυλον Ἀντίπατρος, καὶ μάλιστα ἐπιδείξας αὐτοῖς τὰς Ὑρκανοῦ τοῦ ἀρχιερέως ἐπιστολάς. Cf. also Jos. *BJ*, 1.190.

147. For this interpretation of Lentopolis, see E. S. Gruen, "The Origins and Objectives of Onias' Temple," *SCI* 16 (1997): 47–70, with bibliography. For a different view, see D. R. Schwartz, "The Jews of Egypt between Onias' Temple, the Jerusalem Temple, and the Heavens" (in Hebrew), *Zion* 62 (1997): 5–22. The authority of the High Priest in diaspora communities is attested also by the request of Saul (Paul) for letters from the High Priest to the synagogues in Damascus, authorizing him to arrest Christians in their midst and bring them back to Jerusalem; Acts, 9.1–2.

148. Jos. *Ant.* 17.300–301.

149. Jos. *Ant.* 17.321–38.

150. Philo, *Flacc.* 45–46.

151. Philo, *Flacc.* 124: κοινὸν ἐχθρὸν τοῦ ἔθνους. Cf. 1, 117.

152. Philo, *Leg.* 184: ἕτερον κατασκήπτει βαρύτατον ἐξαπιναίως ἀπροσδόκητον κακόν, οὐχ ἑνὶ μέρει τοῦ Ἰουδαικοῦ τὸν κίνδυνον ἐπάγον, ἀλλὰ συλλήβδην ἅπαντι τῷ ἔθνει. Cf. 178, 351, 373.

153. Philo, *Leg.* 193–94.

154. Philo, *Leg.* 213–17: ὀλίγου δέω φάναι πᾶσα ἡ οἰκουμένη.

155. Philo, *Leg.* 277–83. Cf. 330: οὐ μόνον τοῖς τὴν ἱερὰν χώραν κατοικοῦσιν ἀλλὰ καὶ τοῖς πανταχοῦ τῆς οἰκουμένης Ἰουδαίοις.

156. Philo, *Leg.* 371; cf. 159–61.

157. Philo, *Spec. Leg.* 2.168. Cf. Schaller, in Strecker, ed., *Das Land Israel*, 176–78. Van Unnik, *Das Selbstverständis*, 127–37, who finds no optimistic assessment of the diaspora in Philo, notably omits this passage.

158. Jos. *Ant.* 4.115–16: τὴν δ' οἰκουμένην οἰκητήριον δι' αἰῶνος ἴστε προκειμένην ὑμῖν, καὶ τὸ πλῆθος ὑμῶν ἔν τε νήσοις καὶ κατ' ἤπειρον βιοτεύσετε ὅσον ἐστὶν οὐδ' ἀστέρων ἀριθμὸς ἐν οὐρανῷ. Josephus departs quite substantially here from the corresponding text in Numbers, 23.6–10. See the good discussion by Halpern-Amaru, *JQR* 71 (1980/81): 225–29; *eadem*, in Hoffmann, *Land of Israel*, 81–82; cf. also Price, *SCI* 13 (1994): 171. For comparable statements in Josephus, see *Ant.* 1.282: οἷς ἐγὼ τὸ ταύτης κράτος τῆς γῆς δίδωμι καὶ παισὶ τοῖς αὐτῶν, ὃ πληρώσουσιν ὅσην ἥλιος ὁρᾷ καὶ γῆν καὶ θάλασσαν; 2.213; 14.115; *BJ*, 7.43. On Josephus' generally positive attitude toward diaspora, see L. Feldman, "The Concept of Exile in Josephus," in Scott, ed., *Exile*, 145–72.

2

Coming to Terms with Exile

Howard Wettstein

"Diaspora" is a relatively new English word and has no traditional Hebrew equivalent.[1] It seems closely related to the more traditional concept, *galut*, exile. Indeed, they might seem to be expressions for the same idea. Nevertheless, reflection on the two concepts reveals crucial differences.[2]

"Diaspora" is a political notion; it suggests geopolitical dispersion. It may further suggest—this is more controversial but, I think, correct—involuntary dispersion from a center, typically a homeland.[3] With changes in circumstances like the coming of new generations, new social conditions, and movement from one diasporic location to another, a diasporic population may come to see virtue in diasporic life. And so "diaspora"—as opposed to *galut*—may acquire a positive charge, as today it has for some.[4] Still, I suspect that we would not think of it as "diaspora"—"dispersion" itself has something of this flavor—had the shift originally been a consequence of the people simply deciding to leave, say for want of economic improvement or cultural enrichment.

Galut is, by contrast, a religious, or almost religious, notion. Daniel Boyarin, in discussion, referred to it as a teleological notion. One of its important resonances is a concomitant of involuntary removal from homeland: dislocation, a sense of being uprooted, being somehow in the wrong place. To view one's group as in *galut* is to suppose that what is in some sense the proper order has been interrupted. Perhaps the dispersed group has been punished, or perhaps the world is just the sort of place where awful things happen.

NORMAL DISLOCATION AND THE COSMIC JOLT

Galut is a pervasive theme—perhaps even the dominant motif—in Jewish history. One might even say that from the perspective of the Hebrew Bible and Jewish religious tradition, human (and not only Jewish) history is a study in exile.[5]

The original, as Arnold Eisen emphasizes, is the mythological expulsion of Adam and Eve from the Garden of Eden.[6] Before their expulsion, Adam and Eve were to carry on in harmony with their world, without pain and suffering. After they are banished, Adam and Eve experience life as we know it, an uncanny constellation of richness, even exquisite beauty, along with all manner of awfulness.

At the surface, the suggestion is that our plight is a consequence of some original misbehavior, of choice exercised in a wrong direction. The story may be seen, however, as making a more subtle suggestion, that such choices are themselves human. Our plight, our condition of *galut*, may be seen as a consequence of being the sort of creature that we are in the kind of world in which we live, no formula for bliss. It is only in the mythological past (Eden before the apple) and the mythological future (Messianic times) that human existence is not radically troubled and confused. The human condition is thus one of dislocation—"normal dislocation" I'll call it—as if we weren't quite designed for the world in which we find ourselves.

Central to the religious impulse is the drive to find meaning—even transcendent meaning—in the face of such "exilic" existence. Adversity thus provides raw material for the religious impulse. Even without the well-known horrors of Jewish history, the religious impulse would have an abundance of raw materials. But that history has been supererogatory in this regard.

Ignoring historical detail, let us skip to what is, until our times, the catastrophe of catastrophes: the destruction of the Second Temple in 70 C.E., the subsequent defeat of Bar Kochba in 135, and the dispersion of Israel. The destruction of the First Temple in 587 B.C.E. and the subsequent Babylonian exile was, of course, calamitous, but that prior exile lasted only half a century; exile could still seem unusual, an exception to the order of things. After Bar Kochba and the expulsion of Jews from Jerusalem, however, with no hope for return in the foreseeable future, exile must have seemed like the rule.[7]

If the dislocation inherent in the human condition counted as a kind of *galut*, we now have the real thing. Temple times—when the sacrificial worship practices were in place and there was a taste of the dignity of sovereignty—are seen in retrospect as a kind of Eden. The prospect of living without the foci of national and religious life, and doing so in exile with no prospect for restoration, must have been experienced as a grave threat to— if not a violation of—the very conception of a cosmic partnership between

God and Israel. The *churban* [destruction], by contrast with normal dislocation, was a cosmic jolt.

Judaism as we know it—so-called rabbinic Judaism—is in important respects a response to this catastrophe, an attempt to pick up the pieces, to reconstruct religious and national life in the absence of their central foci.
While one should never underplay the enormous continuities between pre-
and post-*churban* Judaism, the new developments are dramatic. Taking a bit
of dramatic license, one might say that the religion as bequeathed to us both
by the rabbis of the Talmud and by subsequent developments—another
fifteen hundred years of intermittent persecution, expulsion, and, in our
times, *shoah*—is nothing less than a religion of *galut*. And since the attempt
to reconstruct was made in keen awareness of the normal difficulties of the
human condition, it is a religion of *galut,* both normal and catastrophic.

The idea that Judaism is a religion of *galut* might be further supported by
consideration of the wanderings of the patriarchal families and the rabbinic
idea that the reported experiences of the patriarchs signify the later history
of Israel. Discussing this would take us too far afield, but even with such additional support for the "religion of *galut*" idea, that idea is too one-sided.
There are many foci of the Jewish religious outlook, and certainly no adequate single formula. *Galut* is one of the crucial ones and the one under
scrutiny here.

COMING TO TERMS WITH *GALUT*

I said above that residents of a diaspora might come to see their environment in quite positive terms. Postemancipation Jewish diaspora has been
seen in this way, as a condition or situation characterized by liberation from
galut to a host of newfound freedoms and possibilities. Rebecca Goldstein's
novel *Mazel* vividly represents such a diasporic transformation in terms of
the transition from the *shtetl* to the cosmopolitan city. For some the State of
Israel makes possible a perhaps even more radical and liberating transition,
one that involves political sovereignty in addition to the freedoms and opportunities afforded by a liberating diaspora. But Jewish dislocation runs
deep; there may be a lingering taste of *galut* in diasporic cosmopolitan life
as well as in sovereign Israel.

One reason is the long arm of Jewish history, a mixed history that includes
extraordinary and haunting trauma. Equally important is a refined sense of
normal dislocation. Different cultures respond to life's customary travails in
different ways. A virtue of American pragmatic optimism is that for a wide
range of important projects, Americans get the job done with minimum fuss.
The cost is at least a tendency towards a lack of serious focus on the travails.
A friend—suffering mightily from the death of his mother—commented
that what seemed to work best for him was avoidance. This attitude contrasts

dramatically with what one is likely to find in cultures that history has made more intimate with suffering. The lingering sense of dislocation may thus have roots beyond national tragedy; it may be due in part to a culturally induced sensitivity to the substantial limitations of the human condition.

Avoiding *galut*—for example, by turning to, or turning it into, a culturally plenteous diaspora—may thus not be a winning strategy for Jews. I want to consider the attempt not so much to defeat *galut* as to engage and come to terms with it, to wrestle with it. In this essay I will attempt to tell part of the story of how rabbinic culture contended with the cosmic jolt. In the course of telling this story, I'll comment upon its implications for our grappling with normal dislocation, a struggle of great human significance.

It is undeniable that the rabbis took *galut* seriously. For them it was inescapable, a kind of permanently temporary state. What I think of as their distinctive take on human flourishing is heavily influenced by this perception and by their attempt to find solace, meaning, even salvation while in *galut*.[8] It may be instructive to see how a tradition smitten by *galut*, obsessed with it, develops practices and an outlook to cope with exilic existence.

This rabbinic quest might have gone very badly. It would not be difficult, for example, to overemphasize Jewish victimhood—Woody Allen's Russian rabbi who "developed whining to an art unheard of in the West." This would be stultifying. Alternatively, and more positively, the dislocation might be a sensitizing force. Perhaps, seasoned by *galut*, the rabbis were able to develop a manual, as it were, for the successful negotiation of life experience, even when it goes badly. This is the idea I will explore here.

I spoke above of coming to terms with *galut* by developing practices and an accompanying outlook. Clearly a general exploration would be an enormous undertaking. My emphasis here will be on the outlook, the theological side of the matter, as opposed to better-known post-*churban* developments in communal practice. The latter include the increased emphasis on prayer and the study of the Torah as among the highest forms of religious practice, and the shift in the locus of ritual holiness from the sacrificial alter to the family table.

I call the developments that I'll discuss "theological" for lack of a better word. This is not a process of refining doctrine, or adding to or replacing a body of doctrine. Doctrine is not what's at issue; rather developments in what one might call religious sensibility. Indeed, rabbinic literature until medieval times does not much trade in doctrine.[9] When the concerns of the rabbis are not broadly legal, or *halachic*, they are homiletic, parabolic, exegetical, and the like. These *aggadic* passages are less authoritative than the legal discussions. This is not to make little of them or to diminish their significance for the religious life, which is indeed enormous. There is much in Jewish religiosity that operates at the level of religious sensibility, although this is obscured by much of the medieval doctrine-oriented discussion.

THEOLOGICAL DEVELOPMENTS

My primary focus here will be *Midrash Rabbah* on the Book of Lamentations.[10] That commentary is a compilation of materials composed over many generations after 70 C.E., an attempt by the rabbis of the Talmud to bring Lamentations to bear on their latest and by far greatest tragedy. (Lamentations itself was written some 650 years earlier, in connection with the destruction of the First Temple in 587 B.C.E.)

The aspects of divinity a literature emphasizes reflect salient features of the community's experience. Subject a community to great trial or triumph and its way of thinking about God may well alter or enlarge. The Temple's destruction, accompanied by the prospect of an unending exile, certainly qualifies as such a great trial. And the *Midrash* on Lamentations provides evidence of an important theological development, an altered—but, of course, not historically discontinuous—perspective on God. God is, one might say, super-anthropomorphized.

Anthropomorphic depiction was, of course, characteristic of Hebrew Bible.[11] Early in Genesis, for example, God is angry at our antics, even regretful that He initiated the human experiment. But these were the emotions of a being that was—despite the anthropomorphism—somehow wholly other, the awesome Creator of the universe in whose hands was its destruction, a somewhat remote purveyor of rage, passion, justice, and the rest.

It has been said that the biblical narrative is the history of God's learning that He cannot do it alone, that His plan crucially requires partnership with His human reflections. By the time of the *Midrash* on Lamentations, in the perception of its authors, the lesson is well learned. Not only can He not do it alone, the project is not going well.[12] And God's reaction reveals a new level of affective engagement and self-awareness. Indeed, in terms of affect, God has become almost one of us. He suffers, weeps, even mourns. "Woe is Me!" He cries in Proem 24, "What have I done?"

Sometimes the *Midrash* sees God in maternal terms—or, more accurately, God, as the *Midrash* has it, sees Himself/Herself in such terms (Proem 22): "'Just as when you take away its young a sparrow is left solitary,' so spake the Holy One, blessed be He, 'I burnt My house, destroyed My city, exiled My children among the nations of the world, and I sit solitary.'"

Sometimes the imagery is paternal: God is compared with a king who, enraged at his two sons, thrashes them and drives them away. Afterward the king exclaims, "The fault is with me, since I must have brought them up badly" (Proem 2). In Proem 24 God laments: "'Woe to the King who succeeds in His youth and fails in His old age.' . . . The Holy one, blessed be He, said to Jeremiah, 'I am now like a man who had an only son, for whom he prepared a marriage canopy, but he dies under it. Feelest thou no anguish for Me and My children? Go summon Abraham, Isaac, and Jacob, and Moses from their sepulchres, for they know how to weep.'" Indeed, not only does God mourn, God, it would seem, needs instruction in mourning from us.[13]

One aspect of this humanizing of the divine image, interestingly parallel to (roughly simultaneous) Christian developments, is a new emphasis on divine vulnerability.[14] God is, as it were, exposed to the elements to a degree scarcely predictable by what we knew of Him.

Closely related is what we might call divine approachability. In Genesis, God is available to the patriarchs, and to some extent to the matriarchs. But the *Midrash* on Lamentations (in the continuation of Proem 24) imagines the three patriarchs (Abraham, Isaac, and Jacob) and Moses pleading with God for mercy. God, however, is unaffected; He cannot or will not comply. Eventually, He does promise to restore Israel to its place, but the promise is made not to the patriarchs or Moses. The fact that it is only mother Rachel who can move Him, and, indeed, by the way that she succeeds powerfully illustrates God's humanity. She tells God that she knew of her father's plan to substitute Leah for her in marriage to Jacob. She attempted to foil the plan, but when that failed, she says,

> I relented, suppressed my desire, and had pity upon my sister that she should not be exposed to shame. . . . I delivered over to my sister all the signs which I had arranged with Jacob so that he should think that she was Rachel. More than that, I went beneath the bed upon which he lay with my sister; and when he spoke to her she remained silent and I made all the replies in order that he should not recognize my sister's voice. I did her a kindness, was not jealous of her, and did not expose her to shame. And if I, a creature of flesh and blood, formed of dust and ashes, was not envious of my rival and did not expose her to shame and contempt, why should You, a King who lives eternally and is merciful, be jealous of idolatry in which there is not reality, and exile my children and let them be slain by the sword. . . .
>
> Forthwith, the mercy of the Holy One, blessed be He, was stirred, and He said, "For your sake, Rachel, I will restore Israel to its place."

It is interesting that Rachel does not argue, as did Abraham in Genesis 18:23–33, on the grounds of what divine justice requires. Nor does she appeal on the basis of her own merit, as do (earlier in Proem 24) the patriarchs, Abraham, Isaac, and Jacob. Her appeal is more personal, predicated on issues of character.

These developments are underscored and pushed to still another level with the talmudic idea that after the *churban,* God Himself enjoys only an exilic existence, that the divine presence resides in *galut.* This is no doubt in part a matter of empathy. To say that God's presence is in *galut* is to say that He is with us, He feels for us. But it is equally an expression of divine dislocation and a constricted existence. Here we approach discontinuity with what we know of God from the Bible, a kind of anthropomorphic quantum leap.

One might argue that there is no quantum leap here, but that the powerful imagery of divine exile is a mere rhetorically supercharged variation on what we have already seen, God in a state of mourning, weeping bitterly, feeling lost, at times even hopeless. But one has the sense that this is not simply a matter of divine affect, that something more "objective" is at stake here. God's project for humanity, His partnership with Israel for *tikkun olam,* the repair and redemption of the world, has been thwarted.[15] The universe is thus dislocated, thrown off course. Israel's political, social, and national catastrophe is thus transformed into a metaphysical cataclysm, a real cosmic jolt. The universe is shaken to its foundations.

So much for the theological developments. What are the implications for the community's struggle with *galut?*

COMING TO TERMS WITH *GALUT,* PART TWO

Such super-anthropomorphism yields new possibilities of relationship. The possibilities for relationship with a more remote divine presence, for example as depicted in Genesis, are quite limited for the people, if not for a privileged few. Quite another matter is a God who is vulnerable in the ways explored, whose range of affective response is not unlike our own, whose self-perception is of one whose fate is tied up with that of the community. Such a God can function as life partner, as it were, of the community and derivatively of the individual. Here there are intimations of the rabbinic reading of Song of Songs, God and Israel as lovers.

There are then enormous implications for the post-*churban* community's ability to contend with exile, to be effective in the face of exile. For God to cry over their catastrophe, to feel great pain over their loss, indeed, to feel the pain jointly with them, is to mitigate the loneliness of their suffering. The increased emphasis on prayer—Jewish prayer is at once individual and communal—makes sense in this new picture. Frequent contact with one's, and the community's, divine partner has the potential to transform bitterness into a healing outpouring of pains and disappointments. There is now the possibility of nurture and comfort—for the individual and for the community—even in the face of a unyieldingly awful universe.

As my comment about prayer illustrates, the theological development I've been illustrating proceeds in concert with developments in religious practice. Here as elsewhere, one needs to be careful not to overplay the role of ideas in social developments. In the present case, one should not over-emphasize the role of theological ideas in explaining how the community contends with catastrophe. This is especially important given the dominant role of practice in traditional Judaism. Nevertheless, these are powerful developments in religious sensibility.

The cataclysm of *churban* prompts these theological developments, but the engendered religious sensibility has much wider scope. It is relevant to our handling not only of the great catastrophes of human history, but also of difficulties of ordinary life. Indeed, talmudic discussion of the *aggadic* themes I've been discussing is quite often not restricted to *churban:*[16] "Rabbi Meir said, 'When a man suffers, what expression does the *shechinah* [divine presence[17]] use? "My head is too heavy for me; My arm is too heavy for me"'" (Tractate Sandedrin 46a).

In Tractate Berachot 7a, the Talmud argues that it is not only we that pray. God prays as well. It continues, "What does He pray? '. . . May it be My will that My mercy may suppress My anger, and that My mercy may prevail over My [other] attributes, so that I may deal with My children in the attribute of mercy and, on their behalf, stop short of the limit of strict justice.'" (The Hebrew word *rachamim,* translated here as "mercy," suggests something less Christian in the original. The word seems etymologically related to the Hebrew word for womb, and thus suggests something closer to nurture.)

The passage continues with a remark of Rabbi Ishmael b. Elisha, apparently a priest who performed the Temple service prior to the *churban.* He states that he once entered the Sanctuary, whereupon God asked him for a blessing. He replied to God with the formula just quoted as God's prayer: "May it be Your will that Your mercy . . ." "And," continues Rabbi Ishmael, when the blessing was completed, "[God] nodded to me with His head." There is much that is amazing in this passage and there are many suggestions that connect with my discussion: God is vulnerable, subject to limitations. God, not unlike us, needs to work at suppressing His anger; achieving the desired balance is something for which even God needs to pray.

Passages like these are important in connection with my hope for assistance with normal dislocation. But in the last passage quoted there is something else as well. The story of Rabbi Ishmael highlights the reciprocal aspect of relationship, specifically, what we give to God. For in this story God comes to one of us to ask for a blessing.[18] To this theme of reciprocity I now turn.

In Tractate Berachot 3a there is a discussion of the recitation of *Kaddish,* a prayer that occurs in many contexts in every public service. (The recitation of *Kaddish* requires a quorum.) The *Kaddish* is typically recited by the person leading the service (or by the mourners in the case of Mourner's *Kaddish*). Its centerpiece is an enthusiastic communal declaration: "May His great name be blessed at all times." God is said in the passage in Berachot 3a to experience *Kaddish* as bittersweet. But it is the positive side that is relevant here: God is touched, honored, especially by the communal declaration. "He shakes His head and says, 'Happy is the king who is thus praised in this house!'" Less relevant to the present point, but worth mentioning in light of my broader concerns in this essay, God also feels a sense of great loss. He says, "Woe to the father [an alternate reading has "what is there for the father"] who had to banish his children, and woe to the children who had to be banished from the table of their father."

Mourner's *Kaddish* is constituted by (more or less) the same glorification-of-God text as other occurrences of *Kaddish*.[19] It's thus a somewhat strange piece of mourning liturgy, one that never mentions death or the dead. One traditional interpretation begins with the thought that the loss of each individual is heartfelt by God. God, like us, does not take well to the loss of His children. The Mourner's *Kaddish*—also recited communally—thus represents the community's coming together to comfort God for His loss.

God is thus nurtured by our praise and consoled by our community effort at comforting Him. The liturgy, borrowing from Psalms 22:4, speaks of God as enthroned on the praises of Israel, again pointing to our highly significant role in His flourishing. And then there is a centerpiece of the liturgy, the *Sh'ma*, that emphasizes God's oneness.[20] Perhaps the idea goes beyond numerical unity; perhaps what is at issue is a kind of unity or coherence that depends in part upon the success of one's projects, including one's children. Seen in this way, the *Sh'ma* is a kind of messianic dream about God's future, as it were. And seen in this way the *Sh'ma* is closely related to the messianic Zachariah 14:9, also highlighted in the liturgy, "In that day, God will be one and His name one."

The *Sh'ma* is one of the passages inscribed on scrolls found inside our *t'fillin*, the phylacteries that Jews wear during weekday morning prayer. The Talmud, Berachot 6a, asks what passage is to be found in God's *t'fillin*—as if we would all naturally assume that God dons *t'fillin*. The answer, according to Rabbi Hiyya b. Abin, is the passage from I Chronicles 17:21: "And who is like Thy people Israel, a nation one [or unique] in the earth?" The passage continues: "Does then the Holy One, blessed be He, sing the praises of Israel? Yes. . . . The Holy One, blessed be He, said to Israel: 'You have made Me a unique entity in the world [alluding to the *Sh'ma*], and I shall make you a unique entity in the world [alluding to the Chronicles passage].'"[21]

Thus emerges a love relationship between God and Israel. There are ups and downs, as with human love, and the parties likely need to fall in love again and again. Such relationships depend upon mutual generosity and often survive the considerable foibles of the parties. While I have emphasized the comfort afforded in times of travail, a more complete story would give another central place to shared joys. Also important, and worthy of treatment beyond the mere mention I'll make, is that providing nurture and comfort to another nurtures oneself. Generosity of spirit, *chesed,* is a key virtue of God and His human reflections. So each side, as it provides support for the other, expresses its innate *chesed* and so is enriched, fulfilled.

As the rabbis construe post-*churban* religious life, it is lived, if not within the Land, at least within the law—within the four cubits of the *halacha*. The imagery is both negative—emphasizing constriction, a contrast with life in the Land—and positive—insofar as one sees the law as a source of structure for the enhancement of life. The Talmud also speaks of God living, post-*churban*, within the same four cubits, a similarly mixed image, but with a twist. God's so living certainly conveys exilic constriction—a dramatic contrast with His life in the Land, in the Temple, and specifically in the Holy of Holies. But what can it mean that God also lives within the four cubits of the law? I suggest that its import concerns the shared life with Israel. Indeed, perhaps the most significant outcome of the theological developments I've been sketching is this duality: on one hand, exile for both parties, and on the other, God and Israel sharing a life of mutual dependence and nurture.

These theological emphases are inspired by cataclysmic *galut*. But if one were to read them with too much emphasis on this catastrophe, or later ones, one would miss much of the deeper religious significance. The conception of a shared life has powerful implications for our contending with the substantial difficulties of the human condition—normal dislocation.

CONCLUSION

It is acknowledged by foes and friends of religion that a religious outlook affords its adherents comfort during times of trouble. And this is no small matter. At the same time, this comfort is often seen as a bad purchase, the cost being acceptance of false beliefs about all manner of reward, afterlife, and the like. Religion, that is, is often seen as Marx saw it, a dispenser of opiates. I have argued elsewhere that even within a religious framework, theodicy should be rejected in favor of nonopiate approaches.[22] The present essay is an effort in that direction. The theological development highlighted here—notwithstanding the popularity of messianic movements during the post-*churban* period—is distinctly nonopiate. More precisely, the way this perspective facilitates human efficacy in the face of great adversity is nonopiate. We are not provided with a magical solution, or the promise of one. We are provided with, as it were, a helpmate.[23]

Earlier in this essay, I argued that even a culturally rich and liberating diaspora was not likely to liberate us from *galut*. The question was, where we might turn for help. We have now seen one sort of assistance provided by the religious tradition. But even if not tainted as a purveyor of opiates, traditional religion surely does not constitute an answer for all. At the same time, I think some issues that the rabbinic response brings to the foreground are well worth general consideration.

One such issue is that of the stubbornness of our sense of dislocation, both in terms of the long arm of history and what I've called normal dislocation. Such difficulties require considerable attention if one, or a community, is to make headway with them. This is not to advocate an emphasis on victimhood—far from it. But traditional Jewish practice, mourning for example, can constitute a way to put one's difficulties in their right place, a way not to be forever mired in them. Related issues concern the power of community and of community-based ritual.

My own interest is not only in the religiously neutral lessons available, for my ultimate aim is to articulate a contemporary Jewish identity at the heart of which is a *galut*-engendered religious outlook. I've taken dramatic license again, since the notion of *galut* is only one of the pillars of such an outlook. But it is one important pillar.

I will conclude with some remarks on identity that will perhaps clarify my aim and add to the discussion of identity in this volume. In discussions of Jewish identity, the relevant notion of identity is quite a difficult one to pin down. "Identity" is one of those expressions that does fairly well in discourse until we press for articulation. Likely, there are several related notions at work even in our discussions in this volume. The identity question in which I'm most interested concerns the significance of being Jewish, what it means to be Jewish.[24] There should be little temptation to suppose that there is but a single answer to my question, a single or privileged Jewish identity. Who is to say, after all, that there is only one kind of significance, only one way that being Jewish can matter, or legitimately matter? It is sometimes urged—often by those uncomfortable with religion—that a religious orientation will be, in this regard, "essentialist," that it will regard its own approach as the only legitimate one. It is not easy—given the kinds of creatures we are—to passionately embrace a perspective while making room for others. But this phenomenon is all too ubiquitous. It is certainly not restricted to those who occupy a religious perspective. We would do well to keep open minds on the question of Jewish identity, since the variety of answers may well complement one another.

A final point about the concept of identity: In a recent article in *Judaism*, Shirley Kaufman writes with elegance and grace of growing into her Jewish identity. Notice the contrast between Kaufman's idiom and that of *constructing* Jewish identity, so common in contemporary discussion. "Construction" can be understood in two ways. First, there is the idea of putting a construction upon an idea or remark. In this sense, "construct" is related to "construe." The question then is how best to construe Jewish identity, how to understand it. In this sense of construction, constructing is not a matter of engendering, forming, putting together. But second, and more to the point, the usual talk of constructing identity has the ring of something more constructivist (to use a philosophical word), something like deciding upon one's identity. This doesn't mean, of course, making it up out of whole cloth. But it does suggest that it's in large measure an activity of the will.

The constructivist picture seems to me both tempting and naïve. Not that one never makes choices, sometimes crucial ones, about the direction of one's life. Indeed, in our times this is both common and healthy. Still, it is one thing to make choices at crucial junctures and quite another to put to-gether the identity that is attendant upon such choices.(Whether one grows into the identity bequeathed by one's family or wider community, or into the identity that is attendant upon one's choices, one nevertheless grows into it.)One can put various constructions upon one's identity, but one's ability to form it is limited.[25]

NOTES

1. According to the OED, the term first appears in 1876, and in 1881 is used by Wellhausen, in the *Encyclopedia Britannica*, in connection with Jewish dispersion.

2. As originally pointed out to our research group by Murray Baumgarten. Baumgarten attributes the distinction to Cynthia Ozick. That there is an intuitive distinction seems clear, but it is much less clear how this is to be spelled out. In the following paragraphs, I attempt to do so.

3. Carlos Velez-Ibañez suggested this to me.

4. Cf. in this volume both Murray Baumgarten's exploration of Rebecca Goldstein's novel, *Mazel,* and Bluma Goldstein's study of Heine.

5. "Hebrew Bible" and "Old Testament" are not quite names for the same thing. The order of the contained books is not the same, and the former work includes books that were not canonized in the latter. See Jack Miles, *God: A Biography* (New York, 1995), esp. chapter 1.

6. See his seminal work, *Galut: Modern Jewish Reflection on Homelessness and Home-coming* (1986), a book that I have found immensely helpful. I am grateful to Eisen for discussion of the topics of this paper.

7. As Eisen points out in *Galut.*

8. See my paper, "Awe and the Religious Life," *Judaism* 46, no. 4 (fall 1997): 387–407.

9. See my paper, "Doctrine," in *Faith and Philosophy* 14 (1997): 423–43, for a more detailed discussion. A revised version entitled "Theological Impressionism" appeared in *Judaism* (spring 2000).

10. I'll be quoting from the translation of the Soncino Press, (London, 1983).

11. See my paper, "Doctrine," for an exploration of the contrast between, on one hand, biblical and rabbinic anthropomorphic characterization and, on the other, the anti-anthropomorphism of medieval theology that was inspired by Greek philosophy.

12. This is to some extent true of the prophetic literature as well. Thus what is new in the literature under discussion here is a matter of degree and sustained emphasis.

13. As Alan Mintz points out in *Hurban: Responses to Catastrophe in Hebrew Literature* (Syracuse, N.Y., 1996), 60.

14. A key difference, of course, is that in Jewish thought there is no suggestion of God becoming—or having an aspect that is—human in some more serious or literal sense.

15. As Eisen expressed it in conversation.

16. The comments in square brackets in what follows are my own.

17. The *shechinah* is often associated with the feminine side of God.

18. This is a striking feature of the story. What to say in the end about a host of implicated questions is, of course, quite another matter. What is it to give a blessing? What exactly does one do for another by blessing him or her? And so on. These all need exploration. But it remains clear that God is asking us for some sort of important help or something of the like.

19. The same core text of the *Kaddish* gets minor variations in a number of its occurrences. What most distinguishes Mourner's *Kaddish* is the tone in which it is recited. As opposed to the other occurrences of *Kaddish* that are typically chanted, the mourner's version is recited in a somewhat sad tone, put to music in a barely discernible fashion or not at all.

20. I have in mind here the first line of the *Sh'ma,* the famous call usually translated (badly I think) as "Hear O Israel, the Lord your God, the Lord is one."

21. The *Shabbat* afternoon *amidah* (the standing prayer that constitutes the central moment of every service) places the following text in a prominent place: "You are one, and Your name is one, and who is like your people, Israel, one [a unique] people in the land." This *amidah* is chanted in a melody that is sadly sweet, almost melancholy. This service marks the approaching end of *Shabbat,* a day that God and Israel spend together, as it were.

22. "Against Theodicy," in *Proceedings of the Twentieth World Congress of Philosophy* 4 (1999): 115–25. A revised version appeared in *Judaism* (summer 2001).

23. Admittedly there are promises, e.g., God's remark to Rachel in Proem 24, quoted above, that he will restore Israel for her sake. But there is much to the perspective I've been describing that involves no such promises. And even when one hears a promise, as in Proem 24, it by no means dominates the message. I allow that there may be other rabbinic trends during this period. Still, my aim here is to isolate one important trend.

24. When one raises questions about Jewish identity in the context of philosophy—at least in the context of the tradition of analytic philosophy/history of philosophy that is my professional home—one thinks immediately of the classic philosophic literature about personal identity. But the relevance of this literature is far from obvious. Consider John Locke's proposal about personal identity—that persons are constituted by temporal stages linked by memory or consciousness. Let it be so; we would still not have an answer, and probably no help at all, with the question of Jewish identity. My suspicion is that these questions issue from different sorts of concerns and fall into different philosophic domains. Unlike the question that was Locke's concern, that of Jewish identity seems less metaphysical, more in the realm of value. It is a question about significance—what it means to be Jewish. The beginning of wisdom, I want to suggest, is thus to separate ourselves from an important and extensive metaphysical and epistemological literature on identity.

25. I thus disagree with the idea, suggested (at least to me) by Louise Tallen's essay in this volume, that the process of identity formation we can observe in people who have struggled with difficult, radical choices can serve as a model for what we all do with our identities. This is not to diminish, however, the role of struggle in what I'm calling "growing into."

3

A Politics and Poetics of Diaspora

Heine's "Hebräische Melodien"

Bluma Goldstein

Heinrich Heine's "Hebräische Melodien," whose three long poems comprise the third and final part of *Romanzero* (*Romancero*, 1851), has long been scanned by critics for evidence of alterations in his views of religion and his affiliation with Judaism. The overall meaning(s) and structure of the text are often identified and assessed by referring to the religious and psychological changes that resulted from Heine's reaction to his debilitating illness, which confined him to what he called his "mattress-grave." Alternatively, the poetic text becomes the evidential source for ascertaining revisions to his religious orientation. As interesting and informative as interpretations may be that rely heavily on biographical data to document the writer's ideational and attitudinal developments or their literary representations, they often leave important aspects and issues of the poems uncharted and the reading of the whole unsettled. There are, however, approaches and alternate discourses recently explored within cultural studies, in general, and Jewish studies, in particular, that might contextualize this poetry in ways better able to illuminate both the more unyielding sections and the larger ideological and aesthetic significance of the overall text. This essay means to probe the "Hebräische Melodien" for the poetic articulation of the connection between a new understanding of diasporic life and the construction of Jewish identity by situating the text within two different, yet interrelated, frameworks: on the one hand, the "Orientalization" of Eastern European Jewry and glorification of medieval Sephardi culture by early nineteenth-century European Jews, especially German Jews; and on the other, a more nuanced account of diaspora and exile that explores the viability of a truly integrative relationship between subdominant and dominant cultures. Interpreted within these contexts, the "Hebräische Melodien" may be read as a critique—especially apparent in the opening and closing poems—of the devastating consequences of an oppressive exilic life and, in the central poem, "Jehuda ben Halevy,"[1] as an exciting effort to conceptualize a positive and productive diaspora that is not simply exile within a poetic structure that reflects and constructs that imagined reality.

The three poems of this text are all concerned with Jewish life and culture within a diaspora that is more or less associated with Spain and with Jewish, Islamic, and Christian culture on Spanish soil. Even the initial poem, "Prinzessin Sabbat," which makes only minor reference to Spain in the mistaken identification of "Jehuda ben Halevy" as the author of a poem that has become part of the Sabbath liturgy, grounds the transcendent move from weekday to Sabbath in a tale of transformation from the *Arabian Nights,* known only in its Arabic version. Although the event depicted in the final poem, "Disputation," apparently takes place in late-fourteenth-century Christian Spain before the Spanish Inquisition was firmly entrenched but nonetheless perilous for the Jewish population, there is a reference to the Moors, to whom—along with the Jews—King Pedro speaks with civility. The central poem, "Jehuda ben Halevy," which is clearly the most interesting and powerful of the three, follows a complex trajectory between the contemporary narrator-poet and the Sephardi cultural environment of Jehuda Halevy, between the ancient and medieval Mediterranean world and nineteenth-century Berlin and Paris, between a thriving Jewish diasporic life in twelfth-century Islamic Spain and a degraded one in contemporary Europe. This was, of course, not the first time that the significance of Spain and the shifting interaction of its Christian, Moorish, and Jewish populations have appeared in Heine's writings—one thinks, among others, of the two "Almansor" texts (drama and later poem), the unfinished novel *Der Rabbi von Bacharach* and the poem "Donna Clara"—but the "Hebräische Melodien" seems to be uniquely directed toward both articulating a critique of the disabilities of Jewish exilic life and reconstructing a historically grounded diasporic alternative.

During the period of emancipation and modernization in eighteenth- and nineteenth-century Europe, Jews of the Middle East and the Maghreb, who were generally perceived as the "antithesis of 'civilization,'"[2] were referred to as "Orientals." But since connotations of the term "oriental" (in German *orientalisch* or *asiatisch*) often suggested what was considered exotic, sensuous, and sensual, it also could have a positive valence. This is especially pronounced in "Jehuda ben Halevy" with its allusions to the Talmud's Agadic texts as a fantastic garden akin to that wondrous one of the oriental Queen Semiramis of Babylon. And at times, "oriental," when referring to Middle Eastern or Mizrahi Jews, suggested authenticity, especially when "Orientals" were compared with impoverished Eastern European or assimilated Western Jewry. Sometime during the eighteenth-century the term "oriental" began to be used negatively by Germans to designate the non-European origins, archaic practices, "impure" language, and primitive living conditions of the German Jewish population.[3]

By the end of the eighteenth and the beginning of the nineteenth centuries, however, there was another major shift in the term's usage. Almost solely applied to the Eastern European Jew, the *Ostjude*, "oriental" circulated in the discourse of acculturated German Jews eager to separate themselves from the Polish Jewish population on their border, who were perceived as lacking the language, education, and refinements necessary for participation in modern Western society. Steven Aschheim, who considers the "modern" Jew as well as the *Ostjude* to be products of Enlightenment thinking, regards the stereotype of the orientalized Eastern European Jew as a "convenient foil upon which German Jews could externalize and displace 'negative' Jewish characteristics."[4] By thus identifying the *Ostjude* as an unacceptable "other," German Jews could both distinguish themselves from their brethren to the East, who maintained archaic "oriental" practices, and adopt for themselves a position equal to German nationals.

The German Jewish orientalization of the *Ostjude* may best be understood within the broad horizon of European hegemonic thinking because this so-called Jewish problem was in fact a European problem of modernity. Edward Said has noted that Orientalism has little to do with the reality of the Orient, but everything to do with Western strategies to construct and reinforce occidental superiority over oriental backwardness.[5] Not unlike the Europeans, but of course on a far smaller scale, German Jews, who tried to distance themselves from *Ostjuden* by subjecting them to what Virginia Dominguez calls "the orientalizing and primitivizing Eurocentric gaze,"[6] sought to control the discourse applied to Jews and to appropriate a position of superiority to their Eastern brethren and of equality with Germans.

"Hebräische Melodien" was written during the period of Western European Jewry's struggle for emancipation. Heine's focus on Sephardi culture in medieval Spain was no doubt not idiosyncratic, but reflected an interest of some considerable political and social importance to the larger community of acculturated German Jews seeking emancipation. This interest in Jewish participation in the classical Islamic culture of medieval Spain represents a positive view of Orientalism, that is, a model of religious, social, and cultural tolerance and integration that also functions as a critique of intolerant and separatist "orientalized" Eastern European Orthodoxy. In "The Myth of Sephardic Supremacy," the historian Ismar Schorsch notes that since the sixteenth century, progressive Ashkenazi Jews had deemed the rich Sephardi legacy of biblical exegesis, grammatical research, and philosophical inquiry as a model to replace Ashkenazi Judaism's rigid, insular educational system that was devoted almost exclusively to the study of the Talmud. But it was not until the Enlightenment and the intensified opposition to Polish Jewry by German Jews that Jewish intellectuals turned to Spain for historical exemplars of the benefits of equality and a secular education for Jews.[7] It is, of course, not fortuitous in the late eighteenth and early nineteenth centuries—when many German Jews were trying to demonstrate their readiness, even their inherent capacity, for participation as equals in the body politic—that they sought simultaneously to distance themselves from Eastern European (primarily Polish) Jewry and to propagate a myth of a golden age of culture in twelfth-century Spain. After all, a nineteenth-century Jew could see in medieval Spain a period of European history in which Jews enjoyed social and political equality and actively contributed to a vibrant culture and flourishing intellectual life that benefited the entire population. Non-Jewish Germans, on the other hand, might discover in the ameliorative effects of cultural openness and symbiosis reasons enough to support emancipation for the Jewish population.

HEBRÄISCHE MELODIEN

The juxtaposition of the titles "Hebräische Melodien" and *Romanzero* suggests variance between the cycle of poems and the volume in which it appears, but tensions between discrepant aspects of the texts may be precisely what these titles are meant to reflect. *Romanceros,* that is, Spanish collections of romances, ballads, and legendary tales, became very popular in mid-nineteenth-century Spain and France when many *romancero* anthologies appeared featuring a broad array of chivalric adventure tales. The texts in Heine's *Romanzero,* traversing as they do vast periods of time and many continents, a multitude of cultures, histories, and legends, employing a variety of genres and poetic modes, present a kind of discursive textual diaspora, a conception underscored by the title of the final poetic cycle, "Hebräische Melodien," taken from the title *(Hebrew Melodies)* of a group of poems largely about biblical figures and events written in 1815 by Lord Byron, one of Heine's favorite writers. Although critics have noted the dissimilarity between the two collections of poems, Heine's appropriation of the title may have significant aesthetic reverberations: it calls attention not only to the importance of textuality, particularly of his work's poetic textuality, but to the nexus between language and music, between the ancient Hebrew and modern languages (English and German). It may also identify the ironic German poet, who often spoke of Byron as his "cousin," with an admired iconoclastic, satiric, subversive writer who was of the nobility, English, and a Christian, but was also as critical of religion as Heine was. Such multiple possibilities suggest a kind of textual and cultural diaspora that I find demonstrated in complex ways in Heine's "Hebräische Melodien."

The opening verses of "Prinzessin Sabbat" compare the transition from weekday to Sabbath with the fable from the *Arabian Nights* about an all-too-brief transformation of bewitched princes into their original princely form.[8]

This may question the likelihood that a struggling impoverished Jew could actually experience a pure joyous spirituality even one day a week. Yet if this reference to fairy tales also functions to distance the poet-narrator from Jewish religiosity, to present him as an outsider who, in "singing his song," is relying on extraneous texts to explain and communicate the divided existence of an unassimilated Jew, then it may be that the poem has less to do with the Sabbath celebration itself than with the significance of the narrator's intervention into matters of Jewish religious observance. Once the prominence of the narrator's perspective is recognized, two large textual issues are brought to the foreground. On the one hand, there is the system of values and strategies through which his own social environment as well as that of Jewish piety are represented and critiqued, perhaps at the expense of what some critics have understood as the poem's concern with the "poetry of Judaism," the tragic division in Jewish life, or with empathy for Jewish religion and its practices.[9] On the other hand, there is the issue of the ability of an outsider, here probably a nontraditional Jew, to sing this song of the Sabbath—a problem that haunts "Jehuda ben Halevy" as the question of whether the exile from Zion is able to sing Zion's song ("How shall we sing the Lord's song in a strange land?" Psalm 137 asks). In addition, read from the point of view of the narrator, those errors in the text that are usually attributed to Heine's inadequate knowledge of Jewish culture or to a poet's deliberate move to maintain meter or enhance reader recognition may better be understood as a way of identifying the narrator as the one who possesses a flawed knowledge of things Jewish.[10] Indeed, the narrator's treatment of the three texts he cites—the *Arabian Nights,* the Sabbath song "Lekha dodi likras kalla" [Come, beloved, the bride awaits you], and Schiller's "An die Freude" [Ode to Joy]—characterizes him as a rather cultured cosmopolitan writer who, by situating the sacredness of the Sabbath within a rather broad horizon of religious, folk, and high literary culture, can portray and perhaps even honor the Sabbath, but also deride certain aspects of Jewish life and ritual.

Since it is impossible to analyze the poem in depth here, let me explore a segment in which the narrator shifts the focus from the sanctity of the Sabbath service to a rather broad and perhaps even subversive critique of Jewish diasporic life. "Prinzessin Sabbat" is divided roughly into two parts: the Sabbath eve service in the synagogue where the traditional liturgical song "Lekha dodi likras kalla" welcomes the arrival of the Sabbath, and its waning hours in the home where, after the luxury of the Sabbath meal, the final ritual, the *havdala* service, ushers out the Sabbath and the poem. The segment under consideration here, which forms the bridge between synagogue and home, begins, once the atmosphere of piety in the synagogue is depicted, with a portrayal of the cantor that, given the unpleasant descrip-

tion of his preciosity, vanity, and pomposity, may very well coincide with the
Reform movement's attack on the "oriental" (here signifying overly orna-
mental) renditions of the traditional cantorial performance.[11]

> Schmuckes Männchen, das sein schwarzes
> Mäntelchen kokett geachselt.
>
> Um die weiße Hand zu zeigen,
> Haspelt er am Halse, seltsam
> An die Schläf den Zeigefinger,
> An die Kehl den Daumen drückend.
>
> Trällert vor sich hin ganz leise,
> Bis er endlich lautaufjubelnd
> Seine Stimm erhebt und singt:
> Lecho Daudi Likras Kalle!
> Lecho Daudi Likras Kalle—
>
> Komm, Geliebter, deiner harret
> Schon die Braut, die dir entschleiert
> Ihr verschämtes Angesicht! (126)
>
> [Dapper little man who shoulders
> His little black cloak coquettishly.
>
> To display how white his hand is,
> He fidgets with his neck, oddly
> Index finger pressed to the temple,
> Thumb reposing on the throat.
>
> He hums to himself very softly,
> Until finally loudly exulting
> He raises his voice and sings:
> Lekha dodi likras kalla!
> Lekha dodi likras kalla!
>
> Come, beloved, already there awaits you
> The bride who for you unveils
> Her blushing face! (652)][12]

Written by Solomon Halevy Alkabets, a sixteenth-century kabbalist and
mystical poet, the esoteric poem "Lekha dodi likras kalla" is considered obscure even by religious scholars, but it has nevertheless been incorporated
into the liturgy and is known by almost every observant Jew. It depicts the
mystical union of the nation Israel as royalty and the Sabbath as Israel's
bride. Given the citation of its opening line in the original Hebrew and the
narrator's obvious knowledge of the text's allegorical content, his reference
to the song as a "hübsches Hochzeitscarmen" [charming nuptial verse] in

the secular tradition of romances confronts the poem's exclusively religious significance with a possible secular literary reading. Indeed, the move to connect the sacred and the profane appears throughout the poem and is supported by his incorrect attribution of authorship to "dem großen/ Hochberühmten Minnesinger/Don Jehuda ben Halevy" [the great/ highly celebrated minnesinger/Don Jehuda ben Halevy], that is, not only to the religious poet and scholar, "Jehuda, son of the Levite," but to "Don Jehuda" the courtly bard.[13] In this instance, by introducing alternative secular cultural/aesthetic perspectives into the discussion of traditional practices in Jewish life, the narrator is able to challenge and yet augment the religious significance of the Sabbath. There are, however, moments in the poem where the narrator clearly (and usually with considerable irony and wit) undermines religiosity or calls it into question. For example, in an elaborate paean to one of the traditional dishes—*Schalet* in the German, *Chulnt* in the Yiddish (and subsequently in English)—served on the Sabbath in Ashkenazi communities, the narrator, in a comedic paroxysm of jubilation, claims that, had Schiller tasted this dish, his poem "An die Freude" [Ode to Joy] would have begun with "Schalet, schöner Götterfunken,/[14] Tochter aus Elysium" (186) [Chulnt, beautiful sparks of the gods,/Daughter of Elysium (653)]. He also claims that the cooking instructions for this dish, which is "des wahren Gottes/Koscheres Ambrosia" (128) [the kosher ambrosia/of the true God (653–54)], were given, as were the Ten Commandments and the Mosaic teachings, by God himself to Moses on Mt. Sinai. Furthermore, it is not the holy practices of the Sabbath, but the *chulnt* just devoured that allows the Prince, "as if transfigured," to evoke the marvelous sights and sounds of the biblical lands with its Jordan river, Bethel valley, and hills of Gilead.[15]

The critique of traditional Jewish life subtly but significantly pervades this entire segment. Observe, for example, the narrator's curious preoccupation with silence, a silence that, in this text, prevails in the synagogue and also emerges as a primary attribute of the Princess Sabbath, who is referred to several times as "die stille Fürstin" [the silent Princess] and as "die personifizierte Ruhe" [personified stillness]. His interest in silence is probably neither merely arbitrary nor idiosyncratic, directed as it is at argumentation and polemics, regarded as an abhorrent trait often associated with Jews. This is an issue that appears marginally in "Jehuda ben Halevy" and is the agonizing subject of the final poem, "Disputation." The narrator's aversion to intellectuality was already alluded to early in this poem in the transformation of the miserable "weekday" Jew from a "Hund mit hündischen Gedanken" [dog with doggish ideas] into the Sabbath Jew as a "Mensch mit menschlichen Gefühlen" [human with human feelings]. This shift from "doggish ideas" to "human feelings" may seem innocent, but its importance is exposed in the narrator's admiration for the silent princess who, he notes, is surely more beautiful than the Queen of Sheba and definitely not the intolerable person that the clever "Ethiopian bluestocking" [Blaustrumpf Äthiopiens] is. After all, "Die Prinzessin Sabbat, welche / Ja die personifizierte / Ruhe ist, verabscheute alle / Geisteskämpfe und Debatten" (127), [The Princess Sabbath, who / Is indeed personified / Stillness, loathes all / Polemics and debates (653)]. What seems to be merely a discussion of the attributes of the Sabbath is in fact an attack on what was perceived as the stereotypical behavior of the Jews, but an attack that may also have a larger, perhaps constructive, agenda. For just as the narrator can, by identifying the author of one of the most recognized and recondite liturgical texts as a great minnesinger, locate within Jewish history and culture an opportunity for an alternate, more secular, and modern conception of Jewish life; so too may it be possible to uncover in the silent but profoundly spiritual union of the nation Israel with the Sabbath an aspect of Jewish tradition that might serve as a model for more productive or acceptable social interaction in the modern world.

What is intimated in "Prinzessin Sabbat"—that is, the possibility of integrating substantive aspects of Jewish tradition and secular culture into an alternative diasporic life in which the modern Jew (and poet) could thrive as Jew and European—develops more explicitly during the course of the long "Jehuda ben Halevy" poem. Although the narrator-poet of "Jehuda ben Halevy" seems to amble rather effortlessly through a complex text replete with digressions that span thousands of years; widely separated geographical areas; and different cultures, religions, and genres; the poem nevertheless has a surprising coherence, the coherence perhaps associated with an extensive diaspora in time and space that nonetheless secures identity amid great variation. This sense of coherence may, in fact, issue from the relationship between the text's explicit interest in the dynamics of exile and diaspora, which is depicted in two ways. First, there is the poem's extensive temporal and spatial journeys of people, objects, texts, stories, and ideas. Second, the diasporic poet traverses the often uncharted borderland between multiple cultures and linguistic groups, between diverse social and discursive constructs. So vast a territory cannot, of course, be covered in this essay, but it may be possible to survey the area.

The importance of exilic existence cannot be overlooked in "Jehuda ben Halevy," given the fact that the first two parts of this four-part poem commence with paraphrases of and allusions to Psalm 137, which is often identified as the "great psalm of exile," and which in the Luther Bible is entitled "Wehklage der Gefangenen zu Babel" [Lamentation of the Prisoners in Babylon].[16] The poem opens with the psalm's fifth and sixth verses in which, although the psalmist speaks from the predicament of exile, the actual subject is not exile, but the connection between memory, which is, to be sure, precipitated by separation from origins, and the possibility (or impossibility) of singing and writing should memory cease:

"Lechzend klebe mir die Zunge
An den Gaumen, und es welke
Meine rechte Hand, vergäß ich
Jemals dein, Jerusalen—" (129)

["Dry with thirst [longingly] may my tongue cleave
To my palate, and let my right hand
Wither, should I ever forget
You, Jerusalem—" (655)]

Had the first verses of the psalm been cited here,[17] attention would certainly have been drawn to a cessation of creativity that exile had brought about, to the recognition that loss of the homeland behooves the exiles, in the psalm's words, to "hang our harps upon the willows." But verses 5 and 6 articulate a possibility other than silence, for it is precisely the absence of homeland and center of meaning and the memory of their presence in the past that gives rise to the poetic creativity, that activates the poet's voice and hand when harps are silenced. The narrator-poet of "Jehuda ben Halevy" may be in exile, but it becomes clear from the first verse, which cites the psalm, and the next five that it is not from Zion that he is exiled, but from Jehuda ben Halevy. These six verses comprise an introduction to the entire poem and function as an overture to the ensuing extended biography of the medieval Sephardi poet. Indeed, the narrator seems able to venture into the substance of this poem, which, in part, consists of constructing the monumental Spanish diaspora poet, only after he has struggled with the "Traumgestalten" [dream-figures, phantoms] and "Gespenster" [ghosts] that occupied his mind. Only then does he recollect the figure of Jehuda ben Halevy, whom he finally recognizes not by definite physical characteristics but rather by an ephemeral "rätselhaften Lächeln / Jener schön gereimten Lippen, / Die man nur bei Dichtern findet." (131) [enigmatic smile / Of those beautifully rhyming lips, / Which are found in poets only. (655)]. This narrator-poet is himself obsessed not with Jerusalem, as his Jehuda ben Halevy was, but with re-membering the renowned poet.

Cast here as an important scholar of Bible and Talmud, a leader of the nation Israel "[i]n der Wüste des Exils" (134) [[i]n the wasteland of exile (659)], and a poet who, though writing in Hebrew and Arabic, could match or surpass any European courtly poet, Jehuda ben Halevy is clearly a central figure in this text, but, the title of the poem notwithstanding, he is not the only—or perhaps even the main—protagonist. It is, after all, the narrator-poet who takes great pains not only to reconstruct the life of the Sephardi poet from his birth to his death and even thereafter to heaven, but also, in fine modernist fashion, to reveal the intricacies of the complex poetic construction that houses the Sephardi poet as well as others. There are other bards (Ibn Ezra, Gabirol, and Rudello) and other lives and deaths. There are the wandering pearls that travel east to west, from the treasury of Darius, King of Persia, into the diaspora, and are transferred by the initial largesse of Alexander the Great to, among others, Queen Atossa, the courtesan Thais, Cleopatra, the Moors of Spain, and the Spanish Catholic royalty, finally to their resting place on the neck of Baroness Solomon, Baron Rothschild's wife. There is also the beautiful cask—it once held the pearls, but in it Alexander stored the works of his favorite poet, Homer—and the narrator's fantasy that, had he possession of the cask and had poverty not forced him to sell it, in it he would store "die Gedichte unsres Rabbi—/ Des Jehuda ben Halevy (146)" [the poems of our great Rabbi—/Of Jehuda ben Halevy (668)], which the narrator sees as pearls that emanated from a profound, beautiful soul.[18] And then there is the search for the origin of the name "Schlemihl," who figures here as the forefather of both Jew and poet, a search that takes the narrator to Berlin where the baptized Jew Hitzig unlocks the secret of the origin of the name, which even Adelbert von Chamisso, author of the famed *Peter Schlemihls wundersame Geschichte*, did not know. And thence to Bible and Talmud, to Greece and the God Apollo; and, of course, there is more, much more, including a critique of French and probably European education that makes no mention of these great Spanish Jewish poets. By constructing an unfinished tapestry—the poem is a fragment—of disparate aspects of life in which everything and everyone, including the Jews, of course, move about and disperse and by making apparent the complex structure of the routes he has designed, this narrator-poet has created for himself, under the title "Jehuda ben Halevy," the role of poet-protagonist in charge of the world.

But if Jehuda ben Halevy is not the protagonist of the poem bearing his name, what then is his function in the text? Has the narrator merely colonized this extraordinary figure of the golden age of Spain in order to create his own *ars poetica;* or is Jehuda ben Halevy actually central to this work, perhaps indeed its center, as much of a center for the narrator-poet as homeland, Zion, or Jerusalem may be for an uprooted or dispersed people? I would argue that, without a doubt, the latter is the case. In this text, Jehuda ben Halevy is presented as having a dual function for the narrator-poet: on the one hand, he is a rabbi with a formidable Jewish education for whom Jerusalem provides but one site of religious and national identity; on the other, he is a quintessential representative of productive diasporic life for which the narrator longs. He is, after all, presented as the renowned Jewish scholar and philosopher; the poet admired in both the Jewish and European cultural communities; the Spaniard able to write in Hebrew and Arabic using complex Spanish, Arabic, French, and Jewish literary forms and genres; the Jew who, in this poem at least, was driven not by miseries of exile to venture to Jerusalem, but rather by stories of its decimation;[19] and a person who, by integrating into his life and work the complexities of the cultures around him, provided the dominant society with a marvelous creative oeuvre. Surely if, in this poem, the troubadour and minnesinger's proverbial object of desire, namely the lady, could be replaced by Jerusalem, as it is for Jehuda ben Halevy, then for this nineteenth-century narrator-poet awash in the diaspora, the lady and Jerusalem could also be replaced by this world-renowned and generally untroubled Sephardi troubadour and rabbi. Of course, having inherited the ill luck of a double *Schlemihltum* as poet and Jew, and having finally reached his beloved Jehuda ben Halevy, this narrator-poet might best take heed that he not die at that poet's feet as his Jehuda died at the ruins in Jerusalem.[20] One wonders whether he considered that when he left the poem a fragment.

This text's preoccupation with the integrative diasporic life represented by Jehuda ben Halevy seems not to denote a detached intellectual interest on the part of the narrator, but rather to derive from painful experiences of exile—his own and the age-old one of the Jewish people—and of homelessness, depicted in the poem by the continual wanderings of people and things through time and space. If the narrator-poet's yearning for the paragon of Sephardi culture he finds in Islamic Spain is indeed rooted in the anguish of exile and homelessness, then exploring some of the ways in which exile and homelessness are communicated may illuminate not only their effects on the narrator as person, poet, and Jew, but also conceptual differences between exile and diaspora represented in the poem.

To explore some of the distinctions made in this poem between exile and diaspora, let me focus on the first nine verses of part 2, which elaborate the detrimental effects of exile. Part 1 opened with verses 5 and 6 of Psalm 137, which underscored the importance of memory for exiles who write or sing about the homeland. Part 2, however, commencing with a reference to the psalm's recognizable opening lines about grief and silenced song—"By the rivers of Babylon, there we sat down, yea, we wept, when we remembered Zion. We hung our harps upon the willows in the midst thereof" (1–2)—places in the foreground the pain of exile and the harm it engenders. Furthermore, just as the first six verses of part 1 comprise a preface to the biography of Jehuda ben Halevy's formative years, the first nine verses of part 2 function as a preamble to a discussion of the poet's creative activity and yearning for Jerusalem. Focusing on the pain and anger that exilic life causes the narrator and the Jewish people, these nine verses encompass a series of discursive journeys that bespeak broad cultural and social despair, from the lamentations of the Babylonian exiles to the anguish of the contemporary narrator who struggles with a "westöstlich dunkler Spleen" [westeasterly dark spleen] that subsides only after he echoes the rage for revenge expressed in the concluding verse of the psalm;[21] from the elegiac rhetoric of the biblical passage to the folk idiom of home and hearth; and from an ailing narrator's miserable condition comparable to Job's to the dream of a mythological Pegasus waiting to carry him aloft and back to the "great poet" Jehuda ben Halevy. The scope and power of these exchanges and transitions reverberate in the first four verses of the prelude:

Bei den Wassern Babels saßen
Wir und weinten, unsre Harfen
Lehnten an den Trauerweiden—
Kennst du noch das alte Lied?

Kennst du noch die alte Weise,
Die im Anfang so elegisch
Greint und sumset, wie ein Kessel,
Welcher auf dem Herde kocht?

Lange schon, jahrtausendlange
Kochts in mir. Ein dunkles Wehe!
Und die Zeit leckt meine Wunde,
Wie der Hund die Schwären Hiobs.

Dank dir, Hund, für deinen Speichel—
Doch das kann nur kühlend lindern—
Heilen kann mir nur der Tod,
Aber, ach, ich bin unsterblich! (135–6)

[By the waters of Babylon sat
We and cried, our harps
Leaned against the weeping willows—
Do you still know the old song?

Do you still know the old tune,
Which at the start so elegaically
Wimpers and hums, like a kettle,
Which is boiling on the hearth?

Long already, millennia long
Has it boiled in me. A dark woe!
And time licks my wound,
As the dog did Job's ulcers.

Thank you, dog, for your spittle—
But that can only coolingly soothe—
Only death can heal me,
But, alas, I am immortal! (659–60)]

Although the immortality alluded to here seems to refer specifically to the narrator, it becomes clear, within the context of references to the Babylonian exile and a millennia-long exilic condition, that it applies as well to the Jewish people and to poets, whose pegasus-flights can recover and resuscitate the literary production of great poets of the past, such as Jehuda ben Halevy. Thus, the Jew, poet, and ailing individual—designations all applicable to the narrator—may each suffer from exile, but they can also hope to live beyond their mortal lives. Indeed, the narrator's reconstruction of Jehuda ben Halevy's creative life as Jew and multitalented, heterogeneous poet and scholar, which comprises the substance of part 2 of the poem, not only attests to the possibility of transcendence and immortality, but also suggests that an integrative diasporic life may be able to ameliorate or even overcome the grief and paralysis of exilic existence. Witness, for example, how the narrator's involvement with the golden age of Spain seems to provide him with a model not only for transcending his own physical and existential suffering, but for transforming it, within a poetic text and through its construction, into a positive conception of diaspora. The centrality and importance of such a diaspora is also apparent, when speaking of Jehuda ben Halevy and the other Sephardi poets, in the absence of the narrator's biting irony, sarcasm, ridicule, and humor that pervades much of the text, especially those parts pertaining to his contemporary nineteenth-century society.

The activity of the narrator-poet, who delights in the creative construction of a text, comes to an end in the closing lines of "Jehuda ben Halevy." It seems not to be present in the final poem of the "Hebräische Melodien," "Disputation," which depicts a public debate in fourteenth-century Christian Spain about whether the Christian or Israelite God is the true one. Although fictional, this confrontation between the Capuchin monk Friar Jose and Rabbi Judah of Navarre is certainly reminiscent of a famous debate that took place in Barcelona in 1263 between Rabbi Moses ben Nachman, known also as Nachmanides or Ramban, and a learned baptized Jew, Friar Paolo. Debates like these were very serious encounters, but not because of their subject matter. They were, in fact, generally staged for the express purpose of converting Jews, who could therefore hardly be expected to win, and a loss meant that the losing debater, namely, the Jew, and a group of his coreligionists would be forced to convert or be severely punished.

Since the details of this poem's disputation are hardly difficult to grasp because of the commonplace dogmas and cliches exchanged by the parties, let me concentrate on an issue more difficult to assess, namely, the relationship of this final poem to the earlier ones. This may bring us closer to an understanding of the aesthetic and ideological contours of the "Hebräische Melodien" and return us to a central focus of this essay, the problems and poetics of diaspora. Critics, especially (but not exclusively) those primarily interested in Heine's relation to Jews and Judaism, have registered dismay at "Disputation" because it seems to countermand what is regarded as the significance of the first two poems; that is, as one critic put it, "Heines wiedererwachte Liebe zur Tradition des Volkes, dem er entstammt, zu jüdischem Brauchtum und jüdischer Poesie" [Heine's reawakened love for the tradition of the people from which he descends, for Jewish practices and Jewish poetry].[22] Prawer even thinks that because "Prinzessin Sabbat and Jehuda ben

Halevy had both been paeans to the spirit of the Jewish faith," Heine felt obligated to reaffirm "the tartness of his unsweetened imagination and the re-
fusal of his free-ranging intellect to be fettered by orthodoxies of *any* kind."[23]
Although Sammons' insight that the poem "is an attempt to expose the vulgarity of zealous religious faith where it is not ennobled by poetic imagination" is closer to my own, the implication of some of his language is disquiet-
ing.[24] It is not, it seems to me, the "vulgarity" of rigid religious positions or
their articulation that is at stake in this poem, but the social and cultural conditions they represent and reproduce; and I rather doubt that the crass and
vicious dogmatic views presented by monk and rabbi could be ennobled
even by "poetic imagination."

A striking feature of this final poem of the "Hebräische Melodien" is, as
already mentioned, the absence of an identifiable, interactive narrator, an
absence that seems to be connected to a substantive change in the social
and cultural environment from that represented in "Jehuda ben Halevy."
There the narrator had the flexibility and creativity to weave together tem-
porally, geographically, and ideologically diverse cultures, and he clearly
identified with the dynamic diasporic situation in which the major figures
represented—Jehuda Halevy, Gabirol, Ibn Ezra—integrated substantial aspects of several cultures (Christian troubadour poetry, Moslem poetic
forms, Jewish midrashic tradition) into their lives and work. This kind of interactive possibility is absent in "Disputation," where the parties representing immutable positions do not seek common ground or insight into their
opponent's views, but rather desire to gain ascendency for their own fixed
ideas. The intellectual and cultural immobility that reigns in this text is also
reflected in the static scene presented in the poem: an Aula in Toledo, a
royal audience and their servants sit and listen, the disputants argue, and
Queen Donna Blanka casts the final judgment—"Daß sie alle beide stinken"
(172) [That both of them alike stink (688)]. Neither the transformation realized in "Prinzessin Sabbat" nor the continual movement of people and
things, of temporal position and geographical location, of genre and idea
in "Jehuda ben Halevy" is to be found in "Disputation," whose opaque narrator is also so completely absorbed into the narrative that no comment on
this grim yet grotesque and potentially bombastic paralysis is even possible.
Both the structure and the subject matter of this poem suggest that when
religion becomes institutionalized and dogmatic, cultural exchange, perhaps culture itself, is obliterated, and the individual is either confined to
fixed roles—rabbi or monk—or disappears completely, as does the narrator, in an anonymous authoritative script without agent or author.

One may well wonder whether any remnant of the creative cultural vitality represented in "Jehuda ben Halevy" remains after "Disputation," which
marks the end of both the "Hebräische Melodien" and *Romanzero*. In my reading of the "Hebräische Melodien," it is precisely the grim moral vacuity,

intellectual stagnation, and the absence of individuality and creativity so conspicuous in "Dispuation" that prompts the reader to revisit that earlier golden age, be it myth or reality, that stirred the modern poet to construct such a marvelously complex and multivalent cultural document as "Jehuda ben Halevy." Thus, despite, or perhaps because of, the bleak and foreboding social and ideological circumstances portrayed in "Disputation," that golden age continues to reverberate.

Indeed, negative images of exilic life and identity haunt all three poems, whether it is the miserable situation of the "weekday" Jew in "Prinzessin Sabbat" and his insulation within traditional ritual; or the impoverishment of the narrator-poet in "Jehuda ben Halevy," who still hears "das alte Lied . . . die alte Weise" [the old song . . . the old melody] of Babylonian exile stirring in him: "Lange schon, jahrtausendlange / Kochts in mir. Ein dunkles Wehe! / Und die Zeit leckt meine Wunde, / Wie der Hund die Schwären Hiobs." (135) [Long already, millennia long / Has it boiled in me. A dark woe! / And time licks my wound, / As the dog did Job's ulcers. (659)]; or the rabbi and Jews of "Disputation" who, threatened with death or loss of identity, are forced to defend the exclusivity of their religious beliefs and practices, despite the fact that the defense itself would most likely lead to conversion or death. But the "Hebräische Melodien" as a whole addresses the possibility of another model of diaspora. Daniel and Jonathan Boyarin have noted that "[d]iaspora culture and identity allows (and has historically allowed in the best circumstances, such as Muslim Spain), for a complex continuation of Jewish cultural creativity and identity at the same time that the same people fully participate in the common cultural life of their surroundings."[25] The Boyarins' conception of diasporic cultural identity is a disaggregated one that is constructed anew whenever circumstances and conditions demand, an identity protected only by interaction with other cultures. James Clifford underscores the importance in diaspora cultures of the social interaction among groups and of the construction of communities that allow for the active intersection of different cultures: "Diaspora discourse articulates, or bends together, both roots *and* routes to construct . . . alternate public spheres, forms of community consciousness and solidarity that maintain identifications outside the national time/space in order to live inside, with a difference. Diaspora cultures are nonseparatist, though they may have separatist or irredentist moments."[26] It is precisely the possibility of interactive cultures and communities that inform the environment of "Jehuda ben Halevy"; and it is their complete impossibility that is critiqued in "Disputation."

The impetus for the plethora of recent discussions of diaspora (rather than exile) was probably the burgeoning interest in postcolonial and multicultural studies and the enormous increase in the transnational circulation of peoples, goods, and information. The focus on diaspora theory, discourse, and identity has been particularly helpful in distinguishing diaspora as an integration of dominant and subdominant cultures from exile, which is understood as forced homelessness and an anguished longing to return to the homeland, the center of national identity. Of course, each position—diaspora or exile—presupposes an identity very different from the other: the former would construe distinctiveness through connection and coexistence; the latter would stress the necessity of uniqueness, separatism, and sovereignty. Understood in this context, the "Hebräische Melodien" seems invested in establishing the importance of an integrative diaspora that promotes interactive dialogue across borders—cultural and social, temporal and geographical—and in developing a poetics that communicates that possibility. It accomplishes this in two ways: negatively in "Disputation," by depicting the menacing effects of absolutist thinking and practice in a completely polarized society; and positively in "Jehuda ben Halevy," by portraying not only the rich creativity of Sephardi culture in medieval Spain, but especially the imaginative narrator-poet who, using a variety of poetic techniques and genres, ingeniously connects multiple cultures across vast areas of space and time, from the Middle East to the European West, from biblical and hellenistic times through the Middle Ages to the nineteenth century. A challenging performative enactment of the politics and poetics of diaspora.

NOTES

1. The poet's name is actually Jehuda Halevy or Jehuda ben Samuel Halevy, which means Jehuda, son of Samuel the Levite. One cannot normally abbreviate the name as Jehuda ben Halevy, which means Jehuda, son of the Levite. For discussion of the possible implications of Heine's designation, see note 13.

2. Daniel Schroeter, "Orientalism and the Jews of the Mediterranean," *Journal of Mediterranean Studies* 2, no. 2 (1994): 189.

3. Paul Mendes-Flohr, "Orientalism, the *Ostjuden,* and Jewish Self-Affirmation," in *Studies in Contemporary Jewry*, vol. 1, ed. Jonathan Frankel (Bloomington: Indiana University Press, 1984) 100.

4. Steven Aschheim, "The Eastern European Jew and German Jewish Identity," in *Studies in Contemporary Jewry*, vol. 1, ed. Jonathan Frankel (Bloomington: Indiana University Press, 1984) 7; see also his *Brothers and Strangers: The East European Jew in German and German Jewish Consciousness 1800–1923* (Madison: University of Wisconsin Press, 1983), especially chapter 1.

5. Edward W. Said, *Orientalism* (New York: Pantheon) 1–28.

6. Virginia R. Dominguez, "Questioning Jews," *American Ethnologist* 20, no. 3 (1993): 622.

7. Ismar Schorsch, "The Myth of Sephardic Supremacy," *Leo Baeck Institute Year Book* 34 (New York: Leo Baeck Institute, 1989), esp. 47–53. See also 57–66 for a discussion of the many works about medieval Sephardi philosophy, poetry, and culture written in Germany during the first half of the eighteenth century.

8. The Sabbath is traditionally described as a queen, not a princess (see, for

example, *Babylonian Talmud,* "Baba Kama," 32 A–B: "Rabbi Hanina would say on the eve of the Sabbath: 'Come let us go out to meet the bride, the Queen.'"); and it is God (traditionally the King) who sends the Queen Sabbath to Israel as a bride. Since the narrator in "Prinzessin Sabbat" compares the Sabbath transformation of the Jew/Israel to *Arabian Nights* fables of enchanted princes who are returned for a time to their former princely selves, it would seem appropriate that the Jew/Israel be figured as a prince and the Sabbath bride as a princess.

9. See S. S. Prawer, *Heine's Jewish Comedy: A Study of His Portraits of Jews and Judaism* (Oxford: Clarendon Press, 1983) 554–61; Jeffrey L. Sammons, *Heinrich Heine, The Elusive Poet* (New Haven: Yale University Press, 1969) 387–89; Hartmut Kircher, *Heinrich Heine und das Judentum* (Bonn: Bouvier Verlag, 1973) 266–70; see also Israel Tabak, *Judaic Lore in Heine: The Heritage of a Poet* (Baltimore: The Johns Hopkins University Press, 1948) 156–61; and Ludwig Rosenthal, *Heinrich Heine als Jude* (Frankfurt am Main: Ullstein, 1973) 89, 292–95 for Heine's sources and for a discussion of the significance of references to Jewish history and the practices and traditions of Judaism.

10. Sander L. Gilman, *Inscribing the Other* (Lincoln: University of Nebraska Press, 1991) 132–33 states that in this poem Jehuda Halevy was identified as the author of the famous Sabbath song "because" readers would associate him with the golden age, whereas that would not be the case with the actual author, Solomon Halevy Alkabets; Prawer 797, n. 10: "Heine seems to have chosen the form 'Jehuda ben Halevy' for reasons of euphony." See note 13 for further discussion of the possible significance of Heine's designation.

11. Mendes-Flohr, 100.

12. Heinrich Heine, *Sämtliche Schriften,* ed. Klaus Briegleb (Munich: Carl Hanser, 1978) vol. 6, part 1, page references in parentheses after citation. *The Complete Poems of Heinrich Heine: A Modern English Version,* trans. Hal Draper (Boston: Suhrkamp/Insel, 1982), page references in parentheses after citation. I have made changes to the English translation where necessary.

13. The translation of Heine's rendition of Jehuda Halevy's name, that is, Jehuda ben Halevy, is Jehuda, son of the Levite, and the form may have an important aesthetic function in the text. After all, the Levites had the function of reciting or intoning the psalms and hymns in the Temple; and today the *mizmor* (sung poem) recited in the synagogue is preceded by a statement indicating that this was a song "which the Levites used to recite in the Temple." Thus, since Heine casts his figure as a troubadour and minnesinger, the name Jehuda, son of the Levite, would enunciate his descent from a singer/intoner within an old traditional Jewish context. I am indebted to Chana Kronfeld for this information on the function of the Levites in Temple and synagogue. See also note 1.

14. Instead of "Freude [Joy], schöner Götterfunken, / Tochter aus Elysium."

15. On the connection between food, aesthetics, and texts in Heine's writings, see Jocelyne Kolb, *The Ambiguity of Taste: Freedom and Food in European Romanticism* (Ann Arbor: University of Michigan Press, 1995, especially chapter 4, "Heine and the Aesthetics of the Tea Table," 115–224; Barker Fairley, "Heine and the Festive Board," *University of Toronto Quarterly* 36, no. 3 (1967): 209–19.

16. The importance of this psalm for Heine has been discussed in different contexts in two excellent articles: Inge Rippmann, "'Wir saßen an den Wassern Baby-

lons': Eine Annäherung an Heinrich Heines *Denkschrift über Ludwig Börne,"* *Heine-Jahrbuch* 34 (1995): 25–47 is largely concerned with the relationship between Heine's experience of exile and homesickness in Paris and his sense of linguistic isolation as a German writer living in France. Rippmann maintains that Heine expresses homage to Zion (30–31), but it seems to me that his reference to verses 5 and 6 in "Jehuda ben Halevy" is interested less in homage and more in the importance of memory for writing. Ruth Wolf, "Versuch über 'Jehuda ben Halevy,'" *Heine-Jahrbuch* 18 (1979): 84–98 is concerned with the importance of the psalm for Heine (he speaks of the psalm in a letter to Moser in 1826 in relation to his unhappiness about his conversion the previous year), but not with how it functions in the poem. See also Hans-Joachim Kraus's commentary on the psalm in *Psalmen* 2 (Neukirchen-Vluyn, Germany: Neukirchener Verlag, 1978) 1081–86.

17. The first two verses are cited at the beginning of part 2 of the poem; I shall return to their significance.

18. Michael Sachs, *Die religiöse Poesie der Juden in Spanien* (Berlin: Veit Verlag, 1845) 287. There is an interesting reference to pearls in a passage about Jehuda Halevy's works that Sachs quotes from a poem by Rabbi Judah ben Solomon Alcharisi: "Das Lied, das der Lewit Jehudah gesungen,—ist als Prachtdiadem um der Gemeinde Haupt geschlungen,—als Perlenschnur hält es ihren Hals umrungen." [The song that the Levite Jehuda sang,—is as a magnificent diadem twined about the head of the community,—as a string of pearls it holds its neck surrounded.] (The translation is mine.) Heine was indebted to Sachs' work for his knowledge of medieval Spanish Jewish poetry and culture. See Rosenthal, 290–96.

19. Sachs 300–301 comments that Jehuda was not driven to go to Jerusalem by an oppressive situation, but by "ein klares reines liebendes Verlangen, das bald kindlich einfach, bald in glühender Innigkeit sich äußert," [a clear pure loving yearning, which expressed itself sometimes in childlike simplicity, sometimes in glowing inwardness]. (Translation is mine.)

20. Sachs 291 notes that the evidence indicates that Jehuda Halevy did not, as legend had it, die when he entered Jerusalem, but most likely en route from Egypt to Palestine. Heine, however, adopts the legendary narrative in the poem.

21. "Jehuda ben Halevy" reads: "Heil dem Manne, dessen Hand / Deine junge Brut ergreifet / Und zerschmettert an der Felsenwald." (136) [Hail to the man, whose hand / that grabs your young children / And smashes them against the rock wall (660)]. The Luther Bible reads: "Wohl dem, der deine jungen Kinder nimmt und zerschmettert sie an den Stein" (Psalm 137.9) [Happy shall he be, that taketh and dasheth thy little ones against the stones] (King James translation).

22. Kircher 280.

23. Prawer 599. Emphasis in the original.

24. Sammons 395.

25. Daniel Boyarin and Jonathan Boyarin, "Diaspora: Generation and the Ground of Jewish Identity," *Critical Inquiry* 19, no. 4 (1993): 720–21.

26. James Clifford, *Routes: Travel and Translation in the Late Twentieth Century* (Cambridge: Harvard University Press, 1997) 251.

4

Dancing at Two Weddings

Mazel *between Exile and Diaspora*

Murray Baumgarten

CITY AND *SHTETL*

My essay is informed by a question: why have the Jews and modern Jewish writers persisted in their love affair with city life? The folk proverb "die Stadt-luft macht frei" [the city air liberates] suggests one kind of explanation. Episodes ranging from the Book of Esther—"The city of Shushan was perplexed"—to scenes and works from the contemporary Brazilian writer Moacyr Scliar, the Israeli A. B. Yehoshua, and the North Americans Saul Bellow, Grace Paley, Philip Roth, and Rebecca Goldstein reinforce the claim.[1] But our fascination has not been limited to cities and, especially in recent years, has extended to its geographical and cultural opposite, the *shtetl*. Several recent works, including Eva Hoffman's *The Shtetl* and Allen Hoffman's *Small Worlds,* have focused on that smaller world, perhaps in response to its utter destruction by the Nazis, perhaps also in the effort to find a way to respond to the suburbanization of modern life, in particular American Jewish life, and the simultaneous increasing secularism and piety of its Jewish urban villagers.

The contrast between city and suburb could be analyzed historically, relegating the city-centered fictions to an older generation and seeing in the new suburban-centered novels the wave of the future. Although such a typology is, at present, speculative, it is clear that we are at a moment of change in the literary and social history of Jewish writing. Here, Rebecca Goldstein's work is particularly important. It encompasses both suburban and urban worlds, as well as that of the *shtetl,* as it explores their meanings and points us to a fuller understanding not only of the sociological but also the literary, political, and (even) spiritual dimensions of our contemporary situation.

What is striking about *Mazel,* published in 1995, is the powerful dialogue between *shtetl,* suburb, and city around which it is constructed. *Mazel* recapitulates many of the themes of Goldstein's earlier work, especially her first novel, *The Mind-Body Problem* (1983), and her collection of stories, *Strange Attractors* (1993), in which the central characters of *Mazel* first appear. In this novel, suburb, *shtetl,* and city illuminate an abiding concern of Jewish life, the relation of exile and diaspora. *Mazel* is in part a response to the suburban appropriation of some of the central values of the *shtetl.* However, the *shtetl* is a world obsessed by the dislocation of exile, while the city provides the chance to construct an empowering diasporic homeland within the larger condition of differing ranges of Jewish powerlessness and the suburb, though similar to the *shtetl,* partakes of both conditions,[2] for her central characters are caught in dancing at two weddings, unable to abandon either world. Living in *shtetl,* suburb, and city, they are marked by the political, sociological, spiritual, and cultural values of each and thus enact the full range of modern Jewish life. They are caught between exile and diaspora.

People change their names as they change their places in this novel; yet their new identities do not allow them to relinquish the old. Instead of fitting in because of their new identities, they become outsiders in a different way. Personalities, situations, and events are doubled. Some figures take on the life histories of dead siblings and elaborate their narratives as their own. These doubled lives echo the worlds of gothic fiction and an interspersed realist narrative, and these mixed genres of modernist fiction are reinforced by classical Jewish forms, including chasidic parable, talmudic dialectic, and fables approaching the brevity and continuing resonance of biblical narrative. Some characters seem at times to partake of a second soul, as if the *Shekhinah* had awarded them its Sabbath gift permanently and thus taken them out of the condition of exile. Though they are worldless *luftmenschen,* they are also seekers of the way. Time plays tricks on us in *Mazel.* Scenes years apart merge into each other; events that changed the lives of grandparents are relived by grandchildren; the future becomes past and the past, present. The reader joins the characters in this process of decentering. Neither past nor present is anchored to a central scene or figure or place; instead, experiences flow into each other.

Rather than the individualist character of the realistic novel, we encounter a different literary mode. *Mazel* lacks the narrative challenge thrown at the reader by a Bellow novel and the strategy of entrapment in the seemingly autobiographical narrative characteristic of Philip Roth's fictions. Rebecca Goldstein's novel invites us into the conversation in an action that combines the almost lost art of Jewish conversation and the woman's world of sharing discourse. In this fictional universe, events don't move in a linear progression, but are fluid and shifting, "like circles in water," the dominant metaphor of the novel. Instead of being forced with Bellow's Herzog to resolve contradictions at the heart of Western culture or struggling with Roth's Portnoy in the middle of a Jewish joke to avoid becoming a scapegoat for an immigrant family's and community's habits, Goldstein's characters move through a landscape of possibility. Sharing their difficulties rather than competing for resources, they dwell in a potentially revolutionary time-space of their own construction.

In *Mazel* many characters travel great distances, and their personalities change in response to their new circumstances. Such travel marks the Son-nenbergs—the children, Fraydel, Sore, and Tzali, and their parents, Leiba and Nachum. Wandering into the fields adjacent to Shluftchev, Fraydel thinks of going off with the gypsies. Sore travels with the Bilbul Art Theater to Lemberg, Brest-Litovsk, Grodno, Lodz, Pinsk, Krakow, Bialystock, Lublin, and Vilna. Their younger brother, Tzali, travels from Shluftchev to Vilna to study in the "prestigious Ramalyes Yeshiva" (180). Leiba wanders far and wide in her commercial pursuits, and she and Nachum, like their children, move from Shluftchev to Warsaw. Family relationships change as the characters move from the *shtetl* to the city, where the Sonnenbergs encounter distant relatives, who reshape their lives in urban terms. The Saunders boys begin their travels for career purposes: Jascha and Maurice move to Warsaw and then keep going. Maurice moves from Poland to Palestine to America and never settles down. Wandering becomes a way of life for him: "He never could sit out a New York summer. Once, in desperation, he had joined a freighter headed for Iceland, offering himself as a cook's assistant. He had figured that all he'd have to do was stir the pots and peel the potatoes. But then the cook had gotten seasick, and he had been ordered to take over. Dis-covered as an impostor, he had been relegated to swabbing the decks until they reached Reykjavik, where they had put him ashore. He had eventually made his way back to New York by way of Labrador, bringing home a bunch of good stories, filled with his wonder at the endless variety of human lives to be found on this planet." (327–28) [3] Sore leaves Shluftchev for Warsaw, where she becomes Sasha, moves to Vilna, conceives Chloe there, gives birth to her in Palestine, travels to America, and, though happily settled in New York, continues to travel. Her daughter, Chloe, who grows up and makes an academic career in Manhattan, also has a vagabond spirit. Their constant movement marks them as diasporan figures, who, in James Clifford's witty phrasing, exchange roots for routes. Theirs is the "wandering meaning" ar-ticulated by Shirley Kaufman; to borrow the title of her essay, their roots are in the air. [4]

These characters are at home in cities. Having abandoned their *shtetlach*, they respond to the dynamism of modern city life with energy and enthusi-asm. Although some characters, like Phoebe and Nachum, [5] retreat into themselves in part, perhaps, as a result of the urban overload analyzed by Georg Simmel in his classic work, *The Metropolis and Modern Life,* most of the people in this novel—among them Sore, Hershel, Rosalie, Feliks, and Mau-rice—respond to the incessant urban stimulation by seizing opportunities. Embracing Emancipation, they abandon religious practice and study and, instead, frequent coffeehouses, create a theater company, compose music, write learned articles, fall in and out of love, study at the university, devour and devise the cultural treasures of urban life. What they discover in Warsaw they carry with them and use to reshape all the cities they inhabit: "Jewish Warsaw, which was roughly a third of Warsaw proper, was a city of rabbis and swindlers, capitalists and poets, but, most of all, it was a city of talkers. There were so many ideas in the air you could get an education simply by breathing deeply" (206). In the city, they make ideas into realities and in the process turn themselves from *luftmenschen* into cosmopolitan citizens.

Although their experience in Warsaw crystallizes their characters, the deep structure of their personalities has been shaped by the experience of the *shtetl*. *Mazel* explores the range of experience offered by that *shtetl* world, revealing its determining power at the critical moments of their life histories: birth, the onset of puberty, marriage, career decisions, childbearing, old age, and death. Shluftchev-on-the-Puddle, to cite its full name, occupies more than a third of *Mazel*. It does not relinquish its hold on the characters when they move elsewhere, belying its name, which roughly translates into Sleepy Hollow. Furthermore, this *shtetl* world is doubled in suburban Lipton, New Jersey, where the opening and closing sequences take place. Sasha characterizes Lipton, as the Sabbath before the preparations for Phoebe's wedding comes to an end: "Lipton is Shluftchev with a designer label" (333). The sarcasm of her comment recalls the satire of Mendele Moycher Seforim and is echoed in Shluftchev, the name he also gave to his generic *shtetl*. Despite her polemic views—the result of her sister Fraydel's suicide and her own escape from Shluftchev—Sore/Sasha's view of the deadening power of the *shtetl* is only one of several central to *Mazel*.

Whether positive or negative, Shluftchev forms the structure of their memory as well as providing the content of its images; it is the material their urban street smarts will have to contend with, sort out, and make sense of. Shluftchev is a bounded world, governed by Jewish law and tradition, Jewish habits and ways of life. In it, the logic of *Halakha* holds. Dominated by that religious system, Shluftchev shapes the personalities, choices, and life histories of its inhabitants.

When they leave Shluftchev for the city, *mazel*—the principle of chance—comes into play. In an interview coinciding with the novel's publication in 1995, Rebecca Goldstein calls *mazel* "the imp of metaphysics" and provides her shorthand definition: it is "the sly saboteur of cosmic coziness," carrying the force of "Jewish chaos." Her phrasing alerts us to the serious issues she explores in the novel. As a philosopher she is led to questions that she explores in terms articulated by Jewish tradition—she notes in her interview that her "knowledge of Jewish texts informs her writing 'in almost unconscious ways.'"[6] For Chloe, *mazel* parallels David Hume's analysis of causation: "All events seem entirely loose and separate. One event follows another, but we never can observe any tie between them. They seem *conjoined,* but never *connected"* (26). The principle of *mazel* thus calls into question the power of *saychel* [reason] to determine human life. Reason, in the form of the *Halakha,* cannot control these characters: as Chloe thinks about the problem, she realizes that "David Hume sounded just like Sasha." She wonders if "Hume's scathingly rigorous analysis of causality" was "nothing more than Sasha and her insistence that there's *such a thing as mazel?*" (26) Even if Shluftchev is governed by iron rules of causation, Hume's analysis and Sasha's *joie de vivre* provide a way out of the *shtetl.* Urban life offers them change, transformation, new possibility, in short, a place of *mazel.*

The first chapter concludes on the note struck by the novel's opening parable, a dialogue of Mazel and Saychel. This dialogue reappears throughout the novel, constructing a metanarrative on the level of parable to the events and experiences of the characters.

> Mazel, which is luck in Yiddish, encountered Saychel, or brains, on the road one day, and the two fell into a conversation. Before too long, they began to bicker about which of them was the more important.
>
> Saychel claimed that with brains anything is possible, but Mazel argued that without luck all the intelligence in the world will come to nothing.
>
> Soon Saychel and Mazel had reached the point in an argument when there's no going forward without going backward, and at this moment a baby boy was born. Both Saychel and Mazel agreed that one of them should enter the boy, and they would see what would come of it. It was Saychel who slipped himself in, while Mazel settled back and watched.

With this parable, the novel marks several of its distinguishing themes. Mazel and Saychel meet "on the road," thereby striking the travel note so important in the book. Their argument involves opposing claims about how to make one's way in the world. Time enters the algorithm in the form of the birth of a baby boy, who is informed by Saychel, the masculine principle of reason, while the feminine Mazel watches, bemused and amused, both guardian angel and inquisitor. The parable also sets the key signature of the novel. A Yiddish folk-situation, this dialogue of the different gender principles puts into play a Yiddish cultural world with which the characters of the novel, whatever their situation, will have to come to grips, as will the reader.

Shluftchev, however, does not offer the only Yiddish dimension to the novel. The triumphant performance of *The Bridegroom* by the Bilbul Art Theater throughout the cities and *shtetls* of eastern Europe echoes the embrace of the Yiddish world of its own theatrical traditions from *The Dybbuk* to Second Avenue. The Bilbul Art Theater was the spiritual heir to the legendary Vilna Troupe, whose fame grew from their connection to *The Dybbuk,* "a dark and brooding drama about a dead lover who possesses the soul of his intended bride, after she has been betrothed by her father to another man. Its author had been a Yiddish folklorist named Shlomo Rapaport, who had written under the name S. An-ski. Rapaport had based his play on an old Chasidic legend that he had recorded during one of his ethnographic expeditions, but he had never been able to convince any of the Yiddish actors that he'd known to perform it" (308).[7] We learn this as the Bilbulniks are about to conclude their triumphant tour in Vilna, where, after Anski's death, "the still obscure Vilna Troupe had decided to produce their friend's play as a memorial to him. They had put everything together in great haste, wanting to open on the night that marked the end of the thirty-day period of mourning. When they opened, they had found themselves with a smash hit. For a few brief years, they had lived at the feverish pace of fame, there within the nimbus of the limelight. They had toured Western Europe and then gone on to America. And there, in America, they had somehow or other fallen apart, a mishpocheh no more, each of them going his or her own separate way and claiming to represent, in his or her very own person, the former Vilna" (309). Success in this world does not appear to last; it is tinged with the melancholy and early death that is Rapaport's lot. It is a moment echoed at the end of the novel, at the wedding of Phoebe: "And then Jason stamped on the glass that symbolizes the destruction of Jerusalem, always remembered in even the happiest of moments" (353). Although the city makes possible the flight of inspiration and of art, it cannot sustain the transient moment or transform it into a lasting monument. The modern city of enlightenment—of *Haskalah*—does not negate the *shtetl*.

Shluftchev is thus inflected as the premodern world of traditional pious Jewish culture, governed by the *daled amot* [four cubits] of the Law, while the Bilbulniks—whose name appropriately enough means "confusion"—speak for modern Yiddish urban culture. That vibrant city world, with its dazzling array of Jewish identities both religious and secular, was also destroyed by the Nazis. The utter *khurbn* of the Eastern European Jewish world has, through nostalgia's inappropriate claim, at times conflated the city and the *shtetl*, blurring the distinctions and depriving us of our necessary history, an error Rebecca Goldstein's novel does not fall into. In Shluftchev people exist in a dream-like world, which has the completeness of meaning of a classical work of art. In Warsaw, by contrast, the novel's personages must function in a clangorous realm, whose blaring meanings are also subtle and complicated. They depend on chance, that is, on *mazel*, rather than on *saychel*'s inexorable logic. And this contrast between *shtetl* and city calls to mind many of the novels of I. B. Singer, notably *The Magician of Lublin*. In her interview, Goldstein notes that "Singer even makes a brief appearance in the novel as a red-haired 'newly modernized yeshiva boy' (207). His is the voice I've been able to internalize." Goldstein adds that Singer's autobiographical writings about Warsaw proved particularly important in her work on *Mazel*.[8]

In the city, these *shtetl* Jews turn their status as *luftmenschen* into the creative possibilities of modern life. Their marginality becomes a resource.

They continue to learn the lesson of the Exodus from Egypt: having been marginal themselves, they are fascinated by marginality everywhere and do not seek to escape from it so much as to understand its ramifications. Here again Maurice is representative. "No person was too quirky or marginal for Maurice not to want to know how the world looked through his eyes. In fact, the more quirky and marginal, the better. Maurice himself had a great weakness for life in the margins" (328). Maurice, the wanderer, understands the ambiguities of experience.

As in the classic texts of modern Jewish writing, the characters in Rebecca Goldstein's novel cluster around an informing myth: the marginal person emerges from the *shtetl* and seeks a place in the freer, complex, and cosmopolitan life of the city.[9] Rooted in the urban experience of the modern Jewish writer, this myth articulates the strategies by which the protagonists might escape from the traditional tribal realm, as it simultaneously explores the possibilities of citizenship in the newly found civic arena. Paralleling the historical process, the literary work gives that process a conscious shape and purpose, defining an ideal city, at the least a city of imagination, in which protagonist and people might participate in the general enterprise of Western culture. This act reflects the modern Jewish status and situation, for the emancipated Jew is "the first cosmopolite and citizen of the world," by virtue of being both stranger and city person.[10]

Mazel puts this myth of liberation into play, explores it, and complicates it. In this novel the city world is balanced by the *shtetl* world of Shluftchev and of suburban Lipton, in which some characters feel more at home. The dialogue between city, *shtetl,* and suburb changes the trajectory of the characters. Instead of giving the freethinker center stage and legitimating the supposedly inevitable move from tradition to modernity, from communal status to ethnic and personal identity, *Mazel* helps us to envision the possibility that the city—the bridge between tradition and modernity—may also lead to re-traditionalization. That is, the freethinker—Sasha in all her glory—must share the stage in this novel with other characters, including her granddaughter, Phoebe. Together they function, in the words of Hannah Arendt, as a "conscious pariah"—as someone committed to the difficult problem of critical thinking and living. Phoebe, in contrast with her grandmother, attempts to bring the values of tradition into the modern world, as part of the effort to devise a coherent history for herself and her people.

A comic version of this process occurs when Aunt Fruma/Frieda returns from Hamburg and takes her niece Sore/Sasha, whom she calls Sorela, to the Yiddish theater.

> She couldn't anticipate too much. After all, she had seen the dramas of such Germanic geniuses as Wedekind and Hauptmann, performed by the greatest tragedians of the German stage. On the other hand, sitting and watching a good Yiddish play, she couldn't keep her heart from kicking up like a Chasid

at a wedding. Somehow—and completely in spite of her own better judgment, you should understand—she ended up having such a wonderful time. It was like when you go back to the old neighborhood after you've, thank God, made good. You get all *ferputzt,* change your dress a million times before deciding, wear your fur even if it's ninety degrees in the shade, just so there shouldn't be the slightest bit of doubt in anybody's mind. And then what happens but that the sight of the old places and the old faces makes you go limp with memories, and before your better judgment can step in and slap some sense into you, you're actually overcome with the bittersweetness of nostalgia. (184)

The comedy of manners elicits the problem in a different register.

Phoebe, unlike Sasha or Maurice, is not willing to remain an outsider; exactly what kind of an insider she becomes is an issue the novel raises and leaves open for the reader to decide, though it emphasizes the direction of Phoebe's action. At the beginning of the novel Phoebe appears under her apple tree in her suburban *shtetl,* Lipton, a figure of rootedness evoking a biblical image of the centering power of home, in contrast to her wandering cosmopolitan grandmother.

Much of the energy of the novel is invested in the exploration of the impact of wandering on Sasha and her colleagues in the Bilbulnik Art Theater. They exemplify Thorstein Veblen's characterization of the modern Jewish freethinker, "It appears to be only when the gifted Jew escapes from the cultural environment created and fed by the particular genius of his own people, only when he falls into the alien lines of gentile inquiry and becomes a naturalised, though hyphenate, citizen in the gentile republic of learning, that he comes into his own as a creative leader in the world's intellectual enterprise." Furthermore, "it is by loss of allegiance, or at the best by force of a divided allegiance to the people of his origin, that he finds himself in the vanguard of modern inquiry."[11] The social meanings of the historical process are brought into even sharper focus by Robert Park, "When . . . the walls of the medieval ghetto were torn down and the Jew was permitted to participate in the cultural life of the peoples among whom he lived, there appeared" a person "living and sharing intimately in the cultural life and traditions of two distinct peoples; never quite willing to break . . . with his past and his traditions, and not quite accepted, because of racial prejudice, in the new society in which he now sought to find a place. He was a man on the margin of two cultures and two societies."[12]

Sasha leads the characters of *Mazel* in dancing at two weddings—that paradox enshrined in the Yiddish proverb "mit ein toches ken men nit tanzen oyf tzvar chasenes" [with one tush you can't dance at two weddings]. The proverb points to the difficulties of this enterprise, while obliquely underlining the power central to its pursuit. One way of calling attention to the ways in which these characters come to a realization of their situation as social outcasts is offered by Hannah Arendt. Though they are intellectuals and

perhaps thoroughly attuned to the demands of the host culture, these individuals are still deeply linked to their native Jewish people and tradition.
They reflect the political status of all Jews. "It is therefore not surprising,"
Arendt goes on, "that out of their personal experience Jewish poets, writers,
and artists should have been able to evolve the concept of the pariah as a
human type."[13] Given their social and cultural experience, these artists enact the structural role of the conscious pariah.

Mazel deploys characters all along the spectrum from true believer to
freethinker to conscious pariah. They are *shlemiehls* and *shlimazels,* as Jascha
calls himself at one point in the novel, *luftmenschen* and *artistes,* yet the
comedy of their interaction captures the difficulties of their struggles with
identity-politics. Thus, for example, Jascha, the assimilationist, despite the
isolation he suffers as a result of increasing antisemitism, thinks of Hershel
Blau as a conscious pariah: He was a "disciple, a veritable Chasid, of secular
Yiddishism," devoted "to the disentanglement of the condition of Jewishness from its unfortunate and embarrassing theological underpinnings,
thereby to weave it into a high and noble culture: radically and uncompro-
misingly secular, but still, somehow or other, Jewish." Jascha realizes how
they are all caught between past and future: "Hershel Blau and all the other
Yiddishists, who hung out at the Writers' Club on Leszno Street and here at
the [Cafe] Pripetshok, were all stuck in some untenable middle-ground,
stalled halfway between the past and the future, trying to think of some
means or other of being good Jewish sons and daughters, even though they
no longer believed anything their fathers and mothers had taught them.
The Bundists and the Zionists were the same at heart, none of them able to
follow the path to the simple, unavoidable conclusion" (221–22).

Freethinker and conscious pariah are as closely related in this novel as
Sasha and Phoebe. For both, meanings are not rigid, but rather wander, wa-
ver, and move about as their lives have. In their chaotic city world, meaning-
making, the construction of the self, and social formation are functions of
mazel. Their urban experience depends on the opportunities of chance, and
not, as Shluftchev or Lipton would have it, the rigors of *saychel.* Similarly,
though Sasha often appears to win the confrontations with her mother-in-
law, Beatrice, who espouses the traditionalist views of Lipton—note the
meaning of her name, originally Brucha, "blessed one"—by the end of the
novel the two are paired as strong Jewish women in opposing yet comple-
mentary modes. Even though Sasha can out-perform Beatrice and parody
her habits in a delicious skit at the beginning of the novel, at its end the
wedding of their children takes place in Lipton, not Manhattan. And, Sasha
ruefully acknowledges, it is Lipton where Jason and Phoebe have decided to
settle.

In its rendition of these characters and their situations, Rebecca Goldstein's novel recapitulates the history of Yiddish literature. We have not only

the *Haskalah* critique of the *shtetl* of Mendele in Sasha's sarcasm, but the spiritual confusion of the characters of Lamed Shapiro's "Eating Days" or "White Chalah" in Jascha. The urban spirit of I. J. Singer's strong-willed, world-creating figures reappears in Hershel's creation of the Bilbul Art Theater, tempered by Anski's and I. B. Singer's evocation of the world of spirits roosting in the folk imagination central to Fraydel's and, in one sense, Sasha's experience. But the novel is not simply a rehearsal of Yiddish literary history; it also poses the question of agency in putting these characters and situations into play, making us wonder if *mazel* can indeed lead us to new possibilities. Are we still in the world of the Enlightenment and Emancipation, with the illusory promises of citizenship to the Jews, wandering in nothingness once we have abandoned the inexorable grip of the Law? Or can we, like some of these characters, take advantage of the urban moment and turn its transience into the occasion for revolutionary action that changes the conditions of living? Can the theater—can art—make such a difference?

Like the greatest theater, *Mazel*'s magical art inserts the reader into the tale as one of its actors. "It happens sometimes like this, although very rarely: a collaboration between spirits that steps over the footlights, drawing the spectators up out of their seats and into the art, so that they are as inspired as the players, and an entirely new work emerges between them" (309).

> Out there in the dark were sensibilities refined by the untold generations of scholars from whom they had issued. They were worldly men and women, dressed like any other citizens of Europe, and informed by Europe's culture, and yet they were unworldly, too. What they took from the world was meshed with that sensibility which was their birthright, which they could no sooner have put off than their own faces. There was a sort of subtlety sitting out there in the darkness this night that had been centuries in the making, and it was from it that these spirits had soared over the footlights, to join themselves with those on the stage, creating an entirely new work. And even Hershel, with all the torments of his ambitions, knew a moment of complete and perfect satisfaction. (309)

This magic is accomplished, in part, by the interplay of genres, to all of which the reader lends credence, though most of the characters remain wedded only to one. Change in this novel is signalled when a character leaves one genre—as when Sasha leaves the bounded, almost pastoral world of Shluftchev for the open arena of Warsaw with its novelistic possibilities, or when Phoebe reverses this trajectory when she leaves Manhattan for Lipton. Goldstein works similarly with genres in *Strange Attractors,* the collection of stories in which Sasha, Chloe, and Phoebe first make their appearance, where Goldstein creates a resource guide and literary compendium of these genres. Unlike *Mazel,* where the characters are fixed, at least to begin with, in one genre or another (the gothic, the parable, or realist narrative), in *Strange*

Attractors the reader gets situated in the in-betweenness of the conflicting genres, caught between *saychel* and *mazel,* participating in the unfolding of the tale that depends on their interaction. Living in all the genres at once, audience becomes actor here in a moment worthy of Dickens's art.

Throughout *Mazel,* urban life offers hope and breathing space, opportunity and possibility. Enlightenment has brought the heady possibilities of modern life, including the *goyim-naches* [gentile habits] of romance.[14] The desire of these "young people" has a messianic force: they are "so hungry for the world at large, that, no matter how much they took in, they still felt themselves famished. It was a hunger that would be felt unto the seventh generation" (201). Taking possession of urban possibility, they insist, *"This is mine! I am here and this is mine!"* (201) The hunger to participate in modern life translates into a dominant image: "How could there be time enough to touch it all, absorb it all, and then—yes—contribute something of one's own? A piece of melody, an equation, a theory, a canvas—something of one's own that will make a difference. It doesn't have to be big, though all the better if it is. But *something* to show that one is there, *there,* inhabiting the text itself, no longer stranded in the despair of those despicably narrow margins" (202). Yet this city is also a place that does not by itself redeem. These urban secular Jews who "will no longer be confined to the narrow, grimy margins," repudiating the places where "father and mother were born and will die, having never even learned the language of the text," have not emerged into a normal existence. Rather, "so many we passed on the street had the feverish look of consumptives. Desire for the world at large was consuming us alive" (202). And though they believe they can make a home and world for themselves in the modern European city, they are threatened by the prowling antisemites of right-wing Polish nationalism and are forced at times to hide in entranceways on what is no longer the public street. Such danger is but another indication that their chosen city of Warsaw is but another stop in the long Jewish journey of homelessness.

Having left Shluftchev behind, the characters return to it in thought and lived experience; it becomes the conundrum that their lives must somehow decode and resolve. Sasha, the spirit of *mazel* and of the city, cannot and does not want to leave her dead sister Fraydel behind. Fraydel haunts the novel, as the meanings of her storytelling inform and shape it. Fraydel, for example, brings Maurice and Sasha together in a moment of recognition that ignites their love.

"I've wished so many times that we really had run off with the Gypsies," she suddenly said, so softly that for a moment Maurice wondered whether he had only imagined it. . . . "She took her own life. She drowned herself in the river."

She was staring at him, and he stared back into her long gray eyes, overlaid with their shimmering sea-blueness, and it was hard to shake off the sense that this moment wasn't happening at all.

"She could have been anything, my sister Fraydel. She could pull knowledge from out of the air, even there in the shtetl. You don't know what it was like there"—her voice suddenly became fierce—"especially for a girl like Fraydel, Fraydel, Fraydel, *da meshuggena* . . ."

Sasha's sobs cut short her sentence.

When Maurice, who was also crying, just a little, reached out his arms to her, she collapsed into them and clung, clutching him, so that for the first time in his life, Maurice Saunders forgot to think. (291)

It is loss that has brought them to love, in a moment of mourning, not exhilaration. This exemplifies the mysteriousness of the characters in *Mazel*, their contradictions and the conundrum of their personalities. They will be possessed by love and attempt to sort out its meanings, and yet they will not be able to evade Fraydel's story. Presented on stage by the Bilbulniks, Fraydel's gothic experience is doubled as a Yiddish folktale. Haunting gentile and Jew alike, it is a liminal moment between classical Western and Jewish modes and invents a third way,[15] "No matter how enlightened or assimilated, the story of the young bride meeting her doom on the very night of her wedding cast a long shadow of meaning" (278). For *The Bridegroom* rivets by its oppositions, as Misha, the critic, acknowledges: "The play had at once exhilarated and depressed him, and it continued to do so all through that unusually warm Warsaw summer. The artistry was superb, and yet the net result of all this artistry had been to induce in Misha an overwhelming sense of life's futility. 'The drunken lift their cups to Life / To strange powers of unseeing and forgetting.' Misha wasn't able to get these lyrics out from his head" (276). Despite themselves, they must remember and retell the play's meanings, as a way perhaps of recovering and reclaiming the sources of their being. Their experience thus turns upon them; city life in all its gaiety yet evokes the deep guilt of exile. What is it they remember? What experience do they retell?

REMEMBERING AND RETELLING

In Jewish tradition, remembering and retelling have an honored place, from the tales of grandparents to the biblical commandment to remember the Sabbath and keep it holy. Recollection shapes the future not only in anticipation but as its informing structure. Memory matters not as literal repetition but as that process that reshapes and defamiliarizes; it opens the world of the everyday to the demands of the uncanny. As a recent critic has noted, what Goldstein recognizes "is the complex narrational interconnection between teller and interpreter. Further, she recognizes the hopelessness of the desire for some omniscient interpreter or impersonal narrator—some third-person interpretive perspective that can simply bracket the intentions of the agent as that agent understands them. Goldstein helps us to see part of what is at stake in all discussions of storied lives, as well as what is at stake in the idea that the self or subject of action is produced through the stories that we and others tell."[16] The intertwined tale of Mazel and Saychel, which opens the different sections of the novel, involves the telling of a story of how the tailor's apprentice seduces the princess into speaking. *Saychel* brings him to resolving the conundrum, but only *mazel* can bring him to a happy ending. The performative magic of *mysahs* [Yiddish tales] depends on the participation of speaker and hearer; it is like the greatest theater-magic, and like that experience it is one that calls out for repetition and re-experiencing.

In Exodus the commandment enjoins us to "remember the sabbath day," *(zachor et yom hashabbat)* (20:8); in Deuteronomy, we are commanded to *observe* the sabbath day *(shamor et yom hashabbat)* (5:12). The differences between the two versions of the Fourth Commandment reinforce and elaborate the relationship between remembering and retelling. In Deuteronomy the imperative mood leads to a narrative: "Remember that you were a slave in the land of Egypt and the Lord your God freed you from there with a mighty hand and an outstretched arm." Here the action of remembering brings the epic sweep of the Exodus from Egypt into the summary retelling. Moses' personal account of Deuteronomy brackets the people's story of Exodus, his first-person testimonial recalling the national events whose lessons his account elicits. Concluding the brief citation, the statement ends as a commandment bridging past and future: "Therefore the Lord your God has commanded you to observe the sabbath day" (5:15). In this way the commandment to observe and to remember the Sabbath is linked to the Passover commemoration, both historical re-creation and contemporary retelling, of the Jews' Exodus from Egypt. In this discourse they are inseparable: to remember is to retell the history of communal beginnings and to reiterate its defining structures—and thereby to build a bridge between narrator and reader/listener. And it is in the great kabbalistic hymn of Shlomo Alkabetz, the *Lecho Dodi* of the *Kabbalat Shabbat* Friday evening prayer service welcoming the Sabbath, that this bridge between narrator and reader/listener is articulated as *Zachor* and *Shamor* are brought together: *Shamor veZachor BeDibur Echad*. As the later Spanish commentator Don Isaac Abrabanel elucidates Alkabetz's formulation, the two commandments are separated in the two versions, but were uttered as one: *BeDibur Echad*.[17]

This informing power of remembering and retelling situates Rebecca Goldstein's work in a Jewish tradition rather than a (post)modernist, more-or-less secular, Western, or Christian one.[18] By contrast with other efforts to reconstruct cultural memory resulting from responses to modernization,[19] the Jewish imperative to remember and retell is anchored in its scriptural text and its two-thousand-year-old interpretive practice, in constant reference to the *mitzvah* central both to the Book of Deuteronomy and the *Shma*, where we are enjoined to recall "these words which I command you this day," and to remember that they "shall be in your heart, teaching them diligently to your children," calling us to speak "of them when you sit in your house, when you lie down and when you rise up."[20]

Remember and retell: Goldstein's exploration leads us into the uncanny, that is, in this universe of discourse "alternately nothing seems to be connected and everything seems to be connected" and "everything is constantly in movement between the poles." *Mazel* puts this question of connection to the reader and its characters in chapter 22, when "Maurice, in the course of arguing a point of philosophy with Aleksander Meisel, had declared that everything in the world connects, a fundamental axiom of Spinoza's. All of a sudden, Sasha, who Maurice had thought wasn't even listening, had whirled around and almost hissed at him, the contempt in her voice hitting him like a knock in the head, *'Nothing connects!'*" (288) The subsequent course of the novel leads Sasha to experience what Maurice has, in the name of Spinoza, pointed out, while his own life appears to bear out Sasha's prediction.[21] In fact, what happens in the novel is an exchange of roles between Maurice and Sasha. At Jason's *aufruf*—when the groom is called to the reading of the Torah—Sasha, sitting in the women's section of the synagogue, "had suddenly been visited by a sense of Maurice so strong that she had actually turned in spite of herself to scan the faces of the men wrapped in their talaysim on the other side of the mechitza. Like a superstitious old bubba who had never wandered far from darkest Shluftchev, she had searched to see if her beloved were really there." For the moment she assumes the role of the women's world of the *shtetl,* and Maurice answers: "'Everything connects,' Maurice had mouthed to her silently through the swaying forms of the davening men. 'There's always a reason'" (340). While she is in Lipton, Sasha is also in Shluftchev. Her conversation with Maurice, dead now many years, which has continued for so long and articulated her self-consciousness, leads not to a resolution of the question of connection, but to a moment of meditation on some of the experiences of his wandering: "She had slowly shaken her head in answer. For Maurice she had no more of the vehemence with which she had too often tormented him. But even so, with all of her tormenting, he had always made his way back to them, back to New York, a city he had hated. There was something in the life here that had oppressed him. Sooner or later he'd begin to feel the sheer colossal waste of it all. He liked cold places, sparsely populated. Even human life is worth something more in places where there's little of it" (340). The uncanniness of the moment is emphasized by the naturalness with which their conversation takes place, a mark of their being "sealed together," and yet "worlds apart" (335).

This turn in narrative strategy has an additional function, however, for it helps to overcome the apparent division between the discussion of modernity and that of Jewish tradition, as Goldstein's narrators discover that remembering and retelling can only be partial functions: in the act of remembering they cannot retell, and in retelling they momentarily block out the process of remembering. Such an act of forgetting, Freud notes, "creates a division within us and allows an uncanny experience to occur." Shuttling between remembering and forgetting, this discourse is characterized by "the tension between the two competing frames of reference or double perspective that characterizes uncanny experience. Without such a 'forgetting' the familiar never can become strange or romantic to us."[22]

Part of the power of Goldstein's fiction derives from the recognition of the informing power of the uncanny. It leads to the acknowledgment that cultural mapping cannot be separated from the context of what it is to have a memory, to forget as well as to remember, and to chart the effort of retelling. Thereby, they locate the power of memory in this uncanny and doubled process.[23] Furthermore, by suggesting that Jewish women have tended to function as the primary producers of those values through their storytelling, values recalled ritually by Jewish men in their traditional liturgical practice, Goldstein's tales focus on the process of the engendering of Jewish life, echoing the phrase in Genesis, when God creates humanity, that emphasizes difference while proclaiming equality, for "male and female created He them."[24] As she noted in her interview, she is "always intrigued by 'women of tremendous vitality in settings in which they're not allowed to express themselves.'" Furthermore, she comments that in looking at the Jewish women she knew, she would think that "there must have been some incredibly brilliant and energetic and totally neurotic women" in the shtetl.[25]

In Goldstein's first novel, The Mind-Body Problem, the implications of remembering and retelling are translated into questions about what her narrator calls our mattering map. As she embarks upon the explorations that shape the narrative's boundaries, the engaging narrator assures the reader that our mattering map orients each of us. "Mattering map" is the unfamiliar, perhaps onomatopoetic phrase that carries the overtones of many language-games and academic disciplines, ranging from topology to psychoanalysis, and we hear in it the effort to bring together the reasoned, powerful methods of mathematical logic and the intimate, associative tactics of the analyst's couch. The mattering map is a set of ideals and values organized like a belief system that informs us what "matters" and thus guides us in our own lives. Together, it signals the polar extremes of this novel.

Goldstein's work is distinguished by its wide range of American Jewish literary and cultural reference. There are allusions to Bernard Malamud, Henry Roth, Anne Frank, Alix Kates Shulman, Erica Jong, Tillie Olsen, Kate Simon, and Grace Paley, and an acknowledgment of the determining presence, importance, and central achievement of Cynthia Ozick for modern Jewish writing. There is also an effort to bring Saul Bellow and Philip Roth together and sort out the meanings involved in being the heir of both. In her narrator's voice we hear the mediating and synthesizing project of the contemporary American Jewish woman, unwilling to relinquish any of her modern possibilities, sorting out their benefits and consequences—and a rethinking of the relationship of exile and diaspora, center and periphery.

Like *Herzog, The Mind-Body Problem* deploys a dialectic of remembering and forgetting. Renee, narrator and protagonist, discovers that dialectic at the moment when she is most modern. She needs to recall her past, when memory is indispensable to make sense of the present, just when the very condition of being modern has tended to deny it to her. Married to a genius and awarded his status, she loses her ability to remember who she is, enacting once more her mother's role. As her husband eclipses the memory of her father and mathematical logic sweeps away the melodies and rituals of synagogue and the Jewish home, she begins to lose her way. The genius theme echoes Philip Roth's studies of Nathan Zuckerman, and the emphasis on the philosophy of the body recalls Roth's exploration of sexuality and identity, as Goldstein evokes the experiences, unique as they are, that make up ordinary sexual life. The intimate, confessional aspect of the novel further reinforces the link to Roth. Both create a rhetoric of self-expression that is also an act of disguise in which nimble city talk and joking serve the most serious purposes. When Renee's friend, Ava, a physics graduate student fond of taking strong, lower-class, unacademic and non-intellectual young men as her lovers, whom she designates "the elementary particles," accuses Renee of believing that "the male sexual organ is the human brain" (92), in a direct quote from *Portnoy's Complaint,* Renee must confront the problem of the relationship of sexuality and thought. Responding to Roth's and Bellow's objectification of women, Renee, the woman, acknowledges their power and defines their clear limitations as novelists in recounting how in the course of a love-affair, her partner has revealed the shape of his mattering map: "He was worshipful, offering me again and again the highest praise of which the Jewish male is capable: You don't look at all Jewish" (232).

A parallel moment occurs in *Mazel* in chapter 11, "A Little Yiddish Theater," when Aunt Frieda dresses Sorela and imagines she is not Jewish but a Russian aristocrat fleeing the revolutionary hordes. They make a dramatic entrance into the theater and Sorela's regal bearing gives her the air of "the beautiful shiksa" (188). It is not, however, a role Sorela accepts. She refuses the meaning of this image in which she looks "so very un-Jewish. People were always telling her this. She was, to be perfectly frank, perfectly sick of it. People always said it as if it constituted a compliment of the highest order. Well, Sorela didn't consider it such. It rankled in her, this dismissal of Jewish beauty" (183). The punch line follows this image: "There could be no doubt: everyone assumed she was a young Polish aristocrat, a beautiful shiksa. By following the general flow, they soon made their way to one of the two buffets. There was a crush of people before it. Again heads turned. And then one of the greatest tributes that can be paid to someone, especially when performed by Jewish people waiting in line to get food: the crowd parted for Sorela" (193).

Goldstein dramatizes and then opposes what Bellow and especially Roth express about American Jewish men. In *The Mind-Body Problem,* her narrator defends what Portnoy and Herzog, classic examples of Jewish American princes, have done their best to escape from—the beauty and power of the Jewish woman:

> Our brothers always expect us to thrill at the words, because of course in their scheme of things there's nothing so desirable as a *shiksa.* I've never understood it. Jewish women seem to me so much juicier and more *betampte* (tasty). It's like the difference between a Saltine cracker and a piece of Sacher cake. The latter may be a bit much at times; but it's moist, it's rich, and it's layered. My symbolic logic professor in college, who regarded himself as a great connoisseur of women, once told me that I was his first Jewish lover and that, judging from me, he had made a great mistake in never sampling from his own kind before. I recognized the compliment, although I was pricked by its suggestion that my qualities could be duplicated in any other daughter of Jacob. And I certainly didn't respect my professor any the more for it. It was as if someone who professed a great love and knowledge of wines told me he had just sampled a Bordeaux for the first time and thought these wines merited further investigation. (232)

In the comparison of Bordeaux wine to the complexity of the sexuality of the Jewish woman, we discover what Portnoy's implacable reductive logic has led him to miss. And unlike Portnoy, who journeys to Israel only to discover the extent of his inner confusion and personal malady, Renee encounters the sweetness of the Sabbath even amid the devastating memories of post-Holocaust Vienna.

Roth's obsessions are further parodied in this novel, for Renee expounds the philosophy of the body when, spurned by her linguistically minded colleagues, she affirms her worth denied her in the realm of mind by seducing "various graduate students who lived, like me, at the Graduate College." *The Mind-Body Problem* also echoes the episode of *The Counterlife* when Jimmy Lustig demands that Nathan Zuckerman help him force the State of Israel to close Yad Vashem and thus turn the Jews away from the task of remembering. "Forget Remembering" is Jimmy's motto; for him the Jews must give up the function of superego and become nations like all others. Embracing the mindless functions of the id, they will cease to elicit the moral guilt of the other nations.

Renee discovers that the mind she cannot still, the questions she cannot repress, create the opposite of Jimmy Lustig's demands: what she needs is to "Remember Forgetting." Neither, however, is ultimately possible for her, as she discovers the meaning of the "Jewish idea," which, in Edward Alexander's clear and direct phrasing, is the view that the Jews were called into existence as a people by a covenant with God that is as real and living today as it was at its inception. "I will establish My covenant," says God to Abraham, "between Me and thee and thy seed after thee throughout their generations for an everlasting covenant" (Genesis 17:7). According to this simple and traditional idea, the Jews were chosen by God in order to achieve the universal salvation of mankind: "In thy seed shall all the nations of the earth be blessed; because thou hast hearkened to my voice" (Genesis 22:18). Israel has been chosen, but chosen by a God who keeps admonishing Israel to love the stranger "as thyself; for you were strangers in the land of Egypt" (Leviticus 19:34). The chosenness of Israel, therefore, is directed toward the ultimate unity of mankind.[26]

Discovering the central purposes of Jewish tradition through the process of remembering and retelling, Renee's narrative parallels the work of her husband, Noam Himmel, in discovering the supernatural numbers. When she is about to marry Noam, she is ready to begin to draw a fuller mattering map, translating a particular private vision into an intersubjective experience.[27] Her comments also suggest that what happened to Moses Herzog was the shattering of his mattering map.

It is important to recognize, however, that Renee has reached this point because of the process of remembering and retelling, and it is worth recalling that not only Yom Kippur and Rosh Hashanah that call us to this doubled act of performance. Passover, the central event of the liturgical and communal year for many American Jews, and the recitation of the Passover Haggadah enjoin upon us this uncanny act. Remembering and Retelling: we become a community that draws its mattering map by recalling and retelling the story of our liberation from Egypt. "Bechol dor vador chayav kol adam leerot et atzmo k'ilu hu yatza mimitzrayim": the imperative mood of the Hebrew takes us into the act of remembering and retelling, and helps us to understand that "in each and every generation, every person must regard himself or herself as if he or she went out of Egypt."

This process of remembering and retelling, while not constrained by any language, has a fuller resonance—has its home, we might say—in Jewish languages. Hebrew, Ladino, and especially Yiddish convey the memory of this process of remembering, which alone makes exile (and, I will argue later, diaspora) meaningful. *Mazel* evokes both the bitterness of exile, the hopefulness of diaspora, and the difficulties implicit in the strenuous dialectic of memory, which recalls the arabesques of much contemporary theorizing. Written in late-twentieth-century American English, the texture of *Mazel* bears the imprint of the semantic values of Yiddish.[28] Have its characters, especially Phoebe and Jason, whose marriage frames the novel, reached "the imagined peace of a daily life in which none is afraid"—the terms in which Arnold Eisen reminds us classical Jewish thought defined home?[29] Or are we still amid the bitterness of exile, veiled though it may be?

In what way are these Jews no longer exiles from their country, exiles from themselves?[30]

Goldstein's novel comes at a moment when American Jews no longer live in a transitory or transient urban homeland. Having become suburbanized, they seek to account for their current North American acculturation. Perhaps in this situation, the word "diaspora" can be replaced by "suburb." *Mazel* offers a critique of this conflation of diaspora/suburb/home when Sasha calls Lipton "Shluftchev with a designer label." And yet despite her tart witticism, the conclusion of the novel takes place in Lipton with a traditional Jewish wedding that reenacts the life cycle as "circles drawn in water," and evokes profound emotion and a surprising depth of feeling. It is a scene that functions as wish-fulfillment: yes, exile has ended, for the moment, since marriage is a glimpse into the unmitigated joy of the return to Eden pointed to by one of the traditional seven marriage blessings. And yet the wedding ceremony concludes with the breaking of the glass that is a reminder of the condition of exile. Perhaps what occurs here in this simultaneous reference to the worlds of *shtetl,* suburb, and city, is a moment of joy defined as what Clive Sinclair has aptly called the "diaspora blues."[31]

STORYTELLING AND SELF-CONSCIOUSNESS

In *Mazel,* people live in two separate space-time continua simultaneously. Who is more present in the moment than Sasha, yet who is more engaged in the past through her dialogue with the dead—with Fraydel, Leiba, Maurice—than Sasha? And Hershel, the artistic entrepreneur, centered like a whirling dervish in the frantic activity of the Bilbul Art Theater, is at the same time immersed in the Chasidic world, where he had his first taste of ecstasy (262). Living in two worlds simultaneously, neither of which can be denied or resolved into the other, these characters encounter the world of the uncanny.

They live in a storied world, a world explored and articulated by stories. As such they follow the rules of storytelling with its own logic of surprise and meaning-making. These stories are *mysahs,* tales, accounts, fables. In these stories, experiences are evoked and then suspended; remembered in order to be retold and rerembered. These stories make time move fluidly forward and backward in response to the present-tense action—which is timeless, like meditation—of consciousness and meaning-making. The novel begins with the preparations for Phoebe's wedding yet quickly segues into Chloe's experiences with her mother and leads into Sasha's remembering Warsaw. I say "remembering," for the narration functions in present tense, creating a virtual reality more like what we expect from lyric poetry, in which consciousness is put into action, than from novelistic description of a physical world and its events; in *Mazel* past, present, and future are all available simultaneously. The second chapter repeats the time sequence of the first, only this time Phoebe is pregnant and going to give birth within twenty-four hours.

The exploration of time in *Mazel* thus parallels the scrutiny of causality. Instead of time's arrow having only one direction, it goes in both directions simultaneously; time, too, bears the sign of the uncanny—of *mazel*, the imp of metaphysics. It is also worth noting that in this novel memory is a two-way bridge. This novel enforces reciprocal interpretations by leaving nothing singular and by doubling if not tripling characters and situations, Sasha's memories of Shluftchev are paralleled by Phoebe's memories of New York, which will be her node of recollection and reinterpretation.

Like the time-trickery of this novel, the *mysahs* punctuating the narrative are not singular but multiple; other stories nest inside them. This pattern is most clearly discernible in the way the great theatrical triumph of the Bilbulniks—the play of Death and the bride that echoes Anski's pathbreaking *The Dybbuk*—is the story of Fraydel, which Sore/Sasha has carried with her from Shluftchev.

In this world, storytelling is authoritative, as seen in one exchange between Jascha and Maurice:

> "A good story, huh, Yossela?" Maurice said to his brother, trying to provoke him. He alone could get away with calling his brother by his discarded Yiddish name.
>
> "Not so bad, Mayer," the elder brother responded in kind. "But a story is only a story. It proves nothing."
>
> "Says who? If a story rings true, you think that doesn't count for anything?"
>
> (267)

The Yiddish world of the Bilbulniks functions under the authority of the story. In the world of *efshar*, of shoulder-shrugging possibility—Sasha is noted for her "extravagant shrugs, her eyebrows eloquently skeptical" (342)—stories like Fraydel's sketch a Jewish and a human destiny. As Sidra DeKoven Ezrahi notes of Singer, in a phrase that applies also to Goldstein, "in the figure of Gimpel and others of his species, Singer offers not sentimental recycling of a no-longer viable Jewish character, but a competing figure of authority: the authority of the wanderer-shlemiel-storyteller."[32]

Sasha becomes a storyteller, taking on Fraydel's role; she remembers the story of Fraydel's life and retells it. The story comes upon her unawares, rescuing her at a theatrical audition when she has forgotten her prepared lines. Her spellbinding performance—she enters a trance as Fraydel, and Fraydel's story speaks through her—sweeps her into the theatrical world of the Bilbulniks, and Fraydel's story becomes their great play. The Bibulniks call themselves the *mishpocheh*, the family, and they become her new kin group. The experience of that play—death coming for the bride—is riveting, as attested by their triumphant tour. *Mazel*, however, does not leave the story singular, as the wedding of the play is doubled in the concluding marriage-scene of Jason and Phoebe. Unlike the Bilbulniks' version, the young couple's wedding loops around to the birth of their child at the beginning of the novel. The child is connected by Sasha to Fraydel, whose name she asks be given to Phoebe and written on the *ketuba,* the marriage contract. That is, remembering leads to retelling, and such doubling articulates the relationship of speaker and listener in an act constitutive of community.

Both the Bilbulniks' play and the marriage of Phoebe and Jason reflect back on the *shtetl.* The motivation for Fraydel's suicide—she cannot accept the marriage arranged for her—is reinforced by her inability to leave Shluftchev and go wandering with the gypsies. Although she succumbs to their allure, she is unable to put her feelings into action—unable to repudiate the rigors of the Law of the Father. She is torn apart by these conflicting impulses and, like Ophelia, drowns herself. The stories she tells have a gothic edge, while the life she lives is bounded by the seemingly realistic world of the *shtetl.* Together they plot the dimensions of her identity and elaborate in a kind of cost-benefit analysis the social formation—the "deformation," a *Haskalah* generation called it—of personality and Jewish identity by the *shtetl* and its governing religious ideology.

Henya Saunders parallels Fraydel's experience of oppression, though Henya has a musical outlet denied to Fraydel. "Under the tyranny of their father, the only inclinations Henya was free to develop with abandon were her scores of nervous ailments, the twitchings and grimaces that came and went, and which, at their worst, made almost a freak of this infinitely kind and infinitely intelligent sister." Only "when she played the piano was Henya free from her afflictions. Within the music, she existed whole and harmonious. Her face—with its great high forehead and sunken cheeks and long, thin nose—rested in repose; her fingers flew with perfect control over the keyboard. She stopped playing, and her organism was once again the scene of grotesque, almost mocking, mannerisms" (214).

Both Henya and Fraydel live in a world dominated by a deep sense of exile—of dislocation. This world has been constructed by rabbinic Judaism in response to political, social, economic, and ideological institutions that cast the Jews as the scapegoats, the Others. It is a world desperately trying to articulate and safeguard a space of sacredness in the midst of a polluted, corrupt environment, even at the cost of obsessive behavior.[33] Inside this world, the guilt and shame of exile—the powerlessness of the Jews the Zionists insisted—informs their lives. When confronted with this idea by Zev Ben-Zion, Jascha explodes: "'Homeland?' He had turned the word contemptuously back on the odious little firebrand. 'I suppose by this you mean some wilderness on the other side of the globe, on which I have never laid eyes, and which I don't even know how to picture, but which, from its description, even by those who profess themselves its eternal lovers, can promise me *nothing.'"* The vehemence of his response reveals the power of the exile theme in the shaping of his identity. "Somehow he had let this little fanatic pull a hidden cord in his psyche" (224). The characters' identities circle around the ever present question of exile and homeland, which is made relevant daily by the increasing antisemitism of their Eastern European environment and the powerful attraction of modern Zionism. Most of *Mazel* is played out in the lands of the Jewish dispersion. Of its central characters, only Sasha, Chloe, and Maurice get to Palestine, and all leave before the proclamation of the independence and existence of the State of Israel. Yet Zionism is present throughout the novel as a call from the Center.

The stories that fill *Mazel* interweave different voices and dictions "into what Bakhtin might recognize as a 'composite text'—a term central to polyphonic narrative."[34] In these tales the effort to come to terms with the meanings of exile and diaspora results not in exclusion but inclusion. When the Bilbulniks perform, their audiences respond with tears; though the play dramatizes the difficult experience of their *shtetl* lives, which they have left behind for the city, they do not evade it, but accept it as their own. The Bilbulniks thus offer catharsis in the Aristotelian sense, echoing the therapeutic powers of the novel that proposes a theory of character and culture as palimpsest.

The actors embrace the role-playing of the world of the theater. They are marked as performers by the stage-names they choose, and they proclaim their right to act out their desires on the urban stage. The metropolis, be it Warsaw or Vilna or New York, is their partner and is the enabling condition for their new identities as it participates in their transforming characters. "The glowing windows of the great fine residential buildings they passed provoked something sharp with the ache of longing in Sorel, as she imagined to herself the cultivated existences that go on in such places: booklined walls, artful talk, refined tastes and pleasures. So many lives going on simultaneously! It was wonderful somehow just to know this was so, even though you couldn't hope to partake in all their lives" (186). This sense of city possibility is part of the magic of theater: "Jews and theater may have come together belatedly, but once they were together, it was a match of real love. How could it have been otherwise? You step onto a stage . . . and *become somebody else!* How could Jews not have loved it?" (179). Maurice has a similar experience: "He would have liked, at one and the same time, to be both a *talmid chachem*, a disciple of the wise, and also to be one of those bright lights who danced away every night at the Astoria Hotel, buying drinks for the prettiest and fastest girls in all of Warsaw." These don't slake his thirst: "He would have liked to be a thorough-going rationalist, a professor of physics or philosophy at some famous German university, and at the same time to be a Cabalistic mystic, seeing divine emanations in every puddle." And "he would have liked to be an American millionaire, but also a kibbutznik living in collective penury in Palestine." Since "one life is definitely not enough," Maurice decides, "there was always the theater, where at least a person could *pretend* to try on one life after another" (252). In this novel, everything is overdetermined, condensed, performed.

The theme of exile is similarly overdetermined. Rabbi Nachum watches his daughter go to the Warsaw Theater and, when she is out of sight, turns back to the tract of Baba Bathra, where he reads of the bitterness of exile and the problem of setting limits to mourning the destruction of the Second Temple.

> Our rabbis taught: When the Temple was destroyed for the second time, large numbers in Israel became ascetics, binding themselves neither to eat meat nor drink wine. Rav Joshua got into conversation with them and said to them: My sons, why do you not eat meat nor drink wine? They replied: Shall we eat flesh which used to be brought as an offering on the altar, now that this altar is in abeyance? Shall we drink wine which used to be poured as a libation on the altar, but now no longer? He said to them: If that is so, we should not eat bread either, because the meal offerings have ceased. They said: That is so, and we can manage with fruit. We should not eat fruit either, he said, because there is no longer an offering of first fruits. Then we can manage with other fruits, they said. But, he said, we should not drink water, because there is no longer any ceremony of the pouring of water. To this they could find no answer, so he said to them: My sons, not to mourn at all is impossible, because the blow has fallen. To mourn overmuch is also impossible, because we do not impose on the community a hardship which the majority cannot endure. (181–82)

Though he is concerned to reconstruct the bounds of that world within which exile is palliated through the power of *Halakha,* Nachum acknowledges that "there was no denying that many Jewish people took enjoyment from these productions, so who was Nachum to say? Jewish Warsaw was filled with talk of theater" (180). Perhaps his tolerance for the modern world is due to his understanding that both theater and *Halakha* are performative realms.

Like the *shtetl*'s transformation of the condition of exile into a livable world, the Bilbul Art Theater takes the confusions of everyday life and, by dramatizing them selectively in powerful ways, creates a place of enchantment. The Bilbulniks turn the city of refuge into a place of hope, even in exile, even in the capitalist world of alienated labor, helping to realize the proverb "the city air liberates." Furthermore, their ability to move their audiences to catharsis produces a moment of communal solidarity that, evanescent though it is, also functions as a taste of redemption. During the performance, their audiences enter the Eden of art. And within themselves the Bilbulniks know their power—theirs is the force of theater to remake reality—to create a momentary homeland within the diasporic city that removes the stigma of homelessness and dislocation. Their theater dramatizes the world of exile and the hope of redemption; enacting the process, it engages the reader in realizing an imaginary community.

This fragile, evanescent moment comes into being in the city; its repetitions amid different venues and its reiterated evocations of redemption by means of theatrical catharsis mark it as a modern urban ritual. As such it provides a glimpse of wholeness and allows participants a fleeting moment to overcome the destruction of community and the dislocation of personality. These issues, which Eisen articulates in *Galut,* are the conditions setting the stage for the lives of the characters of *Mazel.* For the moment, the Bilbul Art Theater frees each of these figures from the condition of being "an exile from his own country, an exile from himself."[35] They have arrived at a home, temporary though it may be.

This urban moment of liberation, however, differs from the claim of contemporary diasporic apologists like Jonathan and Daniel Boyarin, who speak for the tent as against the house.[36] The triumph of the Bilbulniks is bittersweet. Even amid their urban theatrical success they cannot abandon the *shtetl;* they are in exile and in diaspora, homeless and at-home simultaneously. They live at the periphery and in the center at the same time. No politics can extricate them from their metaphysical irony. Their situation recalls that which Clive Sinclair discovers on a visit to Israel. Visiting Masada in the company of a beautiful Israeli, he realizes that "She was not mine to possess, any more than was Israel, and I left both, because my language was English and I had ambitions to be a writer. I didn't know then what my subject would be, nor that I would eventually attempt to possess with the written word what I couldn't otherwise, that I was destined to haunt Masada . . . forever spying upon the history of the Jews, stuck at the base camp with the diaspora blues."[37] Within exile, there can be no individual action; to take action outside the fold of the community is to engage in a form of suicide. To stray from the four cubits of the Law, which guarantee the possibility of right action and guard against the misprision of exile, is to move into unmarked territory and lose your way. As one of Singer's characters in *Meshugah* notes, "What *is* important? I could understand if you were a pious Jew, as your father was, or a Zionist who wanted to rebuild the Jewish land. What you are doing, your entire conduct, is sheer suicide."[38] That is, like Fraydel, to wander out of the homeland of the *Halakha* is to invite confusion, terror, and death.

Given this condition, how can the city redeem? Do we believe that Goldstein's characters escape the condition of exile and the four cubits of the Law by making a homeland in the city, in Warsaw or Vilna or New York? Although we admire their courage in leaving the bounded world, we must also ask if right action is possible in the city—the arena in which such action can be articulated through the art of the theater, amidst the theatricality of urban life. These questions circle back into Sasha's presence and are explored at the end of the novel when she participates in the student takeover of Columbia University in 1968. Is the idealism of the students—her idealism as a revolutionary woman—viable? Or does an acknowledgment of the power of exile and self-consciousness lead us inexorably to the *shtetl* of Shluftchev/Lipton and a return to the four cubits of the Law? This novel reveals how each of the central women in the Sonnenberg family—Leiba, Sasha, Chloe, and Phoebe—struggles to a choice that shows different mitigations of, if not ways out of, the condition of exile. Like the narrator of Isaac Babel's story, "Gedalia," each asks for "a little bit of that pensioned-off God" in the glass of Sabbath tea and has the courage and will to make her own way in the chaotic, revolutionary world.

The home they make in the city suspends, for the moment, the bitterness of exile. Undermining what Hannah Arendt calls worldlessness—the deeper condition of all Jews between the destruction of the Second Commonwealth by the Romans in 70 C.E. and the founding of the State of Israel in 1948—these Jews make a diasporic world by force of imagination. Like Kafka, they put into play a representation of their worldlessness. Like rabbinic Judaism, this exilic image gathers, bounds, and thus restrains the metaphysical and political dimensions of exile. It draws out the sting of exile, as does Nachum's quoted talmudic passage about how one manages to live in this narrowed exilic realm. As a result of this process of catharsis and boundary-making, these Jews are freed to conduct their lives with a measure of freedom—though still governed by the ever-present possibility, seen in Hitler's destruction of European Jewry, that they are not finally secure.

Diaspora, thus, no matter how comfortable, is not redemption. The messiah, despite the strident claims of the political left and the metaphysical right, has not yet arrived.[39] As Eisen notes, "Zionism has significantly altered the facts but not the nature of Jewish existence. It has dealt the Jewish people a far better political hand. But the deck remains the same. The metaphysical condition of the Jews remains as it always has been."[40] The dimensions of the world these Jews construct in Shluftchev, Warsaw, Vilna, Palestine, and New York in *Mazel* simultaneously reveal their diasporic triumph and exilic failure.

In constructing a city that, in the classic Jewish phrasing is an *Eer VaEym BeYisrael*—a city that nurtures learning, we might say, echoing one of the glories of Jerusalem—they articulate what Andre Aciman calls a shadow city. It is a place like his New York, which resembles Sasha's and Isaac Bashevis Singer's, for it exists simultaneously at multiple addresses. It thus has its being in an Einsteinian rather than an Aristotelian space-time.

> What I was looking for, and had indeed found quite by accident, was something that reminded me of an oasis—in the metaphorical sense, since this was . . . an oasis of the soul, a place where, for no apparent reason, people stop on their

various journeys elsewhere. Straus Park, it seemed, was created precisely for this, for contemplation, for restoration—in both its meanings—for retrospection, for finding oneself, for finding the center of things.

And indeed there was something physically central about Straus Park. This, after all, was where Broadway and West End Avenue intersected, and the park seemed almost like a raised hub on West 106th Street, leading to Riverside Park on one side and to Central Park on the other. Straus Park was not on one street but at the intersection of four. Suddenly, before I knew why, I felt quite at home. I was in one place that had at least four addresses.

Depending on where I sat, or on which corner I moved to within the park, I could be in any of four to five countries and never for a second be in the one I couldn't avoid hearing, seeing, and smelling. This, I think, is when I started to love, if love is the word for New York. I would return to Straus Park every day, because returning was itself now part of the ritual of remembering the shadow cities.[41]

Aciman's essay is a meditation on exile. "I had come here, an exile from Alexandria, doing what all exiles do on impulse, which is to look for their homeland abroad, to bridge the things here to things there, to rewrite the present so as not to write off the past. I wanted to rescue things everywhere, as though by restoring them here I might restore them elsewhere as well." As it evokes the multiple, overlapping worlds of shadow cities, his essay simultaneously elicits the meanings of exile. "I wanted everything to remain the same. Because this too is typical of people who have lost everything, including their roots or their ability to grow new ones. They may be mobile, scattered, nomadic, dislodged, but in their jittery state of transience they are thoroughly stationary. It is precisely because you have no roots that you don't budge, that you fear change, that you'll build on anything, rather than look for land. An exile is not just someone who has lost his home; it is someone who can't find another, who can't think of another. Some no longer even know what home means." Aciman helps us to see that exile is not only a state of being but a linguistic condition. Exiles "reinvent the concept [of home] with what they've got, the way we reinvent love with what's left of it each time. Some people bring exile with them the way they bring it upon themselves where they go" (35). Wittgenstein's comment, "The limits of my language are the limits of my world," serves as a gloss on Aciman's articulation.

In a shadow city, the lucky or plucky exile can construct a diasporic space by bridging his or her worlds and bringing the past into the present. It is no accident that Straus Park, Aciman discovers, is presided over by the statue of Memory—of "Mnemosyne, Zeus' mistress, mother of the Muses." This mother endows her daughters, the Muses, with the ability to inspire the art of exile, the imagination that can make a (temporary) home in a homeless world. This world of the creative art of the homeless, Aciman comes to realize, is what leads him again and again to Straus Park. "My repeated returns to Straus Park make of New York not only the shadow city of so many other cities I've known, but a shadow city of itself" (37). In this shadowy world, the condition of exile can be transformed into the diasporic world of hope through the creation of the rich and layered city language of which Wittgenstein speaks. "Our language can be seen as an ancient city: a maze of little streets and squares, of old and new houses, and of houses with additions from various periods; and this surrounded by a multitude of new boroughs with straight regular streets and uniform houses."

Though in *Mazel* these Jews apparently come to be rooted in their American home, they do not cease their wanderings, as all the characters attest. Nevertheless, they have found a still point and temporary center from which to leave and to which they return. They have given the book that is their portable homeland—the Torah—a local habitation and a name. Of the transience and evanescence of urban experience, they have articulated a permanent virtue, the power and presence of memory. This home is where the theater of their imagination functions; it is the place where they perform the experience of homelessness and, by delimiting it, create a home for themselves.

What Aciman articulates as a personal journey, *Mazel* expresses in familial terms. At the end of the novel the relationship of Chloe and Phoebe, mother and daughter, Sasha's child and grandchild, engages the issue of agency. Phoebe tells her mother she has "begun to keep kosher" and the puzzled Chloe acknowledges that "being Jewish had seemed to Chloe to be nothing more than an incidental feature in both her own and her daughter's biographies" (335). The narrative of events pauses for an inquiry into the difference between accidental and substantive features of personality. We enter the intersubjective world of these three women and their entangled family history.[42] "These family stories had constituted Chloe's elusive sense of herself as Jewish. Her mother and her father had lived through extraordinary events, largely because they had been born into a Europe in which being Jewish was no incidental feature in a person's biography. The world from which these stories had derived had always seemed so remote to Chloe, existing almost at the level of mythology. And this was true even though Chloe, of course, had been conceived right in the middle of all that inconceivable history, just as the old world had come crashing down around her father and mother" (335). Chloe had thought that "being Jewish had figured" in the "back pages of the family history," aware of how the utter destruction of European Jewry by the Nazis had deprived her of grandparents and cousins and an extended family.

Sasha had escaped from the *shtetl* world of family only to reconstitute it for the moment in the *mishpocheh* of the Bilbulnik Art Theater in Warsaw. Now, however, Phoebe has decided to "start taking being Jewish so very seriously, insisting on removing it from the level of mythology" (336). Chloe—

the in-between figure—"had no idea whether this was, in itself, a good thing. But she did find herself believing, increasingly, that it was a good thing for Phoebe" (336). The chapter articulates Phoebe's choice, against Sasha, and Chloe's acknowledgment that in so doing "Phoebe—who had always been an extraordinarily gifted problem-solver, first as a little chess prodigy, and then as a mathematician—had hit upon a quite brilliant solution to the problem of being Phoebe" (336). The phrasing simultaneously enforces the sense of the mysteriousness of personality that informs the novel and leads to the notion of agency: Phoebe chooses to make Judaism central to her life. What had seemed a suffocating condition of being for Sasha and outside the realm of adult experience for Chloe has become the focus of Phoebe's life. This chapter ends with Sasha being outmaneuvered by Phoebe, who explains her choice by interpreting a story Sasha had told about her great-great-grandfather, who had reburied a suicide inside the cemetery. As she tells Sasha, "I always loved what the dead man said to Rav Dovid. That even the dead need the comfort of their own kind" (338). With this phrase, Phoebe solves the conundrum and the contradictions of her life, asserting her right not to Fraydel's death-dealing gothic storytelling and Sasha's heroic world-creating self-consciousness, but to what Chloe understands is "an almost unbearably poignant innocence, the air-sweetening breath of the very wise child" (331). This choice to return and thus become a *ba'alat teshuvah* [a penitent] takes her to the old ways. Chloe recognizes that "Phoebe had found something here that she loved, and Chloe was trying her damnedest to see what it might be, if only for the sake of understanding her daughter. She was trying to peer past the limits of irony . . ." (332). The phrase—the *limits of irony*—takes us out of the modernist world of Sasha with its dominant self-consciousness and into the world of classic Jewish tradition. We are left with a conundrum, which we as readers have to resolve: is Phoebe, in reenacting that return to tradition, simply reentering the stagnant world of the *shtetl*, of Shluftchev with its puddle. Fraydel had said "that all of the memories of Shluftchev had sunk to the bottom of that puddle, and these memories were of such a nature as to give off just such a stink" (334). Or has a different and new possibility come into play that might reconcile modernist city and traditional *shtetl* life?

Mazel articulates central themes of Rebecca Goldstein's work, including chaos theory, gender concerns, theatrical mise-en-scene, and the shifting narrative point of view. We move from the first-person narration of *The Mind-Body Problem* to the shifting narrative of *Mazel*, like *mazel* itself constantly changing course, even in mid-sentence. This is a novel relying on free indirect discourse that flows from character to character and offers us a shifty, shifting narrator whose point of view keeps switching not only from character to character but from inside to outside—entirely appropriate to a tale of four women's overlapping generations. Its many storytellers and stories invite us in their multiplicity into the world of chaos, chance, and the capriciousness of life. With Sasha, Chloe, and Phoebe we experience the uncontained, uncontainable, and surging power of life. Leiba acknowledges the world left outside by the *Halakha,* just as Phoebe discovers the Law as a Jewish religious experience, Chloe as generic Greek paganism, and Sasha as the fullness of the world of Emancipation. In Warsaw Sasha transforms Fraydel from the ugly duckling of Shluftchev into a Sasha-theatrical-swan. Together, these women articulate not the chain of tradition but the circles of life in water; as women their experience is flowing, fluid, and dynamic, by contrast with the masculinist closed systems of ideological institution-building; as women, they live in experience. That is, they are part of the world of *mazel,* in the world of chance and change. They are, as the novel concludes, "all dancing together, their arms linked around one another's waists and their feet barely touching the billowing floor, as they swirled in the circles drawn within circles within circles" (356–57).

Theirs is the pleasure of wit, from the skewering phrase—"Lipton is Shluftchev with a designer label" (333)—to the surprising turn of syntax that changes the meaning of the sentence—"Yes, Sorela will be the *Jewish* Sarah Bernhardt." "The Jewish Sarah Bernhardt, Fruma? But wasn't the woman herself Jewish?" "Oh, for heaven's sake, Leiba. You *know* what I mean" (175). Here the barb turns upon the speaker; the exchange begins with an assertion intended to define the object, only to double back upon the person making the assertion. Then there is one of my favorites, which is worth hearing once more: "Jewish Warsaw, which was roughly a third of Warsaw proper was a city of rabbis and swindlers, capitalists and poets; but, most of all, it was a city of talkers. There were so many ideas in the air you could get an education simply by breathing deeply." (206) And any mention of linguistic fun in the novel cannot ignore the delicious wit in names: in the "Bilbul Art Theater," *bilbul* is the Hebrew (and Yiddish cognate) for "confusion," and in "Shluftchev," which echoes the sound of the word for "sleepy" in Yiddish. Nor is the following exchange to be ignored: "Sherlock Holmes *is* Jewish. He changed his name. Watson's a *goy.* The thing I've always wondered about is whether or not Watson ever suspected. My dear friend Holmes: filthy Yid" (248).

This cornucopia of linguistic pleasure does not proceed from an omniscient narrator, but from many different characters, who apparently can't help making such remarks. The comments emerge from the contradictions of their lived experience and as a result often surprise by returning to pierce them with a boomerang effect. Some of them sound like direct translations from Yiddish—"When the penis stands up, then the brains fall down" (256)—and all of them color the novel, providing a kind of Yiddish inflection to the experience it chronicles. Like Yiddish proverbs, these comments have a bite and often a reverse turn, which parallels the dominant narrative habit of the novel. Such wit sticks stories into the memory and encourages us not only to remember but to retell them.[43]

Mazel concludes by returning us, via Lipton, to the *shtetl*. The urban moment of Sasha's participation in the student takeover of Columbia, when she leads them in dancing, parallels the joyous dancing of the wedding of Jason and Phoebe. The revolution seems to Sasha to be a version of Purim, while the wedding, with its theme of fasting and subsequent joy—by contrast with the Bilbulniks' staged version of *The Bridegroom*—we recognize as Yom Kippur and Sukkot—the festival of our rejoicing—rolled into one. The novel balances them against each other: there is the evanescent creation of a diasporic homeland in a theatrical moment in the city by Sasha and the structured space of the ritual of the wedding that extricates Phoebe and Jason from the wanderings of exile and creates a space under the *Khuppa*, the marriage canopy, where the logic of joy can function and the itch of self-consciousness can for a moment be laid to rest. The novel balances Phoebe against Sasha—touring performer against the *wunderkind* mathematician whose academic specialty is the geometry of soap-bubbles. In this way Mazel and Saychel for the moment are reconciled, chance and reason, the bride who understands from her fascination with soap-bubbles the evanescent, fragile beauty of floating and wandering, and her grandmother who recovers a lesson in the meanings of home.

Can it be an accident in this brilliantly organized novel that Chloe always remembers Maurice's arrival, her first glimpse of her father, and focuses on "the funny sandals her father had been wearing" (327)? These sandals echo Maurice's encouragement of Sasha to go to Israel with Zev Ben-Zion; they are the mark of the kibbutznik. They also echo Hershel's wonderful tale of the sandal-wearer: A leaf from the Tree of Knowledge was blown out of the Garden of Eden by a windstorm and became stuck on the bottom of one of the man's sandals, which enables him to cure the King's daughter of her ailments. The King exchanges half the kingdom for the sandals. "But it stands to reason that a king can't wear dirty sandals. So he gave them to his servants to be cleaned, and the servants, of course, scraped away the leaf from the Tree of Knowledge along with the other *shmutz*, and when the King put then on he was no wiser or more sensible than before." With its reference to the Tree of Knowledge, this *mysah* returns us to the Edenic world prior to the first exile. It also recapitulates the uncanny division of this world, and in the culminating exchange between Jascha and Hershel, punctuates the effort to accept all the experiences of Israel. "'You say there's wisdom buried somewhere in all the shmutz we've picked up along the way. I say shmutz is *shmutz*.'" "'Oh,' Maurice says to his brother, 'I know how you think it will end. There won't be anyone left who still wears sandals.' 'Precisely. In a few generations, three or four at the most, nobody will even remember who was a sandal-wearer and who wasn't.' 'So,' said Hershel, finally pushing back his chair and reaching for his hat, 'we will have to see whose is the more improbable fairy tale'" (266–68). The phrase echoes the Zionist enterprise and the effort to construct a new home for the Jewish people, a most improbable dream and tale-come-true.

The novel concludes in the second person address of an invitation, "The *bris* of little Mayer will be—'God willing,' his parents have requested that I add—next Thursday morning, at seven o'clock A.M., in Congregation Z'chor Et Ha-emeth in Lipton, New Jersey. You are all, each and every one of you, invited. Beatrice has taken over all the arrangements, so it's sure to be an event that will be well worth the trip—even to such a place as Lipton.

"And may we all only meet at happy occasions, the face pressed up outside the window kindly disposed toward the fragile life that lies within" (357).

Remembering Fraydel, retelling her story, Sasha, despite her conscious choice in leaving, participates in the reconstruction of Shluftchev in modern Lipton. In re-creating the past so brutally destroyed by the Nazis in this brilliant fiction, Sasha's and Phoebe's actions and force of character merge into an emblem of our work of recovery, reclaiming, and reconstruction.

NOTES

1. Nor should the comment of Wittgenstein be ignored: "Our language can be seen as an ancient city: a maze of little streets and squares, of old and new houses, and of houses with additions from various periods; and this surrounded by a multitude of new boroughs with straight regular streets and uniform houses." Ludwig Wittgenstein, *Philosophical Investigations,* trans. G. E. M. Anscombe (Oxford: Basil Blackwell, 1953), entry 18, 8e.

2. See David Biale's important book, *Power and Powerlessness in Jewish History* (New York: Schocken, 1986).

3. "He came back once, after an absence that had seemed particularly long, and told Chloe of the months he had spent driving a cleche, a horse-drawn carriage, in old Quebec. His horse, a temperamental nag, he had named Miessa, the Yiddish for 'ugly.'"

4. Clifford's book focuses on diaspora from an anthropological perspective: *Routes: Travel and Translation in the Late Twentieth Century* (Cambridge: Harvard University Press, 1997). Shirley Kaufman's essay, "Roots in the Air," appeared in *Judaism: A Quarterly Journal Of Jewish Life and Thought* 47, no. 2 (spring 1998): 161–68; her book of poems is entitled *Roots in the Air: New and Selected Poems* (Port Townsend, Wash.: Copper Canyon Press, 1996).

5. "Between the crowds and the streetcars and the invention of Mr. Edison, it was difficult for a man to think. And this overwhelming confusion—a maze of so many streets you could live your whole life in Warsaw and never see them all—this, according to his sister-in-law, was no more than an overgrown Shluftchev! How much more noise and tumult could there be squeezed in between the heaven and the Earth!" (169).

6. Sandee Brawarsky, "Rebecca Goldstein: Mining Intellectual Dilemmas," *Publishers Weekly*, October 23, 1995, 48–49.

7. The best modern version is by Golda Werman, in *The Dybbuk and Other Writings by S. Anski*, ed. David Roskies (New York: Schocken, 1992); also see J. Hoberman, "Repossessing the Dybbuk," *Pakn Treger* 28 (spring 1998/5758): 20–35, for a discussion of the history of its staging, including film versions.

8. Brawarsky, "Rebecca Goldstein," 49.

9. For further discussion see my *City Scriptures: Modern Jewish Writing*, (Cambridge: Harvard University Press).

10. Robert E. Park, "Human Migration and the Marginal Man," in *Classic Essays on the Culture of Cities*, ed. Richard Sennett (New York: Appleton-Century-Crofts, 1969), 141.

11. Thorstein Veblen, "The Intellectual Pre-Eminence of Jews in Modern Europe," *Essays in our Changing Order*, ed. Leon Ardzrooni (New York: Viking, 1954), 229–30, quoted by Allan Guttman, *The Jewish Writer in America* (New York: Oxford University Press, 1971), 136.

12. Park, "Human Migration," quoted by Guttman, *Jewish Writer*, 134.

13. Hannah Arendt, *The Jew as Pariah: Jewish Identity and Politics in the Modern Age*, ed. Ron H. Feldman (New York: Grove Press, 1978), 134.

14. James Joyce uses the phrase in *Ulysses;* also see Daniel Boyarin, "Goyim Naches; Or, the Mentsh and the Jewish Critique of Romance," in *Unheroic Conduct: The Rise of Heterosexuality and the Invention of the Jewish Man* (Berkeley and Los Angeles: University of California, 1997).

15. The range of references includes classic works of Western culture, including *Bleak House*, with its dialectic of connection/disconnection. One could also include Goethe's *Faust* as well as other works, which I have not pursued. My interest has been to elicit and elucidate the Jewish sources, which are the greater force of this fiction and, in any event, are much less well known.

16. Deborah Knight, "Selves, Interpreters, Narrators," *Philosophy and Literature* 18, no. 2 (October 1994): 275.

17. Abrabanel's commentary is found at the two recitations of the Fourth Commandment. *Perush 'al ha-Torah* (Jerusalem: Bene Arbe'el, 1963), *loc. cit.*

18. "When Nachum Sonnenberg began to pay very close attention to the people around him, he saw, with great astonishment, how different a world it was, depending on who was looking at it, and when.

"The Master of the Universe had created heaven and earth, and all that stood and moved thereon. But when, on the sixth day, He saw fit to create a creature in His own image, on that day He had brought into existence a great vast number of separate worlds. Here, too, stood firmaments dividing one world from another.

"Now, at last, Nachum felt that he had come to understand a passage in the Talmud that before had always baffled him.

"The puzzling passage occurs in the book of Sanhedrin. Each person, says the text, has been created absolutely unique as regards his appearance, his voice, and his mind. Therefore, each person should believe that the world was created precisely for him.

"A baffling passage, no? Nachum was to believe that the world was created *for him?*

"But now he saw: the Master of the Universe has created for each person a world that he alone inhabits." (166)

19. It first took shape in the historical novel beginning in England with Sir Walter Scott and the rhapsodic/analytic prose of Thomas Carlyle.

20. Together, remembering and retelling shape the Jewish way of life, as *Shma* is inscribed in the tefillin (phylacteries) that are bound upon the arm as a sign and between the eyes as a reminder, and it is also written in the *mezuzah* affixed upon the "doorposts of thy house and upon thy gates" (Deuteronomy 6:4–9). In capturing a further nuance of the original Hebrew, the 1962 translation of the *Torah* (*The Torah: A New Translation,* Philadelphia: Jewish Publication Society, 1962), underscores their force not only as a constitutive ritual but as the how-to manual of Jewish life and thus suggests their relevance for contemporary fictional practice: "Take to heart these instructions with which I charge you this day. Impress them upon your children. Recite them when you stay at home and when you are away, when you lie down and when you get up. Bind them as a sign on your hand and let them serve as a symbol on your forehead; inscribe them on the doorposts of your house and on your gates." Markers of self-definition, these words articulate the space of meaning, delineating not only the domicile of this discourse but the signified body in which it is inscribed.

21. I owe this observation to Erich Gruen.

22. Robert Newsom, *Dickens on the Romantic Side of Familiar Things: 'Bleak House' and the Novel Tradition* (Santa Cruz, Calif.: The Dickens Project, 1989), 91; also see 54–55, 66–69, and 86–90.

23. See the essay by Heidi Ravven, "Observations on Jewish Philosophy and Feminist Thought," *Judaism* (fall 1997): 422–38.

24. Deploying "mattering map" in her first novel as a phrase that is at once metaphor and metonymy, Goldstein reminds us that the functions of memory are deeply embedded in language. *The Mind-Body Problem* is dedicated "In memory of my father, Bezalel Newberger," and one of its strongest strands is the narrator's account of remembering the sweetness of her father's life as the devoted *chazan* of an American congregation (by contrast with her mother's ever-present worrying). Goldstein's mattering map is not only a defining feature but a figure that stands for the novel as a whole, serving to define the project of this modern fiction as the charting of our cultural situation. As befits the workings of the uncanny, the mattering map is not prior to the narrative; rather, the narrator's central project, like that of the novel as a whole, is to articulate it. Defined as a dynamic process constantly undergoing revision, dependent upon character and reader response as much as the narrator's imagination, the effort to draw it produces the energy with which the novel proceeds.

25. Brawarsky, "Rebecca Goldstein," 48.

26. Edward Alexander, *The Jewish Idea and Its Enemies: Personalities, Issues, Events* (New Brunswick, N.J.: Transaction Books, 1988), 1.

27. Renee's account of the content of the mattering map leads her into the narrative of her married life. Though she has been attracted to his mind and has delighted throughout their courtship in "contemplating the rigor and purity of its executions," Noam, she believes, has turned to her for her body. In his intense gaze, she has found assurance of existence. "Often it had seemed to me that my existence was as ephemeral as the objects in Berkeley's metaphysics; that, like them, my *esse* is *per-*

cipi, my being a function of others' perception. I am thought of, therefore I am. And now I was the object of an adoring attention, not just in *any* mind, but one superior to almost all others. Would I ever again require statements testifying to my existence and worth?" (*Mind-Body* 62) Marriage to a genius, however, does not resolve these questions; instead, it transposes them into everyday life with a greater intensity. Now "what tied me to my body was not so much its desires as the desires it aroused in others—the more (both desire and others), the better. Through it (my matter, so to speak) I mattered to others, and thus mattered. Through it I had mattered to Noam, who himself mattered so much, at least from where I stood" (*Mind-Body* 104). Philosophically speaking, Renee's mattering map bridges the mind/matter division established by Descartes (her namesake, she reminds us). The intersubjectivity of the mattering map as well as its existence as a virtual object releases her from the prison of mind and matter: once located on it as both subject and object, she can both think and feel. Its uncanny qualities make it possible for Renee to rediscover the mysteries of everyday existence and begin to ask about the meanings of ordinary life.

As Renee constructs her map she is forced to confront the reasons for her marriage in ways paralleling those with which Herzog questions himself. "And *I*? Had *I* the right to marry? Other disturbing thoughts pushed themselves forward: One should not marry to save oneself. Anyone in need of saving has no business marrying. Matrimony is not the cement for a cracked self, but is more like someone leaning on the self's point of least resistance. But these thoughts were hurriedly pushed away for the frightening consequences they entailed" (*Mind-Body* 104–5).

28. The world of the novel edges into a query similar to that elicited by Maera Y. Shreiber in "The End of Exile: Jewish Identity and Its Diasporic Poetics," *PMLA* 113, no. 2 (March 1998): 273–87.

29. Arnold Eisen, *Galut* (Bloomington, Indiana, 1986), 131.

30. Vaclav Havel has explored its meanings more fully than most. See, for example, "The State of the Republic," *The New York Review of Books* 45, no. 4 (March 5, 1998): 42–46.

31. Clive Sinclair, *Diaspora Blues* (London: Heinemann, 1987).

32. "Our Homeland, the Text . . . Our Text, the Homeland: Exile and Homecoming in the Modern Jewish Imagination," *Michigan Quarterly Review*, 489.

33. Eisen, 42, 50, 52.

34. Maera Shreiber, "Jewish Trouble and the Trouble with Poetry," (paper presented at the ALA, Florida, 1997).

35. Eisen, 131.

36. Shreiber, "The End of Exile," 277, 275.

37. Sinclair, 77. The diasporic issue is also raised by Jacob Neusner in a slighly different context, when he argues that "the experience of exile and then restoration marked the group as special, different, and select." See Neusner, *Self-Fulfilling Prophecy: Exile and Return in the History of Judaism* (Boston: Beacon, 1987), especially "Field Theory of the History of Judaism," which elaborates this premise.

38. Singer, *Meshugah*, trans. Singer and Nili Wachtel (New York: Farrar Straus Giroux, 1994), 104.

39. See Hayim Soloveitchik, "Rupture and Reconstruction: The Transformation of Contemporary Orthodoxy," *Tradition* 28:4 (1994): 64–127.

40. Eisen, *Galut,* 185.

41. Andre Aciman, "Shadow Cities," *The New York Review of Books,* vol. 44, no. 20 (December 18, 1997): 35–37.

42. I owe this observation to Howard Wettstein.

43. Freud reminds us that part of the power of jokes, whose category these witticisms fit, is to make the listener want to retell them. See "On Jokes and the Unconscious."

5

Portraiture and Assimilation in Vienna

The Case of Hans Tietze and Erica Tietze-Conrat

Catherine M. Soussloff

A mimetic regime of representation dominates painting and sculpture in Europe from the Renaissance to the early twentieth century. The genre of portraiture developed relatively late, "almost like an unexpected gift brought by a visitor no longer waited for," as it was put by the famous cultural historian Jacob Burckhardt in 1898.[1] If, as Burckhardt and every other twentieth-century student of portraiture insists, this genre succeeds above all others in giving us a portrayal that resembles a historical person, where can a portrait be claimed to fail? How does a specific portrait signify a particular human being, including their social-historical context, and how does it hide aspects of the person? Does the interpretation of a portrait and its subject reflect the ambiguities of both representation and subjectivity? Does the representation of a fully assimilated or acculturated subject signal Jewish identity?

In this paper I will be interested in how the assimilated Jewish subject appears in the portraiture of early-twentieth-century Vienna. I will focus on the double portrait of Hans Tietze (1880–1954) and Erica Tietze-Conrat (1883–1958) painted by Oskar Kokoschka (1886–1980) in Vienna in 1909 and today owned by the Museum of Modern Art, New York (fig. 5.1).

Useful definitions of the portrait describe the act of making a portrait, portraiture, rather than the thing. The art historian Richard Brilliant writes that it is the genre that "directly reflects the social dimension of human life as a field of actions among persons": the artist, sitter or sitters, and viewers.[2] This occurs along an axis perpendicular to the image's frame rather than contained within it. The portrait describes subjectivity, the "who" I am, perhaps better than any genre, but this description through its very actions and in its material instantiation, invokes identity. Mikkel Borch-Jacobsen describes the ways in which subjectivity becomes identity in representation:

Figure 5.1. Oskar Kokoschka. *Portrait of Hans Tietze and Erica Tietze-Conrat* (1909). Oil on canvas, 30 1/8 x 53 5/8 inches (76.5 x 136.2 centimeters). The Museum of Modern Art, New York. Abby Aldrich Rockefeller Fund. Photograph ©2000 The Museum of Modern Art, New York.

"But to say *who* I am—who thinks, who wishes, who fantasizes in me—is no longer in *my* power. That question draws me immediately beyond myself, beyond my representation, toward a point . . . where I am another, the other who gives me identity."[3] The representation of subjectivity in the portrait, as elsewhere, is not autonomous, for either the artist, the portrayed, or the viewer.[4] This paper will explore the interpretation of portraits of Jews as representations for artist, sitters, and viewers. I will begin with a brief examination of the history of the portrait of the Jewish subject.

In a chapter entitled "The Rabbi as Icon" of his recent book, *Jewish Icons: Art and Society in Modern Europe,* Richard I. Cohen carefully describes the change in attitudes of European Jewry towards portraits, which coincided with an increasing sensitivity towards the image in general throughout Europe.[5] To be sure, portraits of Jews existed earlier, but in the main, until the eighteenth century they "were deemed idol worship and emulation of a Christian tradition."[6] The first "modern" portraits of Jews were of rabbis, a common genre with clear references to Judaism in dress, attributes, and attitude. In rabbi portraits the subject is always depicted alone within the frame of the painting or print. This is the case even when a number of representations occur together in one work, such as the broadside of rabbis from Breslau (fig. 5.2). In the rabbi portrait the figure is truncated and often

Figure 5.2. *Historic Rabbis*. Printed by the Graphische Kunstanstalt, Breslau. Twentieth century. 66.2872. From the HUC Skirball Cultural Center, Museum Collection, Los Angeles, Calif. Photography by Lelo Carter.

holds a book with visible Hebrew script, such as in the *Portrait of Hakham Zevi Ashkenazi* of 1660–1718 (fig. 5.3). The gaze is invariably focused forward. The clothes and hair distinguish the rabbi as a Jewish religious figure. In fact, these portraits appear to derive in their typology from the Christian visual tradition, in particular from Netherlandish portraits of the Renaissance, such as the *Portrait of a Carthusian Monk* painted by Petrus Christus in 1446 (fig. 5.4). In this portrait the monk can be distinguished from others by his dress and hair, and his figure is truncated. This semiotic coding of the rabbi portrait persists into the twentieth century.

Not discussed by Cohen, whose book deals only with European art, but of equal importance to our understanding of Jewish portraits in modernity, are a large number of portraits of Jews from the American Colonial and Federal periods. In number, these portraits, such as *Moses Meyers* and *Elizabeth Judah Meyers* painted by Gilbert Stuart in 1803–4 reveal the strength of the desire for portraiture among the propertied class of Jewish merchant-traders, shippers, and bankers (figs. 5.5 and 5.6).[7] Unlike the rabbi portraits,

Figure 5.3. *Portrait of Hakham Zevi Ashkenazi.* © Jewish Museum London.

there are no overt signs of Jewishness in dress, person, or attributes. Brilliant finds that such portraits presume a purely domestic context, evident first in the predominance of "paired portraits of worthy husband and equally worthy wife," as he puts it.[8] Paired spousal portraits also derive from an Early Modern Netherlandish tradition, as these examples of 1520 by Quentin Massys demonstrate (fig. 5.7 *Portrait of a Woman* and fig. 5.8 *Portrait of a Man*). The reception of these American portraits must be understood in terms of the "semi-private function of the original display of the painted portrait itself."[9] These portraits would have been seen in the parlor or dining room of a well-appointed urban Jewish home. There the portraits would have been recognized by family and friends as portraying Jewish individuals. Brilliant

Figure 5.4. Petrus Christus. *Portrait of a Carthusian Monk.* All rights reserved, The Metropolitan Museum of Art.

Figure 5.5. Gilbert Stuart (American, 1755–1828). *Portrait of Moses Myers* (ca. 1800). Oil on wood panel, 26 x 33 1/4 inches. Chrysler Museum of Art, Norfolk, Virginia. The Moses Myers House. The Historic Houses are the property of the City of Norfolk and their collections are owned by the Chrysler Museum of Art. M51.1.269.

Figure 5.6. Gilbert Stuart (American, 1755–1828). *Portrait of Eliza Myers*
(ca. 1800). Oil on wood panel, 26 x 33 1/4 inches. Chrysler Museum of Art,
Norfolk, Virginia. The Moses Myers House. The Historic Houses are the
property of the City of Norfolk and their collections are owned by the
Chrysler Museum of Art. M51.1.269.

Figure 5.7. Quentin Massys. *Portrait of a Woman*. All rights reserved, The Metropolitan Museum of Art.

argues that these portraits would have been seen in the context of domestic Jewish religious practices and objects.

The surviving examples of Jewish American paired portraits of the eighteenth and nineteenth centuries are comparable in composition and situation to the so-called marriage portraits commissioned by prosperous Jewish merchant families of Prague beginning in the first half of the nineteenth

Figure 5.8. Quentin Massys. *Portrait of a Man*. All rights reserved, The Metropolitan Museum of Art.

century. My examples here, portraits of Sara and Wolf Moscheles, were painted quite early, in 1790 (figs. 5.9 and 5.10). Like the American paintings of Moses and Elizabeth Meyers, these marriage portraits were usually painted in pairs and reflect the strength of the Flemish precedent. A ceremonial significance has frequently been attributed to these portraits, but the evidence for this religious iconography is scanty.[10] They can be read like the American portraits, that is, as examples of social and economic aspirations made visible.[11]

Without any visual references to religion or religious practices, the central European portraits of Jews, except those of the rabbis, contain no "Jewish semiotic," as Brilliant has argued. When we look at them out of their original context, there is nothing to signify that they portray Jews. It is only when we venture outside the frame of the representation itself and into its history, that we find a Jewish signification, or, if you will, a "Jewish identity."[12] In the case of these early portraits, "place" determines "Jewishness." It is the interpretation of the portrait and its historical context that presses the topic of identity into consciousness. Once there, this identity can be examined as a legitimate aspect of the visual representation itself, even if in the past, in the interpretation of art, it has not been allowed.[13] In addition, if the Jewish identity of the portrait becomes a subject through interpretation, then the interpreter's own subjectivity must also be acknowledged as an integral aspect of the transactions of subjectivity presented by portraits of Jews.

As images, the portraits discussed here represent the Emancipatory ideal of assimilation held by bourgeois, urban Jews in Europe and America, particularly those of Prague and Vienna. Like the assimilated Jewry of modernity, unmarked by dress, no longer residents of the ghetto, these portraits now require a context for interpretation. These portraits signify a desire not to signify ethnic or religious identity pictorially. Just as non-Jewish members of the urban bourgeoisie in Europe and America usually sought to identify with an economic and social class rather than with a particular nation or ethnic background, so too the Jews portrayed in these portraits sought to belong to a dominant social group. Any collective Jewish identity is not carried in the image itself, but only in its context and in the process of interpretation. As we have seen, portraits of rabbis from the same period can be identified by signs and visual symbols internal to the picture itself and visible to the viewer. On the other hand, domestic portraits of Jews from the modern period can only be assembled as "Jewish portraits" if the interpreter establishes their historical context and puts them in a group. Taken "out of place," moved from their initial place of meaning, these portraits require the assignment of identity by the viewer or interpreter in order to be understood.

This last observation provokes considerations of a more historiographical kind. In order to fully interpret these images, we must understand them not purely as images. Rather, these portraits are evidence, if you will, of a social

Figure 5.9. *Portrait of Sara Moscheles.* Courtesy of Jewish Museum Prague.

Figure 5.10. *Portrait of Wolf Moscheles.* Courtesy of Jewish Museum Prague.

act that took place at a particular time and place and whose iteration through interpretation references that historical context. What were no doubt claims of Jewish material success and social/cultural assimilation at the time they were painted translate into claims of class or social status expunged of ethnic or religious difference.

As an art historian, I want to maintain that to deny any distinguishing Jewish identity for these portraits today would be to deny, and perhaps to denigrate, the significance of both place and audience in the interpretation of the work of art. Any such denial goes against our understanding of interpretation itself and of the very means of interpretation, such as provenance, patronage, and the context of the work of art at the time of its production, traditionally considered useful methods of historical analysis for the art historian. And to deny these portraits a Jewish identity negates much recent research in the field of museum studies that investigates the ways that display works upon the viewer to convey the meaning of the work of art.

On the other hand, to deny Jewishness in these portraits upholds a fiction concerning art in the mimetic regime of representation that prevailed in Europe and America until the beginning of the twentieth century: that it gives "an intensified illusion of having unmediated access to meaning."[14] I have already stated the collusion of the genre of portraiture in this assumption. This understanding of the work of art without context contains many dangers associated with the concept of the autonomous work of art. That autonomy should be associated with portraiture depends on the fiction that a portrait represents a complete instantiation of the person portrayed. If one understands that a complete representation of the modern subject is impossible, then the autonomy of this genre of art, at least, seems absurd. The portrait, like the subject, draws us immediately beyond representation to ourselves. To ignore the context of acculturated Jewishness in these portraits may well preserve these works of art within a narrative about the genre of portraiture and its aesthetics, but it denies their historicity. This is an aesthetics based on alienation. Furthermore, it negates an active Jewish subjectivity and maintains a universal and unhistorical view of European and Europeanized subjectivity and of the subject in modernity.

Recent scholarship indicates that the role of the Jewish emancipation cannot be ignored as a factor that allowed, or perhaps even forced, modern Jews not only to assimilate into society, but also to appropriate a universalistic view of art. If the interpreter does not recognize Jewish identity in these portraits, then he or she cannot admit that these portraits required a self-effacement by a minority and, normally, given the usual transaction of commissioning a portrait, an acceptance of it by the artist. Yet, "Jewishness" as well as prosperity in terms of economic status and class would be read when the portraits were in their place in the home of the assimilated Jew. There, these portraits and the family and friends they portrayed would be read as not "too Jewish," to use Norman Kleeblatt's term, and the subjects possibly as not religious Jews.[15] The acts of effacement found in the history of writing about portraits of Jews must also be seen both in the context of assimilation and as a product of portraiture as a social act requiring an aesthetic outcome. These ethics have had a profound effect upon the interpretation of visual culture in the Jewish context.

Emancipation produced an urban, assimilated bourgeois class of Jews in Europe. This social class then promulgated habits of assimilation as an ideal. This contributed to the production of an interpretative frame from which Jewishness itself was foreclosed or excluded by Jewish art historians and critics and by a larger public, who received no encouragement to attribute an ethnic or religious identity to the portraits they encountered. I would argue that, with the possible exception of the portraits of rabbis, the denial of context in the portrayal of Jews went hand-in-hand with the work of assimilation. This is a complex issue, for which judgments of right or wrong prove inadequate. Given the actual social situation of Jews in Europe and America in the eighteenth and nineteenth centuries, what is clear is that many of these portraits represent individuals who in public did not identify themselves as Jewish and did not wish to be identified as Jewish, but who in private were Jewish by dint of their family lineage and social and religious practices.[16] When interpreters view these portraits as essentially "not Jewish," or not "too Jewish," they present an example of why Jewish "visual material, or its appropriation, has been overly compartmentalized and totally separated from research into Jewish society," as Richard Cohen has recently said.[17]

A important example of the absence of the signification of a Jewish subjectivity in portraits of the modern period may, then, appear to exist not only in Oskar Kokoschka's double portrait of 1909, *Dr. Hans Tietze and His Wife, Erica Tietze-Conrat,* but also in his other portraits of assimilated Viennese Jews of the same period.[18] In all previous interpretations, the Tietze portrait has been offered as an outstanding example of the work of a preeminent avant-garde modernist. This signification of the painting can be traced to the association of it with other works by Kokoschka of the same period, which were exhibited in several highly controversial shows from 1908 to 1912 and which solidified his reputation as one of the first avant-garde masters of the century. However, in the case of the Tietze portrait the signification comes through association only. Until the time of its purchase by The Museum of Modern Art, the picture had been displayed only in the Tietzes' home, over the mantelpiece in Heiligenstadt, the rural suburb of Vienna where the couple lived. There it had another meaning. As Kokoschka said of his early portraits: "Most of my sitters were Jews. They felt less secure than the rest of the Viennese Establishment, and were consequently more open to the new and more sensitive to the tensions and pressures that accompanied the decay of the old order in Austria. Their own historical experience had taught them to be more perceptive in their political and artistic judgements."[19]

This painting of oil on canvas, 30-1/8" × 53-5/8" (76.5 cm. × 136.2 cm.), is signed on the lower right by the artist. According to the curatorial files of the Museum of Modern Art, it was brought in its original frame by the Tietzes to New York City, where they were forced to emigrate in 1939.[20] It was approved for purchase by the museum's acquisition committee on December 8, 1939, not long after the Tietzes' arrival. The sale appears to have been brokered through the New York dealer D. Hugo Feigl, who had close ties with the Tietzes. The sale stemmed from their need for funds in order to survive. Prior to the sale of the painting, Feigl wrote to Alfred Barr: "Kokoschka estimated especially this painting very much that hitherto the picture never was exhibited nor was taken a photograph of it, because Mr. and Mrs. Tietze have been extraordinarily anxious and superstitious in connection with all actions concerning their picture."[21] The Tietzes refused to let Kokoschka himself have this portrait for public exhibitions, including the important exhibition at the *Hagenbund* in February of 1911 in which Kokoschka exhibited twenty-five other paintings, most of them portraits from this period.[22] Until the Tietzes were forced to move from Vienna (after Hans had been identified as a Jew) and compelled to sell the painting, this painting affirmed their social status as fully acculturated. Given my discussion so far, it should come as no surprise that interpretations subsequent to the acquisition of the painting by MOMA have failed to address the ethnicity of the sitters in its specific historical context. The documentation of Tietze's religious affiliations parallel the demise of the possibility of Jewish assimilation in Vienna, which had been a striking feature of the Austro-Hungarian Empire before World War I.[23] Hans Tietze was born in Prague in 1880, the son of Siegfried Taussig and Auguste Pohl. In 1893, when Hans was thirteen, his family moved to Vienna, converted to Protestantism, and changed their name to Tietze. Hans attended the elite Schottengymnasium in Vienna and received his doctorate in philosophy in art history at the University of Vienna in 1903, at the age of twenty-three.[24] Two years later Tietze married Erica Conrat, also a converted Protestant and an art historian who had studied at the University of Vienna. Their first son, Christopher, was born in 1908. Kokoschka made his portrait in December of the following year. In 1930 Tietze declared himself religiously "unaffiliated." In 1933, he published *The Jews of Vienna: History/Economics/Culture*. It can be said, therefore, that he never entirely separated from his Jewish heritage, although the image of an Israelite prophet on the title page (fig. 5.11) contrasts greatly with the elegant, beardless, and hellenized portrait of Tietze in 1909. In a document of 1934, Tietze declared himself Protestant and in 1938–39, in order to emigrate to the United States, he declared himself Jewish. The

HANS TIETZE

Die Juden Wiens

Geschichte — Wirtschaft — Kultur

Mit 30 Tafeln, Bildern und Plänen

1933

Leipzig / E. P. TAL & CO. / VERLAG / Wien

Figure 5.11. *The Jews of Vienna: History/Economics/Culture* (book cover). Collection of the author.

International Biographical Dictionary of Central European Émigrés lists his religion as "unaffiliated."[25]

At the time that Kokoschka painted this portrait, Tietze was twenty-nine and Erica Tietze-Conrat was twenty-six. They had been married for four years. In 1953 Kokoschka wrote to the Museum of Modern Art that this "exceptional" portrait, as he called it, "was meant as a symbol of the married life of the two sitters and as such commissioned."[26] In the context of the portraits we have seen of "worthy husband and equally worthy wife," Kokoschka's painting differs significantly by placing the sitters in the same frame, on the same canvas. This format is relatively rare in the history of art. The Tietze portrait may derive from early Dutch examples, such as Jan van Eyck's 1434 *Arnolfini Wedding Portrait* (fig. 5.12). Close comparisons can also be found elsewhere, particularly in Holland, Flanders, and France, such as the seventeenth-century self-portraits with wife by Rembrandt and Rubens, in eighteenth-century examples of married couples painted by Jacques-Louis David, and in an important painting of 1860 by Edouard Manet of his parents (fig. 5.13). However, unlike most of the double portraits of married couples, the Tietzes have no attributes, other than their clothes, to indicate their place in the bourgeoisie, and no background elements to situate them in a particular location. In order to understand the meaning of this portrait, the historical and physical context of the artifact is required, as it was in the earlier portraits of Jews who were not rabbis. The Tietzes' own insistence that this painting's rightful place was hanging over their mantelpiece and not in a public exhibit makes the topic of context particularly apposite.

In the earlier examples of portraits of married couples the active stance and/or foregrounding of the male figures contrasts with the modest pose of the female figures. According to Erica Tietze-Conrat's recollection, Kokoschka said sometime after World War I: "I have not painted you maliciously. . . . The doctor looks like a lion and madam looks like an owl."[27] Whereas the married couple seems the ideal occasion for the depiction of conventional marital relations, Kokoschka was interested in the opposition of the sexes and their psychosexual traits, as is visible in the contrasting gestures and physiognomies of the Tietzes. This interest came, so he said many years later, from the influential studies of Johann Jacob Bachoven.[28] His portrayal of the male as energized activity and the female as balanced stasis can perhaps be discerned in the poses of the figures. Carl Schorske has argued correctly that these oppositions are overtly sexualized in Kokoschka's early work. The artist's illustrations for the children's book *The Dreaming Boys* (1908) reveal that these sexual tensions occurred in many of his images (fig. 5.14), not exclusively in the portraits.

Schorske notes that the "crackling light" behind Tietze and the "sharpened, fin-like scorings" behind his back suggests a male sexual energy.[29] They allude as well to the hand of the artist and support the fiction of the portrait

Figure 5.12. Jan van Eyck. *The Arnolfini Wedding Portrait.* © National Gallery, London.

Figure 5.13. Edouard Manet (1832–1883). *Mr. and Mrs. Auguste Manet* (Parents of the Artist). Musée d'Orsay, Paris. © Photo RMN—Hervé Lewandowski.

as determined by the artist alone. In contrast to the male figure here and elsewhere, Kokoschka's early portraits of women show hands crossed over the breast or abdomen, a gesture of modesty also seen in the figure of Erica Tietze-Conrat. The 1909 *Portrait of Lotte Franzos* is a good example of what becomes at this time an idiosyncratic convention of Kokoschka's (fig. 5.15).

Figure 5.14. Oskar Kokoschka. *The Dreaming Boys* (book illustration). Library, Getty Research Institute, Los Angeles.

In like manner, we might read the gesture of Hans Tietze in the context of Kokoschka's contemporary portraits of men, in which we find active hand gestures emphasized by the foreshortening of the hand. We see these agitated hands in the *Portrait of Auguste Forel* (1910, fig. 5.16) and the *Portrait of Felix Albrecht-Harta* (1909, fig. 5.17).

In the context of their home and this painting, however, Hans Tietze and Erica Tietze-Conrat were more than simply, if such a word can be used to describe the relationship, husband and wife, man and woman. They were both art historians who often published together and who sat at the same desk every day for years to write about monuments and works of art. In 1957, in a letter to the director of the Museum of Modern Art, Julius Held, an art historian and a friend of the Tietzes, demands that Erica Tietze-Conrat be named on the wall-label in the gallery because "she has made sufficiently

Figure 5.15. Oskar Kokoschka. *Portrait of Lotte Franzos* (1909). Oil on canvas, 45-1/4 x 31-1/4 inches. Acquired 1941. The Phillips Collection, Washington, D.C.

Figure 5.16. Oskar Kokoschka. *Portrait of Auguste Forel*. © 2000 Artists Rights Society (ARS), New York / ProLitteris, Zürich.

important contributions to lend additional interest to a painting in which she is portrayed and identified by name."[30]

Since the Renaissance, scholars and writers had been portrayed in their studies at their books. Kokoschka's portrait differs significantly from this tradition, as the comparison with Manet's *Portrait of Emile Zola* (1869) demonstrates (fig. 5.18). As a portrait of two art historians, Kokoschka's painting

Figure 5.17. Oskar Kokoschka. *Portrait of Felix Albrecht-Harta.* © Hirshhorn Museum and Sculpture Garden, Smithsonian Institution.

Figure 5.18. Edouard Manet (1832–1883). *Portrait of Emile Zola* (1840–1902). Musée d'Orsay, Paris. © Photo RMN—Hervé Lewandowski.

might be understood in the context of another category of portraiture, the group portrait, which became popular in nineteenth-century France. For example, Fantin-Latour's *An Atelier in the Batignolles* (1870) depicts a group of artists and writers—all associates of the painter Manet, who sits at the easel (fig. 5.19). Fantin-Latour's painting and others from the French context, differ significantly from Kokoschka's double portrait, or, indeed, from any of his early single portraits, inasmuch as the French examples portray full-length figures grouped around and focused upon the main figure, whereas Kokoschka's early portraits invariably present the figure half-length, with a gaze that encounters the viewer or someone not in the painting. In the case of the Tietzes' portrait, the figures interact both with each other and with the viewer. The case of Fantin-Latour, who based his painting on an earlier image by the Dutch painter Joos van Craesbeeck (*Painter Doing a Portrait*, Louvre), explicitly reveals that the actual source for the group portrait in the studio derives from Dutch group portraits of the Early Modern period.[31] Kokoschka's portrait of the Tietzes can be associated directly with this tradition of portraiture through which the subjectivities in the portrait can be more precisely historicized.

Like the *Militia Company* by Dirck Jacobsz, Kokoschka's portrait depicts half-length figures in a relatively anonymous space, causing the viewer to focus on the figures, particularly the faces and the hands, which in both paintings emerge from their surroundings (fig. 5.20). In both paintings, the heads press at the upper margins while the torsos are cut off by the lower edge of the painting. The curatorial file at the Museum of Modern Art reveals the intense interest taken by both the Tietzes and the artist in the edges of his double portrait. After purchase, the museum removed the painting from its original stretcher and framed it with the canvas edges folded out to increase the margins between the figures and the edges, to the distaste of Erica Tietze-Conrat. In the original framing, the limits of the painting would have been even closer to the Dutch example, causing the hands and heads to be seen more prominently than they are now.[32]

In both paintings the figures are in conversation with each other and with the viewer or the artist, as the gazes of the faces reveal. These gazes are animated by the exaggerated hands and rhetorical gestures. In 1953 Kokoschka wrote that what impressed most in this and other paintings of his "early period was [that he was] the only one to render the vision of people being alive, due to the effect of an inner light, resulting technically from layers of thinly painted colour and fundamentally from a creative approach which in stressing the sense of vision, as the act of seeing, is dramatically opposed to all fashionable theories on art asserting the human being to be seen as a kind of *nature morte*."[33] Like the Dutch painters, Kokoschka desired a mode of energized representation missing in the portraits of his immediate contemporaries,

Figure 5.19. Henri Fantin-Latour (1836–1904). *An Atelier in the Batignolles.*
Musée d'Orsay, Paris. © Photo RMN—Hervé Lewandowski.

such as Gustav Klimt, as in his *Portrait of Margarethe Stonborough-Wittgenstein* (1905, fig. 5.21).

The "liveliness" of Kokoschka's early portraits has been consistently remarked upon since the early twentieth century, but his work has not been compared to these early Dutch examples before. As in the early Dutch examples, the "act of seeing" is determined by the variations in the gazes and gestures of the figures and the relationship of these to the viewer's gaze. In our brief look at Kokoschka's other early portraits we have already seen that the configuration of hand gesture and gaze, enhanced, as Schorske suggests, by the intervention of the artist's manipulation of the paint, reveal an aesthetic of portraiture highly similar to the early Dutch group portraits. In the literature on Kokoschka this kind of portraiture has been called a "performance," to be understood as the artist's performance on behalf of those he represents.[34] However, the issue of subjectivity in Kokoschka's early portraiture can be historicized more precisely.

In *The Group Portraiture of Holland,* an essay published in 1902, Alois Riegl, Tietze's professor at the University of Vienna and still one of the best-

Figure 5.20.   Dirck Jacobsz. *A Company of the Civic Guard.* © Rijks Museum, Amsterdam.

known art historians of the Viennese School of Art History, addressed not only older portraits of the Dutch school but also the portraiture of his own day.[35] He was particularly critical of modern portraiture for ignoring the reciprocation between subject and viewer by focusing solely on the perception of the subject. He wrote: "One must always proceed from the assumption that the portrait figure turning directly toward the beholder served exclusively as an emphatic demonstration of the Baroque dualism of object and subject. Classical antiquity avoided this turn, for it recognized only objects. Modern art can likewise dispense with it, but for the opposite reason. It recognizes only the subject, since according to its view the so-called objects are entirely reduced to perceptions of the subject."[36] He found in the Dutch group portrait a series of representational strategies—gesture, gaze, spatial configurations—in which the spectator and the subject of the painting were implicated in complex relationships that he characterized as "attentive."[37] One of the key illustrations for his argument is the painting by Dirck Jacobsz. As Michael Podro argues: "The subjective life which Riegl sees in Dutch art is not an expression of the will which can issue in action nor of emotional responses to events, it lies in mental alertness, in watchfulness, in attention, expressed pre-eminently by the gaze of the depicted figures. The

Figure 5.21. Gustav Klimt. *Portrait of Margarethe Stonborough-Wittgenstein*. Oil on canvas, 180 x 90.5 centimeters. © Bayerische Staatsgemäldesammlungen, Neue Pinakothek, Munich.

gaze of the figure is interpreted as *attention* where it is dissociated from the movement of the body, or where it is directed at something not visibly present to the spectator, or something which could not be visibly represented to the spectator, as where a depicted figure entertains a thought, or where men attend to each other's speech."[38]

It is entirely possible that Kokoschka's portrait was influenced by the theories of Riegl, the recently deceased teacher of the subjects. The attraction for Kokoschka of this theory of spectatorship and the portrait appears evident in light of his other portraits of the same period, some of which I have mentioned. Certainly Kokoschka brought to his task an awareness of Tietze's intellectual milieu. An interchange about portraiture between the art historian and artist can be imagined on the basis of the visual evidence of the Tietze portrait.

In the moving obituary of Tietze by Julius Held, Tietze's many scholarly accomplishments as art historian, art critic, and museum official are elaborated.[39] Tietze was perhaps the most prolific heir to the older generation of art historians known as the Viennese school. At the time of the Kokoschka portrait and until 1919 Tietze was employed as the executive secretary of the Central Commission for Artistic and Historical Monuments of Austria, where he had succeeded his teacher Franz Wickoff (1858–1905).[40] Tietze engaged a staff in organizing and publishing a thirteen-volume inventory of Austria's artistic and architectural heritage. At the same time, as Julius Held tells us: "Hans Tietze took also a passionate—and lifelong—interest in modern art . . . becoming the spokesman of modern art in his country."[41]

In her book on Riegl, Margaret Olin argues that with his theory of portraiture Riegl addressed the problem of subjectivity in modern times. Riegl sought a "reconciliation of a new 'subjective' element with the respectful separation which unites subject and object while preserving their individual identities."[42] Thus, Riegl's theory of portraiture, which speaks to the assimilation of subject and object through communication between the portrayed and the viewer, may have appealed particularly to Kokoschka and the Tietzes. It also appeals to the present interpreter of Kokoschka's portraits of some of the acculturated Jewish citizens of Vienna.

As Held recognized, Kokoschka's double portrait, as well as Tietze's later writings in support of Kokoschka, testify not only to Tietze's commitment to modern art, but to a specific kind of radical art epitomized by Kokoschka's work in Vienna beginning in 1908, the date of the artist's public debut at the first *Kunstschau* exhibit.[43] The question of Kokoschka's political sentiments during these years has to be addressed in part through the violent reaction of Vienna against him after the first and second *Kunstschau* exhibits, and in terms of the political orientations of his closest associates at this time, Adolf Loos and Karl Kraus. Loos was an architect and critic from Brno, the capital of Moravia. Kokoschka portrayed him in a painting dated 1909. Kraus, also an émigré from Czechoslovakia, was depicted twice by Kokoschka.[44] Both Loos and Kraus scorned the cultural and social backwardness of Austria-Hungary and championed Kokoschka at this time and later. Kokoschka claimed in his autobiography, written many years after the fact, to have had no revolutionary intent during the years 1908 to 1910, but that may be a clean-up job by the later, more conservative man.[45] In his early years Kokoschka was vilified and attacked by bourgeois Vienna and supported by the most progressive critics, such as Kraus, Loos, and Tietze. No one sensitive to art and criticism in those years, as the Tietzes would have been, could have ignored the scandal and the political realities of Kokoschka's stand as outsider, such as when he presented himself in a poster with a shaved head, like a criminal (fig. 5.22). The view of himself as "outsider" resonates with Loos's theoretical writings from the period, particularly his essay on ornament.[46] Like Loos, Kraus, and Kokoschka, Tietze was an "outsider" in Vienna, both as a Jew and as a native of Prague. The many dimensions of the relationship between Kokoschka and the Tietzes established by the portrait contained within it the negotiation of multiple subjectivities.

Interestingly, the portraits that Kokoschka painted in these years were predominately of assimilated Jews, many of them introduced to him by Loos.[47] As Kokoschka relates, however, even before the *Kunstschau* most of his friends with whom he argued politics in the coffeehouse were Jewish bank clerks.[48] If we were to assemble all of the individual portraits of Jews painted by Kokoschka in the years 1908–11 into one imaginary group portrait this aggregate work would produce all of the qualities of representation and attentiveness addressed by Riegl in regard to the Dutch group portrait.

According to Riegl, the figures in the Dutch group portrait maintain their individual identity but depend on each other for their collective identity. The specifics of that collective identity are read by the viewer through gestures and gazes. These are the marks of identity that the portrait conveys. In our imaginary group portrait, Kokoschka does not point ostensively to collectivity, even though he may have had it in mind. He disperses it to the individual portraits, where it must be activated by the viewer. It is with the attributes common to this group of sitters and the artist that we can grasp the sense of a shared identity that is gestured to, but not incorporated in, each of the separate paintings. Again, Kokoschka says of the early portraits: "Most of my sitters were Jews. They felt less secure than the rest of the Viennese Establishment, and were consequently more open to the new and more sensitive to the tensions and pressures that accompanied the decay of the old order in Austria. Their own historical experience had taught them to be more perceptive in their political and artistic judgements."[49] This is the attentiveness of those whose "place" is outside, who must watch for signs from elsewhere—outside the frame—rather than emit, from within the frame, signs of religion, ethnicity, or a shared identity.

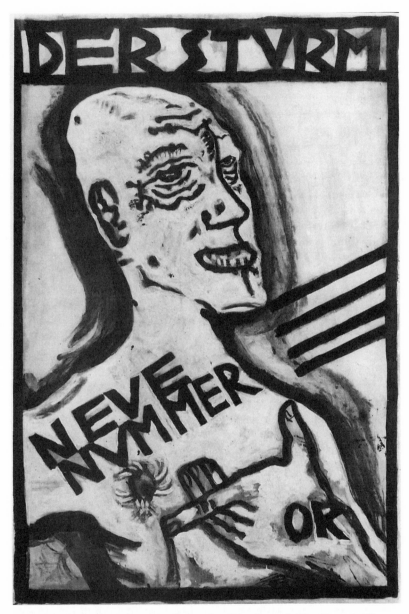

Figure 5.22. Oskar Kokoschka. Poster for "Der Sturm" (The Storm). Water-color on canvas, 102 x 70 centimeters. Szépmüvészeti Múzeum, Budapest. © 2000 Artists Rights Society (ARS), New York / ProLitteris, Zürich.

As I have stated, in the portraits of Jews in the modern period, geographic place or context fulfilled the function of identifying the sitter as a secular, assimilated Jew rather than a religious one. Once the portrait is removed from its place and the relationship of painter, sitter, and viewer it initially invited—be it by physical removal or by the "remove" of an art historical tradition that favors placement within the formal conventions of genre painting over a social reading of the work—we are *ourselves* compelled to exercise an attentiveness that confirms and paraphrases historical contexts. Our context for the reception of the Tietzes portrait and other portraits of Jews from Europe before 1938 includes a knowledge of the events leading up to the exile of the Tietzes from Austria. The Holocaust affects our reception of the visual images of Jews associated with earlier times. The provenance of the painting subjects us to this history as we make an interpretation of it.

Throughout this paper I have assumed that there is no more important genre for understanding "Jewish subjectivity" than the portrait. By subjectivity I do not mean that which is expressed by the phrase "the individuality of an artist as expressed in his work" (OED). This meaning of subjectivity arose in nineteenth-century Romanticism together with an elaboration on the earlier forms of the individual genius and personality of the artist. This concept of subjectivity fulfills a twofold desire. One, that a complete correspondence exists between the mind and personality (sometimes the soul) of the artist and the work of art; and two, that such a correspondence be visible to the observer of the work of art, or at least recoverable to the attentive observer and interpreter, the art historian, for example.

My understanding of subjectivity insists on a basic presupposition of psychoanalysis in regard to the subject: "the subject is not conscious of all 'its' thoughts, is not present in all 'its' representations, not even virtually or potentially."[50] This view of the subject's subjectivity may be particularly productive for the genre of portraiture, where the tensions between the subject and the representation of the subject, particularly in regard to the viewer, has been a topic of discussion ever since the early years of the twentieth century. Significantly for my discussion here, this understanding of subjectivity was the foundation of an influential discussion of the history of Dutch portraiture published in 1902 by Riegl, Tietze's teacher and which, as I have argued, surely influenced Kokoschka's approach to portraits in his earliest years as a painter.[51]

The object of interpretation in portraiture is, by my definition, a subject incapable of complete representation. The portrait, therefore, represents an incomplete subject. At the same time, the received view of the history of portraiture maintains that the portrait is fundamentally a complete picture of the individual at a particular moment in history. This cannot be and was never the case. With the expectation that the representation accurately embodies the particular sitter's physical appearance and personality at a certain time, the power of the portrayed yields to the authority of the artist, whose abilities allow him to represent that which can never be fully shown. Such a view of portraiture not only supports the authority of the artist, it also upholds the definition of subjectivity that I have rejected here. The vacillations between the incomplete representation of the subjectivity of the sitter and the expectation that the genre offer a "complete" representation of the subject concern me because the object of my interpretation, the portrait of an acculturated Jew and his wife, represents historical beings who were themselves engaged in a dialogue over the meaning of subjectivity, both in how they lived in Vienna and in their understanding of Riegl's theories. Thus, the portrait of the Tietzes reflects an active involvement with a theory of portraiture in which subjectivity was understood to reside as much with the viewer as in the portrayed.

For the Tietzes, attentiveness to their subjectivities may not have been altogether optimistic in 1909, but a sign of an unstable place in a changing social order where acculturation could prove imperfect and the study of the art of the past no haven. In 1928 the Viennese Jewish émigré Salo Baron argued that the processes of assimilation had a far more ambiguous character than is usually recognized, particularly for the historiography of Jewish culture in modernity.[52] The difficulties we have today with the "Jewish identity" of the sitters in Kokoschka's early portraits is a strong part of the history of the sitters, the history of the object, and the interpretative tradition that we have inherited. Portraits of Jews in modernity are exemplary "sites of a new and tension-filled social contract," in which displacement reveals identity only when the interpreter beholds the gestures toward identity and collectivity that reach beyond the frame.[53]

NOTES

1. Jacob Burckhardt, *Beiträge zur Kunstgeschichte von Italien* (Basel: Lendorff, 1898), 145–294; see also *Il Ritratto nella Pittura Italiana del Rinascimento*, trans. Daniela Pagliai (Rome: Bulzoni, 1993), 31. I am grateful to both the University of California Institute for the Humanities and The Getty Research Institute for support during the research and writing of this article. I thank Bill Nichols for his editorial advice. This essay was written in 1999. The author has attempted to bring the bibliography up-to-date, but for further and more complete information, see Soussloff, *The Subject in Art* (forthcoming).

2. Richard Brilliant, *Portraiture* (London: Reaktion Books, 1991), 8.

3. Mikkel Borch-Jacobsen, *The Freudian Subject*, trans. Catherine Porter (Stanford: Stanford University Press, 1988), 9.

4. On autonomy and efficacy in relationship to the subject, subjectivity, and subjection, see Judith Butler, *The Psychic Life of Power: Theories in Subjection* (Stanford: Stanford University Press, 1997), esp. 1–30.

5. Richard I. Cohen, *Jewish Icons: Art and Society in Modern Europe* (Berkeley and

Los Angeles: University of California Press, 1998), 27. See my review of Cohen's important book in *Central European History* 33(2000): 122–25.

6. Cohen, 117.

7. Richard Brilliant, "Portraits as Silent Claimants: Jewish Class Aspirations and Representational Strategies in Colonial and Federal America," in *Facing the New World: Jewish Portraits in Colonial and Federal America* (New York: The Jewish Museum, 1997), 1–8.

8. Brilliant, "Portraits as Silent Claimants," 2.

9. Brilliant, "Portraits as Silent Claimants," 4–5.

10. David Altshuler, ed., *The Precious Legacy: Judaic Treasures from the Czechoslovak State Collections*, (New York: Summit Books, 1983), cat. #224 and #225. These portraits have frequently been associated with the part of the Jewish wedding ceremony called "The Veiling" *(Bedeckung)*. The chair or sofa back depicted behind many of the half-length portraits may refer to that particular part of the ceremony, as might the veil worn by the woman, which was put on when the figures were seated. See the portraits of Amalie and Karl Andree, which supposedly represent this event, *The Precious Legacy*, cat. #229 and #230. A wedding couch, dated 1838, originally from Danzig and today in the Jewish Museum in New York, is the only example of this genre of furniture, see Vivian Mann and Joseph Gutman, eds., *Danzig 1939: Treasures of a Destroyed Community* (New York: The Jewish Museum, 1980), 62, cat. #10.

11. Marion A. Kaplan, *The Making of the Jewish Middle Class: Women, Family, and Identity in Imperial Germany* (New York and Oxford, Oxford University Press, 1991), attempts to show the importance of Jewish women in both assimilation and religious practice. Little work exists on the role of the portrait in the formation of the Jewish middle class in Europe, despite the attention to that class by historians.

12. Brilliant, "Portraits as Silent Claimants," 3.

13. On the topic of not allowing Jewish identity into art's history and interpretation, see my *Jewish Identity in Modern Art History* (Berkeley and Los Angeles: University of California Press, 1998). This situation is rapidly changing in the literature on art.

14. Alex Potts, "Sign," in *Critical Terms for Art History*, ed. Robert S. Nelson and Richard Shiff, (Chicago and London: University of Chicago Press, 1996), 27. Pott's definition of the modern work of art comes extremely close to that of "icon" given by Charles Sanders Peirce. In Peirce's semiological system, the icon is the most elemental kind of sign, one that "represents its object mainly by its similarity to it," as the film theorist Peter Wollen wrote in *Signs and Meaning in the Cinema*, 3d ed. (Bloomington and London: University of Indiana Press, 1972), 122. In her book on film theory and semiotics, *The Subject of Semiotics* (New York and Oxford: Oxford University Press, 1983), 14–25, Kaja Silverman explained that Peirce's "icon" has implicit within it the mental image of the thing represented or referred to.

15. Norman Kleeblatt, *Too Jewish*, exhib. cat. (New York: The Jewish Museum, 1997).

16. Similarly, Werner Sollors, *Beyond Ethnicity* (Oxford: Oxford University Press, 1986), uses "descent" as an identity of lineage and private practice and "consent" for an identity of choice or public self-fashioning.

17. Cohen, 9.

18. I will explore these portraits at length in my forthcoming book on portrai-

ture and Jewish identity in Vienna ca. 1900. The literature on the Tietze portrait is large but no attempt I know of has been made to understand the work in terms of the identities of the sitters as assimilated Jews. For the most complete bibliography, see Johann Winkler and Katharina Erling, *Oskar Kokoschka: Die Gemälde, 1906–1929* (Salzburg: Galerie Welz, 1995), 19–20. See also Almut Krapf-Weiler, "Löwe und Eule: Hans Tietze und Erica Tietze-Conrat—eine biographische Skizze," *Belvedere* (1999): 64–83 and Madlyn Millner Kahr, "Erica Tietze-Conrat: Productive Scholar in Renaissance and Baroque Art," in *Women as Interpreters of the Visual Arts, 1820– 1979*, ed. Claire Richter Sherman (Westport, Conn.: Greenwood Press, 1981), 301– 26. An attempt has been made to discuss portraits of Viennese Jewish women by Kokoschka's older contemporary, Gustav Klimt, see Christian Brandstätter, "Schöne jüdische Jour-Damen: Gustav Klimt's Damen-Porträts und seine Auftraggeber—Ein verdrängtes Kapitel österreichische Sammlergeschichte," in *Gustav Klimt*, exhib. cat., Kunsthaus Zürich (Stuttgart: Gerd Hatje), 325–37.

19. Oskar Kokoschka, *My Life*, trans. David Britt (New York: Macmillan, 1974), 35.

20. I am grateful to Glen Lowry, director of the Museum of Modern Art for allowing me access to the curatorial file on this important painting. I have not seen the records on the financial transactions between the Tietzes and the dealer or MOMA. Much of what follows is unpublished and can be found in the curatorial file. According to an article cited in the file, which records the memory of Erica Tietze-Conrat, the portrait was started and completed in December of 1909: J. P. Hoden, *Bekenntnis zu Kokoschka* (Berlin and Mainz: Florian Kupfeberg, 1963), 76. Other research indicates they may have emigrated in 1938.

21. D. Hugo Feigl to Alfred Barr, 26 September 1939, MOMA, New York City.

22. *Sonderausstellung Malerei und Plastik in den Räumen des Künstler Bundes Hagen*, exhib. cat. (Vienna, February 1911) states that the paintings numbered 36–60 were exhibited in rooms two and three. I am grateful to Patrick Werkner of the Kokoschka Archive in Vienna for giving me access to this information, not represented correctly in most of the later Kokoschka literature. Klaus Albrecht Schroder and Johann Winkler, eds. *Oskar Kokoschka* (Munich: Prestel-Verlag, 1991), 70. See also, Edith Hoffmann, *Kokoschka: Life and Work* (Boston: Boston Book and Art Shop Inc., n.d.), 86–108.

23. Of particular interest for Tietze's history is the situation of assimilation in Czechoslovakia; see on this *The Jews of Czechoslovakia: Historical Studies and Surveys*, vol. 1 (Philadelphia: The Jewish Publication Society of America, 1968).

24. Steven Beller, *Vienna and the Jews, 1867–1938: A Cultural History* (Cambridge: Cambridge University Press, 1989), 53 and 53, note 38, identifies the Schottengymnasium as "aristocratic."

25. The majority of this information can be found in *International Biographical Dictionary of Central European Émigrés 1933–1945*, vol. 2, pt. 2: L–Z The Arts, Sciences, and Literature (Munich: K. G. Saur, 1983), 1165. See now the publication of information in Ulrike Wendland, *Biographisches Handbuch deutschsprachiger Kunsthistoriker im Exil: Leben und Werk der unter dem Nationalsozialismus verfolgten und vertriebenen Wissenschaftler*, 2 vols. (Munich: K. G. Saur, 1999).

26. Oskar Kokoschka to Dorothy Miller, 4 October 1953, MOMA, Curatorial File.

27. Erica Tietze-Conrat in Hoden, *Bekenntnis zu Kokoschka*, 76.

28. Kokoschka, *My Life*, 76.

29. Carl E. Schorske, *Fin-de-Siècle Vienna: Politics and Culture* (New York: Random House, 1961), 141.

30. Julius Held to Mr. Alfred Barr, 29 November 1957, MOMA, Curatorial File.

31. Douglas Druick and Michel Hoog, *Fantin-Latour*, exhib. cat., National Gallery of Canada (Ottawa: The Gallery for the Corporation of the National Museums of Canada, 1983), cat. nos. 70–73, pp. 203–14, esp. 204–5.

32. In 1946 the painting was still in its original frame, according to a letter from Hans Tietze to Sweeney at MOMA. He based his assessment on a photograph; see Hans Tietze to Sweeney, 7 March 1946, MOMA, Curatorial File. See also Hans Tietze to Sweeney, 27 February 1946, MOMA, Curatorial File: "looking as it had been meant by the artist and in the frame he had designed for it."

33. Oskar Kokoschka to Dorothy Miller, 10 October 1953, MOMA, Curatorial File.

34. Kirk Varnedoe, *Vienna 1900*, 169. While it may well be useful to follow this line of thinking regarding performance into recent theories of performativity and the construction of subjectivity, deriving from J. L. Austin, Jacques Derrida, and Judith Butler, I choose here to maintain my focus on the contemporary context of the portrait where we can find subjectivity discussed precisely in the interpretation of Dutch group portraiture, but see my "Like a Performance: Performativity and the Historicized Body, from Bellori to Mapplethorpe," in *Acting on the Past: Historical Performance across the Disciplines*, ed. Mark Franko and Annette Richards (Wesleyan: Wesleyan University Press, 2000), 69–98.

35. Alois Riegl, *The Group Portraiture of Holland*, trans. Evelyn M. Kain (Los Angeles: Getty Research Institute, 1999). See the excellent introduction by Wolfgang Kemp to this new edition of Riegl for the publication history of the essay on Dutch group portraiture. I am grateful to the Getty Research Institute for providing me with this translation before its publication and to Juliet Koss for drawing my attention to it.

36. Alois Riegl, "Excerpts from *The Dutch Group Portrait*," trans. Benjamin Binstock, *October* 74 (fall 1995): 20.

37. Margaret Olin, *Forms of Representation in Alois Riegl's Theory of Art* (University Park: Pennsylvania State University Press, 1992), 163–65.

38. Michael Podro, *The Critical Historians of Art* (New Haven and London: Yale University Press, 1982), 94.

39. Julius Held, "Hans Tietze—1880–1954," *College Art Journal* 14 (fall 1954): 67–69.

40. On Wickoff, see W. Eugene Kleinbauer, *Modern Perspectives in Western Art History: An Anthology of Twentieth-Century Writings on the Visual Arts* (New York: Holt, Rinehart and Winston, 1971), 124–25.

41. Held, 68.

42. Olin, 168.

43. Held, 68: "Such 'radical' views and activities, even though only in the field of art, were by no means without risks in the arch-conservative Austro-Hungarian monarchy, but Hans Tietze was never a man to shirk from unpleasantness."

44. On Loos and the background of Vienna in the early years of the century, see Vergo, cited above. See also, Ludwig Münz and Gustave Künstler, *Adolf Loos: Pioneer*

of Modern Architecture, with an introduction by Nikolaus Pevsner and appreciation by Oskar Kokoschka, trans. Harold Meek (New York: Praeger, 1966). On Kraus, see Edward Timms, *Karl Kraus: Apocalyptic Satirist* (New Haven and London: Yale University Press, 1986).

45. Part of that clean-up job has been the criticism by Ernst Gombrich of early Kokoschka and Karl Kraus as essentially nonpolitical. E. H. Gombrich, *Kokoschka in His Time* (London: The Tate Gallery, 1986). In light of my arguments here I do not accept Gombrich's views on either early Kokoschka or Kraus.

46. Adolf Loos, "Ornament and Crime (1908)," in Münz and Künstler, *Adolf Loos,* 226–31.

47. These connections to the radical, artistic, and political Jewish community came in the main through Loos. A fine example of this would be Kokoschka's portrait of the firstborn of the Goldmann family, *Child with Parents' Hands* (Österreichische Galerie im Belvedere, Vienna). In the same year, 1909, Loos was building for the Goldmanns the Goldmann and Salatsch building on Michaelerplatz in Vienna. See Schroder and Winkler, eds., *Oskar Kokoschka,* cat. #6, p. 64.

48. Kokoschka, *My Life,* 23.

49. Kokoschka, *My Life,* 35.

50. Borch-Jacobsen, 3.

51. For further elaboration of the problem of subjectivity in art in the early twentieth century, see my forthcoming book, *The Subject in Art.*

52. Salo Baron, "Ghetto and Emancipation: Shall We Revise the Traditional View?" *The Menorah Journal* 14 (June 1928): 515–26. I am aided in my understanding of the significance of Baron for the Viennese context by the fine introduction by David N. Myers in David N. Myers and William V. Rowe, *From Ghetto to Emancipation: Historical and Contemporary Reconsiderations of the Jewish Community* (Scranton: University of Scranton Press, 1997), vii–xvii.

53. Myers, x.

6

A Different Road to Modernity

Jewish Identity in the Arab World

Daniel J. Schroeter

Agadir is a southern Moroccan Atlantic resort city with a predominantly Berber population. The Jewish community has dwindled to less than two hundred and its synagogue during most the months of the years rarely has more than a handful of congregants. But during the summer, Moroccan Jews from many countries vacation in Agadir and elsewhere in the country. In August 1997, during the Shabbat morning prayers, the synagogue was filled with visitors, many of whom were en route to pilgrimage sites. During the service, the rabbi asked in which language he should deliver his sermon: French, Hebrew, or Arabic? In response, the congregation cried out practically in unison: "bi-l-'arabiyya," [in Arabic]. Almost everyone there would have been comfortable in French or Hebrew. Many had left Morocco at a young age and regarded their new countries as home. And regardless of where they lived, Israel represented to them the Jewish homeland. But Moroccan Jews, including those living in Israel, are living in a kind of exile. Morocco is also home, but for them, a country without borders, a diaspora.

These observations show how difficult it is to define the identity of Jews from Morocco. What is home? What is Diaspora? The conventional response is that Jews living in Morocco were in exile, and the "return" to Israel constituted a homecoming. Yet despite decades of living in Israel, connections to the language and culture of their original home remain strong. This continued attachment to another homeland does not imply dual loyalties to separate nation states. The affiliation of Jews to Morocco is not the patriotism implied by citizenship to a nation state, but rather it constitutes identifying with a Diaspora culture that transcends national boundaries.

These remarks about Jews from one Arabic- and Berber-speaking country complicate the more conventional understanding of Jewish identity in the modern world. Interpretations of Jewish history often stress emancipation and citizenship in the modern nation state as the catalyst for transforming Jewish identities. With the emancipation of the Jews in western Europe and the challenges of citizenship, new ideologies and identities in the Jewish world emerged. Michael Meyer argues that the experience of enlightenment, antisemitism, and Zionism were three forces that "shaped Jewish identity more than any others."[1] Although these generalizations might be applied to Jews in Europe and the United States, they tells us little about the Jews of Asia and Africa, who experienced a different set of forces affecting the modern world: colonialism and Islam. It is the clash of different forces shaping modern Jewish identities in the Diaspora that has caused ongoing ethnic tensions in Israel and elsewhere in the Jewish world.

The identities of the Jews of what later became known as the Arab world escape easy definition. Although immersed in the Arabic language and culture, most Middle Eastern Jews did not define themselves as "Arabs." Besides, the concept of the Arab in a secular and national sense is a construct of the late nineteenth and twentieth centuries.[2] For Jews in Muslim countries, their formal place in society was well defined before the modern era. They were a kind of corporate entity, a religious group that was granted a large measure of self-governing authority and the protection of the state in exchange for an annual capitation tax and the acceptance of a range of legal disabilities defined by Islamic law to underline their inferiority to Muslims. This was known as *dhimma* [protection], and Jews and other legitimate religious groups were called *dhimmi*s [protected people].[3] All members of society belonged to a religious group and were governed by their own laws. Their formal status was also not territorially based: Jews and Muslims, for example, could cross political boundaries, but would still be ruled by the same law.[4] The universal status granted to the Jews by the Islamic state also served to reinforce bonds between different Jewish communities, frequently over great distances.

This system based on the free practice of religion and on the relative freedom of movement is probably one reason why the Talmud and the *halakhah* were so widely disseminated and accepted in the Middle Ages. The Arab empire was created in the seventh century, a century after the Babylonian Talmud was completed. The Babylonian academies relocated in the eighth century to the newly created city of Baghdad, the flourishing capital of the far-flung Abbasid Empire, to be, in effect, under the auspices of the reigning power of those times. The academies exercised a large measure of control over the Jews of the Abbasid Empire (constituting the vast majority of world Jewry of the time).[5] This facilitated the widespread acceptance of a kind of "normative" *halakhic* Judaism.

If the formal status of the Jews was well-defined and more or less uniform throughout the Islamic world, the social conditions under which they lived could vary greatly. There were many kinds of Jewish identities in the Middle

East and vast cultural differences between communities. Local attachments were strong and were legitimized by the sanctification of local shrines (most commonly the graves of venerated rabbis) and the collective veneration of one's own community. In numerous places the home community was legitimized by the epithet, "little Jerusalem." Loyalty to one's place of origin often remained for several generations after one moved to another place. A person, for example, originating in Fez (a "Fasi") and moving to Cairo, would be likely to maintain a Maghrebi identity that would be passed down to future generations.[6] Identifying simultaneously with one's native city and country of origin was especially known for Spain. The expulsion of the Jews from Spain in 1492 did not put an end to their Sephardi identity. They maintained their identity with their Spanish cultural heritage without any particular geographic attachment to the Spanish homeland or desire to return there one day.

However strong local or regional attachments were, Jews also identified themselves and were identified by others as part of a wider community of Jews. Despite the evidence that many Jews did not originate in Palestine, but were converts, all believed that they were descended from the ancient tribes of Israel, maintaining traditions about the time that this dispersion supposedly occurred.[7] Myths of origin were important for legitimizing local identity, but also for connecting to a wider whole. Jews who traveled from the Middle East to Christian Europe considered themselves part of the same religion and believed that they originated in the same place (i.e., the land of Israel). Within the broader category of Jews were a number of ethnic subcategories that also transcended local identities: Rabbanites, Karaites, Sephardim, Romaniyot (Greek speakers), and others. These were not static categories, but often changed over time and were amalgamated into new types of identities.[8]

Jews also became a part of the wider Islamic, and especially Arab, civilization in much the same way that Jews were a part of the Hellenistic world. The majority of world Jewry became Arabic speakers and developed Judeo-Arabic languages and cultures. The intermingling of Arab Muslim and Jewish culture has led the preeminent scholar of the medieval Jewish Middle East, S. D. Goitein, to emphasize the "creative symbiosis" that took place for the Jews of the Islamic world. Most scholars have followed Goitein's path in emphasizing the shared cultural traditions of Jews and Muslims.[9]

This model of symbiosis has been particularly appealing for advocates of a "diasporized identity," which stands in stark contrast to the extreme differences between Jewish and Arab cultures in Israel today.[10] Goitein's model of a tolerant and mobile Mediterranean world has been essentialized for all times and places by a number of scholars. Ammiel Alcalay, for example, invokes Goitein's depiction of the medieval Mediterranean for interpreting contemporary "Levantine" culture where Jews are seen as an integral part of

Arab culture.[11] Based on Alcalay's reading of Goitein, James Clifford suggests that "the Sephardic strand offers a specific counterhistory of Arab/Jewish coexistence and crossover."[12] Clifford, in other words, finds Levantine-Sephardi culture, looked upon disparagingly by Israel's Ashkenazi establishment, as a model of coexistence in a postnational world.

Yet these invocations of an idealized world of Muslim-Jewish symbiosis fail to account for how Jewish identities in the Middle East and North Africa were transformed in the last two hundred years. I propose that it was a more cosmopolitan Jewish identity that was profoundly affected, and in some countries sacrificed, by colonialism. Jews in the Middle East were seen by their European coreligionists as fundamentally different, and under colonialism this was internalized by Middle Eastern Jews themselves. Judaism became much more parochial and localized practices assumed a greater importance than ever before. Members of the elite who acquired a Western education sought to distance themselves from beliefs and practices that they now considered primitive and to join the civilization of the western European powers.[13] The protagonist of *The Pillar of Salt*, Albert Memmi's novel set in Tunisia between the two world wars, reflects on the culture of his community: "Our local dogma was unbelievably primitive: an incoherent mixture of Berber superstitions, old wives' beliefs, and formal rites that could not satisfy the smallest spiritual need. The rabbis were silly, ignorant, and unprepossessing. Their filthy Oriental robes and faded fezzes were part of the life of sordid neighborhoods that I wanted to forget."[14]

Much of the scholarship on the history of Jews in Arab countries accepts the "backwardness" of the Jewish communities and their need to be reformed. Studies written mostly by Israeli scholars tend to find ways to integrate the Oriental Jewish experience with the European, stressing the unifying elements in Jewish history. The reasons for this approach to the history of "Oriental" Jewry are understandable in a sociological sense. For many Jews of the Arab world living in Israel, the positive yet still tenuous assertion of their identity as "communities of the East" (*'edot ha-mizrah*) has become possible only in the last two decades, not unrelated to the decline in Labor ideology and the rise of a new type of Zionism of the political right. For the dominant Ashkenazi-Labor establishment, the in-gathering of the exile ideal of the new state of Israel had not meant the creation of a pluralistic Jewish society through the preservation of the customs of the Diaspora, especially when it pertained to "Oriental Jews." As Ben Gurion said: "We do not want Israelis to become Arabs. We are in duty bound to fight against the spirit of the Levant, which corrupts individuals and societies, and preserve the authentic Jewish values as they crystallized in the Diaspora."[15] The implication is that the Diaspora only refers to the European dispersion, the only place where authentic (secular and Zionist) Jewish values could develop. The "Arabness" of Jews from the Middle East, resembling the culture of Israel's enemy was, to say the least, problematic. To be sure, exotic customs of Jews from the Islamic world had a place, but generally they were to be contained in museum exhibitions and in folkloric spectacles that could stand in contrast to the progressive face of modern, secular Israeli society.[16]

The rise of the right and the growing influence of the Orthodox in Israeli political culture has given the Jews from Arab countries a much larger role in the political landscape. This is reflected in a growth in scholarship on the modern history of Oriental Jewry, but often the emphasis of studies has been in identifying movements in the Arab world that paralleled the movements of the Ashkenazim that led to the emergence of Israel: *haskalah*, emancipation, antisemitism, and Zionism, despite the fact that in the Arab world these movements were marginal and had different meanings. This also came as a response to the dominant Labor establishment view of Oriental Jews: that the kinds of historical forces that were central to Ashkenazi Jewry were entirely absent from their coreligionists in the East, who remained "traditional," and it was only with the birth of the state of Israel that there was an awakening in their Jewish political consciousness.

Such attitudes, it should be admitted, were not only an Israeli product, but were also found in the view of European Jews. For example, leaving aside the question of the importance of the Zionist movements of the Muslim world, relatively little attention or interest was paid to Zionism in Arab countries by the World Zionist Organization until after World War II, with the partial exception of Yemen.[17] In this case, the interest of the Yemenite Jews to settle in the land of Israel in the late nineteenth and early twentieth centuries coincided with the aims of the Yishuv to find a way to avoid employing Arab labor. A solution was sought by importing Jewish workers from Yemen.[18] But for the most part, Zionist settlers associated Middle Eastern and North African Jews with the decadent and unenlightened "Old Yishuv," who they believed lived unproductive lives in Jerusalem and the other few "pre-Zionist" communities of Palestine. The Jews of Morocco, Iraq, and other Middle Eastern countries were hardly seen as prospective clients for the Zionist movement until the latter half of the twentieth century. In perusing the papers of Moses Gaster in London, I discovered a letter from Moses Lugasy, a Jew in Essaouira (Mogador), Morocco, addressed to Theodor Herzl, reporting on the formation of the first Zionist movement in Morocco at the beginning of 1900.[19] The interest in the letter was not only that it represented the beginning of political Zionism in Morocco, but the fact that Gaster never forwarded the letter to Herzl (otherwise the letter would not be found in the Gaster collection today). Lugasy subsequently complained to Gaster: "As soon as I had organised a Zionist society in Mogador (Morocco N.W. of Africa) I had the honour to address a few lines '30 July 1900' to Dr. Herzl, whom I wished to have my letter in time for the congress of 13 Augt 1900 but not knowing that gentleman's address, I have therefore taken the liberty to enclose Dr. Herzl's letter inside one I have also addressed to your goodself and had been duly registered, no reply however has reach me and I would like to know if my communications have arrived at their destinations, for which I would feel greatly obliged."[20]

In 1900, Zionism was understood by its leaders as a movement that addressed the needs of European Jews, who faced the challenges of assimilation, antisemitism, and nationalism. Zionists who paid any attention to the Arab world believed that the pre-emancipation Jews of the Orient had not yet reached a stage in the evolutionary process to be considered part of the Zionist enterprise.

But emancipation did not mean the same for the Jews in the East. How could it, if the advocates of emancipation saw colonialism as a tool for achieving their aims? Many Jews hoped to obtain French or British citizenship, a policy that the colonial powers were unwilling to concede, except in the case of Algeria. Jewish leaders in Baghdad applied on a number of occasions for British citizenship on behalf of the community as a whole at the end of World War I, but their requests were rejected. Some young Jewish intellectuals in Baghdad criticized this overture, stressing instead that Jews had long lived among Muslims in Iraq.[21] But relatively few Jews came to identify themselves with the Arab nationalist movements; only a few believed that the liberation of the Arabs from colonialism would also bring about the emancipation of the Jews.

There were a few exceptions: in nineteenth-century Egypt, for example, one of the early nationalist writers, Ya'qub Sanu', was a Jew.[22] After World War I, when the British granted both Egypt and Iraq a degree of independence, members of the Jewish bourgeoisie participated in the liberal parliamentary politics of the new nation states.[23] With the rise of Arab nationalism in the interwar years, some Jews hoped to find a place in the newly developed concept of the nation. In Egypt and Iraq there was a sizable minority of Jews who began to express the idea of patriotism to their country. An intellectual and literary movement emerged in the 1920s and 1930s in both countries that was integrated with Muslim intellectuals of the same social class; Jews together with Muslims wrote in Arabic and expressed pride and love of country.[24] Some Egyptian Jews saw no contradiction between patriotism to Egypt and support for Zionism in the interwar years, a position that obviously could not be sustained after 1948.[25] Few, however, actually joined the Arab nationalist movements, whose followers argued for the unity of Arabs of all countries tied by a common Islamic heritage. And although an elite of Jews in both countries saw themselves as "Arabs," they mostly avoided participation in the political process, seeing greater security in the umbrella of the yet present British authorities.

Although in Egypt and Iraq the Alliance Israélite Universelle encouraged Jews to integrate into the newly emerging national cultures, in French North

Africa there was no national political arena in which Jews could participate, and the Alliance continued to stress cultural integration with France.[26]

Although there were important differences between the experiences of Jews in different parts of the colonized Middle East, as a general rule few Jews identified with the newly developing political culture. Colonialism was the vehicle by which Jews sought to achieve greater security and prosperity, and they were encouraged by their European Jewish advocates. European Jews described Middle Eastern and North African Jewish communities as "traditional," essentially no different from Jews in pre-emancipation Europe. But they believed that emancipation would bring the oppressed and backward communities of the Arab world into the modern age: East would become West. Many European Jews believed that under colonialism the transformation of Oriental Jews would come about through the instruments of Westernization, especially through modern Jewish schools, which would lead to the demise of the primitive traditional education.[27] The process of modernization, however, proved to be uneven, and "traditional" Jewish culture was often tenaciously maintained. Still, most scholars have assumed the inevitability of modernization of the Jewish communities on a Western model, a kind of modernization theory that was once widely accepted for Middle Eastern society as a whole, positing that modernization would mean the end of traditional society.[28]

The growing focus on Islamic religious expression, responding to the now more evident failure of the modern bureaucratic state to displace the fundamental collective religious affiliation of most of the inhabitants of the Middle East, has challenged scholars to question the assumption that along with modernization would come secularization.[29] The same can be said for the Jewish communities of the Arab world. In most cases modernity did not undermine their religious faith and affiliation to the community. Unlike in Europe, the Middle Eastern and North African rabbis did not need to be concerned about Jews converting to another religion, and although secularization made inroads in some places, it hardly posed the kind of threat it did in the West. There was no Reform movement as in western Europe and the United States and, therefore, the bitter division between Orthodox and Reform or between the religious and secular was entirely absent. Rabbis were able to adopt a much more innovative stance with regard to modern civilization and, with only a few exceptions, were more accepting of modern secular education.[30] Furthermore, large numbers of Jews from Arab countries living in Israel continued to manifest their attachments to traditional religious practice and belief, despite the erosion of strict observance. This demonstrates that collectively expressed religion is not incompatible with modern society, even though many of the founders of Zionism believed that it was.[31]

Fundamental to the transition of European Jewish identity was the granting of citizenship to Jews and the concomitant dismantling of the corporate status of the Jewish community. Remaining a member of the Jewish community became a matter of choice. The actual legal competence of the rabbis and rabbinical courts was greatly reduced and was made binding only to those who chose to accept their decisions. This was seen by advocates of emancipation as desirable—now that Jews were citizens of the countries that they lived in, being Jewish could be stripped of its national component. One became a German or a Frenchman of the Hebrew or Israelite persuasion or faith.[32]

The weakening of Jewish self-government was also one of the outcomes of colonialism in the Middle East. The advocates of emancipation all believed in reducing the competence of the rabbinical courts and the other self-governing organs of the Jewish community. The reform of rabbinical courts was intended to limit their competence to areas of personal litigation and to create a bureaucracy that colonial administrations could easily control. The creation of municipalities under colonialism, for example, often replaced some of the functions of the organized committee *(ma'amad)* of the Jewish communities. The dismantling of the existing structure of Jewish institutions was justified by the backwardness of the communities. European Jewish advocates of emancipation believed that in the modern states of the East there would be no place for a self-governing *kehillah* [Jewish community].

In Europe, the effects of dismantling the communal autonomy of the *kehillah* are well known: secularization and religious reform, the replacement of a universal *halakhic* culture with adherence to the nation state, Zionism, and assimilation. Although religious observance and affiliation to the Jewish community did not disappear altogether, new rituals and values associated with nationalism took a primary place in the identity of Jews. In Germany, for example, the nation state became a formal part of Reform Judaism's ideology and worship.

With the disappearance or the more limited authority of the *kehillah* in Arab countries under colonial rule in the nineteenth and twentieth centuries, it might be assumed that the communities would undergo a process of adaptation to modern society similar to that in Europe. This, however, was not the case (except to a certain extent in Algeria, where the Jews became French citizens). Jews throughout the Arab world maintained strong attachments to their communities despite the more limited authority of their leaders. In some places, such as Egypt, secularization made some advances, but most Jews continued to feel closely connected to a universal *halakhic* culture. Although rabbinical thinkers were critical of the moral laxity of the communities and sought to implement reforms, these reforms were always advocated within a *halakhic* context. In some places, such as Morocco, the undermining of the authority of the *kehillah* caused the Jewish community to turn increasingly to informal leaders, saints, and local practices. Although the veneration of local saints *(tsadikim)* was ancient in Morocco, the great proliferation of pilgrimages on the anniversaries of the saints' deaths *(hillulot)* took place in the nineteenth and twentieth centuries.[33] Some aspects of modernity were assimilated, but the community also drew closer to indigenous and parochial forms of culture.

Religious differentiation barred the Jews from any large-scale assimilation to Arab society. To the extent that it occurred, such as in Egypt or Iraq, it was mostly confined to a certain secularized elite sector of the population where the solidarity of social class transcended religious boundaries. There were advocates of assimilation, especially in countries under French rule, but this assimilation was to France, rather than Morocco, Tunisia, or Syria. Moreover, assimilation to France in the colonial setting had its limits. The Jews often found themselves, as Albert Memmi has so poignantly illustrated in *The Pillar of Salt,* caught between colonizer and colonized, as seen in the frustrated teenage protagonist in the novel.

> I sought—in everything from official documents to my own sharply defined features—some thread which might lead me to the knowledge of who I am. For a while, I believed my forebears had been a family of Berber princes converted to Judaism by Kahena, the warrior-queen and founder of a Jewish kingdom in the middle of the Atlas Mountains. . . . [A]nother time, I found I was descended from an Italian Renaissance painter. . . . Could I be descended from a Berber tribe when the Berbers themselves failed to recognize me as one of their own. I was Jewish, not Moslem; a townsman, not a highlander. And even if I had borne the painter's name, I would not have been acknowledged by the Italians. No, I'm African, not European. In the long run, I would always be forced to return to Alexandre Mordekhai Benillouche, a native in a colonial country, a Jew in an antisemitic universe, an African in a world dominated by Europe. (95–96) [34]

Jews were needed by the colonizers, but full acceptance by the often antisemitic settlers was hardly possible. Furthermore, unlike in France, where secularism was an important form of identity, in the Arab world society remained predominantly based on the religious communities. Jews could selectively assimilate aspects of modern European culture without following the path to secularization.

Zionist culture from Europe was also assimilated by some. In the twentieth century, Zionist movements sprang up throughout the Arab world and, especially in Egypt and Iraq, there were significant followings. But while in eastern Europe Zionism could often become an all-consuming, self-contained culture, the Zionist movements in the Arab world were one of the many forces absorbed into the collective universe of the Jewish communities, but they never really replaced other forms of Jewish identity. For many Jews in the Arab world Zionism resonated with existing cultural patterns, where spiritual attachments to Jerusalem and the land of Israel were never cast in doubt as they were by secular or Reform Jews in Europe.[35]

In short, the Jews of the Arab world traveled along a different road to modernity than the Jews of Europe. The differences cannot simply be attributed to a time lag. Nor can we assume, as does Jacob Katz, that all "traditional" Jewish communities were essentially versions of the same, except to the extent that we reduce the differences to the lowest common denominator in which all communities had the same *halakhic* basis to their social structure.[36] But this does not tell us much.

The modern history of the Jews of the Arab world is closely related to the idea that Arab society in general presents a different picture of modernization. In the Middle East, the emergence of the modern nation state has not meant the erosion of collective religious belief as it has for other parts of the world. The idea of Islamicists to return to the origins of Islam need not be seen, as it often is, as incompatible with modernity, or at least with modern technology. Muslim fundamentalists are usually not adverse to modern technology and figure among the scientists and engineers of the Arab world.[37]

A certain parallel can be found among the Jews of the Arab world. In the *responsa* of Egyptian and Iraqi rabbis studied by Zvi Zohar, we find a clear *halakhic* resolution to technological innovation.[38] Missing is the tension that existed in Europe between Orthodoxy and modernity. This greater flexibility demonstrates that for the Jews of the Arab world there was in some ways an easier accommodation of modernity with religious belief and community than was the case in Europe, where religious tradition often clashed with modern society.

The reasons for these distinctive characteristics could be much debated, but I argue they are related to the exceptional nature of modernization in the Arabo-Islamic world. The distinctive features of Islam in the modern world are rooted in the origins and early development of the Islamic community, which was quite distinct from that of the Christian. The rise of Islam as simultaneously a political and religious entity meant that the Muslim community, the *umma,* never had to define itself in relationship to the state, as did the church. The state and religion were part of the same theoretical whole, where the religious law *(shariʿa)* was all embracing—*halakhic,* if you will—encompassing matters of doctrine; religious practice; and penal, civil, and personal matters. Nineteenth-century Ottoman reforms attempted to create the basis for the development of a civil society by legislating the principle of citizenship, implying that all Ottomans, regardless of religion, were equal before the law, and different types of law courts were established.[39] Colonialism went further in its attempt to develop a civil society, by reducing the legal competence of religious institutions, such as the *shariʿa* courts, and by granting religious minorities further judicial rights.

Despite these changes, secularism only affected a thin stratum of the Arab population. The elaboration of Arab nationalism was instead connected to the notion of Islamic reform.[40] It came as a reaction to the legacy of Western colonialism and its secular, materialist ways. It was in the glorious days of early Islam that cultural authenticity was located. Not surprisingly, the modern bureaucratic state in the twentieth-century Arab world did not engender the development of a civil society. Although the state intervened in more ways than ever before in the lives of individuals, primordial affinities remained closely linked to one's religious faith, and religious minorities have remained quite separate.[41]

In the absence of a secular middle ground, Jewish assimilation, except in the most marginal sense, was impossible in the Arab world. Colonialism contributed to this impossibility by pursuing a policy of divide and rule. But it was not only the association of Jews to the foreign rulers that precluded the participation of most Jews in Arab nationalism, it was also the linking of the modern nation with Islam that made it implausible for Jews to identify with the Arab nation.[42] Although it became legally possible to be, for example, a Moroccan Jewish national, Jews from Morocco really only were considered by others to be "Moroccan" after moving to Israel.

The lack of assimilation did not mean the absence of acculturation. There were many parallels between traditional Judaism and Islam, especially regarding the notion of the law and the community. This did not mean, however, the absence of tension between the two communities, nor any relevant kind of assimilation. Each community led separate private lives. But the structural similarities between the Jewish and Islamic communities had a much greater effect on the culture of the Jews than the relation between Judaism and Christianity did for Jews living in the pre-emancipation Christian world. In most places, Jews spoke Arabic and many of the customs of the Jewish community were similar to those of the Muslims, even though these similarities were almost always denied by both communities. Although the Jewish communities of premodern Europe were not impervious to outside cultural influences, there was more of a sense of cultural isolation, exemplified by the fact that much of the European Jewish world spoke different languages from their neighbors: Yiddish and Ladino. The majority of Sephardi Jews who settled in the Arab world amalgamated into the cultural milieu of their Arabic-speaking coreligionists.

Thus, we see the paradox of acculturation without assimilation, modernity without the erosion of religious faith, and the nation state without the undermining of the religious community. The experience of colonialism and Islam has shaped Jewish identities in the Arab world in ways that are quite distinctive and cannot be understood solely from the Ashkenazi perspective of enlightenment, antisemitism, and Zionism.

Jews formerly of the Arab world are constructing new identities with their countries of origin. Moroccan Jews today living in Israel, France, Canada, and the United States travel regularly to Morocco to reconnect with their native locales and to visit the shrines of saints. If political circumstances permitted, Jews from other Arab countries would probably visit their places of origins with some frequency as well.

NOTES

1. *Jewish Identity in the Modern World* (Seattle: University of Washington Press, 1990), 8.

2. On the rise of Arab nationalism, see Albert Hourani, *Arabic Thought in the Liberal Age, 1798–1939* (Cambridge: Cambridge University Press, 1983); Sylvia Haim, *Arab Nationalism: An Anthology* (Berkeley and Los Angeles: University of California Press, 1974); Rashid Khalidi et al., eds., *The Origins of Arab Nationalism* (New York: Columbia University Press, 1991).

3. On *dhimmi* status, see Norman A. Stillman, *The Jews of Arab Lands* (Philadelphia: Jewish Publication Society, 1979), 24–26; Bernard Lewis, *The Jews of Islam* (Princeton: Princeton University Press, 1984), 3 ff.; Mark R. Cohen, *Under Crescent and Cross: The Jews in the Middle Ages* (Princeton: Princeton University Press, 1994), 52–74; C. E. Bosworth, "The Concept of *Dhimma* in Early Islam," in *Christians and Jews in the Ottoman Empire*, vol. 1, ed. Benjamin Braude and Bernard Lewis (New York: Holmes & Meier, 1982), 37–51.

4. S. D. Goitein, *A Mediterranean Society*, 6 vols. (Berkeley and Los Angeles: University of California Press, 1967–93), vol. 1, 66–70.

5. Robert Brody, *The Geonim of Babylonia and the Shaping of Medieval Jewish Culture* (New Haven: Yale University Press, 1998), 123–34.

6. Goitein, *A Mediterranean Society*, vol. 1, 63.

7. Paul Wexler, *The Non-Jewish Origins of the Sephardic Jews* (Albany: State University of New York Press, 1996). The author somewhat overstates the case for Sephardi Jews, with questionable evidence. Still, there is a degree of plausibility in the argument that a significant number of Sephardi Jews are descended from converts.

8. See, e.g., a discussion on the various communities and identities in Jerusalem in the seventeenth century: Minna Rozen, *Ha-kehilah ha-yehudit be-Yerushalayim bame'ah ha-17* (Tel Aviv: Universitat Tel-Aviv u-Misrad ha-Bitahon, 1984), 93–108.

9. The use of the concept "symbiosis" for early Islam has been reconsidered by Steven M. Wasserstrom, *Between Muslim and Jew: The Problem of Symbiosis under Early Islam* (Princeton: Princeton University Press, 1995).

10. Daniel Boyarin and Jonathan Boyarin, "Diaspora: Generation and the Ground of Jewish Identity," *Critical Inquiry* 19 (1993): 720–23.

11. Ammiel Alcalay, *After Jews and Arabs: Remaking Levantine Culture* (Minneapolis: University of Minnesota Press, 1993), 128–43.

12. James Clifford, *Routes: Travel and Translation in the Late Twentieth Century* (Cambridge, Mass.: Harvard University Press, 1997), 274.

13. See my "Orientalism and the Jews of the Mediterranean," *Journal of Mediterranean Studies* 4, 2 (1994): 188–91.

14. (Boston: Beacon Press, 1992), 149.

15. Quoted in Sammy Smooha, *Israel: Pluralism and Conflict* (London: Routledge & Kegan Paul, 1978), 88.

16. On these questions, see Norman A. Stillman, *Sephardi Religious Responses to Modernity* (Luxembourg: Harwood Academic Publishers, 1995); Alcalay, *After Jews and Arabs;* for a sharp polemic, see Ella Shohat, "Sephardim in Israel: Zionism from the Standpoint of Its Jewish Victims," *Social Text* 19/20 (fall 1988).

17. Norman A. Stillman, *The Jews of Arab Lands in Modern Times* (Philadelphia: Jewish Publication Society, 1991), 90–91.

18. Nitza Druyan, *Be-en "marvad-kesamim": ole Teman be-Erets Yisra'el* (Jerusalem, 1981); Gershon Shafir, *Land, Labor, and the Origins of the Israeli-Palestinian Conflict, 1882–1914* (Berkeley and Los Angeles: University of California Press, 1996), 91–122.

19. Mocatta Library, University College, London, GP 138/135, 30 July 1900, Lugasy to Herzl.

20. GP 91/140, 19 December 1900.

21. Daphne Tsimhoni, "Jewish-Muslim Relations in Modern Iraq," in *Nationalism, Minorities, and Diasporas: Identities and Rights in the Middle East* (London: I. B. Tauris, 1996), 19.

22. Irene L. Gendzier, *The Practical Visions of Ya'qub Sanu'* (Cambridge, Mass.: Harvard University Press, 1966).

23. Nissim Rejwan, *The Jews of Iraq* (Boulder: Westview Press, 1985), 214; Gudrun Krämer, *The Jews in Modern Egypt, 1914–1952* (Seattle: University of Washington Press, 1989), 94 ff., 169; Joel Beinin, *The Dispersion of Egyptian Jewry* (Berkeley and Los Angeles: University of California Press, 1998), 45–47.

24. On Iraqi and Egyptian Jewish Arabic writers, see Sasson Somekh, "Lost Voices: Jewish Authors in Modern Arabic Literature," in *Jews among Arabs: Contacts and Boundaries* (Princeton: Darwin Press, 1989), 9–20. Throughout the Arab world, Jews traditionally did not read or write standard Arabic, but wrote in Judeo-Arabic (Arabic dialect in Hebrew characters).

25. Beinin, *Dispersion,* 34.

26. The activities of the Alliance Israélite Universelle in Morocco have been studied by Michael M. Laskier, *The Alliance Israélite Universelle and the Jewish Communities of Morocco, 1862–1962* (Albany: State University of New York Press, 1983); and on French North Africa generally, Michael M. Laskier, *North African Jewry in the Twentieth Century* (New York: New York University Press, 1994), 27–32.

27. See Michel Abitbol, "The Encounter between French Jewry and the Jews of North Africa: Analysis of a Discourse (1830–1914)," in *The Jews in Modern France,* ed. Frances Malino and Bernard Wasserstein (Hanover, N.H.: Published for Brandeis University Press by University Press of New England, 1985), 31–53. See also Abitbol, *Le passé d'un discorde Juifs et Arabes depuis le viie siècle* (Paris: Perrin, 1999), 216–28.

28. See especially Daniel Lerner, *The Passing of Traditional Society: Modernizing the Middle East* (Glencoe, Ill.: Free Press, 1958). Modernization theory as applied to the Muslim world has had many critics. See, e.g., Leonard Binder, *Islamic Liberalism: A Critique of Development Ideologies* (Chicago: University of Chicago Press, 1988).

29. John O. Voll, *Islam: Continuity and Change in the Modern World* (Boulder: Westview Press, 1982), 275–77.

30. See Harvey E. Goldberg, "Religious Responses among North African Jews in the Nineteenth and Twentieth Centuries," in *The Uses of Tradition: Jewish Continuity in the Modern Era,* ed. Jack Wertheimer (New York: Jewish Theological Seminary of America, 1992), 119–44; Stillman, *Sephardi Religious Responses,* 29–47; Zvi Zohar, "Sephardic Rabbinic Responses to Modernity: Some Central Characteristics," in *Jews among Muslims: Communities in the Precolonial Middle East,* ed. Shlomo Deshen and Walter P. Zenner (London: Macmillan, 1996), 64–80; Zohar, *Masoret u-temurah: hitmodedut hakhme Yisra'el be-mitsrayim uve-Suryah 'im etgere ha-modernizatsyah, 1880–1920* (Jerusalem: Bakhon Ben Tsevi le-heker Kehilot Yisra'el ba-Mizrah, 1993).

31. On religious belief and practice among Oriental Jews in Israel, see Shlomo Deshen, "Ha-datiyut shel mizrahim: tsibur, rabanim ve-emunah," *Alpayim* 9 (1994): 44–58.

32. On this process of change, see especially Jacob Katz, *Out of the Ghetto: The Social Background of Jewish Emancipation, 1770–1870* (New York: Schocken, 1978).

33. For a comprehensive source on saint veneration in Morocco, see Issachar Ben-Ami, *Ha-'aratsat ha-kedushim be-kerev yehude Maroko* (Jerusalem: Hotsa'at sefarim al Shem Y. L. Magnes, ha-Universitah ha-Ivrit, 1984); and the shorter English language version: *Saint Veneration among the Jews in Morocco* (Detroit: Wayne State University Press, 1998).

34. These themes are developed in an essay by Albert Memmi, *The Colonizer and the Colonized* (Boston: Beacon Press, 1991).

35. For an excellent discussion of Zionism in the Middle East, see Stillman, *Sephardi Religious Responses,* 49–64.

36. Jacob Katz, "Traditional Jewish Society and Modern Society," in *Jews among Muslims: Communities in the Precolonial Middle East,* ed. Shlomo Deshen and Walter P. Zenner (London: Macmillan, 1996), 25–34.

37. Henry Munson, Jr., *Islam and Revolution in the Middle East* (New Haven: Yale University Press, 1988), 107–8. On the use of modern technology by Islamists, see Dale F. Eickelman and James Piscatori, *Muslim Politics* (Princeton: Princeton University Press, 1996), 121–31.

38. Zohar, "Sephardic Rabbinic Responses to Modernity."

39. Roderic H. Davison, *Reform in the Ottoman Empire, 1856–1876* (Princeton: Princeton University Press, 1963).

40. C. Ernest Dawn, "The Origins of Arab Nationalism," in *The Origins,* 8–11.

41. Voll, *Islam.*

42. On ideas about the Muslim nation state, see James P. Piscatori, *Islam in a World of Nation States* (New York: Cambridge University Press, 1986).

7

Remaking Jewish Identity in France

Irwin Wall

On October 2, 1997, the Socialist government of France, headed by Lionel Jospin, opened the archives of the period of the Vichy regime to historians with the following explanation: "It is the duty of the Republic to perpetuate the memory of the events which took place in our country between 1940 and 1945. Historical research is in this respect essential. The works and the publications of historians provide an effective weapon with which to struggle against forgetfulness, distortions of history, and the alteration of memory. They thus help permit the recollection of the period to remain vivid and truthful."[1] In the context of French postmodernism this statement may appear to express naive faith in the objectivity of the historian. But given the widely divergent paths of historical inquiry and popular memory in the modern period in France, historical writing has become a matter of critical importance: witness the "Assassins of Memory," as Pierre Vidal-Naquet has characterized the Holocaust-denial industry, which is, or has been, as active in France as in Orange County.[2] The recent exposure of the tortured history of the Vichy era through serious historical inquiry and a series of highly publicized trials has displaced carefully constructed myths and forced the French nation to come to grips with its elusive and troubled past. Jean-François Lyotard, who has characterized belief in the external reality of history as "referentialist credulity bordering on stupidity," refuses to consign historical inquiry with regard to Vichy and the Shoah to the realm of fictive construction. On the contrary, "History as science," he says, "can resist the forgetting lodged in edifying history, prevent it from 'telling stories,' ... critique the inevitable illusion whose victim is consciousness. ..."[3] No group has had a greater interest in pushing forward this process of "critiquing the inevitable illusion" than France's Jewish population, today between 500,000 and 600,000 strong, animated by a new vitality and directly concerned in the face of Holocaust-deniers and Vichy apologists alike to establish some version of historical "truth" as the basis for popular memory.[4]

Forcing France to come to terms with its wartime past has been a victory of sorts for French Jews, but a costly one. It has arguably contributed to the centrality of Vichy and the Holocaust or Shoah to Jewish self-consciousness, and memorializing the Holocaust is in itself a frail reed upon which to hang the prospects for a meaningful Jewish identity. Bernard Wasserstein has recently termed it a "necrophilic obsession" through which "European Jews have succumbed to a potentially destructive sickness."[5] Israeli historian Evyatar Friesel deplores the proliferation of Holocaust monuments and museums. The Holocaust's "acid consequences," he warns, "continue to gnaw away at the foundations of the Jewish people."[6]

The problem is similar for the other pole of contemporary Jewish identity, in France as elsewhere: solidarity with and the defense of the State of Israel. The dilemma facing French Jewry since the Revolution of 1789 has been that of a community trying to affirm its specificity in a society whose Jacobin tradition has seemed to demand complete assimilation and uniformity. Israel offers a paradoxical solution to this dilemma, according to Shmuel Trigano, who has termed Zionism and the infatuation with Israel "the most rigorous and effective rationalization of the structural ambivalence of Jewish life in France: the only way for the Jews to exist in France is to be elsewhere."[7] Lobbying for Israel, "being elsewhere," is the most acceptable way for French Jews to affirm themselves in the French body politic, since France's policies toward the Jewish state are no longer as critical to its survival as they once were. The danger in unconditional support for Israel for diaspora Jews, however, is its dependence on the popular perception of the validity and justice of Israeli policy, increasingly problematic since the accession of the Likud party to power in 1977. More serious is the apparent inability of Israeli society to resist polarization between religious and secular Jews. All this makes ever more cogent the question of whether a political myth, in this case Zionism, can or should function as the basis of a religious and cultural identity, any more than commemoration of a historic victimization like the Holocaust.

The question I want to ask in what follows is, given the unsatisfactory nature of the Holocaust and Israel as sources of meaningful identity for French Jews (or for American Jews for that matter), can that embattled community find elsewhere in its midst the elements for the making of a modern Jewish identity in the diaspora? The question is important, for if the answer is "no," the community with its declining birth rate and high rate of intermarriage, may well be on its way, in Wasserstein's words, to becoming a "disembodied memory." But the answer I want to argue for here is "yes." Powerful voices, for the most part those of intellectuals, have offered meaningful alternatives, two of whom have already had a profound impact: Alain

Finkielkraut and Emmanuel Lévinas. The question that remains is whether their constructions of contemporary French-Jewish identity can be translated into a meaningful program for French Jews.

The diaspora in France is presently composed of a variety of identities, as is typical of Jewish communities everywhere. Identity, like memory, is an object of passionate study and concern in the broader intellectual culture in France, much more so than in the United States; one may even term it a French rather than Anglo-Saxon problem. On one level, to pose the problem of identity is to ask a question that answers itself. Asa Kasher defines identity with a group as the fact that a person considers himself or herself a member, and the group, or a consensus of the group, agrees that the individual concerned should be regarded as a member.[8] But it is precisely this pragmatic kind of definition that French thinkers, concerned crucially with difference and the "other" in the fashioning of identity, eschew. For French thinkers identity has always been an existential question and involves a personal and philosophical consciousness of being and a lived experience. Whether pragmatically or existentially defined, Jewish identity in France today involves a mix of elements: consciousness of a shared family and community history; memory of the Holocaust; a sense of solidarity with Israel; and an awareness of minority status in a broader, non-Jewish society with distinct boundaries between Judaism and Christianity: atheism and noninvolvement by members of the community are more easily accepted among more committed Jews than is conversion to Christianity. French Jews are also part of European and French culture; they share a belief in the unity of the Jewish people worldwide, yet have an acute sense of their difference, as French men and women, from other Jews.[9] Reflecting the contemporary French transition from a unitary to a multicultural state, French Jews have also been redefining themselves, like Jews in Britain and the United States, as an ethnic group rather than as previously, as a religious minority.

The self-definition of French Jews is further complicated by the preexisting definitions that exist in France. French intellectuals have historically fashioned an identity for Jews since the Dreyfus affair. For nationalists the Jews served as the other against which a French identity rooted in the national soil could be constructed, while democratic intellectuals have used the Jews as the bellwether of democracy in France and, in exchange, demanded from them assimilation to the point of the submergence of their identity. Postwar French intellectuals have defined an "essential" Judaism historically and philosophically, as may be seen in the thought of philosophers from Sartre to Derrida. Jean-Paul Sartre defined the Jew in terms of what the antisemite made of him or her. Judaism for Sartre was a "situation," independent of Jews themselves, inherent in the broader society of which they were a part.[10] Antisemites defined the Jew; authentic Jews accepted their situation with pride, inauthentic ones tried to escape it through futile attempts at assimilation. Sartre denied the Jews a history of their own and knew little of Jewish religion or culture; although he was clearly an "anti-antisemite," his construction of the Jew used many stereotypes borrowed from the antisemitic tradition.[11]

In the Sartrean tradition, the influential cultural critic Jean-François Lyotard characterizes the Jews as the quintessential other in the European past: "the jews" (Lyotard uses lower case to distinguish them mythically from real Jews) have the role of remaining in exile and spreading the word of Kant to the world. They bear witness to the forgotten: Europe's or Western civilization's debt to the law.[12] The consequence, for Lyotard, is that "What is most real about real Jews is that Europe does not know what to do with them. Monarchs expel them, Republics assimilate them, Christians demand their conversion, Nazis exterminate them."[13] Lyotard also borrows heavily from Freud and his French interpreter, Lacan: the Jews represent conscience, which Europe often rebels against and would prefer to forget; as a constant reminder of obligation to the law, "real Jews" incur resentment and hatred. Lyotard uses the Jewish condition as paradigmatic of the modern world diasporas and celebrates Jewish intellectuals like Freud, Benjamin, Adorno, and Arendt for their resultant intellectual freedom and creative power.[14] Lyotard's thought is echoed in the ideas of other critics like Maurice Blanchot and Jean-Luc Nancy. For these theorists, the Jews become their role or their function in Europe's past, not independent agents making their own history.

The "real Jews" of France in any case hardly conform to this monolithic picture of a single people defined by an irreducible essence. One way of characterizing French Jewish identities is by degrees of observance and militance: on one end of the spectrum are the religiously observant; a much larger group at the center attends synagogue with varying degrees of frequency and observes tradition in part, while remaining active in Jewish organizations; and at the far edge are those who are mildly or not at all observant but retain a vague sense of identity.[15] One may superimpose on this schematic picture a historical stratification: native French Jews at the time of the Revolution of 1789 numbered a scant forty thousand. About half were Sephardim in the southwest, of Spanish origins: these were well established and prosperous at the time of the revolution and looked down upon their Ashkenaz cousins in Alsace. So distinct were the two communities that the National Assembly emancipated them separately, initially hesitant to apply the "rights of man and citizen" readily granted to the Sephardim equally to the Yiddish-speaking Alsatians.

The communities blended and adopted a kind of Franco-Judaic creed in the nineteenth century that identified France and democracy with Jewish ideals, France was Zion and Paris the New Jerusalem. Napoleon established the Consistory as the corporate voice of the Jews of France, in which capacity it functions to some extent today; from Napoleonic times France has had a "Grand Rabbi" who serves as the religious collective voice of the community, however imperfectly. The Jews of France acculturated well in the nineteenth century, but they did not entirely assimilate; they adopted the French language and became patriotic Frenchmen, but retained and expressed, religiously or otherwise, their Jewish identity. Their synagogues were never formally "Reformed" as in Germany, but there did emerge a modernized French rite with formalized decorous services combining the use of French and Hebrew. Some Jews became entirely secular yet retained their ties to the community and their distinctive lifestyles. Their success in penetrating the professions, the intellectual life of the country, and the highest levels of the French state coincided with the rise of modern antisemitism.[16] The ironies of the Dreyfus affair were that in no other country of Europe were Jews so readily accepted as to rise to the position of aide to the General Staff of the army, which Captain Dreyfus was when he was wrongly accused of treason, and the affair was experienced by French Jews as a victory for justice, in that Dreyfus was finally exonerated, rather than a harbinger of terrible things to come.[17]

Moreover, by the 1890s the immigration from eastern Europe had begun, which was greatly augmented in the 1920s when France was starved for labor after losing 1.4 million soldiers in World War I. Still more came in the 1930s from Poland, Germany, and Austria, refugees from Hitler's oppression or other forms of antisemitism; by World War II the Jewish population of France numbered some 330,000. About two-thirds enjoyed citizenship and most of the Yiddish speakers distinguished themselves from the native French Jews by their radical politics. There were Yiddish-speaking branches of the trade unions and the Socialist and Communist parties in France: the historian Stephen Schuker has argued that the leftist orientation of Jewish politics in the 1930s was at least in part responsible for the virulent antisemitism of Vichy. Pierre Birnbaum rather attributes antisemitism to the role of "State Jews," a group of secular Jewish Republican politicians and state servants who were particularly influential in disestablishing the Catholic Church, legalizing divorce, and implementing other lay reforms that shaped the character of the modern state.[18] Among its "State Jews," France has had several Premiers, among them Léon Blum, who in 1936 and 1937 established the foundations of the modern welfare state, and Pierre Mendès France, who settled the Indochina War in 1954. Mendès France, who was mentored by Blum in the 1930s, in turn sponsored the career of a young associate, François Mitterrand, who went on to be president of the Fifth Republic from 1981 to 1995.

That Jews could accede to the highest office of the French government did not lessen the sense of rupture between France and its Jews created by the war and the Vichy regime. To be sure, this was initially masked by the myth of the French Resistance, which went almost unchallenged until 1970;

Pétain was to be regarded as the shield, and de Gaulle the sword, of French liberation. If de Gaulle, as leader of the Free French, could lay claim to the title of French liberator by the force of arms, Pétain, although imprisoned as a collaborator, had at least tried to protect the French, and particularly French Jews, from a worse fate than the one they actually endured from 1940 to 1944. Pétain's regime had allowed the deportation of foreign Jews resident in France, but it allegedly had done so without knowledge of their ultimate fate, while French Jews remained protected.[19] Thus was constructed a double strategy of forgetting, in which the thought of Sartre was accomplice: all France was said to be Resistant, at least in spirit, while collaboration was un-French, a consequence of seduction by the Germans. Many Jews themselves bought into this mythology, which provided them with a measure of comfort.

The period from 1967 to 1973, sandwiched by the Six-Day and Yom Kippur Wars, was a turning point in the history of postwar Europe, both east and west, but even more specifically for postwar French Jewry. Pride in Israel's achievements galvanized Jews everywhere, but French Jews were embittered when their government appeared to turn against the Jewish state and de Gaulle accompanied his policy turn with a seemingly gratuitous antisemitic remark. The simultaneous shock of the failure of the *gauchistes,* or extreme left, to support Israel forced a rethinking of one of the axioms of Jewish diaspora politics, the historic association of Jews and the political left. In May 1968 some of the most prominent leaders of the student insurrection were Jews, including its putative leader, the media star Daniel Cohn-Bendit. By the 1970s, however, intellectuals like Bernard-Henri Lévy and André Glucksmann were evolving toward the antitotalitarian school of the new French conservatism, while some, most notably Benny Lévy, onetime Maoist and associate of Sartre, spearheaded the Ba'al Teshuva movement, a return to Orthodox practice.[20] After the Yom Kippur War an apparent reappearance of antisemitism in France troubled the tranquility of the community; there were several notorious terrorist attacks on synagogues, Holocaust revisionism appeared, and a new antisemitic political right tried to achieve respectability.

More important in this period was the end of reticence about the Holocaust and the birth of its appearance as a problematic source of identity for French Jews. The French experience of the Holocaust had a specificity of its own in the record of the Vichy regime; preoccupation with it meant reestablishing and coming to terms with the relationship between French Jewry and the nation of which they were a part. France as a whole began coming to terms with its past, a process baptized by one historian as "the Vichy syndrome."[21] French Jewry undertook a simultaneous process of soul-searching that resulted in a variety of attempts to create a meaningful identity in the diaspora.

France's postwar Jewish population was about 250,000; it grew to about 550,000 by the 1970s, by which time slightly more than half were refugees from North Africa. This infusion of North African Jews brought a powerful return to a traditionalist presence. Algerian Jews were the majority of the Sephardim who came to France and, as French citizens since 1870, constitute a curious instance in the history of modern Zionism, having been the only Jewish refugee community to face an absolutely free choice between emigration to Israel and settling in the diaspora, since France also recognized them as citizens. Of 140,000 only about 15,000 chose Israel.[22] There were good reasons for this choice: the French economy was booming in the 1960s, the Algerian Jews were for the most part French-educated, and rumors already were circulating of discrimination against Sephardic Jews in Israel. But Algerian Jews had also suffered during the war; under Vichy's antisemitism even the most assimilated of them were excluded from the French nation and forced to experience their Jewishness, however tenuous it was then felt to be, by having to wear the yellow star, hide, or suffer deportation and death.

The Algerians were augmented by immigrants from Tunisia and Morocco, and North African Jews soon became a majority of the Jewish community of France, profoundly altering the character of Jewish neighborhoods and changing the makeup of Jewish organizations, which absorbed them in large numbers. Religiously they gravitated into the Consistory system, which soon reflected more Orthodox religious practice; in the 1980s the Grand Rabbinate passed from Ashkenazic to Sephardic hands. Although Moroccan and Tunisian Jews retained a powerful sense of identity with their countries of origin, Algerian Jews had been French citizens and French-educated for a much longer time, and the radicalism of the Algerian rebellion had repelled them to the side of the colonialist French. But common to all three communities was the agony of decolonization; for the Algerians, in particular, seven years of bloody conflict followed by sudden massive displacement from countryside and homes they and their ancestors had inhabited for two thousand years replaced or competed with the recent memory of the Holocaust and Vichy in terms of trauma.[23] About half the Tunisian and Moroccan communities, unlike the Algerians, took up residence in Israel. Families were divided between France and Israel and the flow of traffic between the two countries took on large proportions. This cultural flow has had a significant impact on the consciousness of French Jews, making Israel, like the Holocaust, an underpinning of the new French Jewish identity.

The altered historical understanding of the Vichy era in France affected both communities, Sephardic and Ashkenazic. The explosion of the myth of France as a nation of resisters occurred early in the 1970s. Robert Paxton's book on Vichy became a media sensation. Based on a careful study of

German documents of the period, it argued that Vichy was not neutral, but rather aspired to be a junior partner of the Nazis in the "new order" being constructed by Hitler in Europe.[24] Vichy involved both an active policy of collaboration and a process of internal revolution based on repudiation of the Republican tradition born of the Revolution of 1789 and the establishment of an authoritarian regime of fascist allure. Vichy's antisemitism was a part of this policy and was homegrown; the French *statut des Juifs* of October 1940, which excluded French Jews from the body politic and the intellectual and social life of the nation, owed nothing to German pressure and was followed by wholesale expropriations of Jewish property and eventually deportations. Both French and foreign Jews were interned in concentration camps in France.[25] The Vichy regime, despite its blatant antisemitism, initially enjoyed the overwhelming support of the French population, only a small minority of whom participated actively in the Resistance.

As many as 75,000 French Jews were deported directly to Auschwitz, most from a concentration camp in Drancy, just north of Paris. Only about 2,000 of these survived. Perhaps the most despicable act of the regime was the mass roundup of Parisian Jews, over 12,000, on July 16, 1942, their enclosure in squalid conditions in the Vel d'Hiver stadium, and their internment at Drancy for deportation to Auschwitz. The Germans specifically excluded children under 16, but the French insisted for "humanitarian" reasons that the children accompany their parents. The Germans relented, accepting 1,200 of them, who were sent later to join their parents in Auschwitz. This deportation of children made a mockery of French claims to deport only foreign Jews, since they were French citizens by birth. It was organized by René Bousquet, Vichy's head of the police, and later the target of attempts to prosecute Vichy figures for crimes against humanity.

Other historians have mitigated this bleak picture of Vichy France. Of France's 330,000 Jews in 1939, 265,000 survived: some were protected by Vichy as French citizens, some had the good fortune to live in the Italian-occupied zone of France, many escaped across the Spanish or Swiss frontiers, and the majority simply disappeared in the interior, where their strangeness was ignored by their neighbors, who for the most part declined to denounce them to the authorities. If Vichy collaborated, argues Susan Zuccotti, the French people in their totality did not.[26] It is often remarked, and probably a truism, that France was 90 percent for Marshal Pétain in 1940 and 90 percent for General de Gaulle in 1944. The salient question is when one changed and whether one acted on one's new beliefs. In the end there were few who resisted violently (1 to 2 percent, according to estimates, and 20 percent of these were probably Jews), and even fewer who, like de Gaulle, opposed the regime as early as 1940.

The Marcel Ophuls film *Le Chagrin et la Pitié*, which appeared in 1970, focused on the medium-sized city of Clermont-Ferrand, showing that the majority of its population identified with, or accommodated themselves to, Vichy's antisemitism. Vichy now became a topic of debate in the media and film. The most prominent tended to minimize popular complicity in Nazi persecutions, however, and showed individual acts of heroism by French men and women. But Jewish filmmakers, particularly Claude Lanzmann in *Shoah,* sensitized the public to the darker reality of the Holocaust, even though Lanzmann concentrated on Poland. "The Vichy syndrome" obsessed the nation and persisted into the 1990s, exacerbated by the trials of the war criminals Klaus Barbie, Paul Touvier, René Bousquet, and Maurice Papon.

The controversy over Vichy was played out in the media in the late 1980s and early 1990s as a result of these spectacular trials and the increased prominence of the National Front, which is overtly antisemitic. Its leader, Jean-Marie Le Pen, who got 15 percent of the vote in the 1995 presidential election, has called Auschwitz a "detail." Holocaust Revisionism flourished in France; the influential *Le Monde* opened its columns to it for a brief period, although it remains technically illegal. But more than this, the prosecution and trial of Klaus Barbie, whom the Mitterrand government brought back from Paraguay, followed by the affairs of Paul Touvier, René Bousquet, and most recently Maurice Papon, sensitized opinion, riveting it on controversy over Vichy. Barbie, the German Commandant of the area of Lyon, was responsible for massive deportations of Jews. His trial was meant to be used for didactic purposes, but instead it became a milestone in exposing the problematic nature of using the system of justice to address the Holocaust and Vichy. Barbie's overly clever lawyers, one of Vietnamese, the other of Algerian descent, managed to put French imperialism and the State of Israel on trial instead of mounting a defense, making the didactic effects of the trial difficult to judge, but infuriating both the prosecuting attorneys and the numerous Jewish activists who filed briefs as friends of the court.[27] Barbie, the defense argued, had only done in France what the French had done in Algeria and the Israelis in Palestine.

René Bousquet, the chief of police in Paris under Vichy, had been tried for treason after the war. In his defense he had argued that he protected the autonomy of the French police from the Nazis. This meant, in reality, that the French did the dirty work of rounding up Jews instead of leaving it to the Germans, but the court accepted the argument. He was acquitted of treason, but was reprimanded for having committed "national indignity" and received a commuted sentence. The lenient treatment enabled him to become a banker and financier, a bankroller of the Radical Party, and a friend of Mitterrand, who stuck by him even after he was accused in 1978 of having ordered the deportation of Jews. The justice system proved reluctant to try Bousquet, however, and he was not prosecuted until 1989 and was finally indicted for crimes against humanity in 1991. Despite this, he was left at large, and was murdered by a mentally disturbed publicity seeker in June 1993 without having served any time in prison.[28] The delays in this case dramatically illustrated the reluctance of the French judiciary to prosecute and try crimes against humanity; but they also served to keep the issue of Vichy before the public, causing the press to return to it repeatedly, and perhaps fulfilling the didactic purposes of those who brought forth the evidence for the prosecution.

Paul Touvier's prosecution most fully revealed the contemporary French ambiguity about Vichy. As director of *milice* [French gestapo] operations and head of intelligence, Touvier had ordered the murders of prominent public figures and ordered prisoners deported in reprisal for acts carried out by the Resistance. He was convicted of treason after the war and condemned to death in absentia, having escaped to South America before trial. He later returned and was hidden and befriended by contacts in the Catholic Church, who interceded on his behalf with President Pompidou in 1971 and obtained a pardon for him. In 1973 the French Nazi-hunter and historian Serge Klarsfeld charged him with crimes against humanity, leading again to a long procedural wrangle. He was not arrested and scheduled for trial until 1989. The specific crime the prosecution managed to come up with involved his deporting of seven Jews from the village of Rilleux-la-Pape in 1944.

Touvier was released in 1991 because of illness, causing a massive public outcry, and in 1992 the high court overturned his indictment on the ground that the deportations ordered by Vichy were "war crimes," and subject to the statute of limitations. Only "crimes against humanity" perpetrated by the Germans were exempt from the statute. This led to a reversal of tactics by those seeking to prosecute Touvier. In order to get a conviction, it was now necessary to prove that he acted at the behest of the "totalitarian" Germans rather than Vichy, and this necessitated arguments that the *milice* was in fact a tool of the Germans, the opposite of what, for didactic purposes, Klarsfeld and others had originally wanted to prove. Touvier was finally convicted in 1994 and sent to prison, where he soon died.[29] But in the end it was hard to conclude that anything had been achieved, in that the Germans, not the Vichy regime, were blamed for his crime.

Jewish opinion in France was galvanized by these cases, however, and reached a new level of militancy; Jews began actively to commemorate the Holocaust, building monuments and organizing exhibitions. Klarsfeld enumerated all the Jews deported from France and published a memorial book with the pictures and identity cards of twelve hundred Jewish children deported to Auschwitz during the war.[30] Jews demanded that the government drop the fiction that it was not responsible for the crimes committed during the war in its name, accept responsibility for the crimes of Vichy, and apologize. This the government was loathe to do, in particular President François Mitterrand, who wanted the country to put the disputes over Vichy behind it and avoid the burden of paying financial compensation to victims.

The revelations of Mitterrand's personal role in Vichy, where he served in the ministry of war veterans until November 1943, a year later than previous accounts had publicized, further agitated the debate. Mitterrand, who had always been regarded as a hero of the Resistance, confirmed rumors that he had been decorated by Pétain, but denied knowing anything about the persecution of the Jews during the war and asserted on television that Vichy protected native French Jews, which he must have known to be patently false. His fascist transgressions as a youth could perhaps be forgiven, and he did eventually join the Resistance and headed up a group that actively fought the Germans. He did manage to avoid any overt expression of personal anti-semitism, and he had many Jewish associates and political allies, both after the war and during his presidency. But the revelations of his friendship with Bousquet after the war enraged many of his closest associates and made his arguments that the French government was not responsible for Vichy ring hollow. He also was careful to make gestures to the French right by placing a wreath on the grave of Marshall Pétain every year on the anniversary of his death. Although he refused to acknowledge Vichy's crimes as a responsibility of the government or state, in 1993 he declared July 16 a "day of remembrance" of the Jewish deportations. It remained for President Jacques Chirac in 1995 to take the courageous step of admitting the government's responsibility for crimes against Jews during the war and offering an apology. More recently there has been official study of the possibility of compensating some Jews for despoiled property.

Chirac's action opened the way to a rash of apologies. In a public ceremony at Drancy on September 30, 1997, the Catholic Church officially apologized to the Jews of France for the church's complicity by silence in Vichy's persecutions during the war. On October 7, 1997, the day the Papon trial opened, the French police laid a wreath on the monument to the deportees on Île de la Cité and apologized to the Jewish community for the police's role in the roundup and deportation of Jews during the war. But as the trial of Maurice Papon unfolded, voices on the political right dissociated themselves from Chirac's apology. Papon mounted a spirited defense, and the mood in the country seemed to be running against further exposure of Vichy's crimes. Conan and Rousso, in their book *Vichy: un passé qui ne passe pas* had argued two years earlier against the utility of further trials, and Mitterrand revealed to a journalist that he saw no real purpose being served by them either. It is also true that the preoccupation with exposure of Vichy's crimes paralleled the rise of the National Front to a position of prominence in French politics, although the movement was undoubtedly propelled more by the high unemployment rate and resentment of immigrants, mostly

Arabs, than by the trials themselves. Le Pen also never deigned to hide his antisemitism, although its overt expression was forbidden by law.[31]

This tortured history shows that preoccupation with the Holocaust and Vichy has been a troubled and unfortunate way in which to construct a French Jewish identity. The focus on solidarity with and the defense of Israel has unfortunately also been riddled with pitfalls. Enthusiasm among French Jews for the birth of the State of Israel in 1948 was tempered by a feeble history of Zionism in France and the desire not to call attention to themselves. Even after the experience of Vichy, few of the surviving French Jews showed any desire to emigrate to Israel, and relatively few have done so since. However, the French government in the immediate postwar period assisted eastern European Jewish survivors in their efforts to run the British blockade of Palestine, and weapons were exported from France to the nascent Jewish state during its independence struggle. Jews who admired Israel found their feelings mirrored among Resisters in the French government (many Jews also returned to positions of political prominence in the Fourth Republic), and when the Algerian War began in 1954 the French government began to perceive the Israelis as natural allies in what became an anti-Arab struggle. The Franco-Israeli alliance was sealed in 1955 with the delivery of heavy arms, training for Israeli pilots on French Mystère jets, and ultimately nuclear collaboration. The French shared their expertise and uranium with Israel, whose scientists in turn assisted in the production of the French bomb, and the French reactors and the Israeli reactor at Dimona came on line almost simultaneously. In the Suez Crisis of 1956, the French drew first the Israelis and then the British into their scheme to invade Egypt and topple Nasser, whom they regarded as the inspiration behind Algerian nationalism. Although Suez failed, the Franco-Israeli alliance endured through the coming of de Gaulle, who admired Ben Gurion and appreciated the role French Jews had played in the Resistance and in the Free French in London.[32] An astonishing harmony of views existed between French Jews and their government during the Suez crisis, although it did not have the overall effect of galvanizing French Jewry in the way that the Six-Day War did eleven years later.[33]

No sooner had French Jews thrilled to the sight of Israeli-piloted Mirages destroying the Egyptian Air Force on the ground in 1967, however, than the French alliance with Israel was ruptured. In the 1960s de Gaulle gradually reduced French military collaboration with the Jewish state and restored relations with the Arabs. On the eve of the Six-Day War he pointedly warned Israeli ambassador Abba Eban not to attack first. Eban was shocked; among the capitals of Washington, London, and Paris, French support was the one he had most counted on. After Israel ignored his warning, de Gaulle slapped an embargo on further arms sales to the Middle East, which harmed only Israel, then France's sole client in the area. The French president added insult to injury when in a November 27, 1967, news conference he referred to the Jews as "an elite people, sure of itself and domineering." There were no substantive examples of de Gaulle being antisemitic, and he may genuinely have been surprised by the outcry the remark caused. He eventually made a kind of apology, telling Grand Rabbi Kaplan at a New Year's reception the following January that he had meant the remark to be a compliment. Given his ideas, this is not unlikely, but the remark was echoed after the bombing of the French synagogue on rue Copernic in 1980, when Premier Raymond Barre deplored the deaths of Jews and "innocent French bystanders," implying that the Jewish victims were neither innocent nor French.

Damage was done by such official insensitivity. French Jews' enthusiasm for Israel, moreover, continued to grow as French foreign policy turned further against the Jewish state, continuing along these lines until Mitterrand's election in 1981. France openly backed the aspirations if not the terrorist methods of the PLO. Consequently Henry Hajdenberg organized Renouveau Juif and called for Jews to vote against Giscard d'Estaing in favor of Mitterrand in the elections of 1981. This had previously been taboo among French Jews, although their greater sympathy for parties of the left was no secret. Moreover, in no way could a "Jewish vote," even if it were demonstrated to have existed in France, have mattered much, since Jews were only 1 percent of the electorate; only in a few districts that were heavily populated by Jews could it have made a difference. Nevertheless, it is estimated that 68 percent of Jews in 1981 did vote for Mitterrand, and he responded by visiting Israel in 1982, as promised in his campaign. There was no doubt of the centrality of Israel in the affections of French Jews in the 1980s: in a poll among French Jews carried out in 1987 with regard to their attitudes toward Israel, 66 percent put it first as the land of their ancestors and 21 percent as a future place of refuge for Jews "in case." The astounding figure of 80 percent of adults had been there at least once, and less than 2 percent declared themselves opposed to its existence.[34]

The Israeli invasion of Lebanon in 1982 and the ensuing massacres in the Palestinian refugee camps showed the dangers and pitfalls of the Israeli pole of Jewish identity. The French press and media seemed at times to be overtly anti-Israel, and French Jews attacked the media for pro-Palestinian bias. The most prominent intellectual spokesmen for the community, Emmanuel Lévinas and his student Alain Finkielkraut, went on Jewish radio to attempt to mitigate the damage. Finkielkraut also wrote a short, polemical book in defense of the Jewish state.[35] On the other hand, even the periodical of the influential Fonds Social Unifié Juif, *L'Arche,* carried articles critical of Israeli policy, which the Israeli embassy actually protested against.[36]

The difficulty in putting one's Jewish identity in Israeli hands was exposed by Lévinas's insistence that for Jews to exercise political power required a state bound by a moral code of conduct; Israel must be religious, Lévinas wrote, meaning also moral, or it must not be. But does not the function of a modern state lie in its ability to make war and thus to violate moral codes where necessary in the "national interest?" If Lévinas himself could not on that occasion draw the conclusion of the untenable nature of his argument, others like Shmuel Trigano were willing to do so. The Israeli ambassador to France in the 1980s, Ovadia Soffer, said Israel still remained central to the collective life of French Jews: it "alone has the spiritual substance to save their children from de-judaization."[37] The Oslo Accords brought a moment of respite in the tension over Israel between the French Republic and its Jews, but the election of Netanyahu has again brought renewed polemics against the Jewish state in the French and French Jewish press and the withdrawal of French government support from Israel's policies, while the Jewish community in France remained divided, having invested heavily in the prospect of peace. The "Who is a Jew?" controversy in Israel, which threatened to deny the law of return to Conservative and Reform Jews, also divided the community. In all this Israel revealed itself to be as problematic as the Holocaust in serving as the major prop of French Jewish identity. Nevertheless, this did not stop French Jews, particularly the young, from visiting Israel in large numbers and drawing inspiration from it.

For Orthodox Jews in France identity has never been a problem; it is bound up neither with Israel nor with the Holocaust, important as those are, but with their rituals and faith. But though their numbers may be growing, only a small minority of the French Jews are Orthodox. What other poles of identity remain? Jewish culture and memory; the languages of the old country, whether Yiddish, Ladino, or Judeo-Arabic; and a sense of shared destiny all play their part. Advocates of reconnecting with the ruptured Jewish past exist for each of these choices; one of the most eloquent has been Richard Marienstras, a Shakespearean scholar, who has advocated a revival of Yiddish culture in France replete with its Bundist (in the United States, Workman's Circle-Socialist) overtones.[38] To be sure, Marienstras speaks also of the immutable ties between Jews of the diaspora and Israel. When Israel is threatened, so are Jews everywhere. But Marienstras insists that the Jews have always been and can remain a transnational people. He refuses to accept that he must chose between France and Israel, whether the argument that he must do so came from French nationalists or Zionists.

Marienstras is only one of a number of French intellectuals who have advocated ways in which Jewish identity in France can be re-created or reconstructed. Albert Memmi's *Portrait d'un Juif* is an essential text, but his preoccupations with colonialism (he is Tunisian) led him to espouse Zionism as the answer to Jewish identity in Israel and the diaspora.[39] One should also note the works of the political scientist Pierre Birnbaum, whose studies of antisemitism in France have been pathbreaking, and Shmuel Trigano, who scorns the Zionist attachment for French Jewry and instead seems to advocate a kind of diaspora binationalism. Even the maverick Anarchist Pierre Goldman defined his identity in terms of Auschwitz. There has been the Yiddish revival led by a professor at the Sorbonne, Rachel Ertel; the revival of Hassidic activity, peculiarly transcending the Ashkenazy-Sephardic rift; and the Yeshiva organized by the Ba'al Teshuva advocates of the May 1968 generation (Benny Lévy).[40] A generation of young intellectuals inspired by Emmanuel Lévinas has begun to engage traditional Jewish texts, and the community has put a good deal of emphasis on the making of an infrastructure for Jewish education. There has also been systematic inquiry into questions of Jewish identity by a good many French novelists, in particular Georges Perec, who, since his premature death of lung cancer in 1982, has become something of a cult figure.[41]

Two thinkers, Alain Finkielkraut and Emmanuel Lévinas, have done the most in terms of conceptualizing Jewish identity in postwar France. Finkielkraut is very much the stereotype of the French intellectual, in addition to his importance to Jewish issues. The book that brought him immediate fame was *La défaite de la pensée,* which polemically denounced cultural relativism, third-world nationalism, multiculturalism, postmodernism, and German Romantic thought in a scant 125 pages.[42] The book has been compared to Alan Bloom's *The Closing of the American Mind,* although it might better be compared to Robert Hughes's *The Culture of Complaint.* Finkielkraut has also written books on the Barbie trial and the Holocaust-denial phenomenon, which in France has been a phenomenon of a certain left wing as well as the political right. Finkielkraut argues that, like Socialists during the Dreyfus affair who argued that Dreyfus, as a bourgeois, was unworthy of proletarian involvement on his behalf, leftist Holocaust deniers have tried to maintain that there is no objective difference in the scale of cruelty perpetrated by Nazis and the democratic but imperialist regimes of the other countries.[43] Finkielkraut is a convincing media figure, moreover, attractive and soft-spoken, which enables him to take positions that are unpopular in the community but still remain something of a cult hero. In 1994 he spearheaded a group of French intellectuals who tried to contest the European parliamentary elections on a pro-Muslim Bosnian ticket.[44]

It is *The Imaginary Jew* that has shown Finkielkraut most capable of a profound level of intellectual inquiry, although the book is better at defining the problem than offering solutions. In this work Finkielkraut defines his Judaism in terms of absence, or bad faith in the Sartrean sense.[45] That is to say, he feels his Jewish identity is hypocritical; it is proclaimed from the rooftops with pride, but it is empty of content. Finkielkraut rejects claiming the heritage of the Holocaust as an element of his identity: it occurred in his parents' generation, not his own. He was born after the war and although his parents were survivors, he grew up privileged and disdains any sense of victimization. Zionism is also an inappropriate peg for defining his Jewishness: he knows no Hebrew and has no intention of making *aliyah*. Moreover, he rejects ethnically based nationalism and is very much an advocate of the Enlightenment and universal values. His own Jewishness is empty of content; he is assimilated into French culture. He does not know Yiddish, the language that defined his parents' Judaism and its culture. *Imaginaire,* as used in the title of Finkielkraut's work, can have two meanings: it can mean "imaginary" in the sense of a phantasm, devoid of substantive reality, but it also can mean "imagining" in the sense of inventing, reconstructing, or constructing a new Jewish identity appropriate to the diaspora in the twenty-first century.

Hitler, Finkielkraut writes, beyond piling up corpses, succeeded in exterminating Yiddish culture in Europe. One might add that what Hitler did to Yiddishkeit by genocide, the Soviet regime did by forced assimilation, and America by its homogenization of all cultures through attraction. The historical effect was the same in terms of Yiddishkeit's disappearance. It remained the culture of Finkielkraut's parents, but they failed to pass it on to him; in consequence he is left being a Jew without substance, a "luftmensch . . . Jewishness is what I lack, not what defines me; it is the infinitesimal burning of an absence . . . the Jewish people has died twice, once by assassination and once by forgetting." Finkielkraut means to say here that Hassidism has been allowed to monopolize our picture of pre-Holocaust eastern European Jewry, or, we might add, the caricature of it as portrayed in *Fiddler on the Roof,* or even in the paintings of Chagall. "In a deluge of tears the assassination of a senile people is depicted, when in reality it was a living, multiform, creative culture that the Nazis killed."[46] It was not only swaying Hassidim who were murdered by the Nazis, but modern Jews who lived their Judaism through Yiddishkeit, which Finkielkraut would like to see revived as a secular culture with its brilliant literature. Yiddishkeit, he reminds us, was politically and culturally vibrant, and its adherents did not go like "lambs to the slaughter," a caricature created by Zionism to depict Yiddish culture as pacifist and effeminate. Resistance existed and was led by the Zionists and the Communists. The Warsaw ghetto was not an isolated incident; partisan movements existed all over Europe that were headed and staffed by Jews, who made up twenty percent of the armed French Resistance. The issue has been deflected, Finkielkraut argues, by asking how the Jews could allow it to happen to themselves; they did not. The more serious question is where were the allies, where was the church, what did the Polish or European Resistance movements do? Resignation of the victims was not the uniqueness of the Shoah; abandonment was.

Finkielkraut poses his questions well, and Jews should know their history, particularly the effects of the Holocaust and the brilliance and complexity of Yiddish culture. But the question of whether the revival of Yiddishkeit can become the basis for a Jewish renewal, as Finkielkraut appears to suggest, remains problematic. Yiddish is being studied in universities, but some would argue that is even a more certain sign of its demise. There was a considerable vogue for its study among French Jews of Ashkenazy descent in the 1970s, and it was instituted as a course of study at several French universities, including the prestigious Sorbonne. Doris Bensimon noted its stubborn persistence among some fifteen percent of the French Jewish population who still spoke Yiddish in the 1970s and managed to transmit some of it to their children.[47] Some of the Yiddish study circles continue today, but virtually the only real native speakers of Yiddish left today are the Hassidim and they scorn secular Yiddish culture. This leads us to another suggestion for Jewish renewal, that posed by Emmanuel Lévinas, Finkielkraut's teacher, and the person who more than any other, in Judith Friedlander's term, carried the culture of Vilna to the Seine. Finkielkraut acknowledged his debt to his teacher in a book extolling Lévinas's thought and claiming it as the basis for his own.[48] If Yiddish culture cannot be revived, Lévinas argued, and if religious practice remains an ill-fitting "residue," perhaps Jewish ethics can still be a basis for a culture and a guide to contemporary life.

Lévinas was a Lithuanian Jew who emigrated to France following World War I, became a citizen, and built a career as philosopher that culminated in his becoming professor of philosophy at the Sorbonne.[49] His reputation initially rested upon his role as one of the transmitters and interpreters of German thought in France. Lévinas wrote primarily on Husserl, whose student he was, but he knew Heidegger as well and was a critic of both. While extolling phenomenology as a method, Lévinas was also concerned to demonstrate its limitations as the foundation of meaning. Lévinas was a "dialogic philosopher" in the tradition of Martin Buber and Franz Rosensweig, whose thought profoundly influenced his work. That is to say, he found meaning in human relationships above all else. In that sense Lévinas transcended phenomenology in favor of ethics; rather than trying to found a system of ethics on a rational foundation, the Enlightenment project demonstrably impossible since the thought of Heidegger, Lévinas defined the self in terms of an innately felt sense of responsibility for the other. Lévinas thus elevated ethics to a transcendent level, while he sought to forge a philosophy foregrounded in social justice but simultaneously infused with the highest moral teachings of traditional Judaism.[50] He reintroduced a revelatory if not religious message as the foundation of his outlook. Lévinas argued against Heidegger that philosophy must be ethical before it is ontological, and responsible as well as intelligible. In an interview with Richard Kearney he explained that one's relation to the other is prior to one's ontological relationship to the self and he located this concern for interhuman relationships in biblical rather than secular philosophical thought. Thus it is Lévinas's Jewish sensibility and his indebtedness to Jewish texts that informed his philosophy, rather than the reverse.[51]

This becomes apparent in Lévinas's Jewish writings, in which he outlines his project of a return by contemporary Jews to Judaism's traditional texts, in particular the Talmud. If Torah study is important, Jews must never forget that their culture has been defined and constructed around a particular reading of the Torah that is to be found in the Talmud. It is instructive to contrast Lévinas with another Jewish thinker who dominated the postwar scene in France, André Neher; both shared an intimate acquaintance with Western culture and a desire to integrate it with Judaic ethics. But where Neher wrote almost entirely on the Bible and, under the impact of the Six-Day War, emigrated to Israel, Lévinas stressed the Talmud, a literature created by the Jews to sustain them in exile, and focused his attention on the construction of a viable diaspora in France.[52]

Lévinas did not think the Talmud could be studied on its own terms, nor does he fit in among the academic schools of modern talmudic scholarship, in which he had no formal training. For Lévinas the transformation of the Jews is complete, they no longer speak Hebrew, rather Greek, which is to say they are Westernized (Hellenized), and think in Greek (Western) philosophical terms, and believe and excel in Western science. The Talmud remains vital, yet virtually inaccessible, to Jews as the traditional source of Jewish wisdom and a means to humanize and revitalize their existence in the present secular world. The solution for Lévinas is to translate the Talmud into "Greek," by which he means not a linguistic transformation but a philosophical one; to put its elliptical style into Western expository prose, translate metaphors into concepts, and see what Jewish wisdom has to say that is adaptable to the categories of Western thought and life. Talmudic language, obscure as it seems to the uninitiated, is transposable into philosophical language and can shed light upon philosophical problems, according to Lévinas.[53] It can thus provide the basis for a renewed sense of Jewish identity.

Lévinas finds in the Talmud at once a universal message and a particular one. The particular message is the requirement of distancing and isolation from the society at large that has its foundation in Scriptures and rabbinic literature. The universal one is the message of moral responsibility that Lévinas defines as a "surfeit of responsibility toward humanity." Historically Jews have carried this message as an uncomfortable privilege or perhaps a burden, a "peculiar inequality" that imposes on Jews obligations toward others that they historically have not demanded for themselves in return. This is perhaps what it means to be "chosen." But the talmudic message goes beyond the universal ethical precepts of the West. In the specific commandments it enjoins upon the people of Israel, 613 commandments for the Jews, 7 for the children of Noah, it qualifies its universalist message by imposing upon the Jews a withdrawal from society in many of their daily practices. But by doing so it takes them beyond universalism and provides the means to resist the totalitarian temptation inherent in modern life. Thus Israel becomes a kind of peak of human achievement that makes its survival crucial to everyone, beyond the simple argument of the inherent desirability of cultural diversity.

Lévinas notes that modern reason threatens traditional Judaism and modern science destroys its cosmology. Yet Judaism provides a moral absolute, fidelity to law, and rigid standard that are essential to the continuity of civilization and that are exemplified in a way of living that is both a distinctive ritual and an assertion of human fraternity with those in the non-Jewish world. Dispersed Jews, by virtue of their difference, have become society's voice of moral conscience against the absolutist claims of the modern state, and Jewish particularism functions in the modern world as a bastion against the totalitarian tendency underlying universalism. Religion became a source of justice for Lévinas in a way that political ideology could not. Historically, Judaism has suffered the most from totalitarian ideologies precisely because it forces limitations on the claims of any state that pretends to represent the "march of history." However, for most Western Jews, talmudic and Hebraic studies dried up in the nineteenth century, weakening their observance of ritual and breaking the "contract" or bond between their Judaism and its prophetic morality. But Lévinas insists that modern philosophy and philology have remade of Judaism a living thing and object of study, while exegesis in modern terms also makes it a teaching and can renew its capacity to speak. We can thus rediscover the highest ethical teaching that makes the Jews accountable and responsible for the whole edifice of creation.

Lévinas is ambivalent about assimilation—or perhaps one should say here acculturation—but he regards it an objective sociological process and he accepts the fact that Europeanization has captured all Jews, in the West and in Israel. This is not necessarily something to be deplored, for today European science, art, technology, and democratic politics are everywhere acknowledged to be the norm. Judaism, however, does appear consequently in danger of becoming archaic. Lévinas regards assimilation that becomes de-judaification as a form of betrayal, but he attributes it to profound spiritual reasons that require us to go beyond responses of strengthening the curricula of Jewish schools, or providing better social services. Preventing assimilation "requires an effort to create a culture, in other words a new Jewish life."[54] Jews must recapture Judaism's exceptional universal message.

That universal message includes a feminist one, albeit within limits. Lévinas finds the characteristic Jewish woman in the Hebrew Bible, where they are at the "pivot" of sacred history. All the switches in the difficult path of the Jews are controlled by women, their lucidity, cunning, and sacrifice: "Isaac would have been schooled in the violent games and laughter of his brother but for the painful decision of Sarah; Esau would have triumphed over Israel but for Rebecca's ruse; Laban would have prevented the Return of Jacob but for the complicity of Leah and Rachel; Moses would not have been suckled by his mother if not for Miriam; David, and the Prince of Justice who one day was to be born of him, would not have been possible without Tamar's stubbornness, without Ruth the faithful, or the political genius of Bathsheba." Of course, for the Talmud, "the house is woman." Women remain in the background to make the public life of men possible, and the feminine is an essential category of Being, its essence gentleness. Women love, and thus overcome the alienation resulting from the masculine, cold application of all-conquering reason; theirs is the task of the one "who does not conquer."[55] Consequently, for Lévinas, the feminine becomes the original manifestation of all perfection, indeed the fount of morality; Adam is man and woman joined together; and man without woman diminishes the image of God in the world. Woman completes Man (read humankind) as two totalities complete one another, their personal relation can only be equality itself, and eros is the highest form of communication. In phenomenological terms the man-woman relationship is the one in which one's ethical responsibility for the other appears in its purity. Without ignoring the legitimate claims of feminism to the attainments for women of all that modern civilization has to offer, however, Lévinas still insists on the "mystery" of the feminine, and the necessary modesty of female behavior.[56]

This may not seem capable of satisfying the demands of modern feminism, but it probably squeezes out of biblical and talmudic texts all they are capable of giving on this question, or all that a Lithuanian Jew born at the turn of the century can glean from them. Lévinas has had a mixed reception among French feminists. Luce Irigaray appeared captivated by Lévinas's concept of love as the joining of two distinct Beings, rather than the swallowing of one by the other, but in a later piece she accused him of apprehending the feminine as child-like and the embodiment of animality in humans, reduced to the simple object of male pleasure.[57]

Lévinas attempted to explain the universal message of the ancient Jewish texts in his talmudic readings, most of which originally took the form of lectures given to the French branch of the World Jewish Congress.[58] The Talmud, he insisted, is itself a rational document that tries to make sense of the teaching of the Scriptures; its method is rational inquiry. Lévinas's reading of the Talmud may be fanciful from the standpoint of the talmudic scholar but it may appeal to the modern cultural Jew as a source of practical ethics. For example, in the Mishnah we are told, with regard to Yom Kippur, that forgiveness for sins against God is obtained by prayer and repentance, but forgiveness for sins against another person requires appeasement of that person first, after which that person may still refuse us pardon. Thus, forgiveness of a transgression against God is obtained by our will and is not dependent on God, but forgiveness of sin against another is beyond our powers and dependent on the other. God here appears limited: he is obliged to forgive us when we atone for our sins, but he cannot obtain for us the forgiveness of the other. How is this possible? Lévinas answers that by redefining God in terms of the limits of God's power.

God appears in this homily to be not as a supernatural being, but rather as the principle of justice, the embodiment of moral principles in their absolute, justice and goodness inhabiting a realm beyond truth, as we understand "truth" philosophically in "Greek." God is the attributes we describe him to be, neither more nor less. "The word God," Lévinas wrote in a rather extraordinary statement, "is an overwhelming semantic event."[59] Lévinas explains that the word "God" occurs rarely in his commentaries; it expresses a notion that he says may be religiously clear, but remains philosophically obscure. God is in the relation of the I and the thou, human relations governed by a high moral code. God is in the face of the other, which is also the site of our ethical obligation. Lévinas defines revelation as that moment at which humankind becomes aware of its responsibility for the other; for the Jews this moment came with the gift of the Torah at Sinai.[60] This would almost seem to be a version of the enlightenment concept of a "natural religion" of ethics that is taken to underlie all faiths, whatever the differences in their dogmas. Authentic Judaism is an inner morality, Lévinas says, not an outer dogmatism: "The supernatural is not an obsession for Judaism. Its relationship with divinity is determined by the exact range of the ethical."[61] But Lévinas goes further, even implying a kind of practical atheism, or, if not atheism, at least the risk of it: Judaism does not deny God's existence, of course, but it does claim man's existence outside of God. In revelation, God speaks to man, not within him, making humankind a partner almost on an equal level. Man is made to bear the burden of existence alone, experiencing the world as if atheism were the reality.[62]

Lévinas notes that in a tractate regarding business and commerce, the Talmud dictates that the workers be treated fairly, according to custom, as the descendants of Abraham, Isaac, and Jacob. Lévinas deduces from this section something close to the principle of alienation under capitalism enunciated by Marx and a philosophical basis for trade unionism and democratic socialism. Marx, Lévinas explained, was very much like a biblical prophet; his critique of capitalism was in reality that of an ethical conscience cutting through the false identification of truth with existing reality and demanding that theory be converted into a concrete praxis of concern for the other.[63] We need not go into this teaching in detail, but it perhaps explains why, despite Lévinas's popularity in the non-Jewish as well as the Jewish world of the diaspora, his death went almost unnoticed in contemporary Israel, which arguably has forgotten its Labor origins and where capitalism in the spirit of Reagan and Milton Friedman appears to have run amok. Lévinas was a diaspora thinker; on the question of Israel and its relationship to contemporary Jewry Lévinas was almost ambiguous. He regarded assimilation of the Jews to modernity as a problem equally for Israel and the diaspora. The creation of Israel is one of the most important events in Jewish history, but Lévinas warns against the confusion of a religious idea with the prestige humankind is apt to confer on anything bearing the stamp of the state.[64] Israel's prestige stems from its religious past; it must be inspired by its great books, and it can deduce from Torah the necessity of constructing an avant-garde state on the principles of democracy and socialism. But if Jewish identity is responsibility, a "stiff neck that supports the universe" in moral terms, in Israel it bears the danger of becoming confused with nationalism; and a pagan, imperialist, and oppressive state would be the worst form of idolatry.

Whatever his broader role in French thought, Lévinas exemplified in contemporary French Judaism an intellectual richness at least on a par with the much larger American Jewish community. And the popularity of Lévinas in France may represent a challenge by the French diaspora to Israel's claim to be the unique Jewish homeland as opposed to one of several of them. Richard Cohen offers the intriguing suggestion that Jews consider Buber, Rosenzweig, and Lévinas as the the patriarchs of twentieth-century Jewish thought.[65] Arnold Eisen, in analyzing the growing gulf between American and Israeli Judaism, notes that different interpretations of *galut,* diaspora, and the place of Israel in Jewish theology have developed in the two countries. Israeli theologians tend to agree that the only spiritually fulfilling life for a Jew is in Israel, while American Jewish theologians have constructed a theology that assumes a continued diaspora, with Israel as a kind of spiritual support and place of pilgrimage, but not necessarily of residence.[66] It is tempting to make the same kind of argument for modern Jewish thought in France.

However, French Judaism is less structured than, if denominationally almost as variegated as, its American counterpart, perhaps reflecting the weak organizational or associative nature of French society in general. The vast majority of congregations in France are affiliated with official Consistory Judaism, itself more centralized and hierarchical than any American denomination, and since the 1980s headed by an increasingly Orthodox Sephardic Grand Rabbi. But it is flanked by a fractured ultraorthodox community on the right and a small and less well-developed, if expanding, liberal community on the left. The success of the Lubavitch movement in France, particularly its appeal to Sephardic Jews, is noteworthy. It is more difficult to discern distinct theological voices clarifying the diaspora question from these communities, as they tend to have numerous voices. In further contrast to the United States, arguably the best articulated voices of French Judaism have been nonrabbinical, again a very French cultural phenomenon.

Thus in one sense Lévinas speaks only for himself; he represents no official organization, current of belief, or even congregation of Jews. But it is clear that his philosophical-ethical Judaism articulates the beliefs of a large nonorthodox and moderate segment of French Jewry, and judging from the tributes he received in its official publication, a good part of the French Jewish establishment as well.[67] And while he too stresses the emotional attachment and spiritual significance of Israel for world Jewry, he does not regard Israel as its exclusive center. Indeed, he laments that by accident or design Israel may degenerate (if it has not already done so) into a typical state, certainly no worse, but not much better than most of the others, and he turns his attention to building educational institutions for the diaspora of England, France, and the United States that will enable Jews to return to their traditional texts for guidance for contemporary living.

Neher and Lévinas remained friends, but after the former's emigration to the Jewish state the issue of *aliyah* became something of a barrier between them. During a coffee break at a colloquium at the Van Leer Institute in Jerusalem in honor of Franz Rosenzweig, a participant asked Lévinas when he intended to make *aliyah,* since it was in Israel that the Jewish ethics he preached had the greatest resonance. Lévinas replied to the effect that the Jewish state must not be elevated to a totality; Rosenzweig taught, Lévinas said, that the "judgments" of history must not be confused with justice in the abstract. Israel's historic success, however necessary for the Jewish people, does not incarnate the divine plan. Therefore neither the life nor the thought of the Jewish people can or should be completely absorbed in the state of Israel. Jewish thought expressed the reality of Jewish life quite apart from its territorial or institutional configurations, and in case of need must transcend any Jewish organization or state.[68]

The richness of contemporary French Jewish thought is matched by a new pride in growing up Jewish in France, part of the general focus on regional and ethnic identities in pluralist, even multicultural, France. The Mitterrand government reversed centuries of French governmental policies by decentralizing political power, and it simultaneously abandoned the Jacobin tradition by encouraging regional and ethnic cultural expression with government funds. The French Jewish community is no longer threatened by the Jacobin emphasis on centralization and uniformity. Observers rather fear attrition through a high rate of intermarriage and a low rate of birth. The rate of intermarriage has become a particularly contentious issue in the community and is seen by many as threatening its survival.[69] But among the diverse population apparent on the Paris streets and buses and subways one increasingly sees young people wearing the yellow star, and the contemporary variety tends to be fourteen- or eighteen-karat gold and worn around the neck rather than the sinister patch on one's clothing. More young French Jews know their identity and, as Finkielkraut says, they now affirm it with pride and without any complex. Their challenge is whether they will be able to draw from the richness of French thought in the diaspora the means to construct a new identity with sufficient intellectual, cultural, and ethical-religious content to sustain itself in the face of France's new multicultural society.

NOTES

I want to thank Robert Weiner, Nadia Malinovich, and Jonathan Judaken for reading and commenting upon various drafts of this essay. Howard Wettstein, as editor, has been particularly helpful as colleague and friend.

1. "Circulaire du 2 octobre 1997 relative à l'accès aux archives publiques de la period 1940–1945," *Journal Officiel de la République Français,* October 3, 1997.

2. Pierre Vidal-Naquet, "The Holocaust's Challenge to History," in *Auschwitz and After: Race, Culture, and "the Jewish Question" in France,* ed. Lawrence Kritzman (London: Routledge, 1995), 25–34 .

3. Jean-François Lyotard, *Heidegger and "the jews"* (Minneapolis: University of Minnesota Press, 1990), 9.

4. Voices in France are also arguing that it has gone too far. Former conservative President of the National Assembly Philippe Séguin argued in *Le Monde* that the trial of Maurice Papon was part of a scheme to cast discredit on the memory of de Gaulle, who rehabilitated Papon and made him a minister. Séguin also castigated the spirit of self-flagellation in France, which wrongly held the entire nation responsible for the crimes of a few, while Papon's lawyers argued that he had actually helped Jews while working for the Vichy regime and helped run guns to Israel while an official of the Fourth Republic after the war. The latter claim is entirely within the realm of the possible. See *Le Petit Bouquet* (digest of the French press available on the internet), nos. 166 and 167, October 22 and October 23, 1997. Also *Le Monde,* October 21, 1997.

5. Bernard Wasserstein, *Vanishing Diaspora: The Jews in Europe Since 1945* (Cambridge: Harvard University Press, 1996), 130.

6. Evyatar Friesel, "The Holocaust as a Factor in Contemporary Jewish Consciousness," in *Jewish Identities in the New Europe,* ed. Jonathan Webber (London: Littman Library of Jewish Civilization, 1994), 231.

7. Shmuel Trigano, "From Individual to Collectivity: The Rebirth of the Jewish Nation in France," in *The Jews in Modern France,* ed. Frances Malino and Bernard Wasserstein (Hanover, N.H.: The University Press of New England, 1985), 261.

8. Asa Kasher, "Jewish Collective Identity," in *Jewish Identity,* ed. David Goldberg and Michael Krausz (Philadelphia: Temple University Press, 1993), 56–78.

9. See Norman Solomon, "Judaism in the New Europe: Discovery or Invention," in *Jewish Identities in the New Europe,* ed. Jonathan Webber, 88–94; also the introduction by Jonathan Webber and his essay "Modern Jewish Identities," 74–83.

10. Jean-Paul Sartre, *Antisemite and Jew* (New York: Schocken Books, 1948).

11. Jonathan Judaken, "Jean-Paul Sartre and 'the Jewish Question': The Politics of Engagement and the Image of 'the Jew' in Sartre's Thought, 1930–1980" (Ph.D. diss., University of California, Irvine, 1997).

12. Lyotard, *Heidegger and "the jews,"* 22.

13. Lyotard, *Heidegger and "the jews,"* 3, cited in Michael Weingrad, "Jews (in Theory): Representations of Judaism, Antisemitism, and the Holocaust in Postmodern French Thought," *Judaism* 45, no. 1 (winter 1996): 79–98. Thanks to Murray Baumgarten for calling this article to my attention. In the French language it is customary to use lower case when referring to a religion (protestant, juif) and upper case when referring to a people. When lower case is used for Jews it may indicate the writer believes them a religion or is referring to them as a religious group only. Lyotard's use of the lower case is unique to him.

14. Michael Gluzman, "Modernism and Exile: A View from the Margins," in *InsiderOutsider: American Jews and Multiculturalism*, ed. David Biale, Michael Galchinsky, and Susan Heschel (Berkeley and Los Angeles: University of California Press, 1998), 231–33.

15. Domenique Schnapper, *Jewish Identities in France* (Chicago: University of Chicago Press, 1983).

16. See Pierre Birnbaum, *The Jews of the Republic: A Political History of State Jews in France from Gambetta to Vichy* (Stanford, Stanford University Press, 1996).

17. In fact no jury ever dared find him innocent: he had to be pardoned by the president of the Republic and was only exonerated when the high court threw out his original conviction on a legal violation.

18. Stephen Schucker, "The Origins of the 'Jewish Problem' in the Later Third Republic," in *The Jews in Modern France*, ed. Frances Malino and Bernard Wasserstein, 135–80; Birnbaum, *The Jews of the Republic*.

19. This was indulged by the Jewish historian Robert Aron in his early treatment, *The Vichy Regime* (London: Putnam, 1958), and it was echoed by the conservative Jewish columnist and historian of French Communism Annie Kriegel with regard to the Bousquet and Touvier cases (of which more below). See Eric Conan and Henry Rousso, *Vichy, un passé qui ne passe pas* (Paris: Gallimard, 1996), 163.

20. See Judith Friedlander, *Vilna on the Seine: Jewish Intellectuals in France since 1968* (New Haven: Yale University Press, 1990), 6–21.

21. Henri Rousso, *The Vichy Syndrome: History and Memory in France since 1944* (Cambridge: Harvard University Press, 1991), and Conan and Rousso, *Vichy*.

22. Joëlle Allouche-Benayoun and Doris Bensimon, *Juifs d'Algérie hier et aujourd'-hui: memoires et identités* (Paris: Bibliothèque historique Privat, 1989), 228.

23. See Lucette Valensi, "From Sacred History to Historical Memory and Back: The Jewish Past," *History and Anthropology*, vol. 2 (1986), 283–305. Also Joëlle Bahloul, *The Architecture of Memory: A Jewish-Muslim Household in Colonial Algeria, 1937–1962* (Cambridge: Cambridge University Press, 1996), 115–24.

24. Robert O. Paxton, *Vichy France: Old Guard and New Order* (New York: Columbia University Press, 1972). The French edition sold in the hundreds of thousands, unprecedented for a work of history.

25. Paxton went on to collaborate with Michael Marrus in writing *Vichy France and the Jews* (New York: Basic Books, 1981).

26. Susan Zuccotti, *The Holocaust, the French, and the Jews* (New York: Basic Books, 1993). John Sweets has also offered a corrective to Ophuls's film portrait of Clermont-Ferrand in *Choices in Vichy France* (New York: Oxford University Press, 1986).

27. On the Barbie trial see Alain Finkielkraut, *Remembering in Vain: The Klaus Barbie Trial and Crimes against Humanity* (New York: Columbia University Press, 1989).

28. Richard J. Golsan, ed., *Memory, the Holocaust, and French Justice: The Bousquet and Touvier Affairs* (Hanover, N.H.: The University Press of New England, 1996).

29. Conan and Rousso, *Vichy.*

30. Among Klarsfeld's many books on the Holocaust, see *French Children of the Holocaust: A Memorial* (New York: New York University Press, 1996) and *Memorial to the Jews Deported from France, 1942–1944* (New York: B. Klarsfeld Foundation, 1983).

31. See Pierre-André Taguieff, "Antisémitisme politique et national-populisme en France dans les anées 1980," in *Histoire politique des juifs en France: entre universalisme et particularisme,* ed. Pierre Birnbaum (Paris: Presses de la fondation nationale des sciences politiques, 1990), 127–40.

32. Doris Bensimon, *Les juifs de France et leurs relations avec Israël, 1945–1988* (Paris: Editions L'Harmattan, 1989); Daniel Amson, *De Gaulle et Israël* (Paris: Presses Universitaires de France, 1991).

33. Benjamin Pinkus, "La Campagne de Suez et son impact sur les Juifs de France," in *Les Juifs de France, le Sionisme et l'Etat d'Israel: Actes du Colloque International* (Paris: Publications Langues'O, 1987), 343–78.

34. Yves Chevallier, "L'Evolution de la perception d'Israel par les juifs de France: 1967–1987," in *Les Juifs de France,* 417.

35. Alain Finkielkraut, *La reprobation d'Israel* (Paris: Denoel, 1983). The dialogue between Lévinas and Finkelkraut is reproduced in Sean Hand, ed., *The Lévinas Reader* (Oxford: Blackwell, 1989), 290–96.

36. Ovadia Soffer, "La Communauté juive en France et les relations franco-israeliennes," *Les Juifs de France,* 431–34. Soffer was Israeli ambassador to France.

37. Soffer, "La Communauté juive," 436.

38. Richard Marienstras, *Etre un peuple en diaspora* (Paris: F. Maspero, 1975).

39. Memmi's books are *Portrait of a Jew* (New York: Orion Press, 1962), and *The Liberation of the Jew* (New York: Orion Press, 1966).

40. Friedlander, *Vilna on the Seine,* covers the wide expanse of Jewish thought in France and is an essential text here.

41. See Perec's extraordinary novel *W ou le souvenir d'enfance* (Paris: Denoel, 1975), which evokes his childhood as a hidden child in France. Perec was the grand-nephew of Jacob Leib Peretz, the famous Yiddish novelist.

42. Published in English under the title *The Defeat of the Mind,* trans. Judith Friedlander (New York: Columbia University Press, 1995).

43. Alain Finkielkraut, *L'Avenir d'une négation: Reflexion sur la question du génocide* (Paris: Seuil, 1982); *Remembering in Vain.*

44. See Alain Finkielkraut, *Comment peut on être Croate?* (Paris: Gallimard, 1992).

45. Finkielkraut's *The Imaginary Jew* (Lincoln: University of Nebraska Press, 1985), from which this argument is drawn, is one of the most important books to have appeared in recent French Jewish writing and perhaps Jewish writing in general in the late twentieth century. See also Seth Wolitz, "Imagining the Jew in France: From 1945 to the Present," *Yale French Studies* 85 (1994): 119–34. Also the selection in Kritzman, *Auschwitz and After,* 83–97.

46. Finkielkraut, *The Imaginary Jew,* 85–86.

47. Doris Bensimon and Sergio Della Pergola, *Juifs de France: Socio-Demographie et Identité* (Paris: CNRS, 1986), 281–86.

48. Alain Finkielkraut, *La sagesse de l'amour* (Paris: Gallimard, 1984); translated

as *The Wisdom of Love* (Lincoln: University of Nebraska Press, 1997). On the relationship between Finkielkraut and Lévinas, Friedlander, *Vilna on the Seine,* 91–106.

49. See the excellent biography of Lévinas in Friedlander, *Vilna on the Seine,* 80–91.

50. See Richard Cohen, *Elevations: The Height of the Good in Rosenzweig and Levinas* (Chicago: University of Chicago Press, 1994), 117–21 and passim.

51. Jacob E. Meskin, "Critique, Tradition, and the Religious Imagination: An Essay on Lévinas's Talmudic Readings," *Judaism* 47, no. 1 (winter 1998): 90–107. My thanks to Murray Baumgarten for calling this article to my attention.

52. Among Neher's many books note, in English, *The Exile of the Word: From the Silence of the Bible to the Silence of Auschwitz* (Philadelphia: Jewish Publication Society of America, 1981).

53. Emmanuel Lévinas, *Difficult Freedom: Essays on Judaism* (Baltimore: Johns Hopkins University Press, 1990), 64. There is precedence for this in the work of Maimonides, of course.

54. Hand, ed., *The Lévinas Reader,* 284 and passim.

55. Lévinas, *Difficult Freedom,* 32–35.

56. Hand, ed., *The Lévinas Reader,* 45–51.

57. Martin Jay, *Downcast Eyes: The Denigration of Vision in Twentieth-Century French Thought* (Berkeley and Los Angeles: University of California Press, 1993), 545–51. See the poetic gloss on Lévinas's conception of love by Luce Irigaray in *Face to Face With Lévinas,* ed. Richard A. Cohen (Albany: State University of New York Press, 1986), 231–56. Cohen argues that this is a misreading, however. There are pieces by Irigaray and two other French feminists with varying appreciations of Lévinas in *Re-Reading Lévinas,* ed. Robert Bernasconi and Simon Critchley (Bloomington: Indiana University Press, 1991). For Cohen's critique see his *Elevations,* 195–96, especially the notes.

58. Emmanuel Lévinas, *Nine Talmudic Readings* (Bloomington: Indiana University Press, 1990).

59. Cited in Cohen, *Elevations,* 193.

60. Hand, ed., *The Lévinas Reader,* 207.

61. Lévinas, *Difficult Freedom,* 49.

62. For Neher, God is "silent" at Auschwitz: *The Exile of the Word,* 136–37. A similar idea appears in Richard E. Friedman, *The Disappearance of God; A Divine Mystery* (Boston: Little, Brown, 1995).

63. Lévinas, *Nine Talmudic Readings,* 98–103.

64. Hand, ed., *The Lévinas Reader,* 284.

65. Cohen, *Elevations,* 94. Cohen limits his designation to Rosenzweig and Lévinas, however.

66. Arnold Eisen, *Galut: Modern Jewish Reflection on Homelessness and Homecoming* (Bloomington: Indiana University Press, 1986), 165–74.

67. See, for example, the tribute to Lévinas, "Lévinas: philosophe et juif," published by *L'Arche* (February 1996), 62–90, in the months after his death, including articles by a great many contributors and the comments delivered by Jacques Derrida at Lévinas's funeral.

68. Raphaël Draï, "Neher et Lévinas," *L'Arche* (February 1996), 78–80. Unfortunately the author is not clear about the exact date of the colloquium.

69. Wasserstein, *Vanishing Diaspora,* 280–90.

8

"This Is Not What I Want"

Holocaust Testimony, Postmemory, and Jewish Identity

Diane L. Wolf

I believe in testimony more than anything else.
ELIE WIESEL

Mit vemen
ken ikh redn?
Whom can I speak to?

di meyseim farshteyen
mir afile nit
even the ghosts
do not understand me
IRENA KLEPFISZ

To survive was to escape fate.
But if you escape your fate, whose life do you then step into?
ANNE MICHAELS, *Fugitive Pieces*

The past several years has seen a burst of Holocaust testimonials—both in written and oral forms—in great part due to survivors' reaching the end of their lives and feeling a sense of obligation to record these histories (Bartov, 1993).[1] Although many survivors recount that they felt that no one wanted to hear their stories after the war, there is now a great demand for them.[2] After living with their stories for fifty years, it is not uncommon for Holocaust survivors to decide to finally speak in reaction to the denials of Holocaust revisionists or after seeing *Schindler's List*. Many spoke for the first time about their experiences to those videotaping for Steven Spielberg's Survivors of the Shoah Visual History Foundation (VHF), which aims to collect and make available taped interviews of fifty thousand Holocaust survivors. Clearly, one of the main purposes of producing Holocaust testimonials is to ensure that the past is not forgotten, thereby creating a cultural memory that will contribute to the perpetuation of Jewish identity.

Survivor stories provide rich possibilities for contemporary analysis. Such testimonies can be seen as transnational narratives par excellence;[3] they speak of cultural multiplicity (Foster, 1995), of fluid and multiple selves (Langer, 1995), of a dispersed sense of self (Gallant and Cross, 1992), of identity, of the creation of double- or multidiasporic existences, and of negotiation between the language of emotions (often Yiddish), of schooling and of nation (Hebrew, Polish) of the wartime experience (German) and of their new home (e.g., English). Due to these experiences, Holocaust testimonies are both homeless and global (Suleiman, 1996:643), about dislocation and transnational existences. Holocaust testimonials remain, however, surprisingly underanalyzed by sociologists[4] and other social scientists.[5]

The purpose of this paper is threefold. First, based on a survivor's testimonial that I took as an oral history, I will explore how a displaced and stateless Jewish survivor named Jake made his way in post-Holocaust Europe and North America, with particular attention to his emigration decision and his resultant relationship to home and the diaspora. Second, after delineating Jake's wartime and postwar experiences, I will explore the linkages between Holocaust testimonial, "postmemory," and the construction of Jewish identities in the second and third generations and beyond. In this sense, the paper deals with not only the politics of memory but also the politics of Jewish identity. Finally, I wish to connect the richness of Jewish post–World War II refugee experiences with contemporary sociological and interdisciplinary discourses concerning immigrants, refugees, and diasporas, as part of a broader effort to counter "sociological silences" (Kaufman, 1996:6; Bauman, 1991:3) about the Holocaust.[6]

MEMORIES

Collective memory that transmits a group's history and culture and ultimately its identity constitutes an important role in diasporic groups (Chaliand and Rageau, 1995:xv). Collective memory refers to the "common shared awareness of the presence of the past in contemporary consciousness" (Stier, 1996:1). In her book on the politics of remembering, Sturken (1997:1) argues that "memory establishes life's continuity; it gives meaning to the present . . . memory provides the very core of identity." Although there is no monolithic "Jewish" collective memory (Aschheim, 1997:29), contemporary researchers suggest that the Holocaust constitutes the most important basis of American and Israeli Jewish identity, creating a Jewish "civil religion" (Goldberg, 1995; Stier, 1996).[7] One ramification of centering Jewish identity in the Holocaust is the perpetuation of a notion of victimhood, creating a curious paradox, given that Jews today constitute a relatively strong and powerful ethnic group in the United States (Biale, 1986).

The memorialization of the Holocaust has accelerated in recent years

(Young, 1993), incurring political debates in cities all over the world about the form and content of its representation. Linenthal (1995) provides an unusual view onto the politics of producing Holocaust memory in his book documenting the creation of the U.S. Holocaust Memorial Museum in Washington D.C. Contentious and divisive debates on the museum's initial committee focused on who should be represented in the museum (i.e., which groups) and how they should be represented. These debates, however, can also be seen as metadiscussions about what counts as Jewish cultural memory (Sturken, 1997) and how Jewish identity will be shaped. Thus, cultural memory does not simply occur; rather, it is a social construction.

As Oren Stier insightfully writes, an understanding of the processes of collective memory also reveals much about the present milieu, the contemporary sense of identity as it depends on the past. Memory is about the present, or, more precisely, it is about a particular way of imagining and representing the present by turning attention towards the past (1996:10). Indeed, the production of a kind of cultural memory is pivotal in creating and perpetuating links for the second generation and beyond, with an imagined home and imagined community, and with a sense of ethnic identity that for Jews as well as others may be becoming increasingly symbolic.[8] An important question then becomes, as survivors die and the past "passes from living memory to history" (Hutton cited in Young, 1997:49), how is this past remembered, and what is the impact of this past on contemporary and future Jewish identities? Thus, in addition to analyzing what happened to Jake as he emigrated to the United States and rebuilt his life, I also wish to examine the ramifications of the form and content of Jake's testimonial for the production of cultural memory and for the creation of Jewish identity.

THE ROLE OF TESTIMONIALS: WITNESSES AS POLITICAL ACTORS

Testimonials have been an effective way for Holocaust survivors to make their pasts public and to transmit a particular slice of Jewish history. Akin to the Latin American *testimonio,* giving testimony and telling one's story of oppression is a necessary and political act for the teller because it reveals injustice.[9] "It was my duty," concluded a Dutch Jew after discussing how difficult it was to conjure up memories of war and hiding for his interview with the Shoah Visual History Foundation.[10] Giving testimony is a form of remembering (Langer, 1991) that goes beyond the individual, inscribing it in history. At the same time, creating testimony may be a form of "restitution," bringing some order, mastery, and relief "to the unmastered portion" (Hartman, 1992:324).

As Holocaust survivor Saul Friedlander points out, given that the Nazis "invested considerable effort not only in camouflage but in effacement of all traces of their deeds, the obligation to bear witness and record this past seems even more compelling" (1992:3). The contemporary version of Nazi effacement—historical revisionists and Holocaust deniers—has not only catalyzed many survivors to finally recount their histories but it has also activated some younger Jews to work with these testimonials.[11]

Telling one's story is felt to be political because it makes witnesses out of those who listen, thus making it incumbent for them to act in ways that will fight such injustice. Thus, while it is the political duty of survivors to bear witness about the Holocaust, it is the duty of subsequent generations to listen (Hartman, 1996:133), thereby becoming vicarious witnesses and political actors who must "never forget."[12] Indeed, Elie Wiesel, seen by many as the spokesperson for Jewish survivors of the Holocaust, has asserted that being a Jew today "means to testify, to bear witness" to the Holocaust (Goldberg, 1995:25); not to bear witness is seen as a betrayal of one's people (Rubinoff, 1993).

For Jews in general and Holocaust survivors specifically, the importance of bearing witness can be traced back to biblical roots. According to Jewish law, a witness must report an unjust event once he or she has seen it, thereby making "more witnesses by informing others of events" (Young 1988:18).[13] In his book on Jewish memory, Yerushalmi (1996:5) notes that the command "to remember" (*zakhor*) is used 169 times in the Hebrew Bible. The injunction to remember, in addition to the responsibility of reporting injustice, may help explain the proliferation of Holocaust testimonials; indeed, the fact that such rituals already exist (e.g., the Passover Seder) provide a cultural basis: "in light of this divine precedent, it may not be surprising that the great majority of Holocaust scribes locating themselves within the Jewish literacy tradition have adopted 'testimony' as their personal task." (Young, 1988:20)[14] In his book on Holocaust memorials, James Young (1993:7) points out that the first "'memorials' to the Holocaust period came not in stone, glass or steel—but in narrative." Memorial books (*Yizkor Bikher*) in which the destruction of Jewish lives and communities were documented served as "symbolic tombstones" for the millions without graves. The scribes who wrote them envisaged that these books would create a "memorial space." Since survivors needed a place to mourn, these *Bikher* created "imagined grave sites, as the first sites for memory." Thus, such texts embodied history, memory, and mourning, and perhaps the testimonials given by survivors serve the same purpose for some individuals, providing them a space that helps them move beyond their grief.[15]

Of course, a difficult question concerning testimonies in general and survivor stories in particular concerns their veracity, or what some sociologists would term "reliability" and "validity." How do we view testimonies recounted fifty years after the fact in terms of their portrayal of a particular "reality" or "truth"?[16] Primo Levi argued that with the passing of time, memories go through a sieve, with the most painful memories fading away (1986:136;

White, 1988). Others do not believe that the worst experiences are the ones that necessarily fade away over time (Delbo, 1995).[17] As Lawrence Langer (1991:xv) points out in his research on the memory of Holocaust survivors, the credibility of "reawakened memory" is often questioned, but for many, such memory does not need to be reawakened, since it never died. While it is not clear that the worst memories fade away, it is fairly apparent that the prewar past, particularly accounts about family and community life, are often remolded. Most survivors speak nostalgically of the prewar past; conflict, fights, and problems are not mentioned or are glossed over. In such narratives, childhood is presented as a kind of "nature reserve," a "paradise lost" (Ezrahi, 1997:368; Goldenberg, 1998:329). While the need to uphold this kind of memory is understandable, the result is that we have less sense of prewar family and community conflicts from such survivor testimonies.

It is interesting to note that while academics might be concerned with the question of truth and validity in these testimonies, those giving testimony are often concerned with the listeners' ability to understand them. Some survivors feel that it is difficult if not impossible to transmit their experiences through language, because that would mean speaking the unspeakable, explaining the inexplicable, and portraying the unimaginable. They share with historians, but from a different standpoint, the problem of wrestling with "the exceptionality of the event, its representability, its (un)speakability, indeed, its very (in)comprehensibility" (Haidu, 1992:277).[18] A survivor of Auschwitz-Birkenau repeatedly told me, "You don't can't understand; es is impossible to understand what was. . . . you don't can't imagine. . . ." echoing the poem of Irena Klepfisz that begins this essay. Thus, from the perspectives of academics and the subjects of Holocaust testimonies, we are dealing with "partial truths" and "partial understandings," respectively.[19]

Methodologically, testimonies share the same advantages and disadvantages as oral histories in general. Some find oral testimony to be more "real" and closer to the truth than written forms, due to the spontaneity of a interview. An author can rewrite text (Langer, 1991), but an interviewee cannot rewind the tape and erase what he or she just said. Oral testimony may be more spontaneous than written testimony. It is perhaps easier to get an unexpected response, but it is not necessarily closer to the "truth."

Testimonies can provide a rich personal account that complements historical works. At the same time, they are partial accounts and, as I have mentioned, partial truths, mediated by time, history, and memory. Indeed, what seems important in these testimonials is not only what happened during the war but how subjects come to understand their lives and create meaning and a new life after the war. Clearly, many Jews had similar experiences—boycotts of Jewish stores, being taunted, being herded into a ghetto, train rides to concentration camps, the camp experience, death marches—but due to various configurations of personality, family history, age, class, life

cycle state, nationality, culture, and availability of family members, all of
these stories have their own particularities and they were experienced and
processed differently. What varies is not so much that what happened to
each and every Jew, but *"how* victims and survivors have grasped and related
their experiences" (Young, 1997:56). The ways in which Holocaust survivors' lives have been reconfigured in a post-Holocaust world, as displaced
persons, as refugees and transnational subjects, most of them in diasporic
settings far from their native homes, then, is what is intrinsically different.
This focus on a reconfigured post-Holocaust life guides my reading of
Jake's narrative below.

While it is not possible to generalize from one case, certain arguments
and themes that emerge are relevant for further analyses of the construction of Jewish cultural memory and identity. My concern here is to explore
the mechanisms underlying certain decisions and the meanings that ensue.
Such "data" cannot be reaped from extensive interviews but tend to emerge
from longer in-depth interactions. Clearly, Jake does not represent all
Holocaust survivors although aspects of his narrative may resonate with
those of others.

METHODS: "OUTSIDERS WITHIN" WORKING
WITH HOLOCAUST SURVIVORS

I first met Jake in his and his wife's corner grocery store in Ithaca in 1980 as
I was preparing to go to Java, Indonesia, to do fieldwork. Never having had
a course on how to do fieldwork, something I now teach with great pleasure,
I wanted to "practice" doing an oral history with someone from my own cultural background before trying to do so in a foreign language. A professor
of anthropology at Cornell connected me with Jake and I was immediately
taken with his story and his cheerful personality, particularly in light of what
he had been through. I visited weekly for some months, taking his oral history, which I presented at a course at YIVO (the Yiddish Scientific Institute).
We maintained contact over the years through correspondence, phone
calls, and an occasional visit to Ithaca. I returned in 1996 to redo his oral
history, more professionally and systematically, and it is this later version
that will be presented here.[20]

My work with Jake was different than all my previous research experiences. Having Jewish identity in common with my subject constituted the
first time in my professional life as a fieldworker that I was an "insider" as a
Jew and therefore could be both honest and unfearful about that aspect of
my background and identity (see Wolf, 1996). However, while my Jewishness got me in the door and provided the basis for our initial contact in
1980, it is constituted differently from Jake's highly religious Polish Hasidic
background and Orthodox practices. Clearly, essentialist notions of ethnic

identity do not necessarily provide common grounds between people any more than gender or racial identities (Williams, 1996). Despite having a common Jewish denominator, our backgrounds and notions of that identity were vastly disparate, creating for me a sense of both insiderness and outsiderness in this research.

We now turn to Jake's story, both his wartime and postwar experience. In order to present it with a more natural flow, my analysis will follow his narrative.

JAKE'S NARRATIVE

Before and during the War

Jake was born Jakob (pronounced Yakov, but called "Yankel" in Yiddish) in 1921 in Osweicim, Poland, a city that was later to be renamed by the Germans with a word that came to be synonymous with the terror of the Third Reich—Auschwitz. He was born into a religious Hasidic family of solid middle-class status with five children, when Osweicim was approximately 80 percent Jewish. His life followed a path typical of a young male destined to follow in his father's and grandfathers' footsteps—he went to a Polish public school (and Jewish school in the afternoon) from six until ten years of age, and then was sent to Krakow to live with his paternal grandparents and to attend *cheder* (Jewish school for males) full-time. In 1936, at age 15, he was also sent to a school to learn the leatherwork trade, so that once married, he could support a family.

As a religious Jew, Jake was raised to think of himself and other Jews outside of Palestine as living in exile: "All Hasidim felt themselves to be exiled; you were always a stranger in the land." Home was *eretz Yisroel,* the land of Israel, then Palestine, and the biblical image is that when the *moshiach* [messiah] comes, all Jews will return there. While a religious and textual notion of a true home elsewhere existed for Jake and other Hasidim, Osweicim and Krakow were also home, consisting of a large extended family, embedded in a strong and religiously and politically diverse Jewish community. For Jake and those around him, the Jewish religion and family life were interdependent, constituting the raison d'etre of their lives.

When the Germans invaded and enforced registration and identification cards, Jake's family resisted and did not register him and his next youngest brother, but instead obtained fake identification cards for the two. They had realized that young Jewish men who were registered had been called away by the Nazis to work elsewhere and either did not return or, in the case of their neighbor, was returned a few weeks later in an urn for which the family was forced to pay. In 1940, Jake tried to return to Osweicim clandestinely from Krakow and was captured by the police and jailed for a week, but his family was able to pay for his release. The two brothers were able to hide in the family's house and cellar, avoiding being caught by the Germans during several house-to-house searches. In April 1941, Osweicim was made *Juden-rein*, [free of Jews] and his family (his parents, siblings, and maternal grand-parents) was sent to the Sosnowiec ghetto. He and his next youngest brother went as well, but stayed inside their house in Sosnowiec for over one and a half years, studying Talmud and trying to avoid being seen and sent away.

In August 1942, obeying German orders, his family and all other Jews in Sosnowiec reported to a soccer field while he and his brother hid in the cellar. A day or two later, on a Friday night when the entire family remained at the stadium, he despaired: "I did my prayers, *lecha-dodi* and the *kabbalat shab-bat*, I was crying, tears, I'd never cried in my life like this here, because I was alone, I was the oldest one at home. I'm alone. . . . Where am I going to get something to eat? I was in such a desperate situation." His father and maternal grandfather both escaped and eventually returned to Sosnowiec, and his sisters were also sent home as part of an agreement that the Nazis would release fifty children from the stadium. His grandmother, mother, and baby brother did not return. In early 1943 all Jews in Sosnowiec were sent to Srodula, where Jake and his brother successfully hid for another three months until Jake, at age twenty-two, was caught by the police as he went outside to use the outhouse. As he found out later, his brother was caught shortly thereafter.

After being caught, Jake was sent to a labor camp, Sachenheim, in Upper Silesia in Poland, then under the administration of the Third Reich, where he was a slave laborer for I. G. Farben for one year. Prisoners in that labor camp were allowed to wear civilian clothes and keep their prayerbooks; indeed, Jake received a package from his father with work shoes, matzo for Passover, and a prayerbook with a special prayer taped inside that his father instructed him to say daily.[21] After one year, Jake was sent to an SS camp, Blechammer, where all personal items were taken from him and he was given his first of two tattooed numbers. It was there that he became number 184685. He met up with his brother in that camp and they stayed together until after liberation. After nine months in that camp, in January 1945, Jake and five thousand others were sent on a death march for about two weeks in the brutal cold of winter, wearing one layer of clothing and a thin blanket. During the march, they were not given food or water, but forced to survive on whatever grass or roots they could forage themselves. Jake and his brother were among the approximately two thousand who survived, but he suffered from frostbitten toes. The march ended in the camp Gross Rosen, in Lower Silesia, where they stayed for a short period, after which they were sent to Buchenwald in Germany. In February Jake and his brother were sent to a camp called Zweiberger in the Harz Mountains in Germany, where for almost two months he labored in Hermann Goering Werke, under conditions he feels he could not have survived for long. They worked in a mountain that had been carved out by prisoners, where the V-1 and V-2 rockets were being made: "hell was in there. Every time you got in there, the guards were screaming and yelling, 'faster, faster.'" His job consisted of carrying concrete pieces of twenty-five kilos into the mountain and sometimes up a ladder, subsisting on a subminimal diet and suffering poor health. In addition, he and others had to carry out the bodies of those who died on the job or during the night.

On the last day of Passover, the prisoners realized they were about to be liberated. Jake and the other prisoners were at the breaking point and many were dying. Jake told the 17-year-old Belgian boy standing next to him during the hours of roll call: "'you know something, now we can sing *V'heesha amdah.*' [a Passover prayer about freedom from slavery] And guess what? He drops dead right there. He falls, and I'm saying 'Come on, I tell you we're going to be liberated.' I talked to the wall." The Germans tried to get the prisoners to leave the camp with them, reassuring them all the while. Although most prisoners agreed to go, Jake, remembering his grandfather's advice to stick with the first thought that comes into one's mind when a decision needs to be made, told his brother that they would not go. The twelve hundred or so people the Germans led out of the camp were killed—they were put on a bridge that was then dynamited from below.

The next morning the remaining prisoners slowly realized that liberation had come, as they noticed that the SS were gone, and cautiously ventured out of their barracks, an act that one day earlier would have meant severe punishment or death on the spot. In April 1945, wearing striped prisoners' garb, twenty-four-year-old Jake was near starvation and almost toothless, but free.

In this brief summary, I have skipped over descriptions of beatings, cruelty, starvation, illness, injuries, resilience, of Jake's risking disease while caring for an ill friend who later died, of watching others be killed or drop dead, of resistance, of inhumane acts that defy description, and of a few acts of courage by some Germans who tried to help. However, I am being brief in order to focus on the postwar period, to examine how such displacement led to particular decisions and a long-term multidiasporic life.[22]

After the War

In the several months following the war, Jake, his brother, and some friends lived as squatters in a house that had belonged to a Nazi in Halberstadt, Germany, slowly repairing their bodies, eating many meals daily, regaining weight, and searching for their families. Jake found out from other survivors and eyewitnesses that his grandmother, mother, and baby brother had been sent from the stadium in Sosniewiec on a train to Auschwitz and were never heard from again. He does not know how long they survived there, but we know now that the elderly and women with small children were sent directly to the gas chambers, so it is likely that they were only in the camp for a few hours before they died. How they died and the conditions in the gas chambers is something he can only imagine, but the crowding, the terror, and the screams that accompanied it are things he witnessed in camp. He heard later from someone who had been in the same ghetto as the rest of his family that his father, grandfather, and two sisters hid in a bunker but were eventually found by the Germans. He does not know exactly how they met their end, but simply said, "you can imagine what happened." Thus, Jake's liberation and searching for his family confronted him with some harsh realities: most of his immediate family had been killed. Jews who returned to Poland were often met with contempt if not outright hostility and violence—pogroms and murder. Clearly, home and family as he knew it were gone. Thus, although Jake was now freed from the threat of Nazi violence as a Jew and a human being, he was a citizen of nowhere, a displaced person.

All the survivors were searching for their families and, in confronting the aloneness of their condition, made close connections with other survivors. Many married other survivors during this period and had children. The kinds of ties created between survivors after the war became a kind of surrogate family tie; these were friendships that lasted until death. Jake met his future wife Shayna (later renamed Jeannette) during the immediate postwar period. She was part of a group of women liberated from Auschwitz-Birkenau and searching for their family members who had heard that there were some young men in Halberstadt. She had hoped to find some of her five brothers among them. The group of women, along with Jake, his brother, and friends, moved to Bergen-Belsen in July 1945, which had been turned into a DP (Displaced Persons) camp. Jake and Jeannette married nine months later and had a son a year and a half after that. Those years were spent searching for family members, trying to survive through rations and the black market, and trying to heal the emotional and physical damage that had been done.[23]

In 1948, Jake's brother left for Palestine (Israel), but was then sent by the British to Cyprus. Unlike Jake, who had a surviving brother and a few other family members (an aunt, uncle, and two cousins), his wife Jeannette was the sole survivor of her natal and extended family in Poland. Her widowed mother, her five brothers, all her aunts, uncles, and cousins in Poland had been killed. The magnitude and poignancy of how she felt can only be imagined by watching the video of her interview with the Shoah Visual History Foundation fifty years later, the first time she spoke about her wartime experiences. In the beginning of the interview, she was asked to name those who lived in her house when she grew up. In an extremely moving segment, in which she attempts to name her five murdered brothers, she broke down crying and could barely state their names. If this was still unspeakable fifty years later, one can only attempt to imagine how she felt after the war, when she realized that everyone in her family had been brutally killed. Indeed, she told me that when she first met Jake, he reminded her of one of her brothers. At the end of her video interview with VHF, sitting with Jake, she states, "He's not just my husband, he is my father, my brother, my friend." Clearly, she needed and desperately wanted to replace what had been lost.

Of her extended family, Jeannette had only one aunt, who had emigrated to Rochester, New York, before the war and had a family of her own there. Jeannette set about finding her in hopes of reconnecting with kin. Although Jake would have preferred to go to Palestine with his brother, Jeannette's desire to be reunited with the only blood relatives she had left in the world made their decision. Jake said that Jeannette "felt very strongly that 'this would be my mother.'" Eventually, her aunt sponsored them and in April 1949 the three emigrated to the United States.

Welcome to America

After a week or so visiting Jeannette's aunt in Rochester, they moved to Ithaca, where Jake went to work for Jeannette's cousin (the aunt's son) in his grocery store. They lived in a tiny apartment connected to the store. Barely able to speak English, Jake was asked to do all kinds of tasks, from stacking cans and unloading deliveries to sweeping the store. After two weeks, they "put me in front of the cash register to take in money. I didn't even know the money yet. You know, like somebody came in and said, 'Here's a nickel and two dimes' and says, 'Give me two bits back.' And I looked around, I said 'What's two bits?' I finally found out that two bits is a quarter. I made errors but they probably didn't know it. I found out afterwards, you know like 'oh, it's not eighty-one cents, it's eighteen cents." [He laughs.]

"I was supposed to work from 7:30 A.M. to about 5 P.M. or 6 P.M. every day with one afternoon off, after 2 P.M. on Mondays. Thursday, I came in, the first Thursday [he sighs], I said, [in anticipation of the Sabbath on Friday] 'it's Shabbes, Shabbes, I'm not going to work.' [In a voice imitating their surprise and anger] 'What? Everybody works, look at the stores here, all the Jews work who have stores; nobody closes.' So she [the cousin's wife] sends after Jeannette's uncle to come to talk to me. And here I was already moved in to Ithaca, 'Where am I gonna go? Even if I go to New York, I don't know anybody, where am I gonna go? What am I gonna do?' So I had no choice, you know, I had to work on Shabbes."

For those who observe Rosh Ha-Shanah (Jewish New Year) and Yom Kippur (the Day of Atonement), this is a time to pray and to be with family. On their first Yom Kippur in Ithaca, approximately six months after their arrival, Jake, Jeanette, and baby Joe went to "Kol Nidre at the shul. We came out from shul and said, 'Let's go over to the cousins in Ithaca.' . . . We walked there, with the baby on the hand in the dark to a bad part of town. We got there to their house and they weren't home! They weren't there! They went to Elmira, to her brother and we didn't know that. They had their own family; she [the aunt] didn't think about us the way we thought about them. Like the boy is more in love with the girl than the girl with the boy. It was a disappointment; there was a lot of disappointment." Although Jeannette had hoped that her aunt would be a second mother to her, "her aunt had her own children and was a mother to her own children."

Working for Family

When he first started his job, Jake returned to the store in the evenings simply to hear people speak English, so that he could learn the language. "So while I came to the store after supper to listen how people speak English, they made me do things up, up until ten-thirty at night. Every night. After I had started doing it, they wanted me to come every night. So that's when I came early in the morning until night. I worked about ninety-three hours." The minimum wage was $0.75 an hour at that time, which would have brought Jake a weekly wage of $70.00; instead he made $37.00, half that amount.

Jake's hard work and excellent memory made him an indispensable part of the store: "I knew every price; I marked it and I put it on shelves and sometimes at night when I came home, I couldn't feel my fingers because of everything what I was doing. . . . Sometimes a price falls off or something like this here so they'll come ask, 'Boss, what is the price?' He had to go take the book to find out what it is. But it got so that he didn't have to look at the book for the price. He called, 'Jake, what's the price?' I already knew it by heart. I knew every single thing in the store."

In the store, Jake worked under abusive conditions: "She [the cousin's wife] was [lowering voice to a whisper] just like a Gestapo or something. They used to come in about 9:30, 10:00 A.M. When we opened up the store, we had to have already the displays made—meat display out, every morning we had to take out all the displays and clean everything meanwhile. So when she came in about 9:30, she expected everything to be right. But what happened, sometimes a delivery came. Nobody wanted to go, to take in the delivery. Why? Because they knew that it takes a half-hour and she comes in here in the store, she wants to have everything done. So I said, 'To heck with it [laughs], I'll do it.' And when she came in at 9:30, she sees the case is not made, she screams [imitating angry voice] 'What are you guys doing in here!?' She didn't know that you had something else to do. So that's the way how she was."

As his English improved, Jake found out that in a nearby Air Force base, other immigrants were making $50 to $60 weekly for half the amount of time he worked. After his daughter was born, he asked for more money and was given $55 weekly; after two years of working at highly exploitative wages, he finally got a raise. "If you didn't scream about something, they'd never give you any more." Even though his wages improved, working conditions did not.

"A lot of times she used to come in and get, you know, get mad or something. Once, I remember, she used to buy turkeys after the season. And she used to sell the turkeys to the fraternity houses, and you could sell all year long. Once she bought turkeys and the freezer, the freezer was packed with turkeys. You opened up the door, it was packed. So she needed something, we opened up the door and there were about a hundred boxes of turkeys. So I go in, I go in, I knew where this stuff is. And I start taking out about fifty or sixty boxes of turkeys, till I get to this here. And, one of the customers was waiting over there. And, so finally, she comes out here, and she says, [angrily] 'Uh, how come it takes you so long? You, you—.' So I said, 'If you wouldn't buy that many turkeys [laughs], it wouldn't have taken me so long.' And she said, [angrily] 'You gonna teach me how to run my business? You gonna tell me, eh?' She starts yelling at me. I was taking off my apron, I was gonna go, she goes and grabs me, 'Jake, Jake, Jake,' starts kissing me, 'Don't go, I have two kids to go to college.' She only paid four hundred dollars for [laughs] help. . . . So, I went back [chuckles]. She didn't let me out. [chuckles] And that happened several times. She started kissing me, you know."

One day, in 1962, after Jake had worked for them for thirteen years, "after Yom Kippur, I come to the store, the butcher doesn't show up. So if nobody's here, Jake is gonna be the butcher too. So, I started doing it. And, she starts talking to me, telling me what she did yesterday [on Yom Kippur]: 'Gertrude from Binghamton came to visit me yesterday morning. I was fasting, too, I only had a cup of coffee in the morning.' [laughs] That's what she said. And, I knew, eh, it's not right [that she didn't really fast on Yom Kippur] so I didn't say nothing, but she knew I didn't approve. So, she got mad. And she starts, you know, screaming at me, you know, 'Why did, why it takes you so long to cut the pork chops. You cut the pork chops just like a carpenter.' And all this here, and walks by, trying to, you know, rile me up, to, to make me mad. And I was already mad [chuckles], but I didn't want to start a fight. I didn't start a fight, I didn't want to. So, I kept going, I kept quiet, I figured in another five, ten minutes, she'll calm down. But she didn't. She kept going on like this here. So finally, she tells me to bring out the kosher salami, she's gonna help me 'cause we had all those orders, you know. So, I came out, because I was doing something else and I throw the salami at her, 'Here you are—have it' and I go and take off my apron.

"A customer, there was a customer over there, he said, 'Jake, I don't blame you!' And I took off my apron and that was it. So finally I quit. I quit [sighs] so that was one day. I was home, at night the cousin comes over and asks me to come back. And I said to Jeannette, 'No way. I want out—Even if I have to eat a piece of dry bread—I'm not going back anymore.' Always, you know,

I try to quit a few times, but I didn't go up, but this time I went out, and no matter what. Then, he [the cousin] comes to me and tries to offer me a partnership. So I said, 'Thank you. [laughs] We don't want it.'"

After quitting, Jake went job-hunting: "So, I started, eh, looking around. I didn't know how to drive a car yet at that time. And I started looking, I go to, wherever I go to for jobs, I can't find a job, [whispering] and I see it's bad, I can't find a job, you know. . . . and . . . I didn't have any money, what to eat, what to feed my family." Jake was unemployed for a short but stressful period and was disappointed that no one in the Jewish community tried to help him during that time. He ended up working in another grocery store for some months.

Later in 1962 Jake bought his own store in Ithaca and his entire family worked in that store. But "even when I opened up the store, I kept feeling that 'This is not what I want. I don't want the kids to get into this kind of business. I'll build up the store as much as I can and then get out and go to Israel.' I thought this when I had the store. I wanted to sell it in the 70s and maybe had a buyer but he didn't buy it. I would've sold it because I wanted to go to Israel. We even looked at apartments there." I asked him why he and Jeannette didn't move to Israel when they sold the store in 1982, since their children were already grown. He explained that it was too late by then because his brother had died in the meantime, so "we forgot about it. Now it's too late; we can't; it's too much at our ages." Thus, they had missed their chance in 1949 to emigrate to Israel and by the time family and finances made it possible once again, their primary reason for moving, Jake's brother, was dead.

Family

"This is the trouble, because I was working that long, I didn't have time [for the family]. [Imitating his son speaking in reference to Jake] 'When I was playing ball, he never came to see me playing ball.' I still remember the one day I made that effort to go see . . . until I got there the ball game was over. This was the one time I was gone over there, you know, I get over there, there's the whistle; it's all over." Jake was supposed to get off by 2 P.M. on Mondays but he described how they never let him leave until 3 or 3:30, always finding one more thing for him to do.

"Because I was working that long, with my son, I didn't get the chance to teach him anything [in terms of Jewish education]. I didn't get the chance. When he was small, I was all the time in the store. When he got bigger, I had a business. I didn't come from the business till 10:30 at night, until I was catching up, it was 11:30 P.M. Six o'clock in the morning, I had to get up and go work again. Somehow, my life was like this here, that I couldn't do things what I want usually I would have done. . . . Well, maybe it had to be like this, and maybe, I don't know why, why I came here to Ithaca in the first place."

As I asked Jake to reflect on how his relations with his children and grandchildren might have been affected by his experiences, he explained by way of a parable. "I was mostly bought up with my grandfather. He went to the *mikvah* [ritual bath], I went with him to the *mikvah*. And we went to the rabbis, I went with him, it was just like a friendship or something. Every night, when he comes, you know, I went to bed, he had to go tuck in my feet so they won't be cold. We didn't hug. We didn't kiss, because it's not our style, it's not our custom to do this here."

Retired since 1982, Jake lives an active life, praying daily with a group of Orthodox Jewish students on the Cornell campus. He and his wife see their children and grandchildren whenever possible. Yet he still feels himself "to be a stranger" living in the United States. Had Hitler never come and had Jake continued the life he was brought up to lead in Poland, he imagines that today he'd "probably be a Jew with a nice, long white beard [chuckles] with probably six or eight children [chuckles]. And many grandchildren. And great-grandchildren." Thus, his image of home revolves around the interdependency of religion and family, conjuring up memories of home as he knew it in Poland.

ANALYSIS OF NARRATIVE: FAMILY, HOME, AND DIASPORA

In this section, we turn to the themes of family, home, and diaspora as evoked in Jake's narrative. Given their Orthodox backgrounds, it was unimaginable for Jake and Jeannette that fellow Jews would force Jake to work on a holy day, the Sabbath, denying him the weekly rest, prayer, and family time they felt was sacrosanct. And that it was *family*, the only kin Jeannette had left in the world, who forced this on Jake and his family, after the Shoah, shook their very core. Jeannette described this sense of treachery and subversion to their souls more graphically: "We came from the ovens to work on Shabbes? We came for this?"

This transgression made Jake and Jeannette realize early on that they had erred in choosing to emigrate to the United States over Israel, but they had few resources and nowhere else to go. The constraints Jake confronted often overwhelmed his ability to make meaningful choices. Under such conditions, "agency" becomes little more than reacting to circumstances beyond one's control. In other words, we should take care not to romanticize notions of human agency given that most immigrants and refugees confront debilitating and overwhelming constraints.

Jake and Jeannette had to confront their intense sense of aloneness in the diaspora during their first High Holy Days in Ithaca when they walked to her family's house and found that the cousins had been invited by other family members who were also related to Jeannette. And, of course, the painful point is that Jake and Jeannette were not invited and were not treated as family. Ironically, the decision to emigrate to the United States was made so that Jeannette could join her aunt in the United States and reconstitute a notion of home, family, and belonging. Instead, this decision resulted in exactly the reverse—the pain of her orphaned state and her sense of displacement in a diasporic place far from home were both intensified.

This aspect of Jake's narrative provides an excellent example of why it is important to explore, rather than make assumptions about, the natural altruism of kin, particularly for (trans)migrants. I mentioned earlier that Holocaust survivors tend to romanticize their prewar family life. It is also important not to project similar assumptions about the ties between kin and co-ethnics after the Holocaust. In some sense, the exploitative behavior of Jeannette's relatives seems extraordinarily cruel in light of what Jake and Jeannette had just lived through. Furthermore, it is also likely that Jake tolerated a high degree of exploitation for thirteen years not only because he felt obligated to his wife's relatives for sponsoring them as stateless refugees, but also because the concentration camp experience had raised his level of tolerance for exploitation. During his camp years, he had worked at many jobs, including slave labor for the large industrial firm I. G. Farben and building German war rockets. Jake and his fellow inmates quickly learned that survival was based on working hard and not complaining. In other words, Jeannette's relatives perhaps were able to exploit Jake to such a high degree because of what the Nazis had ingrained in him.

Although what Jake experienced was not the norm among receiving Jewish American families, certainly some European Jews did experience similar difficulties and disappointments when reunited with kin on American soil (Helmreich, 1992:39–41). This finding resonates with contemporary (post-1965) migrants and transmigrants who work for kin or co-ethnics in ethnic enclaves in the United States and elsewhere. Scholars have pointed to the degree of exploitation upon which these enclaves are built (Bonacich, 1994; Guarnizo, 1996), again challenging romantic assumptions about the receiving family of immigrants, about co-ethnic solidarity, and about family in general.

It is ironic that the fight that made Jake's quit his job focused on how he was not properly cutting pork, meat he has never knowingly consumed because it is against Jewish law. Additionally, this criticism came on the day after Yom Kippur, the holiest and most solemn Jewish holiday. It is possible that Jake had finally reached his limits and was ready to quit, but it is also likely that he was even more offended that Jeannette's relative criticized him for the way he handled *trayf*, nonkosher food, right after she admitted transgressing Yom Kippur by drinking coffee but acting as though she had fasted.

Due to the excessive demands at the workplace, Jake had little time with his children, and he reflected on how it had affected his relationship with his son. While Jake's relationship with his grandfather was close, had daily signs of affection, and reflected Jewish learning and practices, his relationship with his son was shaped by the demands of making a living in a foreign culture and a secular society. That chasm speaks of lost possibilities and distance from the one unit—his family—that had been the center of Jake's life. This distance is greatly owed to his diasporic condition, because had he and Jeannette emigrated to Israel, their family life and family relations would have been vastly different. Indeed, his image of what his life would be like today had they emigrated to Israel is centered on the interdependency of family and religious life, much like the prewar life he experienced in Poland.

Jake reiterates his sense of diasporic life outside of Israel: "In World War I, Jews got killed for Germany . . . what good did their medals do later? Jews who were Polish soldiers in World War I were treated like dirt later. You give your life for that country and you're still a stranger. . . . you never know in America either." Among the Cambodian Americans she interviewed, Katharya Um (1998) also found a persistent sense of insecurity in that America offered them both sanctuary and marginality.

In terms of Jake's relationship with Israel, he maintains close connections with his family there and has visited many times; indeed, he continues to visit to attend weddings and bar mitzvahs. He no longer needs to send his family money but instead sends money to various charities. He has been back to Poland twice since the war, once with his daughter and once with his grandson, to show them his roots. He does not, however, maintain any other connection with Poland.

Although he has certain transnational ties with Israel, Jake's ties with Poland can be seen more as an emotional transnationalism. Jake's identity is made more complex by being multilocalized within multiple frames of reference, as he lives a kind of doubly diasporic existence. This case aptly illustrates Guarnizo's contention that "transnationalism, contrary to certain idealized visions," is not necessarily a "socially liberating" force (1997:310). The current academic enthusiasm for all things transnational may neglect its potentially destabilizing impact on family, gender, and class relations (Um, 1998). While forced migrations by the Nazis was clearly imprisoning, the more or less voluntary emigration Jake and his family undertook after the war as transnational subjects did not end up freeing them, but quite the opposite.

The Jewish experience in Europe during and after the Nazi regime might be compared with the multidiasporic experiences of other middlemen minorities such as the Indians in Uganda and the Chinese in Vietnam, both of whom were expelled and became "twice migrants" (Bhachu, 1985). Postwar Jews such as Jake, however, were "twice refugees" if not "thrice refugees," having lost their rights and having been forced from home to concentration camps in Poland and Germany, and then, at the war's end, as stateless subjects who went to the United States or elsewhere.

These multiple and forced movements, added to the experiences of genocide and exile, challenge our contemporary conceptual apparatus concerning refugees and immigrants (Um, 1998). Indeed, the dual frame of reference often used by scholars to analyze home (point A) and diaspora (point B) is not sufficient in such cases complicated by multiple notions of home. However, again we must take care not to make romanticized assumptions about home. As Malkki (1995:509) points out, home is rarely a peaceful, unproblematic place.

NARRATIVES, POSTMEMORY, AND JEWISH IDENTITY

To return to one of the goals of this paper, what are the implications of this narrative for the creation of Jewish cultural memory and the construction of a post-Holocaust Jewish identity? What kind of memory might be imprinted after reading Jake's narrative and how might that affect Jewish identity? As we consider post-Holocaust generations, it is useful to further differentiate the notion of cultural memory.

Postmemory, a concept developed by Marianne Hirsch in her discussion of children of Holocaust survivors, is experienced by those with a generational and historical distance from the Holocaust. Postmemory is a very "powerful and very particular form of memory precisely because its connection to its object or source is mediated not through recollection but through an imaginative investment and creation. Post-memory characterizes the experience of those who grow up dominated by narratives that preceded their birth, whose own belated stories are evacuated by the stories of the previous generation, shaped by traumatic events that can be neither fully understood nor re-created." (Hirsch 1997:22) While a kind of Jewish cultural memory might be shared by the majority of Jews, postmemory is experienced only by those with a particular generational and historical distance from the Holocaust.[24] Here I am utilizing the notion of postmemory somewhat more broadly to refer to second- and third-generation Jews whose notions of the Holocaust are mediated through the memories of others and through the production of Jewish cultural memory.

Earlier in 1996, the same year I took Jake's oral history, volunteers from Spielberg's Shoah Visual History Foundation also took Jake's testimonial. The availability of two different testimonials from the same person offers a unique opportunity to contemplate how they might contribute to different kinds of postmemory and Jewish identity. The two-hour VHF videotape mainly focuses on Jake's wartime experiences, in keeping with the project's goals. Towards the end of the interview, Jake states: "I worked in a grocery store for Jeannette's cousin for thirteen years and that's it, until the end of 1962, and a few months later, I opened up my business by myself." The VHF videotape ends with Jake showing the photos of his two children and six grandchildren and reciting their names.[25] The ten-hour oral history I did with Jake spends approximately half the time on wartime experiences and the other half is divided between prepersecution times, prewar times, and postwar life.

I would like to suggest that the VHF's greater emphasis on the wartime experience creates a clearer division between right and wrong, between victims and perpetrators, and offers a more linear view from obliteration to regeneration, from destruction to redemption, and from destitution to success. Simply put, the message from the VHF video is that Jews were victims and their entire families destroyed, and yet, despite Hitler, some were able to overcome the past and create new generations of Jews. Although I do not wish to suggest that this was Spielberg's intention, such videos are likely to contribute a sense of victimhood to Jewish postmemory and identity. The longer narrative with a focus on the postwar experience demonstrates more ambivalence and ambiguity, scrambles any binaries or linearity and clouds the happy ending.

The longer narrative, with its focus on Jake's postwar experiences, includes persecution, death, proliferation, successful adaptation, irony, discontent, sadness, and possibilities lost. It is of course very positive that Jake and Jeannette were able to have two children who are successful professionals and many grandchildren who are doing well, but the nature and texture of some of those relationships are problematic. Jake and Jeannette survived, worked hard, and succeeded economically in the United States. However, Jake's statement in the VHF video—that he worked for thirteen years for Jeannette's cousin and then opened his own store and "that's it"— obfuscates the difficult life he had for those thirteen years and beyond.

The narrative I presented unsettles a binary opposition between Jews as victims and Nazis as perpetrators because it is clear that Jake was deeply exploited by other Jews after the war. Indeed, it was Jewish kin who took advantage of his vulnerability and marginality, and prevented him from developing the religious life he wished to observe with his family. Thus, the comforting notion of the "extended Jewish family" (Steinberg, this volume) that a viewer of Jake's VHF video might feel as Jake showed photos of his grandchildren, is imploded by Jake's depiction in the longer narrative of how he and Jeannette were treated by kin. Finally, the success story transmitted in the VHF video concerning how he became a self-employed store owner is overshadowed in the longer narrative by his sense of having made a serious error in emigrating to the United States and, as a result, always feeling displaced. In the longer narrative, both the United States and their

Jewish kin are presented as less of a safe refuge, somewhat blurring and perhaps muddying the redemptive quality in the video.

The VHF's focus on the wartime experience of fifty thousand Holocaust survivors will deeply affect the future of Jewish cultural memory, postmemory and the shape of Jewish identity, in that such tapes will become easily accessible for educational purposes. In the decades to come, after all such survivors have died and can no longer present their stories to classrooms, they will still speak posthumously through such videos, instilling a notion of history in the minds of young people. Young Jews will learn about the Holocaust from the diary of Anne Frank, perhaps from the film *Schindler's List*,[26] and undoubtedly from innovative educational packages that the VHF will create. Although Spielberg's VHF project is laudable and the VHF's wartime focus understandable, it unwittingly ends up decontextualizing and simplifying the lives that the survivors have led. Thus, these tens of thousands of testimonials will provide partial and truncated views of the individuals meant to be honored, creating Jewish postmemories focused on Jewish persecution and death, contributing to an identity built on victimhood.

The VHF approach obfuscates more problematic arenas in which Jews exert both agency and power, as well as sites such as the family in which conflict might exist. Furthermore, undercurrents of survivors' post-Holocaust sense of displacement or marginality are swept away by an emphasis on Jewish regeneration. In that sense, recording survivors' testimonials is political not only as an act of witnessing and as a way to rebut Holocaust deniers, but also in its very form and content. Indeed, it is imperative to critically consider the broader social, cultural, and political ramifications of particular narrative styles such as the one adopted by the Shoah Visual History Foundation for the future production of postmemory and its contribution to the creation of Jewish identities.

CONCLUSIONS

For those focusing on psychological well-being and adaptation, I believe that Jake would be judged to be a successful survivor. He is warm, lively, personable, optimistic, and humorous; additionally, he had a successful business, raised two children who became professionals, and is actively involved in his family life as well as the local Jewish community. However, the approach I have taken in this essay is not about seeking out hypersuccessful (Helmreich, 1992; Hass, 1996) or dysfunctional survivors (Niederland, 1964; Krystal 1968; Chodoff, 1980) or judging survivors as such. Rather, I have attempted to present a more holistic portrait of post-Holocaust life that reflects tremendous adaptation, disappointment, hard work, sacrifice, achievement, and loss, while acknowledging ambivalence, conflict, and power. It is a critical analysis of this mélange of marginality despite success, of displacement despite prosperity, and of the dialectic between home and Home that has the potential to contribute further to immigration and diaspora studies and, at the same time, to a more nuanced and complex Jewish identity.[27]

NOTES

1. Some terms I use in this essay—survivor and Holocaust—have, like the term "diaspora," been delinked and decentered from their previous predominately Jewish connection. The term "survivor" previously described "one who has encountered, been exposed to, or witnessed death and has himself or herself remained alive" (Lifton, 1980:117) and tended to refer to a Jew who lived through World War II, particularly concentration camps. However, "survivor" now describes almost anyone who has been through a difficult experience, ranging from "outlasting a bad marriage to lasting through a corporate takeover" (Goldberg, 1995:19). In a society that flourishes on public confessions of lurid victimization, it is not difficult to locate individuals who consider themselves to be "survivors." In this piece, I use the term in reference to Jews who lived through World War II, most of them in concentration camps.

The term "Holocaust" is also used to describe other events (e.g., possible nuclear destruction) and group histories (e.g, the Black Holocaust) such that some scholars now add the qualification, "the Jewish Holocaust" (Buckler, 1996; Steedman, 1996) when referring to the events surrounding the Third Reich and the Jews. In this paper, the term signifies the killing of Jews and others during World War II. Despite misgivings, I will be using the terms "Holocaust" and "Shoah" throughout this paper. Both terms are indirect and obfuscate that it was, in fact, genocide. For example, "Shoah" simply means "disaster" in Hebrew and could refer to an economic, ecological, or other disaster, such as an earthquake; furthermore, that it is in Hebrew seems to suggest that it is a Jewish event rather than a world event.

2. In the United States, there are many Holocaust oral history projects based on taped interviews (at the San Francisco Holocaust Library and Research Center, at Yale University, at the U.S. Holocaust Memorial Museum, and Steven Spielberg's Shoah Visual History Foundation, to name but a few), in addition to collected volumes of survivors' lives (Hass, 1996; Helmreich, 1992; White, 1988; Blum et al., 1991; Linden, 1993; Wolman, 1996; to name a few), and memoirs, (again to name but a few: Halivni, 1996; Friedlander, 1975; Tec, 1984; Winter, 1997; Furst and Furst, 1994; Polt, 1999; Bernstein, 1997).

3. Basch, Schiller, and Blanc (1994:7) define transnationalism as "the processes by which immigrants forge and sustain multi-stranded social relations that link together their societies of origin and settlement." They are termed "transnational" to emphasize that "many immigrants today build social fields that cross geographic, cultural and political borders." While many Holocaust survivors maintain transnational links with their places of origin. In the case of the Holocaust survivor who is the focus of this paper, he was raised in a tradition that configured Israel as Home, as the society of origin and final settlement of all Jewish people, and maintains social, emotional, and economic relations with Israel.

4. While *Psychology Abstracts* had 550 entries under Holocaust, *Sociology Abstracts* had less than half that. To refigure Virginia Domingues' questioning of anthropology,

might this suggest that sociology has a "Jewish problem." (Domingues 1993:621). Similar to anthropology, sociology has a large number of Jews in it but few have focused their academic work on Jewish issues; those who do focus on Jewish issues have been marginalized and "ghettoized to Judaic or Jewish Studies." (Domingues, 1993:622). While the patterns Domingues delineates for anthropology are similar for sociology, I would suggest that the question should not necessarily be limited to why more Jews aren't focusing on the sociological study of the Holocaust, but why more sociologists, Jewish and non-Jewish alike, are not taking up such issues.

5. The few sociologists who have focused on Holocaust testimonials have analyzed them for the ways in which they might inform notions of ethnicity (Climo, 1990), the relationship between human agency and social structures (Berger, 1995), and feminist epistemology (Linden, 1993).

Psychologists have tended to focus on survivor adaptation. Most studies find that survivors' experiences have long-lasting negative effects on their emotional state and ability to function (Niederland, 1964; Eitinger, 1980; Krystal 1968; Dimsdale 1980; Chodoff 1980). A few have focused on the successful adaptation of Holocaust survivors (Hass, 1996, White, 1988), challenging notions of Jewish passivity and pathology. The sociologist Helmreich found that successful survivors had the following ten traits: flexibility, assertiveness, tenacity, optimism, intelligence, distancing ability, group consciousness, the ability to assimilate the knowledge that they survived, the ability to find meaning in one's life, and courage (1992: 267).

6. Jewish experiences immediately following World War II do not figure prominently in contemporary diaspora, refugee, or immigration studies. Although Jews initially presented the "ideal type" for the concept of diaspora (Clifford, 1997) such that the term was more or less synonymous with the Jewish experience, efforts to bring the notion of a diaspora to bear on other, particularly dispersed Third World peoples, has, in effect, pushed the Jewish experience immediately following the Holocaust out of the scholarly picture in these fields (Safran, 1991). In contemporary immigration studies, most authors, myself included (Portes and Rumbaut, 1990; Basch, Schiller, and Blanc, 1994; Espiritu and Wolf, 2001), make a deliberate effort to point out how contemporary (e.g., post-1965) immigrants or refugees from the Third World cannot be compared with the European immigrant analogy in terms of "adaptation" due to the postcolonial context, the global economy, and the racialized nature of American society. Connected to this, contemporary notions of the "refugee" are increasingly seen in the literature as "first and foremost a 'Third World problem'" (Malkki, 1995:503). In the end, there is little, if any, effort in these fields to revisit the Jewish postwar experience.

7. The March of the Living—a tour of concentration camps for Jewish youth, ending in a trip to historic sites in Israel—is one example of the way in which Jewish identity is expressly built upon the Holocaust (Stier, 1996). Anecdotally, it is common on my campus (U.C. Davis) that the most well-attended event during Jewish cultural week is the one focused on the Holocaust. While this is not necessarily problematic, I believe that it does reflect young people's overreliance on Jewish persecution rather than Jewish culture and history as the basis of their ethnic/religious identity.

8. Mary Waters (1990) found that young people refer to their notions of ethnic identity through particular symbols, such as holidays, family get-togethers, and food.

Thus, I found similar answers to the questions "What does it mean to you to be Filipino?" and "What does it mean to you to be Jewish?" when I asked the adult children of Filipino immigrants in my research as compared with third-generation American Jewish students in my course, respectively. Most referred to ethnic pride (e.g., "I'm proud to be Filipino/Jewish"), holidays, and food, but seemed to have little knowledge of their cultural history and background.

9. In Latin America as well, *testimonio* is an accepted and popular form of transmitting personal history that is political, the most famous of which may be that of Nobel Prize winner Rigoberta Menchu, an Indian activist woman from Guatemala. It is interesting to note that Holocaust testimonials and Latin American *testimonios* share certain commonalities.

10. N. H. Wijnperl, personal communication, Israeli Consulate, Den Haag, the Netherlands, November 1998.

11. The first time Jake wrote down his history was in the mid-1980s, in response to an article he read in the newspaper about a Holocaust denier. He describes sitting and writing endlessly, only to be interrupted by his wife due to the arrival of the Sabbath. Also, in my interviews with two people who work for Spielberg's Shoah Visual History Foundation, it was clear that Holocaust deniers gave them a raison d'etre for their work. Thus, their political reaction to such denials is to help facilitate Holocaust testimonials as part of their work.

12. One problem with the way in which this message has been transmitted is the conflation of Jewishness with the Holocaust, contributing to what Goldberg has termed "the Holocaust cult."

13. "And he is a witness whether he has seen or known of it; if he does not utter it, then he shall bear his iniquity" (Leviticus 5:1 quoted in Young, 1988:18). Young explains that a witness is described as someone who both knows and sees an event, but as elaborated in the Talmud, once "an unjust event is known, it must by law be reported" (1988:18). Young also explains that to testify is "literally 'to make witness'—an etymological reminder that as witness and testimony are made, so is knowledge" (1988:19).

14. Young goes on to note that: "It is surprising and even ironic, however, that Elie Wiesel would then overlook what amounts to a long tradition of literary testimony to proclaim that 'If the Greeks invented tragedy, the Romans the epistle, and Renaissance the sonnet, our generation invented a new literature, that of testimony'" (1988:20).

15. For Primo Levi, telling his story in *Survival in Auschwitz* (1959) fulfilled a deep and overpowering need; it was a kind of "inner liberation" that Levi later likened to psychoanalysis (Camon, 1989:41–2). Jake, the subject of the oral history I conducted, said that after he wrote out his story, his nightmares subsided.

16. For the most part, historians have maintained a "forced distinction" between history and memory, creating an "artificial distance" between "history as that which happened and memory as that which is remembered of what happened." As a result, survivors' voices and memories have not been incorporated into works of history (Young, 1997; Friedlander, 1993; LaCapra, 1994), although Saul Friedlander has attempted to counter this tendency. In Germany, academic historians tend not to gather local-level testimonials either but, if at all, draw upon the work of "barefoot historians" *(Barfusshistoriker)*—usually nonacademic second-generation German

non-Jews who have taken it upon themselves to do local and regional Jewish histories (see Kingreen, 1994).

17. French resistance leader Charlotte Delbo wrote, "Auschwitz is so deeply etched on my memory that I cannot forget one moment of it. 'So you are living with Auschwitz?' 'No, I live next to it.'" (Cited in Langer, 1995:xi).

18. The question of representation of Auschwitz and the Holocaust has stirred many journalists and academics more recently, in discussions about *Schindler's List* (see Loshitzky, 1997), a topic beyond the scope of this paper

19. However, by using the term "partial truth," I do not wish to suggest in any way that the anti-Semitic and genocidal policies and acts of the Nazis can or should be doubted. Rather, I am using this term to suggest that we view these narratives as the result of a particularized processing of history and memory within an individual.

20. There were a few differences between the two versions worth mentioning. First, Jake reacted much more emotionally to telling me stories the first time since it had been decades since he told such stories. In the meantime, he has presented his history to many audiences, especially in classrooms, and has become a more seasoned storyteller. Second, I heard more stories the second time that I had not heard before, most likely because we had more time and he was more focused. When I first took his oral history, he talked while he worked in the grocery store.

21. This was the will from the Rambam to his son that Jake's father told him to say daily, so that he would survive.

22. See Jake's entire oral history for further information (Wolf, 2002).

23. As an example of the kinds of business and bartering that existed in the place of shops and proper medical care, during that time Jake had his teeth capped and replaced by a dentist in exchange for a pack of Camel cigarettes. His wedding suit had belonged to a German soldier who was then a prisoner of war; Jake got it from the soldier's wife in exchange for a can of powdered milk; for five pounds of sugar, a tailor made alterations.

24. Although Hirsch originally developed this term in reference to the experiences of Holocaust survivors, she later wrote that it may be useful to describe other "second generation memories of cultural or collective traumatic events and experiences" (1997:22).

25. In other interviews of survivors, where possible, the children and grandchildren are filmed with the survivor as a kind of living family portrait.

26. These two other sources are not unproblematic either. The Anne Frank story also presents some false binaries—the "good" Dutch who hid her and the "bad" Germans who took her away and killed her. This obfuscates the high degree of collaboration between many Dutch citizens and the Nazis, including the person who turned in the Frank family. *Schindler's List* has been the object of considerable criticism by academics, journalists, and filmmakers for multiple reasons (see Loshitzky, 1997).

27. I greatly benefitted from the comments of colleagues and friends alike, including David Biale, Kathie Friedman, Judy Gerson, Erich Gruen, Luis Guarnizo, Richard Hecht, Chana Kronfeld, Max Neiman, Kari Steinberg, Irwin Wall, and Howard Wettstein. My deepest thanks to Frank Hirtz for his tremendous support, which allowed me to participate in the HRI seminar.

BIBLIOGRAPHY

Aschheim, Steven.
   1997. "On Saul Friedlander." *History and Memory* 9, no. 1/2:11–46.

Bartov, Omer.
   1993. "Intellectuals on Auschwitz: Memory, History, and Truth." *History and Memory* 5:87–129.

Basch, Linda, Nina Glick Schiller, and Cristina Szanton Blanc.
   1994. *Nations Unbound: Transnational Projects, Postcolonial Predicaments, and Deterritorialized Nation-States.* New York: Gordon and Breach.

Bauman, Zygmunt.
   1991. *Modernity and the Holocaust.* Ithaca: Cornell University Press.

Berger, Ronald.
   1995. "Agency, Structure, and Jewish Survival of the Holocaust: A Life History Study." *The Sociological Quarterly* 36, no. 1:15–36.

Bernstein, Sara Tuvel, with Louise Loots Thornton and Marlene Bernstein Samuels.
   1997. *The Seamstress.* New York: Berkley Books.

Bhachu, Parminder.
   1985. *Twice Migrants: East African Sikh Settlers in Britain.* London: Tavistock.

Biale, David.
   1986. *Power and Powerlessness in Jewish History.* New York: Schocken Press.

Blum, Lenore, et al.
   1991. "Tellers and Listeners: The Impact of Holocaust Narratives." In *The Meaning of the Holocaust in a Changing World,* edited by Peter Hayes, 316–28. Evanston, Ill.: Northwestern University Press.

Bonacich, Edna.
   1994. "Asians in the Los Angeles Garment Industry." In *New Asian Immigration in Los Angeles and Global Restructuring,* edited by Paul Ong, Edna Bonacich, and Lucie Cheng, 192–221. Philadelphia: Temple University Press.

Buckler, Steve.
   1996. "Historical Narrative, Identity, and the Holocaust." Special Issue on Identity, Memory, and History. *History of the Human Sciences* 9, no. 4:1–20.

Camon, Ferdinando.
   1989. *Conversations with Primo Levi.* Translated by John Shepley. Marlboro, Vt.: Marlboro Press.

Chaliand, Gerard, and Jean-Pierre Rageau.
   1995. *The Penguin Atlas of Diasporas.* New York: Viking.

Chodoff, Paul.
   1980. "Psychotherapy of the Survivor." In *Survivors, Victims, and Perpetrators: Essays on the Nazi Holocaust,* edited by Joel E. Dimsdale, 205–18. Washington, D.C.: Hemisphere.

Clifford, James.
1997. *Routes: Travel and Translation in the Late Twentieth Century.* Cambridge: Harvard University Press.

Climo, Jacob.
1990. "Transmitting Ethnic Identity through Oral Narratives." *Ethnic Groups* 8:163–70.

Delbo, Charlotte.
1995. *Auschwitz and After.* Translated by Rosette C. Lamont. New Haven: Yale University Press.

Dimsdale, Joel E.
1980. "The Coping Behavior of Nazi Concentration Camp Survivors." In *Survivors, Victims, and Perpetrators: Essays on the Nazi Holocaust,* edited by Joel E. Dimsdale, 163–74. Washington, D.C.: Hemisphere.

Dominguez, Virginia A.
1993. "Questioning Jews." Review of *Storms from Paradise,* by Jonathan Boyarin and *Judaism and Modernization on the Religious Kibbutz,* by Aryei Fishman. *American Ethnologist* 20, no. 3:618–24.

Eitinger, Leo.
1980. "The Concentration Camp Syndrome and Its Late Sequelae." In *Survivors, Victims, and Perpetrators: Essays on the Nazi Holocaust,* edited by Joel E. Dimsdale, 127–62. Washington, D.C.: Hemisphere.

Espiritu, Yen Le, and Diane L. Wolf.
2001. "The Paradox of Assimilation: Children of Filipino Immigrants in San Diego." In *Ethnicities: The New Second Generation,* edited by Alejandro Portes and Ruben Rumbaut. Berkeley and Los Angeles: University of California Press.

Ezrahi, Sidra Dekoven.
1997. "See Under: Memory." *History and Memory* 7, no. 1/2:364–75.

Foster, John Burt.
1995. "Cultural Multiplicity in Two Modern Autobiographies: Friedlander's *When Memory Comes* and Dinesen's *Out of Africa.*" *Southern Humanities Review* 29, no. 3:205–18.

Friedlander, Saul.
1975. *When Memory Comes.* New York: Farrar, Straus and Giroux.

1992. Introduction to *Probing the Limits of Representation: Nazism and the "Final Solution,"* edited by Saul Friedlander. Cambridge: Harvard University Press.

1993. *Memory, History, and the Extermination of the Jews of Europe.* Bloomington: Indiana University Press.

Furst, Disider, and Lilian R. Furst.
1994. *Home is Somewhere Else: Autobiography in Two Voices.* Albany: SUNY Press.

Gallant, Mary, and Jay Cross.
1992. "Surviving Destruction of the Self: Challenged Identity in the Holocaust." *Studies in Symbolic Interaction* 13:221–46.

Goldberg, Michael.
1995. *Why Should Jews Survive? Looking Past the Holocaust toward a Jewish Future.* Oxford: Oxford University Press.

Goldenberg, Myrna.
1998. "Memoirs of Auschwitz Survivors: The Burden of Gender." In *Women in the Holocaust,* edited by Dalia Ofer and Lenore Weitzman. New Haven: Yale University Press.

Guarnizo, Luis Eduardo.
1996. "The Mexican Ethnic Economy in Los Angeles: Capitalist Accumulation, Class Restructuring, and the Transnationalization of Migration." Working Paper Series, no. 1, California Communities Program, Dept. of Human and Community Development, University of California, Davis.

Guarnizo, Luis Eduardo, and Michael Peter Smith.
1998. "The Locations of Transnationalism." in Special Issue on Transnationalism from Below. *Comparative Urban and Community Research* 6:3–34.

Haidu, Peter.
1992. "The Dialectics of Unspeakability: Language, Silence, and the Narratives of Desubjectification." In *Probing the Limits of Representation: Nazism and the "Final Solution,"* edited by Saul Friedlander, 277–99. Cambridge: Harvard University Press.

Halivni, David Weiss.
1996. *The Book and the Sword.* New York: Farrer, Straus and Giroux.

Hartman, Geoffrey.
1992. "The Book of the Destruction." In *Probing the Limits of Representation,* edited by Saul Friedlander, 318–34. Cambridge: Harvard University Press.

1994. "Introduction: Darkness Visible." In *Holocaust Remembrance: The Shapes of Memory,* edited by Geoffrey Hartman, 1–22. Oxford: Blackwell.

1996. *The Longest Shadow: In the Aftermath of the Holocaust.* Bloomington: Indiana University Press.

Hass, Aaron.
1996. *The Aftermath: Living with the Holocaust.* Cambridge: Cambridge University Press.

Helmreich, William.
1992. *Against All Odds: Holocaust Survivors and the Successful Lives They Made in America.* New York: Simon and Schuster.

Hirsch, Marianne.
1997. *Family Frames: Photography, Narrative, and Postmemory.* Cambridge: Harvard University Press.

Kaufman, Debra Renee.
1996. "Introduction: Gender, Scholarship, and the Holocaust." *Contemporary Jewry* 17: 3–18.

Kingreen, Monica.
1994. *Judisches Landleben in Windecken, Ostheim, und Heldenbergen.* Hanau, Germany: CoCon Verlag.

Krystal, Henry.
   1968. "Patterns of Psychological Damage." In *Massive Psychic Trauma*, edited by Henry Krystal, 1–23. New York: International Universities Press.

LaCapra, Dominick.
   1994. *Representing the Holocaust: History, Theory, Trauma*. Ithaca: Cornell University Press.

Langer, Lawrence.
   1991. *Holocaust Testimonies: The Ruins of Memory*. New Haven: Yale University Press.

   1995. *Admitting the Holocaust: Collected Essays*. New York: Oxford University Press.

Levi, Primo.
   1986. "The Memory of Offense." In *Bitburg in Moral and Political Perspective*, edited by Geoffrey Hartman, 130–43. Bloomington: Indiana University Press.

Lifton, Robert Jay.
   1980. "The Concept of the Survivor." In *Survivors, Victims, and Perpetrators: Essays on the Nazi Holocaust*, edited by Joel E. Dimsdale, 113–26. Washington, D.C.: Hemisphere.

Linden, Ruth.
   1993. *Making Stories, Making Selves: Feminist Reflections on the Holocaust*. Columbus: Ohio State University Press.

Linenthal, Edward.
   1995. *Preserving Memory: The Struggle to Create American's Holocaust Museum*. New York: Viking.

Loshitzky, Yosefa.
   1997. *Spielberg's Holocaust: Critical Perspectives on* Schindler's List. Bloomington: Indiana University Press.

Malkki, Liisa H.
   1995. "Refugees and Exile: From 'Refugee Studies' to the National Order of Things." *American Review of Anthropology* 24:495–523.

Niederland, William C.
   1964. "Psychiatric Disorders among Persecution Victims: A Contribution to the Understanding of Concentration Camp Pathology and Its After-effects." *Journal of Nervous and Mental Diseases* 139:458–74.

Polt, Renata, ed. and trans.
   1999. *A Thousand Kisses: A Grandmother's Holocaust Letters*. Tuscaloosa: University of Alabama Press.

Portes, Alejandro, and Ruben Rumbaut.
   1990. *Immigrant America: A Portrait*. Berkeley and Los Angeles: University of California Press.

Rubinoff, Lionel.
   1993. "Jewish Identity and the Challenge of Auschwitz." In *Jewish Identity*, edited by David Theo Goldberg and Michael Krausz. Philadelphia: Temple University Press.

Safran, William.
   1991. "Diasporas in Modern Societies: Myths of Homeland and Return." *Diaspora* (spring): 83–99.

Steedman, Carolyn.
   1996. "About Ends: On the Way in Which the End Is Different from an Ending." *History of the Human Sciences* 9, no. 4:99–115.

Stier, Oren Baruch.
   1996. "The Propriety of Holocaust Memory: Cultural Representations and Commemorative Response." Ph.D. diss., University of California, Santa Barbara.

Sturken, Marita.
   1997. *Tangled Memories: The Vietnam War, the AIDS Epidemic, and the Politics of Remembering.* Berkeley and Los Angeles: University of California Press.

Suleiman, Susan Rubin.
   1996. "Monuments in a Foreign Tongue: On Reading Holocaust Memoirs by Emigrants." *Poetics Today* 17, no. 4:639–57.

Tec, Nechama.
   1984. *Dry Tears: The Story of a Lost Childhood.* New York: Oxford University Press.

Um, Katharya.
   1998. "Negotiating Borders: Cambodian Americans in National and Transnational Contexts." Paper presented at the workshop "Transnationalism and the Second Generation." Harvard University.

Waters, Mary.
   1990. *Ethnic Options: Choosing Identities in America.* Berkeley and Los Angeles: University of California Press.

White, Naomi Rosh.
   1988. *From Darkness to Light: Surviving the Holocaust.* Melbourne: Collins Dove.

Williams, Brackette.
   1996. "Skinfolk, Not Kinfolk: Comparative Reflections on the Identity of Participant-Observation in Two Field Situations." In *Feminist Dilemmas in Fieldwork,* edited by Diane L. Wolf, 72–95. Boulder: Westview Press.

Winter, Miriam.
   1997. *Trains: A Memoir of a Hidden Childhood during and after World War II.* Jackson, Mich.: Kelton Press.

Wolf, Diane L.
   1996. "Situating Feminist Dilemmas in Fieldwork." In *Feminist Dilemmas in Fieldwork,* edited by Diane L. Wolf, 1–55. Boulder: Westview Press.

   2002. *From Auschwitz to Ithaca: The Transnational Journey of Jake Geldwert.* Occasional Publications of the Program of Jewish Studies and the Department of Near Eastern Studies, Cornell University. Bethedsa, Md.: CDL Press.

Wolman, Ruth.
   1996. *Crossing Over: An Oral History of Refugees from Hitler's Reich.* New York: Twayne Publishers.

Yerushalmi, Yosef Hayim.

1996. *Zakhor: Jewish History and Jewish Memory*. Seattle: University of Washington Press.

Young, James E.

1988. *Writing and Rewriting the Holocaust: Narrative and the Consequences of Interpretation*. Bloomington: Indiana University Press.

1993. *The Texture of Memory: Holocaust Memorials and Meaning*. New Haven: Yale University Press.

1997. "Between History and Memory." *History and Memory* 9, no. 1/2:47–58.

Zuckerman, Yitzhak.

1993. *A Surplus of Memory*. Translated and edited by Barbara Harshav. Berkeley and Los Angeles: University of California Press.

9

The Ideology of Affliction

Reconsidering the Adversity Thesis

Bernard Susser

A Jew walks along the streets of Minsk (or was it Pinsk?). A bird flying above relieves itself right on his head. He looks up plaintively and says, "far de goyim zingen zey" [for the goyim they sing].

This sense of being embattled and beset—the perennial victim—is perhaps the most prevalent and familiar of Jewish attitudes. It can be found on all levels of Jewish discourse: in the most sophisticated theology, in daily prayer, in folk wisdom, and in the familiar bittersweet character of Jewish humor. Jewish religiosity is often understood to be at its purest when it vindicates itself in trying circumstances. "Believing despite" [im kol zeh ani ma'amin] is a prototypical Jewish posture. If there is a paradigmatic Jewish tale—consider the stories of Pesach, Purim, and Chanuka—it is one of the embattled Jews suffering for their beliefs, resisting the pressures of a hostile world and prevailing nevertheless. Adversity and troubles (that omnipresent Yiddish/ Hebrew term: *tsoros*), it seems, are key elements in the Jewish identity—or at least of the Ashkenazic Jewish identity in the last millennium.

The stress on being beleaguered and oppressed is, therefore, not merely a Borscht Belt trope or a Woody Allen staple; it has been identified by serious thinkers as the linchpin of Jewish identity and survival. It is probably the oldest, simplest, and most popular explanation—certainly among Gentile observers—for the canny ability of Jews to outlive their various oppressors. Adversity, this hypothesis claims, steeled Jewish resistance, it made defection unthinkable, it created the kind of solidarity of both fate and faith that could withstand, indeed gain strength from, the oppressors' blows. In a word, Jews survived not despite their persecutions but because of them.

This argument was advanced more than three hundred years ago by Baruch Spinoza, the first nontraditional Jewish thinker of modern times.[1] There is nothing miraculous about Jewish survival, Spinoza asserted. It de-

rives from a simple source: the Jewish insistence on separatism and the hatred it engenders in others. In Spinoza's own words: "As to their continued
existence for so many years when scattered and stateless, this is in no way
surprising, since they have separated themselves from other nations to such
a degree as to incur the hatred of all, and this not only through external
rites alien to the rites of other nations but also through the mark of cir-
cumcision, which they religiously observe. That they are preserved largely
through the hatred of other nations is demonstrated by historical fact. . . ."[2]

In other words, Jews insulated themselves systematically from all other
peoples by practices (diet, language, rites, holidays, dress) that disciplined
them toward difference. By segregating themselves from others, they
brought universal hatred upon themselves. This hatred, however, did not im-
peril their national existence; it sustained it. First, because antisemitism kept
Jews apart by blocking any exit from their pariah community and, second,
because persecution and humiliation stung a proud and ancient people
into resistance and defiance. In the face of persecution, they found strength
in their traditions and in each other. Jews survived because antisemitism
defined them and preserved them as a people apart.

What is more, history seemed to corroborate Spinoza's adversity thesis.
When conditions did subsequently improve and adversity declined, Jewish
resolve and cohesion relaxed. When, more than three centuries later in the
closing years of our millennium, tolerance and even respect replaced adversity and persecution, the trickle of defections from Jewishness became a
veritable torrent. Proponents of the adversity thesis conclude, therefore,
that the fortunes of Jewish survival rise and fall with the tides of Gentile antisemitism. Heine's untranslatable play on words says it best: "Wie es sich
Christelt, so Judelt es sich." [As Christianity goes, so goes Judaism.]

It is, indeed, an irony that does not cease to fascinate: When pogroms and
crusades carried out their tortures and murders, Jewish resolve never slack-
ened; but when the allures of enlightenment and acceptance were in the
air, Jews tripped over each other to be first and loudest on the side of cosmopolitan modernity. Jews fearlessly resisted brutal Christian assaults on their
Jewish identity, but when they were given the opportunity, they renounced
it voluntarily. If apostasy was repudiated with unparalleled courage, many
embraced assimilation with hardly a second thought. What could be more
compelling evidence for the power of adversity to immunize Jews against
defection?

From inside the Jewish world, however, important reservations need to
be expressed about the adversity thesis. Committed Jews recoil from the as-
cription of Jewish perpetuity to Gentile oppression rather than to Jewish belief and determination. There is something perverse and counterintuitive
in diminishing a remarkable intellectual and cultural tradition with three
millennia of history to the status of an epiphenomenon. Not only does it

trivialize the profound and original, it flies in the face of what Jews understood themselves to be doing in preserving and dying for their faith. Since Jews are what others make of them, there is no reason to enter into the logic and substance of Jewish thinking or to understand how the Jewish world understood what it was doing. Very simply, it defies credibility to reduce a major cultural tradition to a defense mechanism or a social reflex akin to sheep huddling when the wolf approaches.

The alternative explanation insists that the key to understanding Jewish attitudes lies within Jewish thinking itself. If commitment to Jewish survival weakens, the source of that weakening must be sought in the internal push and pull of Jewish ideas. Even if it is true that adversity plays some part in the development of Jewish attitudes, the specific way in which adversity is incorporated into and refracted through the Jewish prism must be understood in specifically Jewish terms.

How then did adversity appear to pre-Enlightenment Jews? Above all, it could be depended upon. Gentile hostility was a consistent, one might even say, reliable source of adversity in Jewish history. It rarely failed to provide the calamities that necessitated ennobling sacrifice and heroism. The brute fact of persecution, I am convinced, has become more than a simple historical datum; over time, it has become an obsessive, tenacious, and pervasive mental fixture of Jewish identity—one might even say it has been *reified*, that is, transformed into a static mental picture that is independent of its empirical referent. It is not too much to claim that Jewish identity, in our millennium at least, has been built around it.

One writer has commented that chroniclers of Jewish history have left the "impression that Jewish life in the Diaspora was uniformly and eternally plagued by the irrational, unpredictable, and all-encompassing evil of anti-semitism."[3] And yet there were periods and places in which reasonably amicable relations between Jews and Gentiles prevailed. Still, historical memories often conspired to regard cordiality with suspicion, to believe that it was tentative and exceptional. The image of Jewish life as insecure, of anti-semitism as a permanent threat, and of violent onslaught as *the* residual condition, was so deeply entrenched in Jewish intuitions and perceptions that at least by the late medieval era it prevails even in periods of relative tranquility and prosperity.

Although the kind of "lachrymose" historiography that portrays Jewish history as a series of unrelenting tragedies has been partially discredited, this does not mean that Jews themselves understood their condition in anything but embattled terms.[4] That Jewish history should be stubbornly perceived as beleaguered and sorrowful even at times when this view was incongruous with reality is, for our purposes, a relevant point. Both leaders and laymen in premodern Europe remained unswayed in their perceptions: they lived with a deep sense of anxiety and dread.[5] What I am suggesting is that for them to have believed otherwise would have entailed a major revolution in Jewish theology, folk wisdom, and communal consciousness.

In the end the dominant attitude was, as the categorical rabbinic epigram puts it: "it is a well-known principle that Esau hates Jacob" [halakha hee k'yadua sh'Esav soneh L'Yaakov]. Which is, of course, to say that Gentiles hate Jews. Notably, when discussions of Jewish-Gentile rapprochement do take place, they almost invariably turn upon messianic deliverance. Messianic deliverance is, in fact, explicitly defined as such: the end to Jewish subjugation by the nations of the world (shibud malkhuyot).

As no other feature of Jewish civilization, the conviction that oppression is permanent and reconciliation is illusory has been faithfully passed on from generation to generation. Deeply encoded and primordial, it often outlives even the decline of Jewish knowledge and the erosion of Jewish commitment. Even among those in the throes of assimilation, it appears to resist easy repudiation. The sense of embattlement is perhaps the only Jewish remnant that persists when all else has been sloughed off. Many for whom Jewishness is only a trivial vestige draw the line when confronting the symbols of the historical oppressor: the cross and the church. "It's not important if I'm a Jew," they seem to be saying, "but I know that I'm *not* a Christian." Many entirely marginal American Jews continue to carry within themselves this stubborn remnant: We have not forgotten persecution and we are not Christians.

This persistent sense of being vulnerable and defenseless is one factor behind many of the well-known paradoxes of American Jewish life. Although Jews are the most financially successful ethnic group in America (with perhaps twice the income of non-Jews), they voted, at least until recently, as if they were a underprivileged minority—roughly like Hispanics. Although the professionals report that there are virtually no areas of American life that are closed to Jews because of discrimination,[6] two-thirds of American Jews continue to believe otherwise.[7] When asked to predict how non-Jews will respond to questions measuring acceptance of Jews as equals in American society, Jews consistently and substantially overestimate Gentile hostility.[8] More piquant still: one-third of the contributors to the Jewish Federation in San Francisco expressed the belief that a Jew could not be elected to Congress from San Francisco—this when (1985) all three members of Congress from the San Francisco area, the two state senators, and the mayor were Jews.[9]

Sometimes these sentiments surface in the most startling places. Erica Jong, queen of the picaresque-risque novel, who led a generation of readers through some of the seamiest nonsectarian bedroom adventures in recent memory, devotes an essay to the subject: "How I Got to Be a Jew."[10] The essay is vintage Jong: all razzle-dazzle and wise-cracking giddiness. But some-how, stuck amidst the banter, the following dead-earnest paragraph unac-countably appears: "A Jew may wander from Egypt to Spain to Germany to America to Israel picking up different languages and hair and eye color, but nevertheless remains a Jew. And what is a Jew? A Jew is a person who is safe *nowhere.* . . . A Jew is a person who can convert to Christianity from now to Doomsday, and still be killed by Hitler if his or her mother was Jewish. This explains why Jews are likely to be obsessed with matters of identity. Our sur-vival depends on it."[11]

There are many younger Jews in the sovereign Jewish state of Israel for whom the experience of antisemitism is theoretical and remote. Yet, even among them the same curiously incongruous sense of being the victim of dark Gentile designs erupts in the most unexpected contexts. Not far from the surface of even the most prosaic diplomatic friction between Israel and other states lurks the suspicion that all is not as meets the eye, that ancient enmities are being surreptitiously rehearsed. Perhaps a moment of reflec-tion scatters these phantasms to the wind, but it says a great deal that these conditioned reflexes get past the gatekeepers of reason in the first instance. When a referee in an international soccer or basketball game makes an os-tensibly bad call against the Israeli team, some primordial string of this perennially wronged people is plucked and begins to resonate uncontrol-lably. In one such instance that I experienced, a thoroughly secular, Western-ized, sabra intellectual with whom I was watching a basketball game became so deeply agitated by a referee's call that out of some cavernous historical recollection and in the most pronounced Yiddish accent came the ultimate curse: *antezemitt!*

The centrality of Gentile hostility in Jewish culture renders alternate in-terpretations of Jewish tradition, history, and practice difficult to sustain. In-deed, there is remarkably little interest in traditional Jewish discourse in con-templating a world in which Gentile hostility has ceased, in which the siege had ended. What Jewish belief and practice would look like in an accom-modating world remains a virtually unbroached subject—at least not in the Ashkenazi world during the past millennium. In short, there has been no widely accepted reading of Jewish existence in terms of Gentile acceptance. Nor, arguably, could there be such a reading that did not undermine inte-gral parts of the Jewish emotional and intellectual constitution.

What emerges for modern Jews is, therefore, a striking dissonance be-tween the cultural assumptions of the tradition and the reality with which they are familiar. The tradition lacks the psychological and cognitive re-sources to account for a positive, accommodating world while it is just such a world that Western, democratic, pluralist societies provide. Embattledness as an instinct has outlived embattledness as a reality. And this discrepancy has created a major crisis of credibility.

Does all of this mean that in the end Spinoza was right, that the Jews "are preserved largely through the hatred of other nations"? Spinoza may have been right in regard to the seventeenth century, but I am convinced that his analysis is no longer relevant. In our era, it is not persecution per se that is critical but rather its having been Jewishly internalized and interpreted in a specific way. If Jewish resolve crumbles when the siege ends, it is not so much because without adversity there is no solidarity; it is rather that having incorporated Gentile hostility deeply into Jewish religious and popular perceptions, there is great difficulty in constructing a plausible worldview when it is absent.

Let me try to flesh out this point. Pre-Enlightenment Jews shared an intense sense of ethno-religious communality in which peoplehood and faith were scarcely distinguishable. It was precisely this unity—communal existence as a religious category—that sustained them in the face of intolerable realities. When confronting degradation and violence at the hands of the Gentile, religious faith aided them in making sense of what was a grotesquely illogical and unacceptable reality. It spoke to the question of theodicy when persecution was a unavoidable daily predicament. Finally, it provided the strength to rebuild after the attack, the comfort to resist despair, and the meaning to carry on.

Just as their religious outlook granted them the strength to deal with adversity, so their faith reinforced the permanent fear of pogroms and expulsion in their minds. Adversity, so the normative Jewish tradition taught, was no passing burden; it was the unalterable Jewish destiny. Judaism both explained and predicted affliction as an integral part of the divine plan.

Few are the normative Jewish texts that fail to repeat the following paradigmatic tale. God loves the Jews, they are his chosen people. He gave to them and only to them, his Torah and his Law. Because God loves the Jews above all other people, he is especially strict and demanding with them lest they depart from his teachings. But the Jews are often not up to the high standards imposed upon them. They abandon his commandments and worship other gods. Forgetting their chosenness, they succumb to the ways of other peoples, aping their customs and adopting their values. They trample his courtyard in feigned piety although their hearts are callous and obdurate. And for all of this, God's wrath is loosed upon them through the fury of the Gentile. In virtually every era, the Jews are struck with the force of this divinely directed retribution and, in the midst of their suffering, they are called upon to recognize their sinfulness and to seek forgiveness.

The opening chapters of the Book of Judges present a illustration of this paradigm. After the passing of Joshua, the Israelites "did what is evil in Yahweh's eyes and served Baals. They deserted Yahweh, God of their ancestors, who brought them out of Egypt, and they followed other gods from those of the surrounding peoples. . . . Then Yahweh's anger grew hot against Israel.

He handed them over to pillagers who plundered them; he delivered them to the enemies surrounding them and they were no longer able to resist their enemies."[12] Hearing their groans under the burden of oppression, God relents and appoints judges to rescue the Israelites from their plunderers. But once again they refuse to listen, once again they abandon the path of their ancestors. "Yahweh's anger then blazed out against Israel." Not having listened to my voice, God says, the nations that Joshua left in Israel after he died will remain where they are. They will put Israel to the test: will the Israelites cling to the paths of their ancestors or succumb to the temptations offered by their neighbors? The next stage should already be clear; if they resist the ways of sin and retain their purity, God will protect them. If, however, they fall under the sway of their neighbors, then these very peoples that God has left among them will rise up to torment them.[13]

What is extraordinary about this account is that Gentile oppression, far from being a problem in the light of God's special relationship with the Jews, serves to confirm it. Gentile hostility demonstrates that Jews are privy to a special status in divine creation. The baffling but consistent hatred of the Jew seemingly in all eras and cultures, serves to prove the centrality of Jewish history in the human odyssey and to verify, in Jewish eyes, how closely God's scrutiny follows them. The fact that Jewish history abounds in extraordinary disasters justifies the conclusion that it is no ordinary history.

In persecuting God's chosen people, the Gentiles act out of unforgivable malice and enmity. They do not, of course, understand that they serve as instruments of God's grand design. Oddly, Gentiles appreciate the special status of Jews in God's eyes. It is, in fact, jealousy of this status as well as resentment of Jewish rectitude—by comparison to which they are convicted of their own deficiencies—that prompts them to lash out violently. In other words, the strange logic of Jewish chosenness plays itself out subliminally in the Gentile mind and provokes the attack that is a wake-up call for repentance. All this without conspicuous divine intervention into the affairs of humankind.

This hidden religious drama, with the Jews cast as heroes playing at center stage, inverted the simple import of a problematic and melancholy fate. Ostensible victims were transformed into secret victors. Humiliation was transfigured into holiness and dignity. Inferior to Gentiles in power and position, Jews prove to be superior to them in their ordained destiny. Aggressive Gentiles venting their rage turn out to be unwitting pawns in divine providence, while the Jews, passively bearing the blows, are cast as the true champions and movers of history. It was this turning of the tables that formed the heart of the Jewish theodicy: what appeared to be unutterably degrading and unjust was, in fact, the chronicle of Jewish redemption.

To put it simply, Jewish religiosity furnished a vindication of Jewish suffering and endowed communal travails with significance. By providing a silver lining to a very dark cloud, Judaism rendered Jewish misfortunes endurable; indeed, it construed the anguish of Jewish history as a source of pride and a harbinger of triumph.

A set of important corollaries follow. First, were Jews to abandon their religious interpretation of their fate, their oppression would be rendered meaningless. Jewish history would be reduced to a tragedy bereft of consolation, a mortifying tale of impotence and humiliation that signified nothing. Without the Jewish theodicy, degradation and injustice would be merely degradation and injustice. Clinging to their faith, therefore, went beyond metaphysical commitments: it was a pressing psychosocial necessity. They could not question their faith without forfeiting the justification for their suffering. It is no wonder then that religiosity and the adversity-centered worldview so deeply implicated each other.

Second, were Gentile oppression to cease, Jewish ethno-religious civilization would need to undergo fundamental reformulations in order to retain its resilience and credibility. Jewish survival would no longer be able to draw its moral and psychological energy from the fortress mentality of the besieged. The meaning of ideas such as chosenness and exile would be open to examination. Jewish isolation and insulation would need to be reassessed. Messianic visions would require new content.

It may well be that to read Jewish history is to develop at least a mild case of paranoia. And after the Holocaust there is understandable resistance to the idea that the siege may well be ending. The fears and sensitivities accumulated over the centuries have had so many painful reinforcements that they will not be easily swayed by a half century of relative affluence and security—even if this new reality gives every sign of being essentially different from everything that preceded it.

But these stubborn fears—whatever their legitimate place in a healthy Jewish identity—are, at present, the source of a serious impasse. Since it is the adversity-centered segment of the Jewish heritage that most powerfully resists attenuation, it often remains the core substance of Jewish identity—particularly among those most vulnerable to assimilatory pressures. Indeed, it becomes the surrogate for virtually all other Jewish content and prevents the creation of a culturally self-affirming and psychologically autonomous understanding of Jewish existence. Moreover, in a welcoming and secure world, the penny will eventually drop. Even the well-known mechanisms of "cognitive dissonance" cannot endure indefinitely. In the end, with the adversity-centered worldview sliding into practical irrelevance, there seems to be no alternative to a natural falling away, a massive silent exit that threatens Jewish survival as it has never been threatened before.

Paradoxically, the adversity-centered worldview that once served to ensure Jewish survival today endangers it. It simulates Jewish substance, which is, in fact, missing. It artificially resuscitates a moribund ethno-religious consciousness although it cannot tell those who are affected why they ought to survive as Jews. Above all, it fails to encourage Jewish commitment or advance Jewish learning or enrich Jewish cultural life. If anything, it preempts just these developments.

On another front, the failure of religious justifications for Jewish suffering renders antisemitism intolerable. If all the blood and tears were not part of a great tale of deliverance, enduring them becomes all the more agonizing.[14] It is no surprise, therefore, that severing the religious umbilical cord encouraged many Jews to search for more immediate solutions to the problem of Jewish affliction. In a word: after the Enlightenment, antisemitism emerges as a problem to be solved rather than as a divinely ordained fate to be endured. If Esau does not really hate Jacob because it is fated, if this hatred is attributable to specifiable causes (Jewish separatism, lack of sovereignty, economic jealousy, or even Christian ignorance), if a different reality and different forms of Jewish life will create a different kind of Jewish fate, the tradition ceases to be the only way to vindicate Jewish existence. In these circumstances it becomes possible to replace the Jewish theodicy with a Jewish sociocultural reformation—whether of the Zionist, socialist, classical Reform, or some other variety.

What then is the place of adversity in the preservation of the Jewish people? In itself, adversity is only adversity. There is no intellectual or moral compulsion resident in the brute fact of adversity. Uninterpreted, it leads to no survivalist imperative. To be grasped as a credible justification for preserving Jewishness, adversity needs to be mediated through categories that give it meaningful consequences. Suffering needs to be appropriated by and construed within a viable Jewish worldview.

To be sure, adversity is always a potent catalyst. But it is far from a simple, autonomous stimulus that evokes a predictable response. A calamitous experience can trigger antithetical reactions depending on how it is decoded. Adversity may, of course, send powerful charges of solidarity through Jewish consciousness. It can even be interpreted, as many revolutionary Jews did at the beginning of the century, in Promethean terms: it is the price Jews pay for bringing the light of progress to a tarrying world. Simply put, for adversity to have a continuity-enhancing effect, sufferers must interpret their travail in the light of a Jewish mission with which they identify.

Prior to the Enlightenment, when the Jewish world was the sole reference point for virtually all Jews, adversity echoed within a closed Jewish chamber. It resonated with Jewish religious categories and was naturally shunted through the grooves of "the ideology of affliction." Hence, when Jews were beset by their foes, their sense of a common fate was inevitably heightened. In this sense, Spinoza spoke historical truth when he enunciated the adversity thesis in the pre-Enlightenment era. In the present, however, when the Jewish context is neither mandatory nor exclusive, adversity can echo off any number of ideological surfaces—each with its own peculiar kind of reverberation.

When suffering befalls a Jewishly "lapsed" sensibility, dramatically different kinds of reactions are possible—for example, the resolution to put as much distance between oneself and the cause of one's suffering as possible. Adversity may well intensify the lapsed Jew's sense that Jewishness is a unfortunate accident of birth, an identity imposed by conventions not of their own making. If it is only the irrational forces of circumstance that hold them to this life-threatening and irrelevant tribal affiliation, they must do all they can to be free of it. When, in addition, there is an attractive ideology of humanist universalism available to them and the humanist community invites them to join its ranks, the repudiation of Jewish affiliations is likely to become all the more forceful and principled.

It is, therefore, by no means the case that (1) Jewish solidarity depends upon the presence of adversity, or that (2) adversity necessarily entails the heightening of Jewish solidarity. The resurgence of Orthodoxy in our generation, for example, has been accomplished without adversity; indeed, it coexists with growing confidence, affluence, influence, and unprecedented freedom. What underwrites the Orthodox revival is, it appears, the power of a religious idea, the spiritual demands it makes, and the human fulfillment that it offers its followers.

On the other side, suffice it to say that in the Weimar Republic, with Nazism on the horizon, more than one-third of German Jews were intermarrying. Despite the palpable menace of antisemitism—signs of which were everywhere—assimilation continued apace. In addition, as one of the most cosmopolitan, progressive cultures of the twentieth century, much of Weimar Germany offered a standing invitation for Jews to shed their particularity and join the German mainstream. For many disaffected Jews the threat of adversity, coupled with the promise of acceptance, translated into redoubled efforts to disappear into the woodwork. Adversity, in this case, may well have hastened assimilation.

Neither does the persecution of Jews in the Soviet Union appear to have triggered any notable return to Jewishness. Bereft of Jewish education and culture, Soviet Jews, for the most part, slid into oblivion. Despite suppression and mistreatment, intermarriage rates soared, Yiddish was replaced by Russian, great centers of Jewish learning vanished, and a community of some three million Jews was on the verge of cultural extinction. Vague nostalgia and quiescent national memories were all that survived. Lacking a Jewish frame through which adversity could be harnessed to Jewish survival, Jewishness all but expired.

Nor did the experience of the Holocaust have a substantially different effect. The destruction of European Jewry—far and away the most harrowing form of adversity the Jews have ever suffered—did not spark revivals of Jewish commitment. No significant return to Jewish identity, learning, belief, or practice followed the full disclosure of the Holocaust's horrors. Although I am unaware of any relevant empirical data that quantifies personal reactions to one's Jewishness in the wake of the Holocaust experience,[15] there is ample experiential and anecdotal evidence that reactions varied widely: at the one pole, the Holocaust was understood to be divine retribution on the grandest scale; at the other, it was perceived to be the most decisive argument imaginable for nihilism. Some drew from it the need to reaffirm their Jewish heritage. For others, Jewishness was a plague to be escaped. Although there were celebrated cases of committed Jews who abandoned their commitment and, on the other side, of lapsed Jews who dramatically returned to their roots, these are, in all likelihood, exceptions. For the most part, reactions followed assumptions. Committed and believing Jews assimilated the Holocaust into their worldview; for them adversity, comprehended in traditional terms, fostered Jewish continuity. Estranged Jews, on the other hand, drew their own ineluctable conclusions.[16]

If, as has been remarked, modernity means the movement from destiny to choice, then adversity too has become modernized: it has gained its own interpretive latitude. One needs to choose the interpretation of adversity that one favors. It no longer cuts only one way. The era when adversity instinctively quickened the Jewish sense of identity is over. The adversity-centered worldview, although preserving a certain latent momentum that can still occasionally flare into life, is losing its hold. In the absence of a governing Jewish sensibility, adversity is what you make of it.

Parenthetically, the single explicit attempt in recent years to justify Jewish survival in adversity-centered terms has had little or no impact. In 1978 Emile Fackenheim wrote that the Holocaust had added a 614th commandment: Deny Hitler a posthumous victory. Do not assimilate![17] But—as has become clear over the ensuing years—defiance, in itself, is not a program. Without a substantive reason for resisting the assimilatory impulse, even the Holocaust is impotent. Defiance, even when mixed with guilt, has no content: it can perhaps justify momentary stands of pique or irrational bursts of recalcitrance but it cannot underwrite Jewish survival.

If large segments of contemporary American Jewry suffer from advanced disaffection, it is ultimately because Jewish learning and sensibilities have lost their hold upon them. Without internal, positive motivation to vindicate Jewish communal distinction, the force of American pluralist universalism may well be irresistible. After the fall, even adversity cannot put the Jews back together again. The lack of adversity may, in fact, render it easier to exit the Jewish fold without embarrassment or distress, but the lack of adversity is not, per se, the grounds for the mass exit of recent decades.

The guarantor of contemporary Jewish survival is then not to be found outside the Jewish world. It is what Jews think, rather than what Gentiles do, that is decisive. If the "will to live" rooted in a commitment to Jewish ideas, values, and practices perishes, nothing can—perhaps nothing should—retard the natural death of the Jewish people.

The essential question is then: can Jewishness reconstruct itself in a way that substantially reduces the hold of the ideology of affliction? Will Jews learn how to take "yes" for an answer? Can Jewishness avoid understanding itself in the perennial image of a tightrope walker, or the precarious fiddler on the roof whose misstep will mean tragedy? Can Jewish identity be reformulated to account for a pluralist and accommodating world? If it is true, on the one hand, that Orthodox religiosity of the *status quo ante* variety is intellectually closed to most of us and, on the other, that secular national culture in the Israeli style is unavailable in the diaspora, are there forms of sustainable Jewishness gestating in history that can rest more on choice than on destiny, more on well-being and security than on persecution and negotiating one's identity under the pressure of others, more on learning and creativity than on in-group complicity? It is here, I wish to submit, that the question of Jewish identity in the diaspora needs to be engaged.

NOTES

1. See Yirmiyahu Yovel, *Spinoza and Other Heretics: The Marrano of Reason* (Princeton: Princeton University Press, 1989).

2. *Tractatus Theologico-Politicus*, trans. Samuel Shirley (Leiden: E. J. Brill, 1989), 99.

3. Jane Gerber, "Anti-Semitism and the Muslim World," in *History and Hate: The Dimension of Anti-Semitism*, ed. David Berger (Philadelphia: Jewish Publication Society, 1986), 74.

4. Salo W. Baron's work contains a systematic critique of this view. See, e.g., his *History and Jewish Historians* (Philadelphia: Jewish Publication Society of America, 1964).

5. See M. J. Rosman, "Jewish Perceptions of Insecurity and Powerlessness in Sixteenth- to Eighteenth-Century Poland," *Polin*, 1 (1986): 19–27.

6. See *American Pluralism and the Jewish Community*, ed. Seymour M. Lipset (New Brunswick, N.J.: Transaction Publishers, 1990), 18. Among others, Lipset cites Lucy Dawidowicz, *On Equal Terms: Jews in America, 1881–1981* (New York: Holt Rhinehart and Winston, 1982), 131–32.

7. Steven M. Cohen, *The Political Attitudes of American Jews, 1988: A National Survey in Comparative Perspective* (New York: American Jewish Committee, 1989). Cited by Lipset, *American Pluralism*, 22.

8. See, for example, Jerome Chanes, "Antisemitism and Jewish Security in America Today: Interpreting the Data. Why Can't Jews Take 'Yes' for an Answer?" *Antisemitism in America Today*, ed. Jerome Chanes (New York: Birch Lane Press, 1995), 3–30.

9. See Lipset, *American Pluralism,* 22.

10. Appears in her semi-autobiographical book, *Fear of Fifty* (New York: Harper Collins, 1994).

11. Jong, *Fear of Fifty,* 79.

12. Judges 2.11–14.

13. Judges 2.20–23 and 3.1–6.

14. Ben Halpern, *The Idea of the Jewish State* (Cambridge: Harvard University Press, 1969), 3–15.

15. For a recent study, see William Helmreich, *Against All Odds: Holocaust Survivors and the Successful Lives They Made in America* (New York: Free Press, 1992).

16. For a moving literary exposition of these choices, see Chaim Grade's story entitled, "My Quarrel With Hirsh Razeiner," in *A Treasury of Yiddish Stories,* ed. Irving Howe and Eliezer Greenberg (New York: Schocken, 1958). It has been made over into a film of exceptional power entitled *The Quarrel.*

17. See Emile Fackenheim, *The Jewish Return into History: Reflections in the Age of Auschwitz and a New Jerusalem* (New York: Schocken, 1978).

10

Jewish Identity Writ Small

The Everyday Experience of Baalot Teshuvah

Louise E. Tallen

During one of my many conversations with Penina, a Lubavitcher *baalat teshuvah,* she reflected on the importance of a Jewish identity, saying, "in the religious life you are a Jew as your primary identity before you're a woman or a man. If things sway you through your second identity as a woman or a man you have to go back to your primary identity to decide what to do about it. But what does it mean to be . . . a Jew as your primary identity?" What does it mean to be a Jew in America at the close of the twentieth century? With the competing forces of multiple identities inherent in the modern world, Judaism has become only "one resource among others upon which an individual may draw" (Schoenfeld 1988) in creating identity. So, what makes the appellation "Jew" central to the identity of so many Jewish Americans, including those who have no ties to Judaism other than to call themselves Jews? Perhaps most important, how is Jewish identity lived and instantiated on a daily basis?

In this essay I analyze the concept of identity and, by examining the lives of *baalot teshuvah* (newly Orthodox Jewish women),[1] provide one illustration of the way in which Jewish identity is constructed and reconstructed.[2] This research explicates one side of the relationship between individual and collective identity, that of the individual. Through an examination of individuals in "transit" between two incongruent worlds, it is possible to gain a clearer picture of the competing forces of modern Jewish identity. Before turning to the experiences of *baalot teshuvah,* however, I want to explicate the notion of identity in general and Jewish identity in particular.

IDENTITY

Selves do not live in isolation; we exist in relationships with others (Mead 1934).[3] It is our ability (and need) to identify with others, either individuals or groups, that creates the link between self and the outside world. In order to create meaning, self reaches out to others and identifies with them, creating identities. Thus, creating and negotiating identities is a vital task of the self. Identity is "the sense of oneself as simultaneously an individual and a member of a social group" (London and Hirshfeld 1991:33).[4] Identity negotiation is largely an unconscious process (Erikson 1980:122). Yet for *baalot teshuvah,* as for other individuals who undergo radical life changes and for those living in cultural margins and borders, this process is often made conscious as part of the struggle to unlearn old ways of being in the world and learn new, often antithetical, ways.

For *baalot teshuvah,* finding a compromise between their former secular identity and the new identity associated with the ideals and norms of the religious community in which they live is of central importance. Every woman with whom I spoke, either casually or in the context of an interview, discussed the dilemma of managing competing demands between self-desire and the needs, expectations, and standards of her religious community. *Baalot teshuvah* have to learn new ways of behaving and thinking as they adopt an observant identity and they have to unlearn the thought and behavior patterns of their secular lives. Thus, *baalot teshuvah* have a double dilemma, they must negotiate a compromise between self and their new community and must decide what values of secular American culture to let go of and what to retain, if any.

In the research described below, I focus on how identity is experienced by individuals rather than on analytical discussions or cultural models (Hollan 1992; Holland and Kipnis 1994; Wikan 1995), because this focus allows examination of the ways in which individuals struggle to create and sustain meaning in their lives (Obeyesekere 1981; Goldberg 1982).[5] An examination of individual lives is important because it represents the discrepancy between the ideal of cultural models and the reality of lived experience.

JEWISH IDENTITY

Recently there has been a flood of volumes analyzing Jewish identity.[6] A major thread running through these discussions is that, beginning with the rise of the nation-state and the emancipation of the Jews, secular Jewish identity became a possibility for the first time. Zionism in particular caused a radical rethinking by transforming Judaism from "a divinely ordained body of beliefs, norms, and practices into a secular culture created by Jewish people" (Silberstein 1994:2). Jews began questioning their identity, thus rendering Jewish identity "essentially contested" (Silberstein 1994:2). The plethora of books and articles on the subject is ample evidence of its contested nature.

Nowhere is Jewish identity more contested than in the United States, where, in the modern and "postmodern" eras, the social emphasis on individualism, self-fulfillment, and choice are "virtually creedal" (Feingold 1991: 70). Jews in the United States in the late twentieth century have greater freedom than at any other time or place in the diaspora (Friedman 1991). Thus, Judaism, "a faith which commanded at Sinai is today compelled to rely on persuasion" (Feingold 1991:71). Judaism is just one identity facet among many for American Jews, and for a large minority, a rarely surfacing facet. Yet in this era of self-actualization and freedom of choice, increasing numbers of Jews are choosing Judaism as their core identity (Schoenfeld 1988).

Many studies examining Jewish identity focus on external, observable, quantifiable factors such as frequency of synagogue attendance, holiday and Shabbat observance, and attendance at Jewish functions. Yet what is left out are the personal, psychological aspects of identity (Schulweis 1991), what it *means* to choose Judaism as one's core identity (London and Hirshfeld 1991). Additionally, Jewish identity is often discussed at the theoretical level, leaving out accounts of how people actually experience Judaism. Yet, as Herman notes, it is important to study identity at the individual level because, "Judaism cannot be studied as something distinct from the Jewish people who are its carriers—as if it were a disembodied religious philosophy . . ." (Herman 1989:22). Thus, in order to understand how real flesh-and-blood Jews experience identity, it is vital to ask such questions as, how does one live a Jewish identity daily, feel it, experience it? How does one negotiate a path to observance and how does one stay on that path when surrounded by the "temptations" of the secular world? What are the difficulties and what are the rewards? Why do *baalot teshuvah* remain observant in the face of doubts? While other scholars have examined some of these questions, there are no works focusing solely on Chabad women that examine identity negotiation over the long term. Davidman's (1991) work is one of the few examining Lubavitch *baalot teshuvah*. Her research, like mine, seeks to understand women's experiences from their point of view (27). Yet Davidman focuses solely on "new recruits" and their "initial reactions to orthodoxy" (44). Additionally, most of Davidman's research focuses on the experiences of modern Orthodox women; she spent only one month with Lubavitch women at Beis Chana, a "residential institute" run by Chabad in Minneapolis, Minnesota (55). This differs greatly from my work in that I spent one year living within a Lubavitch community, seeing how women functioned in their daily lives. Beis Chana is an intense learning experience and women studying there are divorced from everyday experience.

Davidman's research sample also differed from mine. Davidman notes that almost 85 percent of the women at Beis Chana were 25 or younger (77), with an age range of 16 to 50. This differs greatly from my sample, in which the majority of the women were over 30, with an age range from 18 to 70.[7] So, while Davidman's research complements mine, my research focuses on an area not examined in Davidman's work; namely, how do *baalot teshuvah* maintain a religious identity over the long term? In the following sections I examine this question from the point of view of several *baalot teshuvah* whom I interviewed during the course of my fieldwork. Before introducing these women, however, I want to sketch out the research background.

RESEARCH BACKGROUND

The data for this study were collected during a year of research in San Francisco, California, centered around a Lubavitch Chasidic Chabad House. A Chabad House is a religious center set up by Chabad *shluchim* [emissaries] to serve the needs of local Chabad communities and to serve as outreach centers. Each Chabad House is relatively autonomous and reflects the personalities of the rabbi and rebbetzin [rabbi's wife] who are in charge of the particular house. Part of Chabad's central mission is encouraging unaffiliated Jews to return to Judaism.[8] This is part of a larger program to speed the arrival of *Mashiach* [the Messiah] through increasing the performance of *mitzvahs* [religious commandments]. This aspect of Chabad has created controversy within and without Orthodox circles, especially since the death of the most recent Chabad leader, Rebbe Menachem Mendel Schneerson. A large and vocal minority of Lubavitchers believes Schneerson is *Mashiach,* and this has led some in the Orthodox community to call for excommunicating Lubavitch from Judaism.

My primary goal, as stated above, was to learn how *baalot teshuvah* construct meaning and negotiate identity on a daily basis; how do they live a religious identity? This is an area that is largely unexplored. The few studies focusing on women's experiences explore their reasons for becoming religious (Davidman 1991) or their social roles within Orthodoxy (Kaufman 1991, 1995; Morris 1995), examining the construction of gender identity within a patriarchal religious tradition that limits women's participation in public roles. Yet the continuing struggle to negotiate a meaningful identity is a central issue for all the *baalot teshuvah* with whom I spoke.

As part of my research, I attended weekly religious services, holiday services, women's classes, and women's social events at Chabad House. I also spent time with women in their homes and places of employment. I spoke with sixty women, ranging in age from eighteen to seventy. Of these, I interviewed five women in depth, using an unstructured, minimally directed interview technique.[9] In the following sections I present the experiences of some of these *baalot teshuvah,* using their own words whenever possible.[10]

DISILLUSIONMENT AND SEARCHING

A common thread among the *baalot teshuvah* with whom I worked was a feeling of being exiles on Main Street while growing up. They frequently expressed the feeling that they didn't fit well within the world in which they lived. So they changed themselves in various ways to fit in, yet ultimately each found this unsatisfying. Eventually, these women chose to live in a community whose ethos resonated with their feelings, rather than continue remaking themselves to fit what they felt others wanted them to be. This decision, however, was not the end of the story; it merely marked the beginning of a new chapter of their lives. Even though the Lubavitch community feels more comfortable, *baalot teshuvah* still experience tension negotiating the "delicately variant and intricate" relationship between self and community (Goldschmidt 1995:250).

In their search for meaning some of these women tried finding their identity in feminist consciousness groups or anti–Vietnam War protests; others dabbled in Reichian therapy, Agni Yoga, or Macrobiotics; and still others adopted Christianity, Buddhism, or other religions; some experimented with drugs; and others entered therapy or joined twelve-step programs; one woman even tried belonging to different ethnic groups. Some women tried out many communities in their search for a meaningful core identity.

While active searching did not begin until adolescence, these women experienced discomfort with the world around them at a young age. For some the discomfort was with the Christian-influenced world around them; for others the discomfort was with Judaism itself. Additionally, many of the *baalot teshuvah* with whom I spoke had problematic family experiences resulting from such things as divorce, death, and mental illness. What these *baalot teshuvah* have in common is that in their struggles with identity, they tried to escape or minimize their "Jewishness" in their search for meaning. In the end, however, it was only after embracing Judaism that they began to develop what they feel are meaningful identities. To explore this discomfort and searching, I turn directly to the experiences of two *baalot teshuvah*.

Marcia has been observant for six years. Marcia's experiences growing up in a largely Christian suburb of San Francisco highlight feelings of dissonance and discord in her unsuccessful struggle to "fit in." She recalls feeling "odd" as a child, not fitting in with the other children in her neighborhood. Marcia recalls becoming aware of her family's "difference" after entering elementary school. Prior to that, Judaism was just another unmarked part of her family life. Once she entered the grade-school world, however, Marcia discovered her experiences didn't fit with those of the other children. At home, she lived in a Jewish world. Her parents often spoke Yiddish to each other and, though they did not regularly attend synagogue, her father read the *parsha* with her every week.[11] Yet the world outside Marcia's home was alien to her experiences; a world that did not want to accept her the way she was. She wanted desperately to fit in with the other children, even if it meant giving up her religion. In Marcia's words:

> I remember growing up in—California, feeling very odd . . . once I started to go to school . . . because my mother would pack my lunch and she would give me lox on pumpernickel or herring in a jar. All this stuff which to me was very normal. And I was in school eating this lox and everyone else had peanut butter and jelly. And I didn't care, but they cared. So they made a big thing about it, and said "eewwh, what's that orange stuff, [it's] stinky" and . . . So that was the beginnings of me wanting not to be who I was. . . . I couldn't get my mother to be normal, to be American. I just wanted to be not who I was, actually . . . I wanted peanut butter and jelly sandwiches on white bread. I wanted to, almost, go to church. Whatever I could do to be like them and not to be like me.

Marcia's disillusionment with her identity continued in high school, compounded by her father's death when she was twelve. She tried to distance herself from her Jewish identity by joining other ethnic groups. As she says, "The older I get chronologically, the more I don't want to be who I am. The more I wanna be like anybody. I must have gone through fifteen cultures. Ya know, first I was Filipino and then I was Black and then I was Latin. For a long time I was Latin." Yet none of these identities worked for Marcia; her search for meaning continued. She turned next to drugs as a way of escaping the painful world in which she lived, made more painful by the deaths of her mother and oldest brother when she was in her early twenties. Drugs also proved unsatisfying. It was after going through a drug rehabilitation program that Marcia took the first steps toward observant Judaism. Through a friend, she first encountered Chasidic Judaism at a Chabad House in San Francisco.

Penina has been observant for over twenty-five years. Like Marcia, she was disillusioned with her world when she was growing up. But for Penina, it was the world of Conservative Judaism she found wanting, believing it to be hypocritical and bereft of spirituality. Additionally, she recalls that while her father had an enthusiastic attitude toward Judaism, her mother felt "ambivalent" about it. Penina first experienced disillusionment with the children's services at the Conservative synagogue her family attended. While she enjoyed the services, she did not like that they were mandatory and she came to believe the teachings of Conservative Judaism were "totally hypocritical." She remembers asking each of her Hebrew school teachers about what happens to one's soul when one dies, and each teacher had his or her own belief. She says, "there was really no theology, and it was custom, custom, custom. . . . I never heard the idea that there was a law." Looking back, Penina says that the one saving grace in her Hebrew school experience was a teacher who, as she later found out, was a Lubavitch Chasidic Jew. As Penina recalls:

"There are so many contradictions in Conservative Judaism . . . when you learn that God said this, well He didn't really mean it, so I had to make my own conclusions. At least, thank God, in this one other school that I went to there was this lady who, I found out many years later, was a Lubavitcher . . . and I always remember that this teacher, I felt, believed what she was telling us. And she also taught us about *Ha Shem* and how he was everywhere. . . ."[12] When she was fourteen, Penina refused to attend synagogue any longer. Attending services was "torture," because "it was all such a sham that it was painful for me . . . and I felt like I did wanna have a relationship with God, but I didn't wanna have this relationship." So, she told her mother in the middle of a Yom Kippur service that she was never going to synagogue again: "I told my mother I'm not going back to Hebrew school, this is it. . . . And I almost made . . . a vow that I was never walking into a shul. . . . I thought it was disgusting. I thought it was a desecration of God's name to go there, and it was [a] very powerful thing in my life. . . . I don't remember fighting with my mother too much about it, it just was . . . a fait accompli."

This dramatic departure from organized Judaism was the beginning of a long and painful search for Penina, which she describes as a search for the "ultimate meaning of reality." Like many others of her generation, Penina became involved in anti–Vietnam War protests and was enamored of beat authors such as Jack Kerouac and Lawrence Ferlinghetti. She also experimented with drugs, especially marijuana and LSD. Each of these experiences, however, ended in disillusionment. Eventually her search led her to macrobiotics and through her macrobiotics teacher she was led to Lubavitch Chasidic Judaism.

TURNING TO ORTHODOXY

Eventually their search for meaning led these women to Lubavitch. Yet even though each woman described turning to Orthodoxy as coming home, embracing Orthodoxy represents only the beginning of a radical, ongoing identity transformation.[13] *Baalot teshuvah* believe deeply that becoming observant is the right choice, yet all experience conflict and psychic pain as part of this choice. Much of this conflict centers around giving up certain aspects of secular culture and with justifying becoming observant to themselves and others. Penina remembers that becoming *baal teshuvah* was not an inherently pleasant experience:

> My whole experience of *teshuvah* was not that it was fun. . . . I do feel *teshuvah*'s a wrenching experience for a person. You have to face everything I did up till now was filled with mistakes. That's why the older you are, the harder it is for people to do *teshuvah,* because then they have to say to themselves, all the things I thought were the most valuable things in the world, that I poured my energy into, weren't the most valuable things in the world and I have to trans-

fer over a whole new set of values on to my whatever I did? People do things 'cause they value them. So, I think it's [a] very painful process. . . . Some of it's very exhilarating and very beautiful, otherwise forget it . . . nobody would become *frum* [observant].

As one can see, becoming *baal teshuvah* requires a radical break with one's past, admitting one's old ways were wrong and making a commitment to learn new ways of being. I spoke with women who had been observant for varying lengths of time, from one month to twenty-five years. Even those who have been observant the longest still struggle with the conflict between their own desires and the community ideals of Lubavitch Chasidism. Penina expressed this idea eloquently: "I don't think that by becoming religious you stop having moral issues or you stop having moral choices. You still have the same exact moral choices except on a different level, you know? And I think it's just as difficult ethically and morally the deeper you get into Judaism. No, it's not just as difficult, that's not true, but it's just as complex, emotionally at different times."

Baalot teshuvah believe in the value of their new way of life. They do, however, face a dual dilemma. Not only are they trying to find a compromise between their own desires and those of the Lubavitch community, they are trying to unlearn a lifetime of values and behavior that they believe were mistaken; they are trying to shed an ill-fitting but sticky identity. *Baalot teshuvah* are in an unique position. In the process of confronting their resistance to certain observant practices, they attempt to dig up and root out the unconscious underpinnings of their resistance. Not only are they trying to rationalize their new behavior, they are trying to rationalize the fact that their behavior before becoming observant was, as Penina says, "filled with mistakes." The conflicts *baalot teshuvah* face do not prevent them from carrying on daily activities; rather these conflicts represent the same kind of internal struggle every individual faces as they negotiate a path through life; the struggle to mediate a compromise between self and community that comprises identity construction and reconstruction.

There appear to be three elements that cause conflict for *baalot teshuvah:* giving up those parts of a secular life that cannot be reconciled with a religious life, maintaining relationships with nonreligious family and friends, and learning to surrender one's will to God. The core element, however, is the difficulty of surrendering one's will to God; doing things not because one wants to or because one expects to gain something by one's actions, but rather doing things because that is God's will. As Father Mapple says in *Moby Dick*, "But all the things that God would have us do are hard for us to do . . . and hence he oftener commands us than endeavors to persuade. And if we obey God, we must disobey ourselves; and it is in this disobeying ourselves, wherein, the hardness of obeying God consists" (Melville 1964:72). Learning to disobey oneself in order to obey God creates the greatest tension for *baalot teshuvah;* a tension that persists over time. Penina discussed the difficulty of learning to obey God, highlighting the continuing struggle to maintain an observant identity, saying:

> It goes against the norm to listen to *halachah* [Jewish law] for anybody, even people that are brought up *frum*. Listening to an authority outside of yourself and your own personal desires is really antithetical on a certain level to the human condition, the not-evolved human part of us. So, everybody comes up with ten million excuses why not to do *xyz*, which is, basically, I feel, where I'm at right now with certain things in yiddishkeit. [When I first became observant] I never would have had a discussion within myself, well should I do this, or should I not do this? . . . I say, "no of course it matters in the cosmic scheme of things." Now I say, "who cares if I don't say my blessing after I just ate my whitefish?" . . . Sometimes I just get into that kind of attitude which is my *yetzer harah* [evil inclination]. . . . It becomes too comfortable. It becomes a culture, rather than a relationship with God after a certain point . . . and the Rebbe . . . said that Chasidus is totally against this. This is the point of Chasidus almost. The point of Chasidus, . . . I think the *Tzemak tzeddik* [the third Lubavitcher rebbe] said this, is that you should change the nature of your nature.

Chaya, a woman who has been observant for twelve years, discussed the idea that, even with conflicts, *baalot teshuvah* believe in the overwhelming rightness of maintaining an observant identity. While Chaya finds great fulfillment in living an observant life, it has also meant sacrificing certain things she might have if she lived a secular life. She has had trouble finding work because she will not work on Shabbat or on Jewish holidays, and even though it is illegal for employers to deny employment for religious reasons, it happens. In addition, even though she is firmly committed, there are times when she misses some events she enjoyed when living a secular life:

> I think that there's always aspects of it [being observant] that are difficult, particularly when you live in some place like San Francisco. There's just times I don't want to pray. I can't honestly say that I've had an overwhelming desire to go to the movies on Saturday, or anything like that, for a very, very long time. No, that doesn't really interest me. Sometimes it's frustrating when there's somebody in town that I wanna see. I had like[d] Bonnie Raitt since the sixties and when she started becoming popular again she started playing the area. . . . She plays Friday night every single time she plays in San Francisco, without fail. . . . So, that's frustrating. But, I certainly wouldn't trade going to see anyone for keeping Shabbos. But, it's hard. Sometimes I just wanna say, "oh I hate this *kashrut*." [14] I just wanna go in and buy a nice brie and eat it without guilt. So it's a constant thing and you think, what if this is all a big joke? This stuff goes through your mind, it goes through everybody's mind. What if [it's] not for real and I'm doing this for nothing . . . but it's not persistent enough and . . . I know that there is a truth to it all that I really believe, on a core basis, so these are just fleeting [thoughts] these are just your mind running.

Chaya reiterated her commitment to an observant life, saying:

> I do it [live an observant lifestyle] because the rewards are greater doing it
> than not doing it, and I think that's true of anybody that starts on a Torah
> path . . . at whatever level people are when they're making the journey, they
> don't generally go back for very long. That once you've taken a step into ob-
> servance on whatever level it is . . . they're not gonna go back on their obser-
> vance. There's no way that I'm ever gonna drive a car on Shabbos, not a
> chance, not unless it's a matter of life and death and then I would do it, but
> otherwise I have no desire to do that, I would never do it. Not because I'm go-
> ing to have some sort of spiritual mud thrown on myself, but just because I
> wouldn't feel good about it, I would gain nothing from it. So that's the moti-
> vator, not fear, just self-interest.

Speaking of her relationship with her family since becoming religious,
Chaya underscores the difficulty in maintaining relationships with nonobservant family members. "I think now that everybody [in my family] accepts
it, everybody's happy for me. They don't exactly understand how I could be
so *frum*. My father says, 'You know you're even more observant than your
grandparents were.' And I know that it makes him uncomfortable in some
ways. . . . Then sometimes I feel like they think I'm judging them, because
they're not doing something and I'm doing it. And I'm not. . . . But from
their point of view, they see somebody who doesn't want to watch television
on Shabbos . . . they don't understand, they really don't."

CONTINUING STRUGGLE AND NEGOTIATION

At the same time *baalot teshuvah* are struggling to resist the pull of the secular
world, they also face resistance to their observance from individuals within
the Lubavitch community who have been *frum* from birth. *Baalot teshuvah*
are, in some ways, not fully accepted into the religious world and are sometimes treated with suspicion by those raised within the tradition. Newly
Orthodox Jews are encouraged to marry other newly Orthodox Jews and actively discouraged from marrying individuals who were raised in an observant
household. There are several reasons for this. One is that Rebbe Menachem
Mendel Schneerson issued an edict saying that because *baalei teshuvah* were
born of women who did not follow *Taharat Mishpachah* [family purity laws],
they can only marry other *baalei teshuvah*. Another is fear of contamination
from the secular world. If someone who is *frum* from birth marries a *baal
teshuvah* and has children, those children might be exposed to the secular
world through contact with the nonobservant relatives of the newly Orthodox spouse. In addition, there is an underlying suspicion, especially if someone has not been religious long, that they might not have a solid commitment to an observant lifestyle and might abandon it. Others fear *baalot
teshuvah* are only practicing the surface aspects of the religion and will never

be able to reach the level of observance that comes with being raised in the tradition.

Squeezed from both sides, *baalot teshuvah* live in a borderland, caught between the secular and religious worlds, unable to fully enter the religious world and still feeling the pull of the secular world. In this way *baalot teshuvah* share many similarities with diaspora populations and others who inhabit cultural borderlands, a place which Anzaldua describes as "vague and undetermined . . . in a constant state of transition. The prohibited and forbidden are its inhabitants" (Anzaldua 1987:3).

DISCUSSION

Negotiating a religious identity is difficult, because adopting an observant lifestyle entails living a life radically different from that of a secular Jew in late-twentieth-century America, in which individual choice is creedal. For the observant person virtually every aspect of one's life is structured: what to wear; when and how to pray; what to eat; how to relate to one's spouse, to one's children, to one's natal family, and to unrelated individuals of the same and opposite sex; and how to behave in various social contexts. Most people who become observant do not adopt an observant lifestyle wholesale. Instead, they may start by practicing just one or two *mitzvahs* and then add more with time. For women, lighting Shabbat candles is often the first *mitzvah* they take on. Perhaps the most striking difference between secular and religious life, as discussed above, is learning to give over control of one's life to God, a concept that is antithetical to the individualist ideal of secular American culture and is the issue with which *baalot teshuvah* struggle the most.

As *baalot teshuvah* learn new community standards and models for living, they strive to attain and maintain those standards. Yet it is difficult for them to let go of secular American values they have spent a lifetime internalizing and utilizing, because, even though they desire change, making the change means consciously acknowledging that one's life up until becoming *baal teshuvah* has been lived incorrectly. This realization can be a wrenching experience. *Baalot teshuvah*, because they are dealing on a daily basis with the dissonance between their experience and new cultural ideals, are in an excellent position to describe and talk about their self-experience (Hollan 1992). What initially attracted *baalot teshuvah* to Orthodoxy was its rigid structure, its strict moral order, its well-defined roles for men and women, and its presentation of an absolute Truth. Yet, paradoxically, it is against this rigidity that they struggle the most, and at times they long for the ease of secular life.

Some *baalot teshuvah* do leave Orthodoxy, unable to find the meaning they are seeking. Yet most stay, even with all of the conflict. What is it that keeps most *baalot teshuvah* within Chabad? There are three factors: one, Chabad acknowledges the difficulty of *teshuvah* and supports it; two, *baalot teshuvah* learn new ways of interpreting their behavior and come to see their struggles as a way of coming closer to God; and three, they invest heavily both materially and spiritually in this new way of living and thus it is difficult to leave.

The majority of the Lubavitch community worldwide is made up of *baalei teshuvah,* many of whom, as with the women in this study, started on their path to observance as a result of Chabad outreach. The outreach program was elaborated under the direction of Rebbe Menachem Mendel Schneerson, and today Chabad's greatest emphasis is on reaching out to unaffiliated Jews (Friedman 1994; Ravitzky 1994). Chabad stresses the importance of *teshuvah* in its teachings, and this is the message of its outreach programs. *Teshuvah* leads one from a secular life to a life centered on Torah and *mitzvahs,* and it is *mitzvahs,* according to Chabad doctrine, that will speed the arrival of *Mashiach.* Belief in the power of *mitzvahs,* "elaborately developed by the Rebbe [Menachem Mendel Schneerson], is so fundamental to the Chabad-Chasidic ideology, as to serve as the premise underlying its entire philosophy and method of Jewish outreach" (Olidort 1995:3).

Chabad also acknowledges that *teshuvah* is difficult. The "Chabad way" is to encourage the performance of *mitzvahs,* even if one is unsure of the meaning behind them, stressing that belief follows action. The encouragement to perform *mitzvahs* even if one does not fully understand their purpose, combined with the recognition that *teshuvah* is difficult, validates the *baalat teshuvah*'s struggle and gives her a way to mediate her self-conflicts. As the majority of Lubavitchers are *baalei teshuvah,* these conflicts are a common experience.

The third reason holding *baalot teshuvah* within Orthodoxy is the great investment made in changing lifestyles. For many women, becoming *baal teshuvah* means leaving jobs, breaking ties with non-Jewish or secular Jewish friends and family, investing in all new kitchen ware to become kosher, buying a new wardrobe and getting rid of many articles of clothing they wore in the secular world. In addition, if a *baalat teshuvah* marries and has children, and those children are raised in an observant household, it is again much harder to go back to a secular life. Thus, learning to accommodate oneself to an observant lifestyle and finding ways to ameliorate self-conflict, is very important for *baalot teshuvah.*

Over time the *baalat teshuvah* experiences changes in her "intellectual habits" (Luhrman 1989:115). She learns new ways of interpreting events, acquires shared knowledge, and gains a "battery of new assumptions" (Luhrman 1989) that help her negotiate her way in the religious world and aid in melding her secular and religious identities.

Performing *mitzvahs* is one of the primary ways in which *baalot teshuvah* learn new assumptions and through which they learn new ways of interpreting events. All of the women with whom I spoke indicated that they could see direct positive manifestations in their lives as a result of performing *mitzvahs*. Belief in the benefits of *mitzvahs* was cited as a reason to continue being observant in the face of conflict.

Over time, the *baalat teshuvah* acquires more shared knowledge regarding aspects of religious observance, and this allows her to "discriminate between events in new ways" (Luhrman 1989:115). This is evident in the way in which *baalot teshuvah* often interpret unlikely positive events as the result of miracles rather than as the result of coincidence or luck. Penina, discussing the sudden reduction of a loan amount by a creditor, said it was "a gift from *Ha Shem* [God]."

Through explicit learning and through the everyday process of living an observant life, *baalot teshuvah* learn to use "a new battery of assumptions" to interpret events. For the observant person the world is filled with divine will; there is no existence apart from God. God, according to Chabad teaching (stemming from Kabbalistic doctrine), is the *Or Ein Sof* [light without end], and each individual is infused with a small spark of this light. Chabadniks believe this spark yearns to connect with God and thus draws individuals to *teshuvah*. Thus, even if one has internal conflicts regarding one's level of observance, it is believed this divine spark will push one toward the right path (Scholem 1974, 1995; Zalman 1966; Steinsaltz 1988).

Becoming *baal teshuvah* requires a radical break with one's past, an admittance that one's old ways were wrong, and a commitment to learning new ways of being. This process is gradual and often fraught with conflict. Yet, *baalot teshuvah*, partially as a result of their accommodation to new batteries of assumptions, believe in the value of their new way of life, and this appears to help ameliorate some conflicts. Yet, as illustrated above, conflict never ceases; the issues that cause conflict merely change. Changing the "nature of one's nature" is a long and continuing struggle.[15]

NOTES

1. The research on which this is based was funded in part by grants from the UCLA department of anthropology and the UCLA Social Psychiatry Student Research Training Program. The write-up of the research was funded by a UCLA Chancellor's Dissertation Fellowship. I spent a year living within a religious community in northern California. I used a combination of participant-observation and in-depth nondirected interviewing to obtain the data presented here. For a description and discussion of participant-observation see: Johnson (1978) and Langness and Frank (1981). For a discussion of methods and importance of in-depth interviewing see: Langness and Frank (1981); Levy (1984); Hollan and Wellenkamp (1994).

2. This research focuses only on a small subset of *baalei teshuvah;* thus I am not making claims that these experiences are "normative," nor necessarily representative. The experiences of these *baalot teshuvah*, however, resonate with the experiences of other *baalot teshuvah* written about by such scholars as Lynn Davidman and Debra

Kaufman, and they illuminate some of the issues facing secular Jews striving to balance Jewish and other identities in the modern world.

3. For more detailed information regarding the concept of self in anthropology see: Mead (1934); Hallowell (1955); Kohut (1971); Lee (1982); Crapanzano (1982 and 1992); Shweder and Bourne (1991); Baert (1992); Hollan (1992); Murray (1993); Spiro (1993); Cohen (1994); Cohen and Rapport (1995); Goldschmidt (1995); Wikan (1995).

4. For seminal work on identity see Erikson (1980 and 1993). For an overview of developments see Fogleson (1982).

5. Mead seems to hint at psychological processes by saying the way in which an individual "gets inside himself (experientially) in such a way as to become an object to himself . . . is the essential psychological problem of selfhood or of self consciousness. . . ." Yet Mead places this process firmly within the social realm, stating that the solution to this problem "is to be found by referring to the process of social conduct or activity in which the given person or individual is implicated" (Mead 1934). Durkheim also stressed the role of society, which he believed was prior to the individual in constructing self (1965, 1984).

6. See for example: Zenner (1988); Herman (1989); Meyer (1990); Gordis and Ben-Horin (1991); Bershtel and Graubard (1992); Goldberg and Krausz (1993); Silberstein and Cohn (1994); Kleeblatt (1996); and Boyarin and Boyarin (1997).

7. I excluded anyone under the age of eighteen from my sample because of human subjects protection regulations.

8. For background on Chabad and Chasidism see: Buber (1948, 1958, 1960); Mindel (1971, 1972); Hundert (1991); Mintz (1992, 1995); Landau (1993); Idel (1995).

9. See Levy (1973); Hollan and Wellenkamp (1994); and Langness and Frank (1981) for a discussion of this type of interview format.

10. The transcript portions used have been edited only to remove expressions such as "like," "you know," and "I mean," parts of spoken speech that are generally ignored by the listener, but which make for difficult reading.

11. The *Torah*, comprising the first five books of the Hebrew Bible, is divided into fifty-four weekly readings. Each week's reading is referred to as the weekly *parsha*.

12. *Ha Shem* [The Name] is one of the many ways observant Jews refer to God. Observant Jews generally do not use the word "God." Instead they use descriptive terms such as *Ha Shem*.

13. I am using the term "Orthodoxy" here in its general sense as the adherence to traditional teachings. And when I refer to *baalot teshuvah* as turning to Orthodoxy or being Orthodox Jews, I also am referring to this in its general as one who strictly observes the laws of Judaism. I do not mean to imply that Lubavitch in any way stands as a symbol for all Orthodoxy; indeed, it is but one example of many. Some scholars refer to Lubavitch and other Chasidic sects by the appellation "ultraorthodox" rather than Orthodox, but I don't feel that is a useful distinction because the reasons for the separation are often vague.

14. *Kashrut:* the laws for keeping kosher.

15. An earlier version of this paper was presented at a meeting of the University of California, Humanities Research Institute Residential Research Group, "Jewish Identity in the Diaspora." My work has been informed by discussion with various

members of this group and I am grateful for their insightful comments. This paper also benefited from discussion with Douglas Hollan and Anna Simons. Finally, I am grateful to the *baalot teshuvah* who shared their lives with me.

BIBLIOGRAPHY

Anzaldua, Gloria.
  1987. *Borderlands/La Frontera: The New Mestiza.* San Francisco: Aunt Lute Books.
Aviad, Janet.
  1983. *Return to Judaism: Religious Renewal in Israel.* Chicago: University of Chicago Press.
Baert, Patrick.
  1992. *Time, Self, and Social Being: Temporality Within a Sociological Context.* Aldershot, England: Avebury.
Bershtel, Sara, and Allen Graubard.
  1992. *Saving Remnants: Feeling Jewish in America.* Berkeley and Los Angeles: University of California Press.
Boyarin, Jonathan, and Daniel Boyarin.
  1997. *Jews and Other Differences: The New Jewish Cultural Studies.* Minneapolis: University of Minnesota Press.
Bozza, Anthony.
  1998. Random Notes. *Rolling Stone Magazine,* August 6, 1998.
Buber, Martin.
  1948. *Hasidism.* New York: The Philosophical Library.
  1958. *Hasidism and Modern Man.* Edited and translated by Maurice Friedman. New York: Horizon Press.
  1960. *The Origin and Meaning of Hasidism.* New York: Horizon Press.
Clifford, James.
  1997. *Routes: Travel and Translation in the Late Twentieth Century.* Cambridge: Harvard University Press.
Cohen, Anthony P.
  1994. *Self Consciousness: An Alternative Anthropology of Identity.* London: Routledge.
Cohen, Anthony P., and Nigel Rapport.
  1995. *Questions of Consciousness.* London: Routledge.
Crapanzano, Vincent.
  1982. The Self, the Third, and Desire. In *Psychosocial Theories of the Self,* edited by Benjamin Lee, 179–206. New York: Plenum Press.
  1992. *Hermes' Dilemma and Hamlet's Desire: On the Epistemology of Interpretation.* Cambridge: Harvard University Press.
Davidman, Lynn.
  1991. *Tradition in a Rootless World: Women Turn to Orthodox Judaism.* Berkeley and Los Angeles: University of California Press.

Durkheim, Emile.

1965. *The Elementary Forms of the Religious Life*. Translated by Joseph Ward Swain. New York: The Free Press.

1984. *The Division of Labor in Society*. Translated by W. D. Halls. New York: The Free Press.

Erikson, Erik.

1980. *Identity and the Life Cycle*. New York: W. W. Norton.

1993. *Childhood and Society*. New York: W. W. Norton.

Feingold, Henry.

1991. The American Component of Jewish Identity. In *Jewish Identity in America*, edited by David M. Gordis and Yoav Ben-Horin, 69–80. Los Angeles: The Wilstein Institute.

Fogelson, Raymond.

1982. Person, Self, and Identity: Some Anthropological Retrospects, Circumspects, and Prospects. In *Psychosocial Theories of the Self*, edited by Benjamin Lee, 67–110. New York: Plenum Press.

Friedman, Howard.

1991. Response to Harry Feingold. In *Jewish Identity in America*, edited by David M. Gordis and Yoav Ben-Horin, 81–89. Los Angeles: The Wilstein Institute.

Friedman, Menachem.

1994. Habad as Messianic Fundamentalism: From Local Particularism to Universal Jewish Mission. In *Accounting for Fundamentalisms: The Dynamic Character of Movements*, edited by Martin Marty and R. Scott Appleby, 328–57. Chicago: University of Chicago Press.

Goldberg, Arnold.

1982. The Self of Psychoanalysis. In *Psychosocial Theories of the Self*, edited by Benjamin Lee. 3–22. New York: Plenum Press.

Goldberg, David Theo, and Michael Krausz, eds.

1993. *Jewish Identity*. Philadelphia: Temple University Press.

Goldschmidt, Walter.

1995. An Open Letter to Melford Spiro. *Ethos* 23(2):244–54.

Gordis, David M., and Yoav Ben-Horin, eds.

1991. *Jewish Identity in America*. Los Angeles: The Wilstein Institute.

Hallowell, A. Irving.

1955. *Contributions to Anthropology: Selected Papers of A. Irving Hallowell*. Chicago: University of Chicago Press.

Herman, Simon.

1989. *Jewish Identity: A Social Psychological Perspective*. New Brunswick: Transaction Publishers.

Hollan, Douglas W.

1992. Cross-Cultural Differences in the Self. *Journal of Anthropological Research* 48(4):283–300.

Hollan, Douglas, and Jane Wellenkamp.

1994. *Contentment and Suffering: Culture and Experience in Toraja.* New York: Columbia University Press.

Holland, Dorothy, and Andrew Kipnis.

1994. Metaphors for Embarrassment and Stories of Exposure: The Not-So-Egocentric Self in American Culture. *Ethos* 22(3):316–42.

Hundert, Gershon David, ed.

1991. *Essential Papers on Hasidism: Origins to Present.* New York: New York University Press.

Idel, Moshe.

1995. *Hasidism: Between Ecstasy and Magic.* Albany: State University of New York Press.

Johnson, Allen.

1978. *Quantification in Cultural Anthropology: An Introduction to Research Design.* Stanford: Stanford University Press.

Kaufman, Debra.

1991. *Rachel's Daughters: Newly Orthodox Jewish Women.* New Brunswick: Rutgers University Press.

1995. Engendering Orthodoxy: Newly Orthodox Women and Hasidism. In *New World Hasidism: Ethnographic Studies of Hasidic Jews in America,* edited by Janet S. Belcove-Shalin, 135–60. Albany: State University of New York Press.

Kleeblatt, Norman.

1996. *Too Jewish: Challenging Traditional Identities.* New Brunswick: Rutgers University Press.

Kohut, H.

1971. *The Analysis of the Self.* New York: International Universities Press.

Landau, David.

1993. *Piety and Power: The World of Jewish Fundamentalism.* New York: Hill and Wang.

Langness, Lewis L., and Gelya Frank.

1981. *Lives: An Anthropological Approach to Biography.* Novato: Chandler and Sharp.

Lee, Benjamin, ed.

1982. *Psychosocial Theories of the Self.* New York: Plenum Press.

Levy, Robert.

1973. *Tahitians: Mind and Experience in the Society Islands.* Chicago: University of Chicago Press.

1984. Emotions, Knowing, and Culture. In *Culture Theory: Essays on Mind, Self, and Emotion,* edited by R. Shweder and R. LeVine, 214–37. Cambridge: Cambridge University Press.

London, Perry, and Allissa Hirshfeld.

1991. The Psychology of Identity Formation. In *Jewish Identity in America,* edited by David M. Gordis and Yoav Ben-Horin, 31–50. Los Angeles: The Wilstein Institute.

Luhrman, Tanya.
1989. *Persuasions of the Witch's Craft: Ritual Magic in Contemporary England*. Cambridge: Harvard University Press.

Mead, George H.
1934. *Mind, Self, and Society: From the Standpoint of a Social Behaviorist*. Chicago: University of Chicago Press.

Melville, Herman.
1964. *Moby-Dick, or, The Whale*. Indianapolis: Bobbs-Merrill.

Meyer, Michael.
1990. *Jewish Identity in the Modern World*. Seattle: University of Washington Press.

Mindel, Nissan.
1971. *Rabbi Schneur Zalman of Liadi*. Volume 1: *Biography*. Brooklyn: Kehot Publication Society.

1972. *Rabbi Schneur Zalman of Liadi*. Volume 2: *The Philosophy of Chabad*. Brooklyn: Kehot Publication Society.

Mintz, Jerome.
1992. *Hasidic People: A Place in the New World*. Cambridge: Harvard University Press.

1995. *Legends of the Hasidim: An Introduction to Hasidic Culture and Oral Tradition in the New World*. Northvale, N.J.: Jason Aaronson, Inc.

Montefiore, Alan.
1993. Structures of Personal Identity. In *Jewish Identity*, edited by David Theo Goldberg and Michael Krausz, 212–42. Philadelphia: Temple University Press.

Morris, Bonnie.
1995. Agents or Victims of Religious Ideology? Approaches to Locating Hasidic Women in Feminist Studies. In *New World Hasidism: Ethnographic Studies of Hasidic Jews in America*, edited by Janet S. Belcove-Shalin, 161–80. Albany: State University of New York Press.

Murray, D. W.
1993. What Is the Western Concept of the Self? On Forgetting David Hume. *Ethos* 21(1):3–23.

Obeyesekere, Gananath.
1981. *Medusa's Hair: An Essay on Personal Symbols and Religious Experience*. Chicago: University of Chicago Press.

Olidort, Baila.
1995. Tzaddik and Baal Teshuvah. *Wellsprings* (fall 1995):20–24.

Ravitzky, Aviezer.
1994. The Contemporary Lubavitch Hasidic Movement: Between Conservatism and Messianism. In *Accounting for Fundamentalisms: The Dynamic Character of Movements*, edited by Martin Marty and R. Scott Appleby, 303–27. Chicago: University of Chicago Press.

Schoenfeld, Stuart.
1988. Integration into the Group and Sacred Uniqueness: An Analysis of Adult Bat Mitzvah. In *Persistence and Flexibility: Anthropological Perspectives on the American*

Jewish Experience, edited by Walter Zenner, 117–35. Albany: State University of New York Press.

Scholem, Gershom.

1974. *Kabbalah.* Jerusalem: Keter Publishing House.

1995. *The Messianic Idea in Judaism and Other Essays on Jewish Spirituality.* New York: Shocken Books.

Schulweis, Harold M.

1991. The Role of the Synagogue in Jewish Identity. In *Jewish Identity in America,* edited by David M. Gordis and Yoav Ben-Horin, 159–65. Los Angeles: The Wilstein Institute.

Shweder, Richard.

1991. *Thinking through Cultures: Expeditions in Cultural Psychology.*Cambridge: Harvard University Press.

Shweder, Richard, and Edmund J. Bourne.

1991. Does the Concept of the Person Vary Cross-Culturally? In *Thinking Through Cultures: Expeditions in Cultural Psychology,* edited by Richard Shweder, 113–55. Cambridge: Harvard University Press.

Shweder, Richard, and Robert LeVine, eds.

1984. *Culture Theory.* Cambridge: Cambridge University Press.

Silbersten, Laurence.

1994. Others Within and Without: Rethinking Jewish Identity and Culture. In *The Other in Jewish Thought and History: Construction of Jewish Culture and Identity,* edited by L. Silberstein and R. L. Cohn, 1–34. New York: New York University Press.

Silberstein, Laurence, and Robert L. Cohn, eds.

1994. *The Other in Jewish Thought and History: Construction of Jewish Culture and Identity.* New York: New York University Press.

Spiro, Melford.

1993. Is the Western Conception of the Self "Peculiar" within the Context of the World Cultures? *Ethos* 21(2):107–53.

Steinsaltz, Adin.

1988. *The Longer Shorter Way: Discourses on Chasidic Thought.* Translated by Yehuda Hanegbi. Northvale, N.J.: Jason Aaronson, Inc.

Wikan, Uni.

1995. The Self in a World of Urgency and Necessity. *Ethos* 23(3):259–85.

Zalman, Shneur of Liadi.

1966. *Sefer Ha-Tanya* (in Hebrew). Brooklyn: Mekos L'Inyonei Chinuch.

Zenner, Walter, ed.

1988. *Persistence and Flexibility: Anthropological Perspectives on the American Jewish Experience.* Albany: State University of New York Press.

Contesting Identities in Jewish Philanthropy

Kerri P. Steinberg

UNITY VS. PLURALISM

In a 1997 essay called "The Politics of Philanthropy," David Biale takes to task the United Jewish Appeal's fundraising strategy of linking Jewish identity to an illusory sense of Jewish unity. The UJA's slogan, "We are one," proclaims the theme of unity and agreement against which Biale reacts. Instead, Biale argues in favor of promoting the diversity of American Jewish opinion. He invokes the New Israel Fund as a philanthropy that works toward the more progressive goals of religious pluralism, democracy, and Jewish-Arab relations. Biale illustrates his argument with an advertisement from the *New York Times* featuring a child with the heading, "He's Not Reform, Conservative or Orthodox. He's Poor and Hungry." The accompanying text reads, "Wherever you stand on the debate about religion in Israel, he's not the enemy." For Biale this ad prompts a discussion about the politics of mainstream Jewish philanthropy. His article concludes: "Only by accepting and affirming these diversities publicly can a true pluralism be allowed to flourish and only by affirming a true pluralism can a much more realistic sense of Jewish unity emerge."[1]

Biale's choice to expose the politics of American Jewish philanthropy through a photograph and advertisement—the fabric of material culture—is important. All too often these visual artifacts are overlooked as incidental to larger historical or sociological phenomena. Such materials frequently offer insight into a particular problem, supplementing and enhancing political and intellectual arguments. Indeed, pictorial representation in its multiple forms—from drawings and paintings to engravings, lithographs, and photography—must be consulted as the silent agents that often fuel social and political reform or preserve the status quo.

This essay investigates American Jewish identity by examining a part of the the material culture of the organized Jewish community—the 1995 annual reports of the New Israel Fund and the American Jewish Joint Distribution Committee (JDC). I am interested in how both mainstream Jewish philanthropies like the JDC (the overseas arm of the United Jewish Appeal [UJA]) and alternative philanthropies such as the New Israel Fund shape American Jewish identity. More specifically, what does Jewish identity look like when it is represented in the photographs of these philanthropic institutions, and how do these agencies use photographs to reinforce and perpetuate their ideological positions? Equally at stake are the identities these photographs assign to both the donors and recipients of Jewish welfare. On the surface, the photographic production of the JDC supports the political philosopher Marla Brettschnieder's claim that mainstream philanthropy, intent on preserving a strong and coherent Jewish community, exemplifies a static, undialectical philanthropic model where difference or dissent is understood as a threat to group solidarity.[2] The alternative paradigm, by contrast, champions the process of dynamic exchange while struggling toward a vibrant and coherent Jewish community.[3] If the photographs we shall consider present competing claims for ascendancy within the American Jewish community, what they share is a utopian and romanticized conception of American Jewish affiliation or identity, only seen from opposite ends of the political spectrum.

The UJA's slogan, "We are one," declares the solidarity of American Jews with their Jewish brethren abroad. The American Jewish community itself, however, is anything but monolithic. In 1990 the Council of Jewish Federations conducted a National Jewish Population Survey to study the social, demographic, and religious structure of the American Jewish community.[4] This survey confirmed the reality of a splintered community and illustrated the plummeting tendency of Jewish affiliation by pointing to a pattern of assimilation, conversion, and secularization. As a result of the astounding statistics outlined by the study, the organized Jewish community responded with a campaign espousing continuity and a redoubled commitment to Jewish unity.

The unyielding pledge to unity in a reality of discord causes us to question to what extent the UJA's plight is illusory, or alternatively, what purpose does this recalcitrant emphasis on unity serve? I would suggest that this insistence on unity corresponds to the yearning for a universal essence that unites Jews worldwide. Whether such an essence actually exists is beyond the scope of this paper. For now, suffice it to say that in order to realize such an intrinsic or "authentic" contour of Jewish identity, one must gloss over the cultural, social, and political differences that distinguish Jews both within and without the American Jewish community. This homogenous and stark understanding of identity corroborates the tenets of a modernist paradigm and its promotion of transcendent and often essential values. A more nuanced or postmodern ideological position would accept and embrace the contingencies and vast differences that inevitably result from the dispersion of Jews throughout the world, thus recognizing multiple Jewish profiles.

In their capacity as philanthropies, both the JDC and the New Israel Fund may be understood as symptomatic of an American Jewish hegemonic enterprise that has a vested interest in Jewish continuity. However, they present two distinct models. As models of mainstream American Jewish philanthropies, the UJA and its JDC beneficiary represent highly established, coordinated philanthropic machines that, in enforcing the Jewish tradition of self-help, disseminate a message of Jewish solidarity. By contrast, the New Israel Fund fashions itself as a proactive and reflexive philanthropic alternative whose stated mission is to celebrate the diversity of Jewish existence. Certainly the New Israel Fund's emphasis on diversity situates it more on the margins of the established philanthropic system. I propose that the photographs of the JDC and the New Israel Fund clearly reflect multiple interpretations of Jewish identity. These differences are attributable to various causes, including the social and political backgrounds of each institution's membership and the divergent priorities of a mainstream versus an alternative philanthropy. Upon closer examination, however, we shall see that the New Israel Fund may not ultimately be as distant from the mainstream as it would have us believe.

THE PHILANTHROPIC ROAD TO JEWISH IDENTITY

In the late-twentieth-century era of American Jewish identity in turmoil, philanthropy has functioned to anchor that identity in the task of rescue and relief.[5] Philanthropy, as an expression of the values of righteousness and charity, has interceded to mitigate the competing values of integration and survival in America that have tugged at the identity of American Jews since the nineteenth century. In a 1995 article, Ofer Shiff examines this tension through a discussion of two American Jewish leaders, Isaac Leeser (a traditionalist) and Isaac Mayer Wise (a spokesman for Reform Judaism) and their competing philanthropic attitudes toward Palestine in the second half of the nineteenth century.[6] Early on, philanthropic activity, especially on behalf of Palestine, was recognized as a means of strengthening American Jewish solidarity. Of these two positions, Wise's gained ascendancy and evolved into the integrationist response that has characterized American Jewish existence for much of the twentieth century. Schiff explains that philanthropy provided a legitimate means through which Jews could pursue their objective of survival while "injecting American values into the traditionalist perception of Jewish solidarity."[7]

To a certain extent, therefore, we may view the escalating importance of philanthropy as a manifestation of the integrationist response to American Jewish survival that reflects a concern, as sociologist Jonathan Woocher has

argued, that American Jews not jeopardize their successful efforts toward assimilation.[8] This concern is an important factor in what Woocher has designated the *civil religion* of American Jews. Unlike traditional religion, civil religion represents a group effort to express itself as a moral community, independent of traditional religious institutions.[9] Woocher defines the civil religion of American Jews as a "model of Jewishness which synthesizes ethnicity and religiosity and places both firmly within the embrace of American pluralism."[10] Through their civil religion, American Jews have been able to embrace the economic and social opportunities in America while supporting Jewish perpetuation both at home and abroad.[11] Civil religion ties American Jews to the larger *family* of Jewish peoplehood.[12] As Woocher asserts, it "gives American Jews a transcendent purposiveness by holding out to them a vision of Jewish destiny and mission in which they have a central role to fill."[13]

So vital is the philanthropic current within American Jewish life that Jewish theologian and historian Jacob Neusner has written a book entitled, *Tzedakah: Can Jewish Philanthropy Buy Jewish Survival?* wherein he claims that philanthropy may be the single most unifying force in a Jewish community defined by fiercely held differences. This leads Neusner to determine that if Jewish philanthropy cannot buy Jewish survival, no other program can: "if we are to shape a way of life common to us all, a way of life to define what makes us a community at all, it will have to emerge from the world of philanthropy."[14] Neusner recognizes the power of philanthropy and its potential to confer a sense of purpose for American Jews. Bearing in mind the long-standing tradition of Jewish self-help and the integrationist-survivalist contest that has vexed American Jewry throughout the twentieth century, we may cast new light upon an old deed to understand philanthropy as a conduit that enables many otherwise unaffiliated Americans to center their Jewish selves.

THE NEW ISRAEL FUND ALTERNATIVE

"With thirteen million Jews in the world, including over four million in Israel, there is much diversity among us. So when we talk about 'unity,' we do not mean uniformity. Our diversity keeps us healthy, vibrant, and responsive. It must be accommodated and respected."[15]

In comparing the goals and values of Jewish philanthropies, I do not mean to reproduce the binary opposition frequently established by mainstream organizations like the UJA, between a dominant or hegemonic contour of Jewish identity and more marginalized positions. Marla Brettschneider designates this the "either/or" approach, in which difference is distorted into polarization. She ascribes such tactics to a narcissistic community whose hegemonic push for unity requires the silencing of dissenters.[16] As a philanthropic alternative with a vastly different agenda from the UJA or the JDC, the New Israel Fund underscores the reality of Jewish diversity. At the same time, however, the New Israel Fund is just as determined, if not recalcitrant, about the validity of its own position regarding the politics and social conditions that contour Jewish life.

Regardless of their different self-presentations, we must bear in mind that the existence of both philanthropic models depends on how successfully each can promote the relevance of its current campaigns and interest potential donors. Consequently, their photographic campaigns must always be situated within this promotional context. Though there are certainly differences between the UJA and the New Israel Fund, including methods of allocation and political interests, there are also points of agreement. For example, supporters of both the UJA and the New Israel Fund are highly educated, middle- and upper-middle-class individuals. Religious affiliation tends to be distributed primarily between Reform and Conservative denominations, with a minority of individuals following Orthodox practices.[17] More New Israel Fund members, however, are affiliated with the Reconstructionist movement than are contributors to mainstream philanthropies. Interestingly, three-quarters of the New Israel Fund's approximately ten thousand donors are also UJA donors.[18] Though it is difficult to explain this overlap, it is possible that continued contributions by New Israel Fund donors to the UJA reflects a sentimentality or nostalgia for this preeminent institution, which has occupied a central role in American Jewish history since its establishment in 1939. Further, some donors view their contributions to the New Israel Fund as a complement to mainstream Jewish philanthropies and as a way to fund interests that might not otherwise receive financial support.[19] At the least, this statistic seems to support a larger thesis regarding the multiple facets of Jewish identity within single individuals. In addition, it argues for a link between divergent styles of philanthropic activity and underlying conceptions of identity and, as we shall see, leads to adjustments in each philanthropy as it responds to the actions of the other.

In order to contextualize the differences between the New Israel Fund and the UJA, we must recall that each came of age at a different historical moment. In response to *Kristallnacht* of November 1938, the JDC merged with the United Palestine Committee and the National Committee for Refugees to establish the United Jewish Appeal in January 1939. While this merger signaled the unification of competing American philanthropic interests under the new UJA umbrella organization, it also represented a drive toward rendering fundraising tactics more efficient at a critical historical moment.[20] Built into the UJA philanthropic machine was an impulse toward crisis resolution that still figures prominently in the UJA's modus operandi. We may view this emphasis, then, as part of the UJA's ties to its own past and as its perpetuation of tactics, both laudatory and problematic, that have brought rescue, relief, and rehabilitation to hundreds of thousands of distressed Jews.[21]

Founded in 1979 by Jonathan Cohen and Eleanor Friedman (one of the heiresses to the Levi-Strauss fortune), the New Israel Fund represents a smaller philanthropy with a vastly different agenda from that of more centralized organizations like the UJA. Its establishment was in part a response to the social, cultural, and intellectual revolutions that swept across Europe and North America during the sixties and seventies. In addition, the New Israel Fund was a response to the desire for more direct involvement in social justice and peace in the Middle East. The New Israel Fund presented an alternative venue for a more progressive donor who felt that his or her interests in Israel were not addressed and who wished to circumvent the bureaucracy of mainstream philanthropic involvement.

The New Israel Fund's establishment anticipated the proliferation of Jewish social action groups that would emerge in the next decade. By the early 1980s, particularly in the aftermath of the Israeli invasion of Lebanon, some American Jews began to express alternative political viewpoints. Those who were staunch supporters of Israel began examining just what kind of Jewish state they were supporting, while those who had earlier felt marginalized by the organized community began to explore alternative ways to forge a relationship with Israel.[22] It is within this context of increased concern on the part of the public regarding the limited interests supported by the philanthropic mainstream that the New Israel Fund was able to organize.

The New Israel Fund represents a joint effort by Israelis, North Americans, and Europeans whose endeavor is to build a more humanitarian society in Israel.[23] It funds organizations that foster tolerance, empowerment, and equality. Many of its programs support grassroots efforts on behalf of battered women; abused children; Arab-Jewish coexistence projects; gays and lesbians; and Ethiopian, Sephardic, and Mizrahi Jewish communities in Israel, who are often discriminated against.[24] In its emphasis on tolerance, pluralism, and equality, the New Israel Fund claims to challenge Israel, as a democratic nation, to recognize the human rights of all its inhabitants as a precondition to the peaceful coexistence of peoples. This means that Israel must honor the competing values of its citizens, rather than require certain groups to bury their differences and acquiesce to a hegemonic majority. The New Israel Fund also supports programs to help eliminate gender-based discrimination and bridge social and economic gaps. Such programs have traditionally been excluded from the UJA budget, calling into question the operation of this philanthropic giant, which has relied more upon a singularity of ideological interests in its funding activity.

Why would the UJA insist upon an ideological consensus from its donors, and how might this "oneness" of interests benefit its operation? Inasmuch as this singularity of interests is the glue that holds together this complex philanthropic machine, it depends upon an internal coherence of the individual subjects who make up the larger collective. Clearly, a sense of internal coherence would seem to indicate both a healthy subject and a healthy identity; in this portrait there is no room for fractured identities or divided interests. It is as if internal coherence of the individual subject is a prerequisite for group consensus. In this way, participation in the UJA affirms the value of both the individual as donor and the uniformity of the collective. In order for such a fellowship to emerge, however, individual differences must be downplayed and similarities emphasized. And, as feminist philosopher Judith Butler warns, it is precisely this emphasis on uniformity that obscures the multiplicity of cultural, social, and political aspects of a subject.[25]

Butler's reflections on the category of "woman" and the construction of identity resonate far beyond her own seminal feminist critique and are instructive in discerning the kinds of identities constructed through the New Israel Fund's and the JDC's photographic campaigns. Aware of the illusive nature of the UJA's campaign slogan, "We are one," the New Israel Fund, as a much smaller and more narrowly defined philanthropy, has fashioned itself to address the demands for diversity and plurality that fall through the cracks. Diversity, as opposed to uniformity, figures as the leitmotif of the New Israel Fund's published record. This is announced on the cover page of the New Israel Fund's 1995 annual report, whose subtitle reads "Profiles of dedication, climate of discord." By contrast, the subtitle of the JDC's 1995 annual report reads "One people, one heart . . ." reinforcing how the phenomenon of unity operates within the rhetoric of the philanthropic mainstream. Recognizing the internal coherence of the subject assumed by the UJA model of philanthropy, the New Israel Fund promotes itself as an alternative model that accepts the kind of divergence, splintering, and fragmentation that Butler describes as part of the "often tortuous process of democratization."[26]

The passage quoted at the beginning of this section appeared in the Los Angeles *Jewish Journal* as part of the New Israel Fund's advertisement on November 14, 1997. Clearly responding to the emphasis on unity proclaimed by the UJA's slogan, "We are one," it suggests that respect for diversity is central to the New Israel Fund's vision of the Jewish future. And yet, the second part of this ad reads, "It's hard work reconciling religious difference. But after surviving thousands of years, this family can handle it." Although masked by an emphasis on discord and diversity, also built into the New Israel Fund's campaign is an underlying assumption of ties that bind Jews as a "family." Despite opposing motifs, the metaphor of family unity rather than discord ultimately unites the two philanthropies on the level of Jewish continuity and survival into the future.

IDEALS AND IDEOLOGIES

The photographs that appear in the JDC's and the New Israel Fund's 1995 annual reports underscore how each agency uses a unique visual tradition to confer distinct identities upon Jewish subjects and donors. As we shall see, the JDC's photographs correspond to mainstream American Jewish notions of Western advancement, presenting a teleological thrust wherein underprivileged Jewish subjects are transformed to more closely resemble American Jews. By comparison, the photographs featured in the New Israel Fund's report portray their subjects as more autonomous, implying a more heightened awareness of cultural differences. Laurence Silberstein has argued that ideologies participate in bestowing identities on individuals by situating them in specific subject positions, according to his definition of ideology as a social force, "materialized in concrete practices and rituals," and dependent upon specific apparatuses for its operation.[27] Indeed, the photographic productions of the JDC and the New Israel Fund provide a way to examine the construction of various subject positions by these philanthropies.

Through its photographs, the New Israel Fund suggests that its donors have a sensibility about art and highly contested subjects such as race, gender, and class. This sensibility is visualized by accomplished photographers, who render the New Israel Fund's interests through their professionally trained eyes. Often the New Israel Fund commissions the Magnum Agency, a distinguished international photojournalistic organization, founded in the 1940s by Robert Capa, Henri Cartier-Bresson, and others, as well as acclaimed Israeli photographers like Micha Bar-am to document its projects.[28] By introducing polemical subjects not represented by the mainstream Jewish philanthropies, and by eliminating the portrayal of American donors, New Israel Fund photographs obviate the polarization between donors and beneficiaries that we encounter time and again in the JDC's annual report.

For example, the cover page of the New Israel Fund's 1995 annual report (fig. 11.1) features a photograph of two religious figures. For some observers, these subjects have an equally distant and exotic appeal. The *streymel* [hat], *kapota* [overcoat], and *gartel* [belt] worn by the bearded man to the right presumably identify him as a Hassidic Jew, while the *kafiyah* [traditional male Arab headcover] covering the other man's head identifies him as an Arab Muslim. Framing the chance encounter of these two passing subjects underscores their ethnic and religious differences. Yet the intentionally hazy lens seems to blur their opposition, diffusing their differences in the interest of a romanticized vision of harmony and coexistence. As the New Israel Fund states in its publication, *Power of People:* "The Middle East abounds with conflicts. Between Jews and Arabs especially a profound conflict exists, with right claimed on both sides. . . . The future of Israel depends on two elements: the

New Israel Fund
הקרן החדשה לישראל

1995 Annual Report

Profiles of dedication,
climate of discord

Figure 11.1. Arab and Jew in Jerusalem, ca. 1995.

determination of Israelis to defend their own lives and equal determination not to claim power over others."[29]

By framing tensions in nationality and religion, the image forces the reader to confront his or her own desires and anxieties concerning these "types." The representation of each subject in profile cleverly returns us to the report's subtitle, "Profiles of dedication, climate of discord." This play on the word "profile" prompts various responses from the viewer. On the one hand, the limited profile view is in keeping with the stereotypical rigidity that defines each figure as a religious type. On the other hand, it might be argued that the written text encourages us to overcome these assumptions and rather to see each figure as a profile composite of ideas and practices. The four smaller photographs on the cover page provide a window into the array of racial, ethnic, and class backgrounds the reader will encounter in the report. At the same time, this enigmatic window underscores the artistic sensibility on which the New Israel Fund prides itself.

A comparison with the first two photographs of the JDC's 1995 annual report (figs. 11.2 and 11.3) exemplifies a more normative and patriarchal conception of Jewishness. Opening the JDC's annual report, we see a small girl running down the aisle of a synagogue in Havana toward a male religious figure who stands on the *bima* above and awaits her with outstretched arms. Clearly, this young girl has found her way home. As the opening image, this photograph introduces a visual narrative of reclamation into the fold of traditional Jewish patriarchal society. As the viewer turns to the next page, he or she encounters a formal portrait of the JDC president. This middle-aged white male casually rests his hand on the globe as he addresses the public, reminding the reader of the JDC's far-reaching influence. His presence is self-assured, befitting his position as both JDC president and a United States ambassador. This commanding male presence recalls that historically there has been an uneven gender distribution in the leadership of mainstream Jewish philanthropies.[30] For example, in 1995 when these annual reports were released, only one-fifth to one-fourth of UJA and JDC offices were occupied by women. In comparison, just under half of the New Israel Fund's board of directors are female.

The New Israel Fund's story is told through the profiles of four activists whose diverse involvements reflect the array of interests the organization supports. Each profile is conveyed through the first person, bringing the concerns and ideas of each activist close to the reader. The photographs are carefully composed to appear casual, spontaneous, and immediate as they depict each subject absorbed in his or her respective causes. Each image pays tribute to the direct impact that these individuals, along with those who are not represented, have made in improving relations and fostering social justice in Israel. By deflecting attention from the role of the philanthropists to the role of these activists, the New Israel Fund infers that its donors contribute

Figure 11.2. Young Girl in the Patronato Synagogue,
Havana, Cuba, 1995.

Figure 11.3. JDC President, 1995.

out of strong ideological convictions and not because they are seeking to confirm their Jewish self-worth.

By contrast, the JDC's story of relief, rescue, and reconstruction pays tribute to the impact that American Jews have had "at one time or another in more than 85 countries on every continent."[31] Following the president's and vice president's introductory remarks highlighting the JDC's accomplishments over the past year, the report details its work by geographical region from Israel, to the former Soviet Union, to Africa, Asia, and Latin America. In comparison to the New Israel Fund, which represents a joint effort of North Americans, Europeans, and Israelis committed to fashioning a more equitable Israel, the JDC identifies itself as the overseas arm of the "American Jewish community, reaching out to Jewish communities in distress and improving the quality of Jewish life around the world."[32] As the JDC clearly validates the importance of the diaspora, it equally confirms the far-reaching influence of American Jews. Though the president's and vice president's remarks are presented in the first person, the remaining narrative unfolds in the third person, presenting the voice of an informed but more distanced philanthropic authority. This voice affirms the accomplishments of JDC supporters and invites their continued identification with the JDC cause.

Emphasizing the value of its donors and activists, JDC photographs identify the board members who are pictured, while individual recipients of JDC gifts remain nameless, or are identified only by their disabilities (fig. 11.4). Clearly, such tactics reduce these subjects to their deficiencies, overlooking other important characteristics. At the same time, they validate the American leaders as normative Jews and revere their efforts on behalf of disadvantaged Jews. Indeed, these photographs salute the contributions of the American Jewish public to the UJA, the primary funding source of the JDC. In so doing, they appeal to the donors to regard themselves as givers, thereby modeling their Jewish identities as philanthropists.

Although the JDC operates as an autonomous organization with its own officers and board of directors, the UJA provides the bulk of its funding. In 1995 this amounted to 68 million dollars, approximately 83 percent of the JDC's funding, and 20 percent of the total monies distributed by the UJA. Though the JDC was allocated more money in 1995 than in 1994, generally contributions to the UJA were down approximately 9 percent in 1995 compared to the previous year. The New Israel Fund, however, increased its revenues by approximately 35 percent between 1994 and 1995. While we must recall that the New Israel Fund's contributions represent only a fraction of those collected by the UJA ($12,357,000 in 1995 compared to the UJA's $346,650,000), this reversal in trends seems to signal a dissatisfaction with mainstream philanthropy and, more specifically, with the kind of Israel being fashioned, in part, through American funds. Perhaps more than anything

Figure 11.4. JDC Board Members Observe Hearing-Impaired Child at the Alliance School for the Deaf, Jerusalem, 1995.

else, the assassination of Israeli Prime Minister Yitzhak Rabin in 1995 by an Israeli Jew epitomized the impasse of an Israel rife with conflict.

Given the paucity of studies on the membership profile of the New Israel Fund, we can only speculate why American Jews have either transferred their allegiances to alternatives such as the New Israel Fund, or entered the realm of American Jewish philanthropy through other portals. A telephone survey of eight hundred New Israel Fund donors revealed that eighty-two percent define themselves as liberal and progressive.[33] Its support of organizations that are catalysts for social change coincides with the interests of a new generation of liberal donors. Moreover, the New Israel Fund makes provisions for individual donors to target how and where they choose to allocate their contributions. By contrast, the UJA's donations to Israel are distributed through the Jewish Agency in Israel, allowing it to circumvent Israel's internal social and political conflicts. The concept of personalized Jewish giving satisfies those donors who wish to follow how their contributions are used. Because of its size, the New Israel Fund can take risks and support innovative programs that may not be feasible within mainstream philanthropy.

Some believe that the New Israel Fund's innovation has inspired changes in the philanthropic mainstream. For example, in the 1980s the UJA together with the Jewish Agency launched Project Renewal, in which diaspora

Figure 11.5. JDC Members and Arab Women at Home for Elderly Arabs, Dabburiya, Israel, 1995.

communities were "twinned" with Israeli communities. The recent Partnership 2000 is a modified version of Project Renewal that likewise aims to meet the demands for more direct donor involvement. According to Eliezer Jaffee, a professor of social work at Hebrew University who helped pioneer the idea of Project Renewal, personalized giving represents an effective philanthropic strategy by capturing the loyalties of American Jews and directly engaging them in Israeli programs that they find compelling.[34]

Despite the conflicting attitudes projected by each philanthropy toward donors and welfare recipients, at times their stated interests overlap. For example, both organizations express concern about the rights of Arab Israelis. Like the New Israel Fund, the JDC is working to develop social and community programs in the Arab sector, which lags behind. Through the photographic lens, however, each agency discloses different responses and attitudes toward the Arab subjects. Figure 11.5 captures activities at the JDC-Brookdale Institute, Israel's leading center for applied research in providing assistance to the Arab sector on aging, health policy, and social welfare. The New Israel Fund photograph of Amal el-Sana (fig. 11.6) illustrates

Figure 11.6. Amal el-Sana Instructing Bedouin Women, Beersheva, Israel, 1995.

her position as a Bedouin feminist. While both photographs depict the inroads being made regarding Arab-Jewish coexistence, the differences between these two images are striking. Whereas the JDC's photograph includes the president/ambassador, to whom we were earlier introduced, along with another woman, possibly his wife or a board member, the New Israel Fund's photograph represents only Amal el-Sana and other Bedouin women. The American leaders in the JDC image loom over the Arab women to observe their handiwork. While the Arab subjects are absorbed in their activity, the gaze of the American subjects is elsewhere. This connotes only a superficial interest in the Arab women and the skills they exhibit. Moreover, the arrangement diminishes the importance of the Arab women, while valorizing the role of the American leaders, who establish eye contact with the photographer.

This arrangement of figures recalls Homi Bhabha's claim that the depiction of Others often seems to represent them as contained, without their own desires: "The danger is that in the process of delineating the Other, it is subjected to containment and abstraction, and stripped of specific identities, locations, agency, and its historic desires."[35] And as Silberstein observes, little if any serious attention is given to the voices of Others both within and without the Jewish community.[36] Measuring the weight of these statements against the JDC's visual record would seem to indicate that, indeed, more is invested in reinforcing the status of the donor than that of the welfare recipient. In other words, the real subjects of the photograph are the American philanthropists; the Arab women are merely accessories. Proud of its focus on diversity and no doubt responding to the authority of the UJA's emphasis on oneness, the New Israel Fund makes a conscious effort to avoid speaking for Others. And, for this reason, the information contained in its annual report is presented in the first person.

As a Bedouin feminist, Amal el-Sana is anything but a commonplace subject. As we might discern from the photograph, her portrayal together with other female subjects reflects an archaeology of influences. Certainly an emphasis on tradition manifests itself in this image, as three generations of women are clad in traditional Bedouin attire. In fact, their headdresses are perhaps the most prominent aspect of the photograph. The starkness of these headcoverings presents a striking contrast to the dark chalkboard, thereby providing signposts of tradition and modernity, and a trajectory of advancement through education. Atop the chalkboard is a Bedouin weaving, visually connected to the other woven materials prominently displayed in the center of the table, and a reference to the importance of tradition within Bedouin life.

These references to tradition and modern life embody the tension experienced by these women as they adjust from a nomadic lifestyle to settlement in villages. Amal el-Sana indicates that in their former lifestyle, women were the backbone of Bedouin society, managing the family economy and deciding when the family would move. Now, according to el-Sana, the gender roles have been reversed, and women's traditional skills have been laid aside. As a result, Bedouin women have little self-esteem, a high rate of illiteracy, and generally a sense of displacement.[37] This photograph thus introduces education as a remedy for their feelings of displacement and as a way to build their resilience in a newly defined society. In comparison to the JDC's representation of Arab women framed by American leaders, in this image there are no resonances of New Israel Fund leaders or donors. In contrast to the JDC's concern with the philanthropists, the New Israel Fund infers that its donors surrender their authority as philanthropists in order to empower the recipients.

As an alternative Jewish philanthropy, the New Israel Fund is candid about its objectives. It supports agencies such as the Movement for Quality Government and the Movement for Governmental Reform, which seek to change public policy and influence legislation to realize a more democratic, pluralistic, and tolerant Israeli society. Though at times its objectives require that it step on the toes of the Israeli government, the New Israel Fund is a nonprofit, nonpartisan organization and, therefore, does not raise money for overtly political purposes.[38] Avinoam Armoni, director of the New Israel Fund in Israel, admits that the fund has certain ideological interests and that only organizations whose work coincides with these interests are eligible for New Israel Fund grants.[39] Yet, because it engages internal Israeli issues and supports organizations that fight the status quo, the New Israel Fund has drawn accusations that it is antiestablishment, with an exclusively left-wing political agenda.[40]

In the pamphlet, *The New Israel Fund: A New Fund for Israel's Enemies* (1990), published by Americans for a Safe Israel, Joseph Puder argues that its claim to be a nonpartisan organization is misleading at best.[41] He emphasizes that most of the leaders of the New Israel Fund have long records of involvement in organizations that "specialize in attacking Israel."[42] These leaders, according to Puder, regard the New Israel Fund as a convenient vehicle for furthering their radical agendas. He concludes that the only difference between the New Israel Fund and other groups on the Jewish left, such as the New Jewish Agenda or Friends of Peace Now, is that it intentionally conceals its left-wing political orientation in order to gain respectability and attract donors.[43]

Despite its interest in some sixty countries, the JDC also regards itself as an apolitical, nonpartisan organization. As the president discloses in his address in the annual report: "The JDC has always made it a point to conduct its country operations, wherever feasible, in partnership with local community organizations and to bring as many interested parties as possible together to address issues of mutual concern."[44] While politics are clearly involved in forging allegiances with various governments so that the JDC can work in foreign countries, it does not assume a political stance. Although the JDC and the New Israel Fund both claim apolitical positions, based upon the interests of their leadership and the organizational agendas that work to effectuate programs of relief, it seems that both funds are politically active and engaged, more than they care to admit.

In this context we might compare two photographs representing Ethiopian men who made *aliyah* to Israel in the early 1980s (fig. 11.7; only the JDC photograph could be reproduced here). Each image features an educated, modernized subject in a position of leadership. As empowered individuals, these men have been given the opportunity to help others from similar backgrounds. And yet, upon closer examination, important distinctions in the ideological positions of the JDC and the New Israel Fund emerge. Through Wende Akale's own narrative in the New Israel Fund annual report, we learn that his main job is to accompany immigrants from their temporary dwellings in absorption centers or trailer sites to permanent homes. The photograph of Akale portrays him in front of one such absorption center. Akale stands close to the camera, but his presence does not overwhelm the photographic composition. In fact, a good part of the photograph shows the stark trailers, loose gravel ground covering, and makeshift clotheslines. This photograph does not present a glamorous description of the Ethiopian absorption process in Israel. Rather, the viewer confronts the difficult reality of being absorbed into a new cultural milieu.

Figure 11.7. Ethiopian Immigrant, Shmuel Yilma, Instructing Recent Ethiopian Immigrant Children in Israel, 1995.

In comparison to this image, the JDC's photograph (fig. 11.7) is less polemical. Unlike the JDC photographs considered earlier, where the subjects were nameless, here the Ethiopian teacher is identified as Shmuel Yilma. The written caption further informs us that he is teaching children about their heritage (presumably both Jewish and Ethiopian). Through his autobiography, *From Falasha to Freedom: An Ethiopian Jew's Journey to Jerusalem,* Shmuel Yilma has distinguished himself as an Ethiopian Jew in Israel.[45] The title of Yilma's book corresponds to the teleological narrative charted by the philanthropic mainstream, typically presenting Israel as the panacea to the Ethiopians' former lives of despair. Because Yilma's journey corroborates the narrative charted by mainstream philanthropy, he is represented as a qualified expert to instruct these Ethiopian youngsters.

Compared to the New Israel Fund's photograph, which is arranged to appear haphazard, the image of Shmuel Yilma in the classroom appears much more orderly. Nearly all of the children direct their attention toward the teacher, who towers above them. Even the childrens' artwork hangs in an organized fashion. Here the emphasis is on control and the semblance of an established order. Indeed, the viewer observes the unfolding of a smooth and seamless absorption experience, as opposed to the difficult experiences that have characterized the absorption of so many Ethiopians in Israel. This image appears to support Ella Shohat's observation that American Jews have participated with the Israeli establishment to "reduce the gap" between Ashkenazi, Sephardi, and Mizrahi Jews by "initiating the Oriental Jews into the ways of a civilized, modern society."[46] As these children are shaped by the imperatives of a white, Western, Ashkenazi society, we observe the process of eradicating the racial and ethnic differences that interfere with the conservative agenda of the mainstream's leadership, whose philanthropic program desires the appearance of diversity, but a reality of Jewish unity.

If, as I am suggesting, the JDC's photographs continually return us to the influence of American Jews, whether in a direct or indirect fashion, as part of a political agenda that seeks to propagate the myth of Jewish unity, the New Israel Fund's photographs disrupt such appearances as part of its agenda to introduce marginalized voices into the Jewish fold. Although the New Israel Fund builds an artistic sensibility into its construction of its ideal, politically and intellectually progressive donor, like the JDC, its photographic subjects are carefully delineated as part of a philanthropic agenda that relies upon its photographs to construct and secure the identification of its Jewish donors. By shifting the visual balance from the donors to the philanthropic recipients, the New Israel Fund implies the altruism of its supporters as they fulfill the Jewish mandate of self-help.

Compared to the more journalistic and less reflexive photographs of the JDC, New Israel Fund photographs intend to be provocative, imploding the race, class, and gender assumptions that often define the photographic production of mainstream philanthropies. Consider, for example, the New Israel Fund's photograph of a woman studying what is presumably a religious text (fig. 11.8). This image accompanies a report on Melila Hellner-Eshed and Moti Bar-Or, cofounders of Elul, a learning center that brings together religious and secular Israelis to study Jewish texts as a means of uniting them and engaging them in intellectual debate.[47] Though it is the face of a woman that studies the text in this photograph, the two sets of hands in either corner could belong to men, although we cannot be sure. The ground rules of Elul regard learning through diversity as a right and a privilege, not a "problem" to overcome. This assertion directly responds to what the New Israel Fund perceives as the shortcomings of a hegemonic and monolithic Jewish identity.

Despite the differences in artistic sensibility and attitudes toward donors and philanthropic subjects, at times the New Israel Fund images, like those of the mainstream, border on the sentimental. Sentimentality, for all its contrivances, consistently serves as a powerful emotional catalyst, softening a potential resistance to support the cause. There is no doubt that its overarch-

Figure 11.8. Melila Hellner-Eshed Studying Torah, Jerusalem, 1995.

ing concerns for tolerance, pluralism, and equality, admirable as they may be, correspond to an idealistic agenda, given an Israeli reality overwhelmed by conflict. Likewise, the JDC's overarching theme of unity as suggested by "One people, one heart . . ." also indicates a sentimental emphasis. This sentimentality is captured in the JDC's photograph featuring the hands of an elderly woman crocheting (fig. 11.9). Clearly, the close-up of this woman's aged hands intends to prompt a timeless association with the past. And certainly the fact that these female hands are represented in the act of sewing genders the image, as it ties her to the domestic realm. What is of greatest interest, however, is what this image appears to assert about Jewish continuity. It is as if these age-old hands are weaving the fabric of Jewish life and longevity. This image imparts a dose of sentimentality by using the past to inspire a sense of Jewish solidarity and belonging in the present. This belonging draws upon a common Jewish *essence*, that which underlies the UJA's declaration, "We are one."

Unlike in UJA or JDC photographs, where difference is opposed to sameness, with the New Israel Fund, difference is recast into a softened motif of diversity. Despite this admirable objective, New Israel Fund opponents have accused it of discriminating against Ashkenazi Jews and Jews who happen to be right-wing. Although the UJA and the New Israel Fund occupy distinct positions on the embattled spectrum of Jewish identity, the verbal and visual rhetoric of each discloses their utopic visions. As in the contest for ascen-

Figure 11.9. Hands of Unknown Woman Engaged in Needlework, Israel, 1995.

dancy between any two recognizable names, there is a responsive quality between the two organizations. The name of the game is Jewish fundraising, and the strategies most successful for one agency are likely to be adopted by the competition.

The photographs of the JDC and the New Israel Fund emphasize the multiple manifestations of American Jewish identities as they chart the differences between a mainstream philanthropy organized in response to World War Two–era antisemitism and an alternative philanthropy established in the late seventies. Undoubtedly, each philanthropy must perpetually reinvent itself—its own identity—in order to maintain an up-to-date mission that is responsive to the needs of Jews both at home and abroad. What the philanthropies share is the representation of similar subjects, albeit through different photographic lenses. While this indicates areas of mutual concern, their distinct photographic styles correspond to the differences between their self-construction on an organizational level and, in turn, how each fabricates the identity of its Jewish donors and recipients. New Israel Fund photographs are more cutting-edge, conveying an artistic sensibility and recognition of the power of photography that is lacking in the more conservative, journalistic approach of the JDC. Examining the use and circulation of photographs by each philanthropy—their material culture—enables a more nuanced understanding of how Jewish identity is constructed and, more specifically, the important role photography plays in visualizing the various inflections of this identity.

NOTES

I wish to acknowledge my fellow participants in the research group "Jewish Identity in the Diaspora," at the University of California Humanities Research Institute. Our discussions were provocative and have helped to contour my work. Many thanks also to the HRI staff. I would especially like to express my gratitude to Cathy Soussloff and David Myers, respected scholars in their fields of art history and Jewish history, whose careful readings and editorial comments helped to improve this paper.

1. David Biale, "The Politics of Philanthropy" *Tikkun* 12, no. 4 (July/August 1997): 16–17.

2. See Marla Brettschneider's chapters "Unity" and "Diversity" in *Cornerstones of Peace: Jewish Identity Politics and Democratic Theory* (New Brunswick, N.J.: Rutgers University Press, 1996).

3. Brettschneider, "Unity" and "Diversity."

4. See Barry A. Kosmin, Sidney Goldstein, Joseph Waksberg, Nava Lerer, Ariella Keysar, and Jeffrey Scheckner, *Highlights of the National Jewish Population Survey* (New York: The Council of Jewish Federations, 1991). Currently, the combined UJA and Council of Jewish Federations is organizing an updated National Jewish Population Survey to reflect the status of American Jews at the beginning of the new millennium.

5. The tradition of Jewish self-help goes back to medieval times when each community had its communal system of fund-raising, in which local collectors gathered obligatory contributions from community members. As the spread of secularism and individualism, the *Haskalah* (Enlightenment) and Reform worked to weaken the cohesiveness of the community, voluntary associations were substituted for the communal charity systems. During the nineteenth century, international welfare and fund-raising agencies such as the Alliance Israelite Universelle, the Israelitische zu Wien, and the Hilfsverein der deutschen Juden assumed the functions of the earlier voluntary associations.

6. Ofer Shiff, "At the Crossroad between Traditionalism and Americanism: Nineteenth-Century Philanthropic Attitudes of American Jews toward Palestine," in *Jewish History* 9, no. 1 (spring 1995): 35–50.

7. Shiff, "At the Crossroad," 45. The sociologists Mordechai Rimor and Gary Tobin have also examined the relationship between Jewish identity and philanthropy. They argue that organizational and institutional structures bind the Jewish community together and that fund-raising campaigns play a central role. Moreover, they observe that while the philanthropic Jew may be active in the organized Jewish community, he or she is not necessarily religiously active. Rimor and Tobin's study highlights the correlation between unobservant or secular Jews and those involved in Jewish organized life. See Mordechai Rimor and Gary Tobin, "The Relationship between

Identity and Philanthropy," in *Contemporary Philanthropy in America,* ed. Barry A. Kosmin and Paul Ritterband (Savage, Md.: Rowman and Littlefield, 1991). Also see Marc Lee Raphael, *Understanding American Jewish Philanthropy* (New York: Columbia University Press, 1979), who suggests that Jewish philanthropy, although a prominent feature of Jewish society and religious life throughout the ages, has become the primary expression of Jewishness today.

8. See Jonathan Woocher, *Sacred Survival* (Bloomington and Indianapolis: Indiana University Press, 1986), 44. In fact, even during World War Two, many American Jewish leaders were careful that Jewish group activity not be perceived as in any way removing Jews from the mainstream of American life, as indicated in the following statement by American Jewish leader Philip Klutznick, delivered at the General Assembly (the governing body of the Council of Jewish Federations and Welfare Funds) in 1947:

> When the history of this era is written, let us hope that it will be said of us that we not only heeded the call to relieve the pain and suffering of a desperately miserable Jewish people overseas, but at the same time, in recognition of our duty to the common destiny of all Jews, we found the strength and courage to advance the culture, the mental and physical well-being on our own domestic front. To do less is to destroy on one hand while we succor on the other. This is a contradiction of purpose—this is a deferral of accounting—this is a road toward self-annihilation which is immoral and inconsistent with a Jewish heritage that we seek to save.

9. Woocher, *Sacred Survival,* 28.

10. Woocher, *Sacred Survival,* 20.

11. Woocher, *Sacred Survival,* 28.

12. On the notion of an extended Jewish family see my article, "The Ties that Bind: Americans, Ethiopians, and the Extended Jewish Family," in *Race, Gender, and Class* 6, no. 4 (1999): 136–51.

13. Woocher, *Sacred Survival,* 28.

14. Jacob Neusner, *Tzedakah: Can Jewish Philanthropy Buy Jewish Survival?* (Atlanta, Ga.: Scholars Press, 1990), 69.

15. Excerpt from the New Israel Fund's full page advertisement, appearing in the *Jewish Journal,* November 14, 1997, 7.

16. See Brettschneider, "Unity," 15–16.

17. For more on the religious practices of American Jews involved in the world of philanthropy, see Jonathan Woocher, "The Civil Jewish Activists—A Portrait," in *Sacred Survival: The Civil Religion of American Jews* (Bloomington and Indianapolis: Indiana University Press, 1986), 104–28. Also see Arnold Gurin, "The Characteristics of Federation Board Members" in *Understanding American Jewish Philanthropy,* ed. Marc Lee Raphael (New York: Ktav Publishing House, 1979), and Steven M. Cohen, "Dollars and Diplomas: The Impact of High Social Status upon Jewish Identification," in *American Modernity and Jewish Identity* (New York and London: Tavistock Publications, 1983). On the Orthodox philanthropic tradition see Samuel Heilman, "Tzedakah: Orthodox Jews and Charitable Giving" in *Contemporary Jewish Philanthropy in America,* ed. Barry A. Kosmin and Paul Ritterband (Savage, Md.: Rowman and Littlefield, 1991).

18. Special thanks to Gilbert D. Kulick, director of communications at the New Israel Fund in Washington D.C. for providing this information.

19. See Cynthia L. Mann, "The Rise of the New Israel Fund," in *Moment* (October 1994) 35.

20. For more on the history of the UJA, see Marc Lee Raphael, *A Short History of the United Jewish Appeal* (Brown University: Scholars Press, 1982).

21. I do not mean to suggest that the UJA has remained completely static over the last fifty-eight years. I only wish to emphasize how the crisis factor functions as a motivating principle, perpetuating, in an interesting way, the *adversity* thesis proposed by Susser's paper in this volume. We may trace this through the various operations that the UJA has performed over the years including, "Operation Magic Carpet," "Operation Malben," "Operation Ezra," "Operation Moses," "Operation Exodus," and "Operation Solomon." This list is not exhaustive.

22. Brettschneider, "Unity," 27–30.

23. New Israel Fund, *The Power of People* (New Israel Fund and Jan Krukowski and Co., 1994), 4.

24. See *The Power of People* on SHATIL, 8–10.

25. See Judith Butler, *Gender Trouble* (New York and London: Routledge, 1990), 14.

26. Butler, *Gender Trouble,* 14.

27. Laurence J. Silberstein, "Cultural Criticism, Ideology, and the Interpretation of Zionism: Toward a Post-Zionist Discourse," in *Interpreting Judaism in a Postmodern Age* (New York and London: New York University Press, 1996), 331–32.

28. To my knowledge, the UJA and JDC have not employed the Magnum Agency, though it is possible that some independent photographers who have done work for the UJA or JDC have been Magnum members. In an interview conducted in March 1997 with Robert Cumins, a photographer who has worked with the UJA for some twenty years, I was told of his warm relationship with the UJA and his attempts to do what he can through his photographs to support its cause. Toward this end, Cumins told me about the photographic conventions he employs, such as "going for the eyes" of his subjects and letting himself go emotionally, in order to provide his images with a certain emotional appeal. After many years, Cumins claims to have a lot of leeway when he is on assignment. He assembles his own "Master Packet" including his recommendations of the most effective prints, which he submits to the public relations department of the UJA. It appears as though Cumins is extremely influential regarding the UJA's use of photography. Clearly, there is no conflict of interests in his relationship with this organization.

29. *The Power of People,* 6.

30. A recent study released by the Council of Jewish Federations and its New Advocacy Department clearly underscored the absence of women from leadership positions; see Brettschneider, "Unity," 145, note 62. In 1998 a woman assumed the National "Chairmanship" for the first time in the UJA's nearly sixty-year history.

31. American Jewish Joint Distribution Committee, Inc., 1995 Annual Report, 2.

32. American Jewish Joint Distribution Committee, Inc., 1995 Annual Report, 2.

33. Mann, "Rise of the New Israel Fund," 88.

34. Mann, "Rise of the New Israel Fund," 86.

35. Homi K. Bhabha, "The Commitment to Theory," in *The Location of Culture* (London: Routledge, 1994), 31.

36. Silberstein, 326.

37. See the profile on Amal el-Sana: "The Making of a Bedouin Feminist" in the New Israel Fund 1995 Annual Report, 11–12.

38. I would like to express my appreciation to Judy Lapin, director of the New Israel Fund in Los Angeles, for clarifying its political position.

39. *The Power of People*, 36.

40. *The Power of People*, 36.

41. See Joseph Puder, *The New Israel Fund: A New Fund for Israel's Enemies* (New York: Americans for a Safe Israel, 1990).

42. Puder, *The New Israel Fund*, 2.

43. Puder, *The New Israel Fund*, 5. Likewise in his article, "The New Israel Fund—For Whom?" Raphael Medoff attributes the New Israel Fund's success in part to its ability to entice potential donors who are led to believe that they are being asked to contribute to the cause of "social justice." According to Medoff, these individuals remain unaware that the New Israel Fund invests their money to implement a philosophy of radical sociopolitical change. See Raphael Medoff, "The New Israel Fund—For Whom?" in *Midstream* (May 1986): 13–16.

44. American Jewish Joint Distribution Committee, Inc., 1995 Annual Report, 3.

45. See Shmuel Yilma, *From Falasha to Freedom: An Ethiopian Jew's Journey to Jerusalem* (Jerusalem: Gefen Publishing House, 1996).

46. Ella Shohat, *"Mizrahim* in Israel: Zionism from the Standpoint of its Jewish Victims" in *Social Text: Theory, Culture, and Ideology* 19/20 (fall 1988): 28–48.

47. See the profiles on Moti Bar-Or and Melila Hellner-Eshed: "Seeking Common Ground" in the New Israel Fund 1995 Annual Report, 21–22.

CONTRIBUTORS

Murray Baumgarten is professor of English and comparative literature and coordinator of Jewish studies at the University of California, Santa Cruz. He is the editor of *Judaism: A Quarterly Journal of Jewish Life and Thought,* published by the American Jewish Congress. He is the founding director of the Dickens Project and has written extensively on Victorian literature and culture and modern Jewish writing, including *City Scriptures: Modern Jewish Writing* (1982).

Bluma Goldstein is professor emerita in the German Department at the University of California, Berkeley. She is the author of *Reinscribing Moses: Heine, Kafka, Freud, and Schoenberg in a European Wilderness* (1992), as well as recent articles on Schoenberg and the Bible, Kafka, and Andy Warhol. She is currently completing a work on the representation of deserted wives/*agunahs* that covers writings in German, Yiddish, and English from the seventeenth century to the mid–twentieth century.

Erich S. Gruen is Gladys Rehard Wood Professor of History and Classics at the University of California, Berkeley. His most recent publications include *Heritage and Hellenism: The Reinvention of Jewish Tradition* (1998) and *Diaspora: Jews amidst the Greeks and Romans* (forthcoming).

Daniel J. Schroeter is the Teller Family chair in Jewish history, at the University of California, Irvine. His most recent book is *The Sultan's Jew: Morocco and the Sephardi World* (forthcoming).

Catherine M. Soussloff held the Patricia and Rowland Rebele Chair in Art History at the University of California, Santa Cruz, before becoming professor of art history and director of visual and cultural studies at the University of Rochester in 2001. She is the author of *The Absolute Artist: The Historiography of a Concept* (1997) and *The Subject in Art: Portraiture and Identity in Vienna ca. 1900* (forthcoming). She also edited *Jewish Identity in Modern Art History* (1999). Professor Soussloff has published articles on early modern Italian art and theory, the history of aesthetics, theories of performance, and avant-garde film.

Kerri Steinberg teaches art history at the University of Redlands. Her publications include "From Stereotype to Archetype: Demystifying American Jewish Identity in the Photographic Campaigns of the USA" in *Representations of Jews through the Ages* (1996) and "The Ties That Bind: Americans, Ethiopians, and the Extended Jewish Family" in *Race, Gender, and Class* (1999).

Bernard Susser is Senator Norman Paterson Professor of Politics at Bar Ilan University. His most recent works include *Political Ideologies in the Modern World* (1999), *Choosing Survival: Strategies for a Jewish Future* (with Charles Liebman, 1999), and *Israel and the Politics of Jewish Identity: The Secular-Religious Impasse* (with Asher Cohen, 2000).

Louise Tallen teaches in the departments of anthropology, biobehaviorial sciences, and psychiatry at the University of California, Los Angeles.

Irwin Wall is professor emeritus of history at the University of California, Riverside. His latest publication is *France, the United States, and the Algerian War* (2001).

Howard Wettstein is professor of philosophy at the University of California, Riverside. His most recent publications include *Has Semantics Rested upon a Mistake? and Other Essays* (1991) and *The Magic Prism: An Essay in the Philosophy of Language* (forthcoming). He is the editor (since 1976) of the Midwest Studies in Philosophy.

Diane L. Wolf is associate professor of sociology at the University of California, Davis, where she is also a member of the Jewish studies program. She recently coauthored (with Yen Le Espiritu) "The Paradox of Assimilation: Children of Filipino Immigrants in San Diego" in *Ethnicities: The New Second Generation,* edited by Alejandro Portes and Ruben Rumbaut. Her book *Beyond Anne Frank: Hidden Children and Family Reconstruction in Postwar Netherlands* is forthcoming.

INDEX

Text: 10/12 Baskerville
Display: Baskerville
Compositor: G&S Typesetters, Inc.
Printer and Binder: Sheridan Books, Inc.